PROTECTIVE SECURITY LAW,
SECOND EDITION

PROTECTIVE SECURITY LAW, SECOND EDITION

Fred E. Inbau
John Henry Wigmore Professor of Law Emeritus
Northwestern University
First Director, Chicago Police Scientific Crime Detection Laboratory

Bernard J. Farber
Attorney-at-Law, Chicago, Illinois
Adjunct Professor of Law, Illinois Institute of Technology
Chicago Kent College of Law

David W. Arnold
General Counsel, Reid Psychological Systems
Chicago, Illinois

BUTTERWORTH–HEINEMANN
Boston • Oxford • Melbourne
Singapore • Toronto • Munich
New Delhi • Tokyo

Library of Congress Cataloging-in-Publication Data

Inbau, Fred Edward.
    Protective security law / Fred E. Inbau, Bernard J. Farber, David W. Arnold.—2nd ed.
        p.   cm.
    Includes bibliographical references and index.
    ISBN 0-7506-9279-0 (hardcover : alk. paper)
    1. Private security services—Law and legislation—United States.   2. Police, Private—United States.   3. Police—United States.   4. Criminal procedure—United States. I. Farber, Bernard J. II. Arnold, David W. (David Willis), 1954– . III. Title
KF5399.5.P715 1996
344.73'05289—dc20   95-30395
[347.3045289]   CIP

British Library Cataloguing-in-Publication Data
A catalogue record for this book is available from the British Library.

The publisher offers discounts on bulk orders of this book.
For information, please write:

Manager of Special Sales
Butterworth–Heinemann
313 Washington Street
Newton, MA 02158–1626

10 9 8 7 6 5 4 3 2 1

Printed in the United States of America

Table of Contents

Preface vii

Acknowledgments ix

Chapter 1   The Law of Arrest 1

Chapter 2   The Law of Search and Seizure 31

Chapter 3   Temporary Detention and Inquiries of Detained Persons 57

Chapter 4   The Interrogation of Suspected Persons 69

Chapter 5   Scientific Investigations 81

Chapter 6   Security Surveillance of Customers and Employees 97

Chapter 7   Property Owners' Protection Against Intrusion 107

Chapter 8   The Procurement of Information Regarding the
Dishonesty/Criminality of Job Applicants, Employees,
and Customers 117

Chapter 9   Laws and Governmental Regulations Regarding
Psychological Testing for Dishonesty Among Applicants 131

Chapter 10 Legal Consequences of Impermissible Investigative
Conduct 145

Chapter 11 Civil Liability for Inadequate Security Duties Owed to
Invitees by Business Owners and Their Security Personnel 187

Chapter 12 Crimes, Criminal Law, and Criminal Procedure of
Special Interest to Security Personnel 205

Chapter 13 The Courts and Their Organization 221

Chapter 14 Security Officer's Preparation for Trial and Testimony
in Court 231

Appendix 243

Index 325

Preface

Protective Security Law is a text on the legal rights available to security officers, corporations, partnerships, and individually owned businesses for the protection of their property from thievery by employees, customers, and others. It was prepared primarily for nonlawyers, but it also presents thoroughly documented coverage of the entire legal spectrum for corporate counsel and individual lawyers who must advise clients regarding their security operations.

In addition to its practical application, *Protective Security Law* is a text that is highly suitable for instructional purposes in junior colleges and other educational institutions offering courses relating to protective security. We also suggest its value in police training schools, because it presents a uniquely simplified treatment of the law regarding police powers of arrest, search and seizure, interrogation, and other aspects of law enforcement.

An appendix contains statutory provisions from all of the states, and the District of Columbia, regarding protective issues of particular concern to merchants and security personnel.

Publisher's Note: To avoid both biased language and awkward sentence constructions, masculine pronouns have been used in odd-numbered chapters, and feminine pronouns have been used in even-numbered chapters, wherever the intention is to denote a person or persons who may be of either gender.

Acknowledgments

The present authors are grateful for the contributions of two of the co-authors of the preceding edition—Judge Marvin E. Aspen, who in 1995 became Chief Judge of the United States District Court for the Northern District of Illinois, and James E. Spiotto, a partner in the Chicago law firm of Chapman and Cutler.

Fred E. Inbau

Bernard J. Farber

David W. Arnold

1

The Law of Arrest

In order for a security officer employed by a mercantile establishment or other privately owned business operation or facility to obtain an adequate understanding of his powers of arrest, it is essential that he first know about the powers possessed by public security officers—the police.

ARRESTS BY POLICE OFFICERS

Arrest means the taking of a person into custody. It may be effected by "an actual restraint of the person or by his submission to custody."[1] Police officers, however, may detain persons for any of several purposes without the detention becoming custodial and thereby an arrest.

The questioning of a witness to a crime does not constitute custody, nor does the stopping of a motorist for an ordinary traffic offense or the issuance to him of a "ticket." Also, a police officer's "stopping" and "making reasonable inquiries" of a person reasonably suspected of criminal activity does not constitute an arrest.[2] In other words, an arrest occurs only when it is obvious that the detained person is going to be taken to a police station or before a judicial magistrate.

---

1. This is the definition of one of the most recent legislative enactments upon the subject—Sections 5/102-5 and 5/107-5 of the Illinois Code of Criminal Procedure (Illinois Compiled Statutes, Ch 725). An enlarged definition is "the taking of another into custody for the actual or purported purpose of bringing the other before a court, body or official, or of otherwise securing the administration of the law." PERKINS, ELEMENTS OF POLICE SCIENCE 223, 227 (1942).

2. This practice of stopping and making inquiries of an individual was approved by the Supreme Court of the United States in Terry v. Ohio, 392 U.S. 1 (1968). Moreover, once a person is stopped under such circumstances, he may be "frisked" for weapons that might be used to attack the officer. This additional right, set forth in the same Supreme Court case, gave rise to the designation of the practice as "stop-and-frisk." (See Chapter 3 for a discussion of the police right to "frisk" as well as to "stop," and also the right of some classes of security officers to "stop-and-frisk.")

Arrest Without a Warrant

Prior to the enactment of legislation authorizing arrests without a court order, a police officer could arrest a person only for a felony committed in the officer's presence, or for a misdemeanor involving a "breach of the peace."

A felony was, and still is, generally considered an offense for which the penalty includes the possibility of confinement in a penitentiary, or execution; a misdemeanor carries a lesser period of jail confinement (not more than a year), a monetary fine, or both. In addition to felonies and misdemeanors, there exists a third general category of offenses known as ordinance violations, which are violations of laws enacted by county boards or by city or village councils.[3] Such violations are usually punishable by a fine only. An example is a "breach of the peace," i.e., conduct that does, or very likely will, arouse or disturb a segment of the public.

The right to arrest for these various offenses was originally established many years ago by court decisions, and that collection of law became known as the *common law*. The same rights continue today, although in most cases they have been enlarged. For instance, the requirement that a warrantless arrest for a felony could be made only if the felony was committed in the officer's presence has been replaced by authorization to make an arrest whenever the officer has "reasonable grounds" to believe that the person being arrested is committing or has committed a felony. The same degree of police arrest authority has been extended, in a few states, to misdemeanors. Also, in most states police officers have been afforded the right to arrest for ordinance violations committed in their presence, although there may be available the alternative practice of issuing (as in traffic violations) a "notice to appear" or a "summons." A court-ordered arrest may follow, of course, if the notice to appear or summons is ignored.

The doctrine of the *Terry* case was extended in 1972 to permit a nighttime seizure of a pistol from the pocket of a parked motorist whom an officer had approached for questioning after a reliable informant had pointed him out as an armed possessor (and seller) of heroin. Adams v. Williams, 407 U.S. 143 (1972). In addition to this judicial sanction, many state statutes authorize "stop-and-frisk"; see Chapter 2.

3. California has a rather unusual classification of state crimes and offenses. Its Penal Code provides, in Section 16, that "crimes and offenses," as the term is used in the Code, include "felonies," "misdemeanors," and "infractions." Section 17 of the Code provides that "[a] felony is a crime which is punishable with death or by imprisonment in the state prison. Every other crime or public offense is a misdemeanor except those offenses that are classified as infractions."

The word *infractions*, unaccompanied by a definition, was added to the Code in 1968, and, according to a 1970 court opinion in Castro v. Superior Court, 88 Cal. Rptr. 500 (Cal. App. 1970), "the concept of infraction was developed to provide punishment for low grade violations yet avoid the societal stigma of a criminal conviction." Infractions, therefore, are not punishable by jail confinement. Nevertheless, a person who commits an infraction is subject to arrest not only by the police, but, according to Section 837 of the Code, by private citizens as well, provided the act is committed or attempted in the citizen's presence. As to both officers and private persons there are, however, certain exceptions provided in Section 840.

The Constitutional Requirement of "Reasonable Grounds."   The "reasonable grounds" ("probable cause") requirement stems from the Fourth Amendment to the United States Constitution, which protects against "unreasonable" searches and seizures, and requires that no warrants shall be issued without probable cause.[4] "Probable cause" and "reasonable grounds" do not mean *actual* knowledge. An arresting officer need not personally observe or hear the commission of a crime; he need only have knowledge of facts and circumstances that would lead a reasonable person to conclude a crime has been committed and that in all probability the individual about to be arrested is the one who committed it.

The amount of evidence necessary to satisfy the reasonable grounds test for an arrest is much less than that required to prove in court that the person arrested actually committed the crime. At the trial of an accused person, the prosecution must present evidence to prove guilt *beyond a reasonable doubt.* To make an arrest, however, a police officer need only show enough facts to cause him *to believe,* upon *reasonable grounds,* that the person about to be arrested has committed an offense. A classic definition of reasonable grounds is that it exists if the facts and circumstances known to the officer would justify a reasonable person in believing that the offense has been committed by the suspect.

Following are examples of the fulfillment of the constitutional requirement:

EXAMPLE

Officer Price, while cruising in his patrol car, heard a voice from a jewelry store yelling, "Help! Thief!" Seconds later he observed Smith running down the street away from the store where he had heard the shouts for help. Price chased Smith and apprehended him. Price had reasonable grounds to arrest Smith.

EXAMPLE

A police officer, cruising in a patrol car at 3:00 a.m. in the parking lot of a shopping center where a number of burglaries had recently occurred, observed Carlton carrying a portable television set, a small radio, and several phonograph records. When Carlton saw the police car he dropped the items he was carrying and started to run away. The officer had reasonable grounds to arrest him.

EXAMPLE

Coleman, known by the police to be a "fence" (a trader in stolen property), was seen by Officer Jones walking hastily to get into a cab. The officer arrested and searched him for stolen merchandise. Officer Jones' action was not based upon reasonable grounds, and consequently the arrest and search were illegal.[5]

---

4. Draper v. United States, 358 U.S. 307 (1959); Beck v. Ohio, 379 U.S. 89 (1964); Hill v. California, 401 U.S. 797 (1971). *See also* the shoplifting detention cases of Lucas v. J.C. Penney Co., 233 Or. 345, 378 P.2d 717 (1963), and Coblyn v. Kennedy's, 359 Mass. 319, 268 N.E.2d 860 (1971), both of which are discussed in Chapter 3.

5. *See* United States v. DiRe, 332 U.S. 581 (1948); People v. Beattie, 31 Ill. 2d 257, 201 N.E.2d 396 (1964); Adams v. State, 128 S.W.2d 41 (Tex. Crim. 1939).

The reasonable grounds requirement would have been satisfied in the foregoing examples even if subsequent developments established that the person arrested was actually innocent of the offense.[6] Mere suspicion or a "hunch," however, will not justify an arrest.

Hearsay Evidence and Informants' Tips.   Under most circumstances, hearsay evidence, which may be loosely described as second-hand evidence, cannot be used at the trial of an accused person. However, if corroborated in some way, it may be used to establish reasonable grounds for an arrest.

Hearsay evidence is most often in the form of information received by a police officer from an informant (or so-called stool pigeon). Reasonable grounds, however, cannot be established by hearsay evidence alone. There must be some validation of the informant's reliability. This requirement may be satisfied in several ways:

1.   If a police officer observes certain activities, facts, or circumstances that substantiate the tip given by any informant, reasonable grounds may exist for an arrest.[7]

EXAMPLE

Denison told Officer Nelson that Lacy had been selling gambling tickets on a street corner. Officer Nelson, in an unmarked police car, observed Lacy conducting some type of transactions with about twenty persons who came up to him separately in the course of thirty minutes. As the individuals came up to Lacy, they each gave him something and he handed them something. Although Officer Nelson could not tell exactly what was exchanged, his observations, coupled with the informant's tip, gave him reasonable grounds to arrest Lacy.

2.   If a police officer receives a tip from an informant who has given him consistently accurate and reliable tips in the past, he may place considerable reliance on the tip of such a person for purposes of an arrest.[8] In general, however, unless the officer's personal observations afford some substantiation of the particular case situation, the informant must relate the basis for his own information—for instance, actually seeing a recent sale of narcotics by the suspect.[9]

---

6. An arrest may be valid even though no criminal conviction results from a shoplifting charge. Jacques v. Sears, Roebuck & Co., 30 N.Y.2d 466, 285 N.E.2d 871 (1972), and the cases cited therein.

7. People v. Brooks, 32 Ill. 2d 81, 203 N.E.2d 882 (1965).

8. Draper v. United States, 358 U.S. 307 (1959); People v. Durr, 28 Ill. 2d 308, 192 N.E.2d 379 (1963).

9. United States v. Harris, 403 U.S. 573 (1971). Also, for an excellent analysis of the probable cause issue generally, consult Dawson v. State, 276 A.2d 680 (Md. App. 1971).

With regard to informants other than "stool pigeons," see People v. Waller, 67 Cal. Rptr. 8 (Cal. App. 1968), *cert. denied*, 393 U.S. 1039 (1969), in which the court noted that "a citizen who purports to be the victim or to have witnessed a crime is a reliable informant even though his reliability has not theretofore been proven or tested." To the same effect: People v. Wolfe, 147 N.W.2d 447 (Mich. App. 1967).

EXAMPLE

Oakley told Officer Martin that he had observed Lawson selling narcotics to Nelson. Oakley described Lawson and advised Martin where Lawson would be that night for the purpose of making his sales. On several prior occasions, whenever Oakley gave Officer Martin similar information, Martin always found narcotics on the person "fingered" by Oakley. Under these circumstances, Officer Martin had reasonable grounds to arrest Lawson.

On the other hand, information from an uncorroborated, unknown informant may not be the basis for establishing reasonable grounds.[10]

Of interest in connection with hearsay evidence situations is the fact that, when an informant has furnished such information, his identity need not be disclosed at the suspect's trial unless (a) the informant himself participated in the crime, (b) the informant was a witness to the particular crime for which the arrest was made, or (c) the informant was present at the time of arrest.

"Stop" Short of an Arrest, Followed by an Arrest. As previously stated, in addition to a police officer's right to arrest, he is also empowered to stop a person under reasonably suspicious circumstances and ask for that person's name and the person's reason for being where he is. Although the suspect is under no obligation to answer, if he refuses, the officer may consider that fact along with all the other circumstances in evaluating whether valid grounds exist for an arrest.[11]

EXAMPLE

At 3:00 a.m. one cold morning an officer observed a man in an alley, beside a garage door, with light clothing and tennis shoes. The officer asked him who he was and what his reason was for being there. (Although at this initial encounter there were no grounds for arrest, the officer had authority to stop the suspect and ask these questions.) No response was given. Then the officer observed a screwdriver on the ground near the garage door and also, on the garage door itself, marks which appeared to have been made by a screwdriver. Reasonable grounds existed for an arrest for attempted burglary.

"Reasonable Suspicion," "Reasonable Grounds," and "Proof of Guilt Beyond a Reasonable Doubt": The Relative Differences. Figure 1 indicates, in a very general way, the relative differences between "reasonable suspi-

---

10. Beck v. Ohio, 379 U.S. 89 (1964); People v. Pitts, 26 Ill. 2d 395, 186 N.E.2d 357 (1962); People v. Castaneda, 82 Cal. Rptr. 205 (Cal. App. 1969); Peters v. State, 152 S.E.2d 647 (Ga. App. 1966).

   There are some rare situations in which an ordinary citizen will tell an officer that he has just witnessed a crime and the officer will hurry to the scene before getting the witness's name. A court will usually regard such information as coming from an "ordinary citizen" rather than an "anonymous informant." People v. Hoffman, 45 Ill. 2d 221, 258 N.E.2d 326 (1970).

11. However, the mere refusal to identify one's self to a police officer is not a crime, does not constitute disorderly conduct, and does not by itself furnish grounds for any arrest without a warrant. People v. Bomboy, 229 N.Y.S.2d 323 (App. Div. 1962); Beail v. District of Columbia, 201 F.2d 176 (D.C. Cir. 1952); Leighton v. Getchell, 169 N.W. 649 (Iowa, 1918).

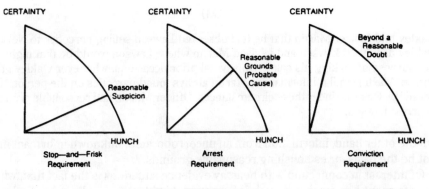

Figure 1

cion" for a police "stop," "reasonable grounds" for an arrest, and the requirement of "proof of guilt beyond a reasonable doubt" for a conviction.

Arrest with a Warrant

An arrest warrant generally may be obtained by presenting to a judge, magistrate, or justice of the peace a *complaint*—a charge made under oath—containing statements establishing reasonable grounds to believe that the person named in the warrant committed the crime therein described.[12] The person who signs the complaint is called the *complainant* or *affiant*.

An arrest warrant is not a courtroom "pleading" as that word is used by judges and lawyers, but rather a written order from a court directed to a peace officer, or to some other individual, specifically named, commanding him to arrest a designated person.

The Reasonable Grounds Requirement for an Arrest Warrant.   The same kind of evidence that may establish reasonable grounds for an arrest without warrant (e.g., hearsay bolstered by other factors, such as the ones previously described) may also justify the issuance of a warrant by a judicial officer.[13]

---

12. Some states, such as Florida, allow clerks of the court to issue arrest warrants. Fla. Stat. Ann. Sec. 34.13(6). The Supreme Court has held this practice constitutional where it can be shown that the clerk qualifies as a "neutral and detached magistrate as prescribed by the Fourth Amendment." Shadwick v. Tampa, 407 U.S. 345 (1972). Therefore, state statutes that permit prosecuting attorneys, corporation counsel, and their assistants to issue arrest warrants have been held violative of the Fourth Amendment. Coolidge v. New Hampshire, 403 U.S. 443 (1971).

13. Rule 4(a) of the Federal Rules of Criminal Procedure provides that "[i]f it appears from the complaint, or from an affidavit filed with the complaint that there is probable cause to believe an offense has been committed and that the defendant has committed it, a warrant for the arrest of the defendant shall issue to any officer authorized by law to execute it."

EXAMPLE

Sanford told Bradley, a hotel keeper, that Sadie Rain was performing acts of prostitution in her hotel room. Sanford said that he, too, had engaged Sadie's services.

On several occasions, Bradley observed six men enter and leave Sadie's room at intervals of about half an hour. Such information, submitted by Bradley under oath, would justify an arrest warrant.

In cases where corroboration of an informant's tip is not possible, the only recourse for the police officer is to have the informant sign the complaint. This is seldom done, however, because the complaint and the warrant are public records and, without the protection of anonymity, most informants would be unwilling to run the obvious risks of disclosure of their identities. An informant-complainant may use an alias in signing the complaint for an arrest warrant, but if he becomes a witness at the trial itself, he must disclose his own name.

Police Obligations in Warrant Arrests.   What are the legal obligations and responsibilities of a police officer who is assigned to make an arrest pursuant to a warrant? When the warrant has been issued on the sworn complaint of another officer or on the sworn complaint of the victim of a crime, or of a witness, the officer who is to make the arrest is not required to check into the warrant's total validity. He need only verify that it is signed by a judge or magistrate, that it contains the name of the person to be arrested, and that it names the charge for which the arrest is to be made. If the warrant is "fair on its face," as the expression is sometimes used, the officer can proceed to effect an arrest. He is privileged to assume the warrant was based on reasonable grounds, because that determination was the responsibility of the judge or magistrate who issued it.[14]

The execution of a warrant is a ministerial act which, by law, the police officer is required to perform and for which he will not be held liable if he acts properly. If the warrant is lawful and regular on its face, it serves as complete protection to the officer, provided it clearly discloses no want of jurisdiction or lack of authority on the part of the magistrate or court issuing it.[15]

---

14. It must be emphasized, however, that only if it is "objectively reasonable" for the officer to believe that the warrant is valid will he be entitled to rely on it. In Malley v. Briggs, 475 U.S. 335 (1986), the United States Supreme Court held that the mere issuance of an arrest warrant by a judge or magistrate would not protect an officer from civil liability if a "reasonably well-trained officer" would have known that the affidavit relied upon failed to establish probable cause and therefore created a danger of an illegal arrest. "[I]t goes without saying," the Court noted, "that where a magistrate acts mistakenly in issuing a warrant but within the range of professional competence of a magistrate, the officer who requested the warrant cannot be held liable. But it is different if no officer of reasonable competence would have requested the warrant, i.e., his request is outside the range of the professional competence expected of an officer. If the magistrate issues the warrant in such a case, his action is not just a reasonable mistake, but an unacceptable error indicating gross incompetence or neglect of duty. The officer then cannot excuse his own default by pointing to the greater incompetence of the magistrate."

15. PROSSER AND KEETON, HANDBOOK OF THE LAW OF TORTS ch. 4, Sec. 25 (5th ed. 1984); Malone v. Carey, 69 P.2d 166 (Cal. App. 1936).

The execution of a faulty warrant will render the arrest invalid. Therefore, when an arrest warrant is prepared, care must be taken to follow the requirements of the specific state criminal code; and a warrant of arrest must comply with all constitutional requirements and statutory provisions. Generally an arrest warrant *must*:

1. be properly captioned;
2. show on its face facts sufficient to demonstrate that it was issued by a magistrate or other officer having jurisdiction to do so;
3. contain the necessary complaint on oath or affirmation;
4. set forth facts sufficient to constitute a violation of law and thus adequately apprise the arrestee of the crime with which he is charged.

Only those irregularities on the face of the warrant that adversely affect the substantial rights of the accused will invalidate the warrant.[16]

EXAMPLE

The name of the person to be arrested was spelled correctly as "John Q. Smith" in six out of the seven places where it appeared in the complaint and warrant. In one place it was incorrectly spelled as "John Q. Smythe." The warrant was valid.[17]

EXAMPLE

A state arrest warrant statute required that all complaints be "sworn to." Complainant Williams told Police Officer Parker about a crime committed by Holcomb. Parker prepared a complaint for Williams' signature. However, in the excitement of preparing the case, Officer Parker neglected to make sure that the complaint made by Williams was sworn to by him prior to making the arrest pursuant to the warrant. The judge who signed the warrant also neglected to notice that the complaint was not under oath. After Holcomb was taken into custody, Officer Parker noticed the error and then presented Williams to the judge, who then had Williams swear that the complaint was true. This irregularity affected Holcomb's substantial right not to be arrested pursuant to a warrant unless it had been issued on a sworn complaint. The arrest was therefore invalid.

The arrest warrant must be signed by a judge or magistrate, who is obligated to first examine the complaint as to the matters related in it. For this reason, it is good practice *always* to bring the complainant to the judge's courtroom when presenting the complaint to the judge or magistrate for the issuance of a warrant. It is also good professional practice, when time and circumstances permit, to have

---

16. *See* Sec. 5, Code of Criminal Procedure of The American Law Institute [A.L.I.] (1930) and Ill. Comp. Stats., Ch. 725, Sec. 5/107-10; and also State v. Barry, 183 Kans. 792, 332 P.2d 549 (1958); State v. Ninemires, 306 S.W.2d 527 (Mo. 1957). Variance between the nature of the offense as alleged in the complaint and in the warrant, however, will invalidate a warrant.

17. Statutes commonly provide that if the name of the accused is not known, he may be designated in the warrant by any name or description by which he can be identified with reasonable certainty. *See* Ill. Comp. Stats., Ch. 725, Sec. 5/107-9(d) (2); Okla. Stat. Ann., tit. 22, Sec. 173; Wis. Stats. Ann., Sec. 968.04. *See also* Holmes v. LeFors, 36 Okla. 729, 129 P. 718 (1913).

the local police department's legal advisor or the local prosecutor examine the complaint and warrant for their legal sufficiency before presenting them to the judicial officer.

Even though time and circumstances may have afforded the police an opportunity to obtain an arrest warrant, an arrest may nevertheless be made without one whenever reasonable grounds are present. In other words, although there are situations where a warrant arrest may be considered advisable, there is no compelling legal necessity for a warrant when the requirement of probable cause can be otherwise established. An exception to this general rule is when an arrest is to be made in the arrestee's home, in which case an arrest warrant should be obtained if time and circumstances permit. Stated another way, an in-home arrest warrant is required for a nonconsensual, nonemergency entry.[18]

Although it is advisable, when circumstances permit, for the arresting officer to have the warrant of arrest with him at the time of arrest, it is not essential.[19] In fact, in most states any officer who has reasonable grounds for believing that a warrant has been issued in that state or in another jurisdiction may make a valid arrest of the person who has been named in a warrant.[20] However, a rumor that an individual is wanted elsewhere will not justify an arrest.[21]

"Quashing" an Arrest Warrant. Where counsel for an arrested person seeks to attack the validity of a warrant, he will file in court, before trial, what is known as a "motion to quash" the warrant of arrest. If he is successful—that is, if the motion is granted—the arrest will be declared illegal and, for reasons to be subsequently discussed, any evidence obtained incident to the arrest will be suppressed and unusable at the trial.

Where a warrant is declared void because of a substantial defect, the arrest itself may still be valid, and the seized evidence admissible at the trial, if the cir-

18. Payton v. New York, 445 U.S. 573 (1980). *See also* Rawlings v. Kentucky, 448 U.S. 98 (1980).

19. People v. Scott, 211 N.E.2d 418 (Ill. App. 1965).

   Statutes substantially the same as Section 8 of the Uniform Arrest Act have been enacted in a number of states: "An arrest by a peace officer acting under a warrant is lawful even though the officer does not have the warrant in his possession at the time of the arrest, but, if the person arrested so requests, the warrant shall be shown to him as soon as practicable." *See, e.g.,* Cal. Penal Code, Sec. 842; Minn. Stats. Ann., Sec. 629.32; Wis. Stats. Ann., Sec. 968.07. Nevertheless, some jurisdictions still require that an officer of the law making an arrest under a warrant when no resistance is offered must show his warrant to the party arrested. *See, e.g.,* Kans. Stats. Ann., Sec. 62.1203; N.D. Code Ann., Sec. 29.06-11; 22 Okla. Stats. Ann., tit. 22, Sec. 192.

20. *See, e.g.,* Ill. Comp. Stats., Ch. 725, Sec. 5/107-2(b). *See also* Section 14 of the Uniform Criminal Extradition Act, which provides: "The arrest of a person may be lawfully made also by any peace officer or a private person, without a warrant upon reasonable information that the accused has been charged in the courts of a state with a crime punishable by death or imprisonment for a term exceeding one year, but when so arrested the accused must be taken before a judge or magistrate with all practicable speed and complaint must be made against him under oath setting forth the grounds for the arrest. . . ." This Uniform Criminal Extradition Act, prepared by the National Conference on Uniform State Laws, has been adopted by all of the states except M.S., N.D., S.C., and the D.C.

21. People v. Humphreys, 353 Ill. 340, 187 N.E. 446 (1933).

cumstances under which the arrest was made would have justified an arrest *without* a warrant.

EXAMPLE

A warrant was obtained for the arrest of Hanson on a charge of rape of a child. Officer Pauls, looking for Hanson near Hanson's home, observed him pick up another child in his car and speed off. Officer Pauls gave chase and ultimately arrested Hanson. In his car, and in clear view of Officer Pauls, there was a child's garment that was later identified as belonging to the raped child. Hanson's trousers were stained with what was determined to be blood of the same type as that of the rape victim. If the arrest warrant contains a defect and is declared invalid, the garment and the blood evidence would be admissible at the rape trial because, under the foregoing circumstances, Officer Pauls could have made a valid arrest without an arrest warrant.

The Area (Jurisdiction) in Which Arrests May Be Made

Authority in Nonwarrant Situations.   In the absence of a special law to the contrary, a local police officer may make arrests only in the jurisdiction of his particular police department. Consequently, although a state police officer may make arrests throughout the state, a county police officer may make an arrest only in his own county, and a city or village officer only in the community served by his department.[22] A police officer outside his own jurisdiction has only the powers of a private citizen of that jurisdiction. If an arrest by a private citizen would be lawful under existing circumstances, an arrest by an officer outside his own jurisdiction would be lawful. However, a police officer who observes a suspect commit a crime in his own jurisdiction may chase that person into another jurisdiction within the state and make the arrest there. This is commonly called the doctrine of "fresh pursuit" or "hot pursuit."

EXAMPLE

Highland Park and Glencoe are adjoining municipalities, but located in different counties of the state. Jones was a police officer in Highland Park, and while on patrol he observed Smith snatch a purse from a woman on a street in Highland Park. Smith jumped into a car and drove away. Jones chased him on his motorcycle. Smith entered Glencoe, where Officer Jones curbed Smith's car and arrested him. The arrest was valid even though Jones is a police officer in Highland Park and not in Glencoe.

22. In early England, the chief peace officer of a village was a "bailiff," and the village was called a "wick." Through time the phrase "bailiff's wick" was contracted into "bailiwick" and came to mean the territory or area throughout which a peace officer exercises his authority under the law. PERKINS AND BOYCE, CASES AND MATERIALS ON CRIMINAL LAW AND PROCEDURE, 909 (5th ed. 1977).

A Uniform Act on Fresh Pursuit has been adopted by most states which authorizes a police officer in fresh pursuit to follow a felon or a suspected felon into another state and arrest him there without a warrant.[23]

Authority in Warrant Situations.   As a general rule, an arrest under a warrant cannot be made outside the territorial jurisdiction of the court or magistrate issuing the writ or outside the territorial jurisdiction of the police officer to whom it is addressed; however, there are some statutory exceptions to this general legal principle.[24] An increasing number of states have provided by statute that an arrest warrant for the violation of a state law may be executed anywhere in the state.[25] It should be noted, however, that the state statutes that confer authority to execute arrest warrants outside the territorial jurisdiction of the issuing court, magistrate, or officer do not similarly extend the authority of the officer to arrest without a warrant.

An arrest warrant has no validity outside the state in which it is issued. To apprehend a suspect who is outside the state and thus a fugitive, a legal proceeding must be commenced for his removal (*extradition*) from the other state. However, a federal arrest warrant for a federal offense may be executed by a federal officer in any state.

Force Permissible in Effecting an Arrest

Generally, a police officer may use the force he *reasonably* believes necessary to make the arrest or protect himself or another from bodily harm while making the arrest. If a police officer uses excessive force—force unnecessary under the par-

---

23. With slight variation in wording, such state statutes provide as follows: "Any peace officer of another State who enters this State in fresh pursuit and continues within this State in fresh pursuit of a person in order to arrest him on the ground that he has committed an offense in the other state has the same authority to arrest and hold the person in custody as peace officers of this State have to arrest and hold a person in custody on the ground that he has committed an offense in this State." Ill. Comp. Stats., Ch. 725, Sec. 5/107-4(b). Similar provisions by other states include Cal., West Ann. Cal. Pen. Code Secs. 852 to 852.4; N.Y., McKinney's CPL 140.55; and Wis., W.S.A. 976.04.

    Some states, by statute, permit police officers in one city to make arrests within an adjacent city in the same county. *See, e.g.*, Ill. Comp. Stats., Ch. 65, Sec. 5/7-4-7, 5/7-4-8. *But see* People v. Carnivale, 21 Ill. App. 3d 780, 315 N.E.2d 609 (1974), *aff'd in part, reversed in part on other grounds*, 61 Ill. 2d 57, 329 N.E.2d 193 (1975), which strictly construed the Illinois provisions, so that in the absence of any of the statutorily expressed emergencies, a police officer is not authorized to arrest in an adjacent jurisdiction. *See also* Cal. Pen. Code, Sec. 852.2; 22 Okla. Stats. Ann., tit. 22, Sec. 221; Mo. Ann. Stats., Sec. 544.155.

24. *See* 34 A.L.R. 4th 328 (1984); 5 Am Jur 2d *Arrest* Sec. 18-19 & 50 (1962); 6 C.J.S. *Arrest* Sec. 12(a).

25. Some statutes of this kind empower officers to execute warrants of arrest in other parts of the state only when such authority is endorsed on the warrant by the magistrate issuing it, or by a magistrate in the county where it is to be executed. (*See, e.g.*, Mo. Ann. Stats., Sec. 544.090, 544.100). An arrest warrant, under some state statutes, may be directed to the sheriff of the county where the accused resides or may be found, and it then becomes the duty of such officer to arrest the accused and take him to the county from which the writ was issued. *See, e.g.*, Neb. Rev. Stats., Sec. 29-1702; Wash. Rev. Code Ann., Sec. 10:31.060.

ticular circumstances of the case—he may subject himself to criminal or civil liability, or both, under state as well as federal law.[26]

The amount of force a police officer is permitted to use when making an arrest depends on the circumstances of the particular situation. The force may not be disproportionate to the resistance offered.[27] The United States Supreme Court has ruled that the proper legal standard to be applied to a claim that an officer used excessive force in the course of an arrest, investigatory stop or other "seizure" of a person is the "objective reasonableness" of the force utilized, a standard required by the Fourth Amendment.[28] Nevertheless, a distinction is generally made between the amount of force which may be used in making an arrest for a felony and that which may be used in making an arrest for a misdemeanor.[29] State statutes usually provide that if a misdemeanant resists arrest, or attempts to escape, the officer may employ such force as may be reasonably necessary to overcome such resistance and subject the offender to his custody; however, an officer has no right to employ deadly force or to inflict great bodily harm on a misdemeanant who offers no endangering resistance but is merely attempting to escape.

Prior to 1985, many states had a "fleeing felon" rule which allowed police officers to use deadly force to stop a felon fleeing from the scene of his crime— regardless of whether the felon was armed, used force in the commission of his offense, or was posing an immediate threat to the life or safety of the officer or others. In some states, private citizens were also allowed to use deadly force in this fashion, standing in the shoes of a police officer in stopping a fleeing felon.

---

26. PROSSER AND KEETON, HANDBOOK OF THE LAW OF TORTS, ch. 24, Sec. 26 (5th ed. 1984); Annot., 60 A.L.R. FED 204 (1982). It has been held that an officer who exceeds the amount of force he is privileged to use under the circumstances is liable only for so much of the force as is excessive. City of Miami v. Albro, 120 So. 2d 23, 26 (Fla. 1960).

The criminal as well as civil liability under provisions of the federal Civil Rights statutes (18 U.S.C. Sec. 241, 242; 42 U.S.C. Sec. 1983) will be discussed subsequently in Chapter 10.

27. 5 Am Jur. 2d, *Arrest* Sec. 80, 81 (1962). *See also* 4 AM. JUR., *Arrest* Sec. 73 (1936).

28. Graham v. Connor, 490 U.S. 386 (1989). This is based on what the officer knew at the time of the arrest, not what is later discovered. For example, an officer may use force appropriate in attempting to subdue an arrestee he reasonably believes to be armed and dangerous, and will not be viewed as having used excessive force even if it is later determined, after the arrest, that the arrestee was not actually armed or that the weapon was a toy or was otherwise inoperable. *See* Wyche v. City of Franklinton, 837 F. Supp. 137 (E.D.N.C. 1993).

29. At common law, deadly force could be used by an officer to effect the arrest of a suspected felon but not of a suspected misdemeanant. This rule, according to a 1976 federal appellate court, "reflected the social and legal context of felonies in 15th century England and 18th century America." The court then went on to state: "Since all felonies—murder, rape, manslaughter, robbery, sodomy, mayhem, burglary, arson, prison break, and larceny—were punishable by death, the use of deadly force was seen as merely accelerating the penal process, albeit without providing a trial. 'It made little difference if the suspected felon were killed in the process of capture, since, in the eyes of the law, he had already forfeited his life by committing the felony.' It was also assumed that a suspected felon facing death upon capture was more desperate than a misdemeanant and that greater force was required for his apprehension. Finally, because there was no network of police forces a felon eluding his initial pursuers would probably escape ultimate arrest." Mattis v. Schnarr, 547 F.2d 1007 (8th Cir. 1976), n. 5, *vacated and remanded,* Ashcroft v. Mattis, 431 U.S. 171, *reh. denied,* 433 U.S. 915 (1977).

In 1985, however, in *Tennessee v. Garner*[30] the United States Supreme Court imposed certain constitutional limitations on the legality of police officers to use deadly force in this fashion. The Court held that an officer may not use deadly force to stop a fleeing felon unless there is a reasonable belief that the felon poses a threat of death or serious physical harm either to the officer or others. The Court therefore held unconstitutional, under the Fourth Amendment, as an unreasonable search and seizure, the use of deadly force against a fleeing unarmed burglar.

The same limitations on police use of deadly force—in addition to whatever other limitations are imposed under state law—will apply to armed security guards. At least one court has explicitly held this in *People v. Couch*,[31] a 1989 Michigan appellate court case. Earlier decisions in Michigan had allowed private citizens to use deadly force to prevent any felon from escaping because "essentially, in that situation, a private citizen is playing the part of a police officer." The court concluded that since the decision in *Garner* limited when the police are allowed to use deadly force, the same limits should apply to a private citizen who "stands in the shoes of a police officer." Security agencies utilizing armed guards, therefore, should be familiar with the following parameters of the rule in *Garner*:

> Where the officer has probable cause to believe that the suspect poses a threat of serious physical harm, either to the officer or to others, it is not constitutionally unreasonable to prevent escape by using deadly force. Thus, if the suspect threatens the officer with a weapon or there is probable cause to believe that he has committed a crime involving the infliction or threatened infliction of serious physical harm, deadly force may be used if necessary to prevent escape, and if, where feasible, some warning has been given.

This rule would appear to preclude the use of deadly force to protect property alone where there is no threat of bodily harm or death to any person. It also needs to be emphasized that state and local law in many instances may impose still other restrictions on the use of firearms, including special licensing requirements for armed security guards.[32]

---

30. 471 U.S. 1 (1985). Four years later, in the context of civil liability for alleged excessive force, the Court made it clear that whether the use of a particular level of force is justified is to be governed by a Fourth Amendment objective reasonableness standard. Graham v. Connor, 430 U.S. 386 (1989). This is to be judged from the perspective of a "reasonable officer on the scene." Under this objective test, the officer's malicious state of mind or intentions will not make a Fourth Amendment violation out of an objectively reasonable use of force; "nor will an officer's good intentions make an objectively unreasonable use of force constitutional." The test must make allowance for the fact that police officers are often forced to make split-second decisions about the amount of force necessary in a particular situation. Factors to be considered include the severity of the crime at issue, whether the suspect poses an immediate threat to the safety of the officers or others, and whether he is actively resisting arrest or attempting to evade arrest by flight.

31. 439 N.W.2d 354 (Mich. App. 1989).

32. *See* People v. Clark, 505 N.E.2d 1179 (Ill. App. 1987) and Commonwealth v. Walton, 529 A.2d 15 (Pa. Super. 1987). Additionally, to the extent that a security guard is acting within the scope of his employment, an employer may be held vicariously liable for his unjustified or negligent shooting of an individual. *See, e.g.*, Weinberg v. Johnson, 518 A.2d 985 (D.C. App. 1986) ($2 million judgment against employer for employee's shooting a customer during a dispute.) For an employer to be held

Some state statutes provide that when a police officer is making an arrest pursuant to an invalid arrest warrant he may use the same force as if the arrest warrant were valid—unless the police officer actually knows that the arrest warrant is invalid.[33]

The Timing of an Arrest

How soon must a police officer act after acquiring valid grounds for an arrest, either with or without a warrant? Will a delay in making the arrest render it invalid? Usually, so long as the delay between learning of the grounds for arrest and the act of making of the arrest can be justified on the basis of proper police work, the delayed arrest will be upheld. Thus, in an armed robbery case, a delay of over eighteen days between knowledge of the offense by law enforcement officers and the arrest of the defendant was held justifiable on the grounds that the added time was necessary to obtain evidence that would not have been obtainable had the defendant been arrested immediately.[34] Also, a delay between the controlled purchase of narcotics by the police and the arrest of the defendant was considered justified because of an attempt to reach the defendant's source of supply.[35] Likewise, police officers can delay effecting the arrest of an offender where such delay is necessary to avoid unwarranted entry, to conceal the identity of an informant, or to conceal an ongoing investigation.[36]

A few states specifically prohibit nighttime arrests under warrant for misdemeanors, unless so directed by the magistrate and endorsed on the warrant.[37] However, such statutes have been held not to affect a police officer's power to arrest at night without a warrant for a misdemeanor committed in his presence.[38]

vicariously liable for the intentional wrong of an employee, the act must be motivated, at least in part, by a purpose to further the employer's business and must not be unexpected in view of the employee's duties. Even if the shooting is *partially* motivated by personal motive, the employer may still be liable. However, if the guard was acting in what he reasonably thought was self-defense, there will be no liability. This principle is illustrated by Carbo Inc. v. Lowe, 521 N.E.2d 977 (Ind. App. 1988), in which the court overturned a $500,000 jury damage award against a store for the fatal shooting of an innocent bystander by its clerk during a robbery. The innocent bystander customer entered the liquor store at the same time that two masked armed men entered. The two robbers flanked the customer. The robbers fired some shots, which were returned by store employees. The customer vaulted over a store counter to seek cover and was fired at by a part-time store clerk who thought he was one of the robbers. The court held that the clerk acted in what he believed to be reasonable self-defense under the circumstances. The clerk was not the initial aggressor and, while the results may be tragic, it was reasonable for him to believe that he was in great risk of death and that the customer might be one of the robbers. For a collection of cases on the use of deadly force in this context, see Annot., *Liability of Private Citizen/Employer For Firing at Fleeing Criminal*, 29 A.L.R. 4th 144.

33. *See, e.g.*, Ill. Comp. Stats. ch. 720, Sec. 5/7-5(b).

34. People v. DeBerry, 211 N.E.2d 26 (Ill. App. 1965).

35. People v. Webb, 208 N.E.2d 639 (Ill. App. 1965).

36. Model Penal Code, Sec. 3.07 Comments (Official Draft 1985); 58 A.L.R.2d 1056 (1958).

37. *See, e.g.*, Okla. Stats. Ann., tit. 22, Sec. 189. *See also* 9 A.L.R. 1350 (1920).

38. Sima v. Skaggs Payless Drug Center, 82 Idaho 387, 353 P.2d 1085 (1960).

Postarrest Police Obligations

State statutes generally provide that when an arrest is made without a warrant, the arrestee must be taken before the nearest judge or magistrate "without unnecessary delay" (referred to in some statutes as "forthwith" or "immediately"). When the arrest is pursuant to a warrant, the arrestee must be taken promptly before the judge who issued the warrant, or, in his absence, before the nearest judge or magistrate in the same county.

"Unnecessary delay" means an *unreasonable* delay, and consequently the police are permitted to retain custody over an arrestee for a *reasonable* length of time, with reasonableness being determined by all the surrounding circumstances of the particular case.

EXAMPLE

White was arrested at 10 a.m. as he left the scene of a burglary. The police put him in a jail cell and kept him there until 10 a.m. the next morning, even though a judge was in a courthouse six blocks away. Such a delay was unnecessary and unreasonable.

EXAMPLE

Five persons observed two men commit a robbery in a tavern at 2 p.m. One of the witnesses, Davis, was shot in the foot as a result of an accidental discharge of the gun of one of the robbers. The police apprehended John Jones, who met the description Davis gave of one of the robbers, but they could not locate Jones' brother Bob, who had a criminal record for robbery and whose physical features were the same as those described by Davis with respect to the second participant. The police retained custody of John Jones as they continued the search for Bob Jones, and as they awaited Davis's release from a hospital so that he and the other witnesses could view John Jones in a lineup. The next morning, after Bob Jones was apprehended and all five witnesses had viewed both suspects in line-ups, John Jones and Bob Jones were taken before a judge. The delay was necessary and reasonable.

The reason for this rule of prohibiting unnecessary or unreasonable delays in taking an arrestee to a judge or magistrate is to afford him an early judicial determination as to whether there are reasonable grounds for continuing to hold him in custody. The judicial procedure for determining whether such reasonable grounds exist is known as a *preliminary hearing*. This requirement does not apply, however, to an offender who is lawfully incarcerated on another charge, because the statutes and relevant case law contemplate an arrest in the sense of an initial restraint of liberty.

Rights of Arrested Persons

An individual who is arrested has certain basic rights as provided by the Supreme Court of the United States and other courts, and by certain federal and state statutes. The right to a preliminary hearing has been discussed in the preceding section. Others are as follows:

When an arrest is made on the basis of an arrest warrant, the arresting police officer must inform the suspect of the fact that a warrant has been issued for his arrest, and the nature of the offense specified in the warrant.[39] When making an arrest without a warrant, the arresting police officer must inform the accused of the nature of the offense on which the arrest is based.[40]

When in custody, the person arrested must be provided with food, shelter, and, if required, medical treatment.[41] He has a right to telephone his family and his attorney. In the event he is moved to a different place of custody, he may make additional telephone calls.[42]

In some jurisdictions, a police officer who arrests a person without a warrant is authorized to release that person without requiring him to appear before a court, if the officer becomes satisfied that there are insufficient grounds for filing a criminal complaint against the arrestee.[43] This procedure not only protects the rights of a properly arrested but innocent suspect, it also affords the arresting officer protection from possible civil liability for exercising his own independent judgment in such instances. (The rights of an arrested person prior to an interrogation of him are discussed in Chapter 4.)

Obligations of Persons about to Be Arrested

A common law rule, followed in many states, recognizes the right of any person to resist an unlawful arrest.[44] However, a few states, by statute, have departed from this rule and provide that a private person may not resist arrest by a known police officer "even if he believes that the arrest is unlawful and the arrest is in fact unlawful."[45]

---

39. *See, e.g.*, State v. Jemison, 14 Ohio St. 2d 47, 236 N.E.2d 538, *cert. denied,* 393 U.S. 943 (1968); Collet v. Commonwealth, 296 Ky. 267, 176 S.W.2d 893 (1943). *See also* Cal. Penal Code, Sec. 841; N.Y. Crim. Pro., Sec. 120.80; PROSSER AND KEETON, HANDBOOK OF THE LAW OF TORTS Sec. 25 (5th ed. 1984).

40. *See, e.g.*, Ward v. Texas, 316 U.S. 547 (1941); People v. Adame, 169 Cal. 2d 587, 337 P.2d 477 (1959), *cert. denied,* 361 U.S. 969; Cal. Pen. Code, Sec. 841; PROSSER AND KEETON, HANDBOOK OF THE LAW OF TORTS, Sec. 25 (5th ed. 1984).

41. *See, e.g.*, Ill. Comp. Stats. Ch. 725, Sec. 5/103-2(c).

42. Escobedo v. Illinois, 378 U.S. 478 (1964); Cal. Pen. Code, Sec. 851.5; Alas. Stats., Sec. 12.25.150; N.C. Gen. Stats., Sec. 15-47; Ill. Comp. Stats. Ch. 725, Sec. 5/103-3.

43. *See, e.g.*, Ill. Comp. Stats., Ch. 720, Sec. 5/107-6; N.Y. Crim. Pro., Sec. 140.20(4); SECOND RESTATEMENT OF TORTS Sec. 134, Comment (f).

44. State v. Rowe, 238 Iowa 237, 26 N.W.2d 422 (1947); Williams v. State, 204 Md. 55, 102 A.2d 714 (1954); King v. State, 246 Miss. 86, 149 So. 2d 482 (1963); People v. Massey, 181 N.Y.S.2d 473, 2 A.D.2d 850 (1959); State v. Mobley, 240 N.C. 476, 83 S.E.2d 100 (1954); City of Columbus v. Holmes, 169 Ohio St. 251, 159 N.E.2d 232 (1959); Walters v. State, 403 P.2d 267 (Okla. Crim. App. 1965); Miers v. State, 29 S.W. 1074 (Tex. Crim. 1895).

45. *See* Ill. Comp. Stats. Ch. 720, Sec. 5/7-7; Cal. Pen. Code, Sec. 834 (a). A Cal. case has held that even where an arrest is ultimately determined to be unlawful, a defendant who resisted the arrest by the peace officer can still be convicted of simple assault or battery upon the peace officer. People v. Curtis, 70 Cal. 2d 347, 74 Cal. Rptr. 713, 450 P.2d 33 (1969). *See also* another California case, People v. Corey, 147 Cal. Rptr. 639, 581 P.2d 644 (1978), in which a moonlighting police officer, while in his

Arrests by Federal Officers

There is no single legislative act regarding the arrest powers of federal officers generally. The matter is dealt with by separate statutes pertaining to particular groups of officers. For instance, there is a separate provision for FBI agents which authorizes an arrest without warrant for "any offense against the United States committed in their presence, or for any felony cognizable under the laws of the United States if they have reasonable grounds to believe that the person to be arrested has committed or is committing such felony." Another statute confers a similar power on marshals and their deputies. Still another prescribes such arrest rights for agents of the Drug Enforcement Administration (DEA). The various arrest rights of agents of the Secret Service and officers of other governmental units, such as the Postal Inspection Service and the Bureau of Prisons, are also separately defined.[46] In the absence of applicable federal statutes, federal officers who make an arrest without a warrant for a federal offense are bound by the law of the state in which the arrest occurs.[47]

As a general rule, a state (or local) police officer has the authority and the duty to arrest without a warrant any person committing a federal offense in his presence.

Legal Alternatives to Police Arrests

As stated earlier, some states, by statute, have provided that persons accused of minor offenses may come before the court by voluntarily appearing in response to a summons[48] or a notice to appear.[49]

police officer's uniform, was kicked and had a finger broken by a shoe-wielding woman whom he tried to prevent from entering a dance hall where the officer was working. She was held to be guilty of only a single battery rather than the greater offense of assaulting a police officer. *Compare* a 1972 Arkansas Supreme Court decision holding that the state may prosecute a person for resisting arrest even though the arrestee was arrested by a moonlighting police officer working for a private employer. Meyers v. State, 253 Ark. 102, 484 S.W.2d 334 (1972). *See also* Williams v. State, 490 S.W.2d 117 (Ark. 1973), and Annot., *Illegal Arrest: Modern Status of Rules as to Right to Forcefully Resist Illegal Arrest,* 44 A.L.R.3d 1078 (1972).

46. *See,* respectively, 18 U.S.C. Sec. 3052; 29 U.S.C. Sec. 549; 26 U.S.C. Sec. 7608; 21 U.S.C. Sec. 878; 18 U.S.C. Sec. 3056; and 18 U.S.C. Sec. 3050.

47. Marsh v. United States, 29 F.2d 172 (2d Cir. 1928), *cert. denied,* 279 U.S. 849 (1929).

48. *See, e.g.,* Ariz. Rules Crim. Proc., Rule 3.1; Del. Rules Crim. Proc., Rules 4, 5; Fla. Stat. Ann., Sec. 901.09; Ga. Code Ann., Sec. 92A-506; Ill. Comp. Stats., Ch. 725, Sec. 5/107-11(a); Mass. Ann. Laws, ch. 276, Sec. 24; N.H. rev. Stats. Ann., Sec. 594.14; N.Y. Crim. Proc., Sec. 150.10 et seq.

In some jurisdictions rules of court have been promulgated to provide authorization for a court in limited types of cases (e.g., traffic offenses or nonindictable misdemeanors) to issue summons instead of arrest warrants. For example: Missouri Rules of Practices and Procedures in Municipal and Traffic Courts (1960); New Jersey Rules of Government Practice in the Local Criminal Courts. The Federal Rules of Criminal Procedure provide in Rule 4(a) that "upon the request of the attorney for the government, a summons instead of a warrant shall issue." For a similar principle, see the ABA Standards for Criminal Justice—Pre-Trial Release, Secs. 3.1-3.4.

49. *See, e.g.,* Ill. Comp. Stats., Ch. 725, Sec. 5/107-12(a); Kans. Stat. Ann., Sec. 8-5; ABA Standards for Criminal Justice—Pre-Trial Release, Secs. 2.1-2.3.

Although the use of a summons or a notice to appear is generally restricted to traffic violations or other misdemeanors, some states, as previously stated, have authorized the use of a summons or notice to appear in any case that merits it.[50] If an accused person fails to appear in response thereto, an arrest warrant will be issued.[51]

ARRESTS BY SPECIAL POLICE OR OTHER GOVERNMENTALLY AUTHORIZED SECURITY OFFICERS

As used in this section, the term *special policemen* refers primarily to individuals who are directly and regularly employed by business establishments or by such institutions as hospitals, colleges, and universities for the protection of their property, customers, patients, students, or other persons on the premises. The term may also cover uniformed guards procured by such businesses or institutions on a contract basis from various security companies for either regular or special protective duties. Excluded, however, are individual private detectives or employees of detective agencies, whose services are of an investigative nature, performed by nonuniformed personnel. The arrest privileges of special policemen and private detectives vary considerably. With rare exceptions, individual private detectives or employees of detective agencies, even though usually licensed and regulated by state statutes or local ordinances, have no greater arrest powers than ordinary citizens. On the other hand, special policemen are often granted arrest rights similar to those of public police officers, but such rights are usually restricted to the premises on which they perform their protective function.[52]

The District of Columbia Code provides very broad arrest powers to special policemen: "A special policeman shall have the same powers as a law enforcement

A summons is usually issued by a magistrate in lieu of an arrest warrant if it reasonably appears to him that the accused person will appear at court in response to it. A notice to appear is a citation issued by a police officer in lieu of an arrest. It will contain on it the date and time when the recipient is to appear in court. Some states refer to a notice to appear as a summons; however, in a strict legal sense such a notice is not a summons because it is not issued by a judge or magistrate.

50. Ill. Comp. Stats., Ch. 725, Sec. 5/107-11, 12; Tex. Code Crim. Proc. Ann., Art. 15.03.

51. *See, e.g.*, Wis. Stats. Ann., Sec. 954.02; Ill. Comp. Stats., Ch. 725, Sec. 5/107-12(c).

52. *See, e.g.*, Md. Ann. Code, art. 41, Secs. 4-901-4-905, and the various ordinances referred to in KAKALIK AND WILDHORN, CURRENT REGULATIONS OF PRIVATE POLICE: REGULATORY AGENCY EXPERIENCE AND VIEWS, Vol. III; R-871/DOJ, National Institute of Law Enforcement and Criminal Justice, LEAA (Gov. Pr. Off. #2700-0139) at 135 et seq. This was subsequently published in 1971 by a private publisher, the Rand Corporation, under the title of THE PRIVATE POLICE INDUSTRY: ITS NATURE AND EXTENT. Listed as according arrest powers to special policemen are: Baltimore, Md.; Cleveland, Ohio; Kansas City, Mo.; St. Louis and St. Louis County, Mo.; Miami, Fla.; Newark, N.J.; and New York, N.Y. Also according arrest powers are the Municipal Code of Chicago (Ch. 173-11) and Peoria, Ill. (Secs. 28-2, 5, 10). For a further general discussion, see *Private Police Forces: Legal Powers and Limitations,* 38 U. CHI. L. REV. 555, 559 (1971).

For an article dealing with the general subject of the *Regulation of Private Police, see* 40 SO. CAL. L. REV. 540 (1967); and, with respect to the *Regulations of Private Detectives,* see the extensive treatment in 86 A.L.R.3d 691 (1978).

officer to arrest without warrant for offenses committed within premises to which his jurisdiction extends, and may arrest outside the premises on fresh pursuit for offenses committed on the premises."[53]

Along with arrest powers, special policemen are often given the right to bear arms. In California, most in-house security guards are exempted from the state law that prohibits carrying loaded unconcealed weapons,[54] and bank guards and messengers are exempted from the law requiring a permit to carry concealed weapons.[55] In Illinois, licensed security guards may carry concealed weapons while performing the duties of employment or, under certain prescribed conditions, while between their homes and places of business, provided the commuting is accomplished within one hour of departure.[56] In New York, a member of the uniformed force of the New York City Housing Authority is termed a police officer and is accorded the right to arrest and to stop-and-frisk. Moreover, while off-duty he is not relieved of his obligation "to preserve the peace and protect the property of citizens."[57]

A rapidly expanding group of special policemen is the "campus police"—those who perform police functions on university and college campuses. The legal limitations on them and the powers they possess may be prescribed by state statutes or local ordinances, or both. According to one federally sponsored study, approximately thirty states permit their state governmental body for higher education to appoint campus police officers with the power of arrest; the remainder permit deputization through the governor, the court, a law enforcement agency, or a city government.[58]

The varying interpretations of the law regarding the authority conferred to campus police necessitate a check of the pertinent state statutes and the local ordinances of the particular jurisdiction in which the campus is located.

Following are two examples of the variations that may occur within an individual state. In California, security officers at *state* universities and colleges have full

---

53. Sec. 23-582(a), D.C. Code (1981). Following is the provision (Sec. 4-114) regarding the appointment of special police officers in the District: The Mayor of the District of Columbia, on application of any corporation or individual, or in his own discretion, may appoint special policemen for duty in connection with the property of, or under the charge of, such corporation or individual; said special policemen to be paid wholly by the corporation or person on whose account their appointments are made, and to be subject to such general regulations as the Council of the District of Columbia may prescribe.

54. Cal. Pen. Code, Sec. 12031(b)(7); d(1),(2)(3),(4), and (5).

55. Cal. Pen. Code, Sec. 12027(e).

56. Ill. Comp. Stats., ch. 720, Sec. 5/24-2(a)(4),(5),(6),(8),(9). Any person working as a security guard for an employer with more than thirty persons on the security force must successfully complete a training course regarding firearms usage.

57. A New York appellate court has held that a member of the Housing Authority police force was entitled to workers' compensation for injuries sustained while in the pursuit and apprehension of a thief. Washington v. N.Y. City Housing Authority, 295 N.Y.S.2d 845 (Sup. Ct. App. Div. 1968).

58. KAKALIK AND WILDHORN, SPECIAL PURPOSE PUBLIC POLICE, Vol. 5; R-873/DOJ, National Institute of Law Enforcement and Criminal Justice, LEAA (Gov. Pr. Off. #2700-0141) at 20. However, no specific references are cited.

police powers while on the campus or "within one mile of the exterior boundaries" of the campus, and "in or about other grounds or properties [of the universities and colleges]."[59] Security officers at *private* universities and colleges within California may also exercise full police powers, provided, however, they have received a special course of training, as prescribed by statute, and the institution "has concluded a memorandum of understanding, permitting the exercise of such authority, with the sheriff or chief of police within whose jurisdiction the institution lies."[60]

In Illinois, by state statute, the campus police of the University of Illinois and its various branches have their arrest powers prescribed by the "University of Illinois Police Department," whose members are appointed by the Board of Trustees of the University of Illinois. As thus prescribed, the state's university police "have all powers possessed by policemen in cities, and sheriffs, including the power to make arrests," but "only in counties where the University or any of its branches or property are located when such is required for the protection of university properties and interests, its students and personnel . . . "[61] A separate legislative provision deals with the powers of campus police at other state universities and colleges in Illinois.[62] Their powers are similar to those of the University of Illinois police force. Members of the security departments of Illinois community colleges also have similar arrest powers.[63]

In contrast to campus police at state universities and colleges in Illinois, there are no statutory provisions concerning campus security officers at *private* institutions of higher learning within Illinois. Consequently, the latter must function within the limited powers they possess as private citizens, or else under the powers accorded them by local units of government empowered by the legislature to enact ordinances dealing with "auxiliary policemen."[64] This has produced an interesting phenomenon within Northwestern University, a private university with its undergraduate branches located in Evanston and its professional schools of law, medicine, and dentistry in Chicago. In Evanston, pursuant to the state statute regarding "auxiliary policemen," the city council has designated Northwestern's Evanston campus police as "auxiliary policemen." As such, they are, according to

---

59. *See* Sec. 89560 California Education Code and Sec. 830.2 of the California Penal Code. Also, for a case in which this statutory power was exercised to arrest a university chemistry professor for manufacturing an unlawful chemical substance, *see* People v. Dickson, 154 Cal. Rptr. 116 (Cal. App. 1979).

60. *See* Cal. Pen. Code, Secs. 832 and 830.7.

61. Ill. Comp. Stats. ch. 110, Sec. 305/7.

62. Ill. Comp. Stats., ch. 110, Sec. 520/8, (10).

63. Ill. Comp. Stats., ch. 110, Sec. 805/3-42.1.

64. The power of local government units to enact such ordinances stems from a state statute (Ill. Comp. Stats., Ch. 65, Sec. 5/3-6-5), which provides that the mayor or village president of any municipality in Ill. may, "with the advice and consent of the corporate authorities," appoint uniformed "auxiliary policemen" who "shall at all times during the performance of their duties be subject to the direction and control of the Chief of Police of the municipality." They are accorded full arrest powers by Ch. 65, Sec. 5/3-9-4, which provision also gives broad arrest powers to mayors, aldermen, and "watchmen." ("Watchmen" is not defined.)

the Evanston ordinance, subject at all times to "the direction and control of the chief of police of Evanston."[65] In Chicago, however, the only ordinance of relevance to Northwestern's security force there is one on "special policemen."[66] Although it requires that "special policemen" receive a certificate of appointment from the superintendent and wear a "suitable badge" (issued by the superintendent) "on the outside of their outer coat," the ordinance says nothing about any "direction or control" by the superintendent. It does provide, however, that "special policemen shall possess the powers of the regular police patrol at the places for which they are respectively appointed or in the line of duty for which they are engaged."[67]

The state and municipal powers that may be conferred on campus security officers, and the extent of direction or control that may be exerted over them by the local police chiefs or superintendents, are significant not only in relation to the power to arrest, but also with respect to the searches and seizures these officers make and the interrogations they conduct of suspected or arrested persons. As shall be seen in the succeeding chapters on those two subjects, the official powers that are conferred or not conferred on campus police will bear directly on whether their conduct brings them within the exclusionary rule respecting illegal searches and seizures, and also whether they are required to administer the *Miranda* warnings prior to the interrogation of arrested persons.[68]

ARRESTS BY PRIVATE CITIZENS INCLUDING NONDEPUTIZED OR NONCOMMISSIONED SECURITY OFFICERS

As already stated, for some offenses, and under certain conditions, a private citizen may make an arrest. A nondeputized or noncommissioned security officer possesses that same power, *but no more*. It is important, therefore, that he knows the extent of an ordinary citizen's arrest power and its limitations.

The General Law

In former times, a private citizen without any statutory authorization had the right to arrest for a felony,[69] and also for a misdemeanor committed in his presence, provided the latter offense involved a "breach of the peace," definable as an

---

65. Evanston Ordinance 99-0-71.

66. Municipal Code of Chicago, ch.173.

67. Sec. 173-11.

68. *See* Chapters 3 and 4.

69. Consider this statement from United States v. Coplon, 185 F.2d 629, 634 (2d Cir. 1950): "At common law a private person . . . had the power to arrest without warrant for a felony . . . actually committed in the past, if he had reasonable ground to suppose it had been committed by the person whom he arrested" (citing 1 BISHOP'S NEW CRIMINAL PROCEDURE, Sec. 168).

occurrence which did or was very likely to arouse or disturb a segment of the public.[70]

The generally prevailing case law at the present time has been summarized in the *Second Restatement of the Law of Torts* by the American Law Institute. It provides, in its essential parts, that a private citizen is authorized to arrest another for a criminal offense (a) if the other person has committed a felony for which he is arrested, (b) if a felony has been committed and the arrester reasonably suspects the arrestee has committed it, (c) if the arrestee, in the arrester's presence, is committing a breach of the peace or is about to renew it, (d) if the arrestee has attempted to commit a felony in the arrester's presence and the arrest is made at once or in fresh pursuit, or (e) if the arrestee "knowingly causes" the arrester to believe that facts exist which would create a privilege to arrest under (a), (b), (c), or (d).[71]

Legislative Enactments

Most states have attempted to clarify or extend their common law by prescribing, in statutes, the conditions and circumstances under which citizen arrest may be made. (These state statutes are presented in the Appendix to this book.) The statutes lack uniformity, however, and in order to understand them fully it is usually necessary to consider additional statutory provisions of the particular state; moreover, their correct interpretation often requires a knowledge of relevant constitutional law decisions, and particularly those of the United States Supreme Court. A good illustration is the 1973 Oregon private citizen arrest statute.[72] It provides as follows: "A private person may arrest another person for any crime committed in his presence if he has probable cause to believe the arrested person committed the crime." To a layperson, "probable cause" may not be very meaningful. As previously stated, however, an awareness of pertinent Supreme Court decisions, as well as those of other courts, supports the view that what this phrase really means is "reasonable grounds," an expression that seems to be a more understandable one than "probable cause."[73]

---

70. PERKINS AND BOYCE, CASES AND MATERIALS ON CRIMINAL LAW AND PROCEDURE (5th ed. 1977). *See also The Law of Citizen's Arrest*, 65 COL. L. REV. 502 (1965).

71. SECOND RESTATEMENT OF THE LAW OF TORTS, Sec. 119 (1966). The comments to this section of the Restatement, and the state decisions cited in them as well as in the Appendix, should be of special value to anyone researching the law of a particular state.

   As will be observed shortly, some states, by statute, have extended the rule stated in the above text to permit a private citizen to make an arrest for any misdemeanor, provided it is committed in that person's presence. (In addition to the statutes discussed in this text, see, in the Appendix, the ones in Idaho, Mont., Nev., Okla., and Tenn.) Usually, however, there is no authorization for a private citizen to make an arrest for a municipal or county ordinance violation.

   Even where a private citizen arrest statute restricts such arrests to misdemeanor violations involving "breach of the peace," at least one appellate court has held that a store owner, or an employee with "custodial responsibility" for the merchandise, may, despite the statutory language, make an arrest for a theft of such property. State v. Santi, 8 Ariz. App. 77, 443 P.2d 439 (1968).

72. Oreg. Rev. Stats., Secs. 133.220(3), 133.225.

73. *See* the clarifying diagram presented earlier in this chapter.

Another illustration of statutory language that authorizes citizen arrests but necessitates a search elsewhere for its meaning is the Alaska statute.[74] It provides: "A private person . . . may arrest a person (1) for a crime committed or attempted in the presence of the person making the arrest; (2) when the person has committed a felony, although not in the presence of the person making the arrest; (3) when a felony has been committed, and the person making the arrest has reasonable cause for believing the person to have committed it." Elsewhere in Alaska's Criminal Code, "crime" is defined as "an offense for which a sentence of imprisonment is authorized," "either a felony or a misdemeanor."[75] And still another Alaska statute defines "felony" as "a crime for which a sentence of imprisonment for a period of more than one year is authorized."[76]

Some other state statutes are considerably more complex than either of the foregoing ones—those in California and New York, for instance, which are reproduced in the Appendix of this book.

The Illinois Code of Criminal Procedure provision on private citizen arrests is one that is stated rather simply, but it, too, presents an interpretation problem.[77] How the problem is resolved may be of interest and value to security officers generally, and most certainly to those in Illinois. The provision reads as follows: "Any person may arrest another when he has reasonable grounds to believe that an offense other than an ordinance violation is being committed." The reader may immediately see that in contrast to the Oregon statute, which uses the phrase "probable cause," the Illinois statute employs the phrase "reasonable grounds," more readily understood by nonlawyers, even though the two phrases have the same meaning. What, however, constitutes "reasonable grounds"? What is an "offense"? And when may it be said that an offense "is being committed"? When we answer these questions, the Illinois private citizen's arrest powers become more clearly understood.

The Meaning of "Offense"

"Offense" is defined elsewhere in the Illinois Code of Criminal Procedure as "a violation of any penal statute of this State."[78] Thus, in Illinois there is no legal authorization for a security officer or other private citizen to make an arrest for a municipal or county ordinance violation.

74. Alas. Stats., Sec. 12.25.030.

75. Alas. Stats., Sec. 11.81.900(9).

76. Alas. Stats., Sec. 11.81.900(19).

77. Ill. Comp. Stats., ch. 725, Sec. 5/107-3.

78. Ill. Comp. Stats., ch. 725, Sec. 5/102-15. This section originally defined "offense" to mean "a violation of any penal statute of this State *or any penal ordinance of its political subdivision.*" It was revised in 1969 by the elimination of the *italicized* portion.

There is another, much broader definition of "offense" in the Ill. Code of Corrections (Ill. Comp. Stats., ch. 730, Sec. 5/1-15), but it pertains only to the matter of sentencing of a convicted person.

EXAMPLE

While on his way to work by bus one morning, a department store security officer, Johnson, observed a very unhealthy looking passenger spit on the floor of the bus. Johnson was very much incensed, because one of his brothers had died of tuberculosis in childhood, and Johnson himself was once afflicted with the disease. Johnson knew that there was a city ordinance that prohibited spitting on a bus. He arrested the violator. The arrest was unlawful, because such conduct was not a violation of a *state* penal statute.

In case situations such as the foregoing, a private citizen has only two options: he may call the conduct to the attention of a police officer, or, if he knows or ascertains the identity of the violator, he may go to a judicial magistrate and file a complaint against him.

Falling within the meaning of "offense," as used in the Illinois provision, is, of course, retail theft (shoplifting). Irrespective of whether the cost of the article places the offense in the felony or the misdemeanor category, the conduct is a theft specifically prohibited by "a penal statute of the State." Another illustration of the kind of criminal conduct that falls within the same category is the offense of disorderly conduct.[79] Because it is proscribed by state law, it is an offense for which a private citizen may make an arrest. However, before any person attempts to make arrests for disorderly conduct, or, indeed, for any offense not fully revealed by its very label, he should become aware of the various elements that make up the offense. To assist the reader in this respect, Chapter 12 discusses the various offenses that security officers are likely to encounter.

"Reasonable Grounds." Whether reasonable grounds exist for a private citizen's belief that a criminal offense is being committed will depend upon the circumstances of each particular case. If any general rule is to be applied, perhaps it should be the citizen's own good judgment in response to this question, which he may ask of himself: "Under these circumstances, how would a disinterested, impartial observer view the matter; would he consider as 'reasonable' that which I am about to do?"

EXAMPLE

A department store security agent, Baldwin, observed a woman at an unattended necktie counter. He saw her pick up a necktie, look around, and then insert her hand in her purse, but he did not actually see the necktie go into the purse. However, since the necktie was no longer on the counter, he had "reasonable grounds to believe" that the "offense" of theft (defined elsewhere in the Criminal Code) was being committed. Consequently, Baldwin was privileged to make an arrest. The arrest would be legal even if it should later be revealed that the necktie was not in the purse but had fallen behind the counter.

In situations such as this one, however, there is a natural reluctance to make an arrest, for fear that a jury in a false arrest suit against the employer and the secu-

79. Ill. Comp. Stats., ch. 720, Sec. 5/26-1.

rity officer will decide that the event did not satisfy the "reasonable grounds" requirement of the arrest provision. Consequently, a security officer would ordinarily refrain from making an arrest unless he actually saw the necktie go into the purse. In other words, he would want to be *sure* the offense was being committed rather than rely on a *reasonable belief,* even though the arrest provision of the Code grants him the greater leeway. He would prefer to rely on the temporary detention opportunity afforded by another Illinois statute (similar to those in some other states) and merely stop and briefly question the person for the purpose of ascertaining what happened to the necktie.[80] (The security officer's right to detain customers in such situations is discussed in detail in Chapter 3.)

A security officer functions under a practical disadvantage when he makes an arrest. Despite the flexibility of the phrase "reasonable grounds," in a suit for false arrest a jury is aware that a security officer has acted primarily to protect a selfish company interest (i.e., the protection of its merchandise), and also, in all probability, believes that the company can well afford to pay for a mistake and should do so even though it be a reasonable one. A different jury reaction may be forthcoming in a case where a private citizen acts in protection of another private citizen's interest, or simply in the public interest.

Following is an illustration of case circumstances which constitute reasonable grounds for a security officer to make an arrest. As a precaution, however, he may resort to the temporary detention alternative.

EXAMPLE

A salesperson in a department store told Security Officer Harrison that she had just seen a woman, whom she pointed out, take a bottle of perfume off a counter and put it in her purse without paying for it.

In addition to the previously mentioned risk of civil liability if the salesperson was in error, a tactical problem may arise at the time of a trial for false arrest. Is the salesperson apt to be available as a witness? Will she still be in the company's employ? This risk of witness unavailability is less likely to occur in those cases where the security officer himself saw the offense being committed.[81]

By general law, escape is considered to be a continuation of the offense. Consequently, even though the offender may have completed the offense of theft by taking and carrying off to some other part of the premises a piece of merchandise with the intention of stealing it, his act of departing with it, even outside the store, is viewed as a continuation of the offense. The act of commission continues until the offender has reached a place of safety and concealment. In other words, the crime of shoplifting is still "being committed" up to the point where the shoplifter has left the store and has reached a place or area where he can say to himself the equivalent of, "Well, I got away with that one."

---

80. Ill. Comp. Stats., ch. 720, Sec. 5/16A-5.

81. Consider Hanna v. Raphael Weill & Co., 203 P.2d 564 (Cal. Dist. Ct. App. 1949), in which the court strictly construed the California citizen arrest statute and held that a security officer must actually see the offense being committed; he cannot rely on the word of another person.

Citizen Assistance in Police Arrests

At common law, when a known police officer summoned a bystander for the purpose of assisting him in making an arrest, the citizen was bound to respond,[82] and some states have codified the common law requirements for assisting police officers in making an arrest. In Illinois, for instance, any person over the age of eighteen is legally bound to aid a police officer in making an arrest when the officer commands assistance.[83] The Illinois Code of Criminal Procedure also provides that the assisting person "shall not be civilly liable for any reasonable conduct in aid of the officer."[84] He is also exempt from the Code's prohibition against the unlawful use of weapons.[85] Moreover, when a person who has been commanded to assist a police officer in making an arrest is himself injured or killed, or his property or that of his employer is damaged in the course of his assistance, that person, his survivor, or his employer has a right of action against the municipality employing the police officer.[86]

Use of Force by Private Citizens in Making an Arrest

A private citizen assisting a police officer in making an arrest may generally use the same force a police officer is entitled to use.[87] The exception to this, as stated in one statutory provision, is where the citizen knows that the arrest being made by the officer is actually unlawful.[88] When a private citizen is making an arrest for an offense other than on command of an officer, the amount of force allowable varies, depending on the nature of the crime and other factors.

By way of generalization, only reasonable force is allowable in any citizen arrest situation. By this test deadly force is impermissible with regard to misdemeanors, and only permissible under certain circumstances in cases involving dangerous felonies such as murder, robbery, burglary, rape, and aggravated assault. Deadly force is force that is likely to cause death or great bodily harm; it includes the firing of a weapon in the direction of the person to be arrested, or the firing at a vehicle in which the person to be arrested is riding.[89] One of the present day viewpoints is exemplified in the Illinois Criminal Code. In Illinois, a private person (except when

---

82. Elrod v. Moss, 278 F. 113 (4th Cir. 1921). *See also* FISHER, LAW OF ARREST 354-365 (1967).

83. Ill. Comp. Stats., ch. 725, Sec. 5/107-8. It also provides that the citizen "shall not be civilly liable for any reasonable conduct in aid of the officer." Another provision, Ch. 720, Sec. 5/31-8, requires citizens to aid in an apprehension or to prevent the commission of an offense. A failure to do so constitutes a "petty offense." Elsewhere in the code, Ch. 730, Sec. 5/59-1, such an offense is punishable by a fine of up to $500.

84. Ill. Comp. Stats., ch. 720, Sec. 5/107-8(c).

85. Ill. Comp. Stats., ch 720, Sec. 5/24-2(a)(1).

86. Ill. Comp. Stats., ch. 65, Sec. 5/1-4-5 and 5/1-4-6.

87. FISHER, LAW OF ARREST 362 (1967). *See also* Ill. Comp. Stats., Ch. 720, Sec. 5/7-5 and 5/7-6.

88. Ill. Comp. Stats., ch. 720, Sec. 5/7-6(b).

89. For an example of a statutory provision containing this definition, see Ill. Comp. Stat., Ch. 720, Sec. 5/7-8.

assisting a police officer) may not use deadly force in effecting an arrest, even in forcible felony case situations, unless he "reasonably believes that such force is necessary to prevent death or great bodily harm to himself or another."[90]

Regardless of statutory delineations as to force that is or is not permissible, deadly force by a private security officer should, as a general rule, be reserved for those situations where necessary to prevent imminent death or great bodily harm to himself or another person. There are two principal reasons for this exercise of restraint:

1. "Reasonable belief" as to the elements that justify the use of deadly force is a matter which in hindsight may be viewed differently by those who are called upon to evaluate a private security officer's action. Even among appellate courts there may be differing opinions as to whether a certain set of facts constitutes "reasonable belief." A private security officer's split-second decision to use deadly force may later be considered an unreasonable belief, regardless of the existence of good faith, and he will thereby subject himself and his employer to liability.

2. If deadly force is needed to prevent the commission of a forcible felony or the escape of a felon, it is better, whenever possible, to relinquish that responsibility to public law enforcement officers. They are usually better prepared and also better protected by law, in making the delicate judgments that are required, especially with regard to the safety of innocent bystanders and fellow employees.

Although "reasonable force" is permissible in effecting a citizen arrest for a criminal, it is well for security officers and others protecting store or industry interests to remember that most persons who are about to be arrested for a nonviolent crime will submit without resistance or commotion of any sort. For instance, if the security officer approaches a shoplifter quietly and inconspicuously, the shoplifter will not become so disturbed as when the arrest is made in a very noticeable and excited manner. Then, by spending a few minutes in conversation, the arrester will be giving the arrestee a chance to adjust to the situation, followed by consent to accompany the arrester to police custody or a court.

Where force is required, the determination of its reasonableness will depend upon the surrounding circumstances of each case. About the only test of reasonableness will be the arrester's own good judgment in answer to the question: "Is what I am about to do something that an impartial observer or a jury would consider necessary, but not excessive, in order to seize and to hold the offender in custody?"

These same rules and principles are also generally applied when a citizen is trying to apprehend someone who attempts to escape after he has been observed committing an offense.[91]

---

90. Ill. Comp. Stats., ch. 720, Sec. 5/7-6(a). With regard to the difference between the right of a police officer and that of a citizen to use force in effecting an arrest, consult People v. Whitty, 292 N.W.2d 214 (Mich. App. 1980), and the references cited therein.

91. On this point it is of interest to note the case of People v. Garcia, 78 Cal. Rptr. 775 (Cal. App. 1961), which also applied the principle that it is unlawful for a person to resist forcibly a lawful citizen arrest. In this case, a building manager arrested the defendant who was seen attempting to burglarize the building.

Required Procedure After Making a Citizen Arrest

Most state statutes do not contain any provision that deals specifically with the procedure a private citizen should follow after making an arrest. Some, however, provide that the arrestee must be taken before a judge or magistrate "without unnecessary delay"; others provide for the alternative of delivering the arrestee to the police.[92] The latter procedure is one that is usually followed by a private citizen, irrespective of whether a statute specifically authorized it, and there is scant doubt as to the validity of such a procedure. After an arresting citizen has delivered the arrestee to the police, he must sign a complaint against him, after which there is the obligation, of course, to testify at the trial itself.

Although a person arrested by a security officer may be taken to the protection office of the store or plant, he should not be detained there any longer than the time needed for police arrival.

After a police officer has made an arrest (even though he had reasonable grounds for doing so), he may become satisfied that the arrestee is innocent of the offense. Although some early court cases have held that the arresting officer has no legal authority, absent statutory authorization, to release the arrestee—that decision being one for a judge or magistrate—the usually sanctioned procedure is to allow the arresting officer, or, preferably, a commanding officer, to release the arrestee.[93] This, obviously, is the humane procedure to follow, and some states have sanctioned it by statute.[94] It is also the rule of reason which should apply to a private citizen or security officer in an arrest situation, with the result of a release without going through the useless and unfair procedure of taking the arrestee to a judge, who would immediately do the same thing. On such occasions, a security officer will usually seek a written release from the arrestee. He may also do this even in those cases where the evidence of guilt is present but other considerations suggest that no further action be taken.[95]

Arrests of Juveniles

Although the law accords special trial and post-trial treatment to child offenders and delinquents, juveniles are subject to arrest, and essentially the same arrest procedures apply to them as to adults. In actual practice, however, security offi-

---

92. The Ill. Code of Criminal Procedure provides that a person who is arrested with or without a warrant "shall be taken without unnecessary delay before the nearest and most accessible judge in that county." Ill. Comp. Stats., ch. 725, Sec. 5/109-1.

  The alternative procedure of delivering the arrestee to the police is authorized by the following: Ala. Code, tit. 15, Sec. 10-7; Cal. Pen. Code, Sec. 847; Idaho Code, Sec. 19-604, 19-614; Mich. Stats. Ann. Sec. 28.873; N.Y. Crim. Proc., Sec. 140.40; Okla. Stats. Ann., tit. 22, Sec. 202, 205; Oreg. Rev. Stat., Sec. 133.225; Tenn. Code Ann., Sec. 40-7-113.

93. FISHER, LAW OF ARREST Sec. 156 (1967).

94. See, e.g., Ill. Comp. Stats., ch. 725, Sec. 5/107-6. See also FISHER, supra note 93.

95. The validity of contractual releases will be discussed subsequently in Chapter 10.

cers, in an effort to cooperate with public officials in their juvenile delinquency programs, will usually notify the local police department's juvenile officer and follow his instructions as to whether the arrestee should be released to the custody of his parents or held for formal police and court action. When the offense is a very minor one, and especially when the circumstances are indicative of a first offense, the security officer may contact a parent directly and release the child to him or her without involving the police at all.

The law with respect to juveniles varies among the states. Security officers, therefore, should acquaint themselves with the juvenile arrest requirements of their particular jurisdiction.

2

The Law of Search and Seizure

A security officer must be aware not only of the rights and limitations with respect to arrests but also regarding searches and seizures. Once again, the discussion will begin with the law on the subject as it affects the police.

SEARCHES AND SEIZURES BY THE POLICE

In general, after a police officer makes a lawful arrest, with or without an arrest warrant, she is privileged to search the arrestee and the area within her immediate control. Also, pursuant to a search warrant—a court order issued on reasonable grounds (or probable cause) to search for and seize specified items—a police officer may search a premise for such items. In either instance, if, as the search is being conducted, the officer finds or observes "in plain view" stolen articles, or articles known as "contraband" (an illegal weapon, narcotics, counterfeit money, or anything the mere possession of which is illegal), she may, as a general rule, make a lawful seizure of them, and they may be used as evidence in court. If, however, the arrest itself is illegal, or the officer exceeded the permissible bounds of a lawful search when she located certain articles, the evidence thus obtained may not be used to prosecute because of the "exclusionary rule," which provides that illegally obtained evidence may be barred in court, subject to some exceptions. Also, under some circumstances, the officer may subject herself to criminal and civil liability for an illegal search. The legal consequences of illegal searches and seizures will be further discussed in Chapter 10.

Search Incident to Arrest Without Warrant

Either by court decision law, particularly as enunciated by the Supreme Court of the United States, or by statutory enactments, a search may be made of a lawfully arrested person without a warrant: (a) to protect the arresting officer from attack;

(b) to prevent the arrestee's escape; (c) to discover the fruits of the crime; or (d) to discover the instrumentalities and evidence of the crime.[1]

Under a 1973 decision by the Supreme Court of the United States in *United States v. Robinson,* any person lawfully arrested by the police, regardless of the nature of the offense, may be subjected to a full search (sometimes known as a "field search"), and whatever incriminating evidence is found on her person or in her clothing may be used against her.[2] This ruling was established in a case where a motorist was arrested for operating a motor vehicle after his license had been revoked and after he had obtained a driver's permit by false representation. In accordance with the police department's regulations, the arresting officer was obliged to take the driver into custody rather than merely give him a ticket or summons. As a full search was being conducted in the *Robinson* case, the officer discovered some capsules of heroin concealed in a cigarette pack, and the Supreme Court held that the evidence was usable in a prosecution of the defendant for possessing the heroin.

It should be kept in mind that the extensive search privilege accorded by the Supreme Court in the *Robinson* case applies only to situations in which an actual arrest is made—in other words, only when a person is taken into custody for the purpose of bringing her to court to face a criminal charge.

One motivation for the *Robinson* decision was to protect an officer who takes a person into custody; even though the offense itself may be a minor one, the arrestee could be a dangerous person, such as a fugitive, who may have a knife or other potentially dangerous instrumentality cleverly concealed on her person or in her clothing. No such consideration is involved in an ordinary traffic violation stop which calls only for the issuance of a ticket, although, to be sure, there have been instances of police officers being killed even under those circumstances. A search of all stopped motorists, however, would obviously be unreasonable and

---

1. For a concise yet comprehensive statute covering the purposes for which an arrested person may be searched, consider the following provision in the Ill. Code of Criminal Procedure (725 ILCS Sec. 5/108.1):

   When a lawful arrest is effected a police officer may reasonably search the person arrested and the area within such person's immediate presence for the purpose of: (a) Protecting the officer from attack; or (b) Preventing the person from escaping; or (c) Discovering the fruits of the crime; or (d) Discovering any instruments, articles, or things which may have been used in the commission of, or which may constitute evidence of, an offense.

   There are numerous court decisions regarding permissible searches of an arrested person. Only some of the most important ones, those closely relevant to the subject matter of this text, can be covered here. For the reader who is interested in a broader coverage, we suggest a resort to the following book: F.E. INBAU, J.P. MANAK, J.R. THOMPSON, AND J.B. ZAGEL, CRIMINAL LAW AND ITS ADMINISTRATION (5th ed. 1990).

2. 414 U.S. 218 (1973). A companion case to the same effects is Gustafson v. Florida, 414 U.S. 260 (1973). In accord with the foregoing cases: State v. Florance, 515 P.2d 195 (Ore. 1973); Hughes v. State, 522 P.2d 1331 (Okla. Crim. App. 1974). A few state courts, relying upon their own state constitutions, have invalidated, on state grounds, the type of searches involved in *Robinson* and *Gustafson:* People v. Brisendine, 119 Cal. Rptr. 315, 531 P.2d 1099 (1975); Zehrung v. State, 569 P.2d 189 (Alas. 1977).

thus a violation of the Fourth Amendment or state constitutional rights. The same restrictive principle would apply with respect to a search of a motorist's car following a stop for a traffic violation, or even after an actual arrest for an ordinary violation. On the other hand, in a case situation such as that in *Robinson,* after heroin or other contraband or stolen property is lawfully found and seized from the person of a motorist, that fact in itself would give the officer reasonable grounds to conduct a search of the car, because of the probability that the car contained more narcotics, or, indeed, other contraband or stolen property.

Following is a hypothetical case situation that reveals, in addition to the reasonable basis for an arrest, the extent of the search that may be made incident to it.

EXAMPLE

In responding to a report of burglary in progress one rainy night in a jewelry shop, officers Adams and Brewster observed Parker and Harmon running from the rear of the shop toward a car about half a block away from the shop. In back of the shop, between it and the location of the car, is an unpaved strip of land about fifty feet wide. Just after Parker and Harmon entered the car, the officers approached, informed them they were under arrest, and ordered them out of the car.

The officers were privileged (1) to search the arrestees for weapons; (2) to remove the car keys so as to prevent use of the car for an escape; (3) to search both the men and the car for stolen jewelry; and (4) to search the car for burglary tools that subsequently could be tested to compare the markings they leave on test lead plates with those on a door or window through which entry was effected into the shop. Moreover, at an appropriate time and place, the shoes worn by Parker and Harmon could be subjected to laboratory tests to determine the similarity between the soil on them and soil specimens from the muddy strip of land; additionally, the characteristics of the shoes themselves could be checked against casts which laboratory technicians may have made of the shoe impressions left in the mud leading from the burglarized store.

In the 1969 case of *Chimel v. California,* the Supreme Court held that a search incident to an arrest must be confined to the person of the arrestee and the area within his immediate control.[3] Although this case involved a warrant for the defendant's arrest, and the arrest was made in his home, the same limitation will prevail as to the area of search pursuant to a warrantless arrest. In general, therefore, if a more extensive search is to be made the recommended practice is to obtain a search warrant, particularly if it involves a home or other premise.[4] However, several courts have held that when an arrest is made in a premise consisting of more than one room, a search is allowable within those areas to ascertain if other per-

---

3. 395 U.S. 752 (1969). The phrase "within his immediate control" was described as "the area within which he might have obtained either a weapon or something that could have been used as evidence against him."

4. Of very practical value to arresting officers in such situations is the procurement of a "telephonic search warrant," a procedure sanctioned by Fed'l. Rule Crim. Proc. 41(c)(2)(A), as well as by statutes in Ariz. and Cal. Ariz. Rev. Stats., Sec. 13-1444, 1445(c); Cal. Penal Code, Secs. 1526, 1528.

    As discussed in Chapter 1, note 18, an arrest warrant is required in order to arrest a person in his home, unless there is an emergency situation.

sons are present who might endanger the arresting officers.[5] Evidence observed in plain view while making such a "protective sweep" search is subject to lawful seizure.[6]

If there is reason to believe that incriminating evidence may be found in the area where an arrest is to be made, and time and circumstances permit, police officers should obtain a search warrant. This is particularly true in regard to a residence, an office, or a shop.[7] However, as will be subsequently discussed, greater leeway exists in regard to movable vehicles.[8]

Search Incident to Arrest upon Warrant for Arrest

The nature and scope of permissible searches and seizures pursuant to an arrest upon warrant are the same as that previously described with respect to a warrantless arrest.

An arresting officer need not have the arrest warrant in her possession at the time of the arrest and search, provided a legally proper arrest warrant has been issued and the arresting officer has knowledge of its issuance.[9]

---

5. United States v. Looney, 481 F.2d 31 (5th Cir. 1973); State v. Toliver, 487 P.2d 264 (Wash. App. 1971); Jones v. State, 272 So. 2d 910 (Ala. 1973). *But see* State v. Ranker, 343 So. 2d 189 (La. 1977). *See* Maryland v. Buie, 494 U.S. 325 (1990), in which the U.S. Supreme Court held that a police officer, incident to an in-home arrest, could as a precautionary matter and without probable cause or reasonable suspicion, look in closets and other spaces immediately adjoining the place of arrest from which an attack could be immediately launched. Such "properly limited" protective sweeps did not violate the Fourth Amendment when carried out in conjunction with an in-home arrest, and when the officer possesses a reasonable belief based on specific and articulable facts that the area to be swept harbors an individual posing a danger to those on the arrest scene.

6. *Supra* note 5.

7. The Supreme Court of the United States has vacillated considerably regarding the validity of seizures incident to arrests in such places when there was ample time to secure a search warrant. The latest decision is that a warrant must be obtained. For a history of these vacillations, see both the majority and minority opinions in Chimel v. California, *supra* note 3.

8. The present chapter, page 43.

9. People v. Jeffries, 31 Ill. 2d 597, 203 N.E.2d 396 (1964). Officers may not, however, use the fact that they are on the premises to execute an arrest warrant for one individual to conduct a warrantless, nonconsensual "dragnet" identity search of others present. *In* Community for Creative Non-Violence v. U.S. Marshals Service, 797 F. Supp. 7 (D.C. 1992), U.S. Marshals raided a homeless shelter looking for a fugitive named in a warrant who they believed was there, but they brought along a long computer printout of all fugitives in the D.C. area and checked all identifications of homeless persons in the shelter against that list. This, the court ruled, was clearly "beyond the scope of what an arrest warrant for one person thought to be in the shelter would permit." "Homeless" persons may still have some expectation of privacy in the place where they dwell. *See* Commonwealth v. Gordon, 640 A.2d 422 (Pa. Super. 1994) (homeless person living in room in abandoned house had a reasonable expectation of privacy violated when an officer made a warrantless entry of his room after entering the house through a half-opened door).

Time of the "Arrest Search"

As a general rule, a search incident to an arrest must be closely related in time to the arrest itself. This means it must be contemporaneous with the arrest or follow immediately thereafter. There are cases holding, however, that if at the time a person was searched there existed legal justification for her arrest, it is of no consequence that the actual arrest occurred at a later time or date.[10]

Force Permissible in Making a Seizure Incident to an Arrest

A police officer may use reasonable force and employ reasonable means to seize evidence during a search incident to an arrest. The following actual case examples illustrate that which is reasonable and that which is unreasonable:

EXAMPLE

Police officers arrested Johnson for a narcotics violation. Upon seeing the officers, Johnson attempted to swallow two narcotics capsules he was carrying. The officers grabbed Johnson and shook him and forced him to cough up the capsules before he could swallow them. The police conduct was reasonable and proper.[11]

EXAMPLE

In a similar situation, Thomas actually swallowed the capsules. The police officers took him to a hospital and ordered that his stomach be pumped (without Thomas' consent) in order to retrieve the capsules before they dissolved. This kind of police conduct is considered excessive and unreasonable,[12] and therefore the seized evidence could not be used against Thomas.

The lack of consent and actual resistance to a search on the part of an accused person does not convert an otherwise reasonable search into an illegal search or seizure. However, evidence obtained by methods so brutal and violent as to

---

10. Cupp v. Murphy, 412 U.S. 291 (1973). In this case the Supreme Court held that since the police had reasonable grounds to arrest a husband for killing his wife, an arrest did not have to precede the taking of scrapings of his fingernails against his will. The actual arrest occurred one month later.

11. People v. Johnson, 223 N.E.2d 321 (Ill. App. 1966).

12. Rochin v. California, 342 U.S. 165 (1952). In this case the Supreme Court held that even though the police conduct did not violate the arrestee's Fifth Amendment privilege against "self-incrimination" (because it involved the forceable procurement of physical rather than "testimonial" evidence), there was a violation of that Amendment's protection of "due process of law" by virtue of the use of a tactic "shocking to the conscience" of the Court.

"shock the conscience" of a civilized society is considered to be unconstitutionally seized, and it is thus rendered unusable at the trial of the accused.[13]

"Frisk" Instead of "Search"

As noted in the preceding chapter, in the 1968 case of *Terry v. Ohio,* the Supreme Court validated the police practice of stopping and "making reasonable inquiries" of a person reasonably suspected of criminal activity, or, as the Court expressed it, when the police have a reasonable suspicion that "criminality may be afoot."[14] Additionally, the Court held that if under such circumstances the police officer reasonably concludes that the person whom he has stopped "may be armed and presently dangerous," he is entitled "for the protection of himself and others . . . to conduct a carefully limited search of the outer clothing . . . in an attempt to discover weapons which might be used to assault him." Any weapons seized in the course of such a frisk were declared admissible as evidence against the person from whom they were taken.[15] In a later case, the Court held that the officer may base his belief on information supplied by someone else, not just on his own observations.[16] However, in contrast to a permissible full search incident to an arrest, in stop-and-frisk situations a search is not allowed for anything other than weapons, although evidence discovered while searching for weapons is subject to lawful seizure.[17]

13. Rochin v. California, *supra* note 12. In contrast to the *Rochin* case, however, consider Schmerber v. California, 384 U.S. 757 (1966), in which the Supreme Court held it was lawful for the police, who had arrested the defendant for driving while under the influence of alcohol, to have a nonconsensual blood specimen taken by a physician in a hospital to which the defendant had been transported for the treatment of injuries received in an automobile accident.

14. 392 U.S. 1, at 30 (1968). See Chapter 1, pages 1 and 2, and particularly note 2.

15. 392 U.S. 1, at 30.

16. Adams v. Williams, 407 U.S. 143 (1972).

17. Tinny v. Wilson, 408 F.2d 912 (9th Cir. 1969). A relevant case which involved a shoplifting situation is Whitten v. United States, 396 A.2d 208 (D.C. Ct. App. 1978). A store employee called the police to report the suspicious conduct of a person who had been in the store. She was instructed to call again if he returned, and she did. The police stopped that person as he was about to enter another store. The officer requested identification, but the suspect could offer none. He also gave contradictory accounts about the absence of his wallet. He was carrying a raincoat over his arm, although rain was falling at the time. When asked what was under the raincoat, he replied, "Nothing," whereupon the officer lifted it up and observed a leather jacket which was identified as one stolen from the store whose employee had called the police. The Court of Appeals for the District of Columbia held that the jacket could not be used as evidence because the officer had made a search rather than a mere frisk as authorized by Terry v. Ohio.

   In an important decision, the U.S. Supreme Court adopted a "plain feel" doctrine for stop and frisk situations. In Minnesota v. Dickerson, 113 S. Ct. 2130 (1993), the Court ruled animously that a police officer conducting a Terry v. Ohio frisk of a suspect based upon a reasonable suspicion that he is armed and dangerous may seize evidence other than a weapon if, in conducting the frisk, the contraband nature of the evidence is "immediately apparent" to the officer based upon his feel of the object through the suspect's clothing during the pat down.

Many states have enacted statutes that codify police officers' power to stop-and-frisk.[18] These statutes generally provide that a police officer, after having identified herself as such, may stop any person in a public place for a reasonable period of time whenever the officer reasonably suspects, from the circumstances of the situation, that the person she stopped is committing, is about to commit, or has committed an offense. Moreover, the officer may ask for the detainee's name and address and an explanation of her actions. The detention and temporary questioning must, however, be conducted in the vicinity where the person is stopped. If, thereafter, the officer reasonably suspects that she or some other individual is in danger of attack, she may search the detained person for weapons. If the officer discovers a weapon, she may take it until completion of the questioning, at which time she shall either return the weapon, if lawfully possessed, or arrest the person so questioned.

"Plain View" Seizures of Contraband

The following example illustrates the already mentioned rule that articles not subject to lawful possession—for instance, contraband such as narcotic drugs—may be seized if they are within plain view of a police officer in a place where she is lawfully present.

EXAMPLE

Officer O'Malley, equipped with a warrant to search Yates' home for stolen property, observed in plain view a sawed-off shotgun. Since its mere possession is unlawful, the gun may be lawfully seized, and Yates may be arrested for its possession.[19]

The fact that a police officer may have had to crane her neck, bend over, or squat—while in a public place—does not render the plain view rule inapplicable, so long as what she saw would have been visible to any curious passerby.[20] Moreover, the same rule may be applied even where binoculars or flashlights have been used to obtain a view of something, or of an activity that would have been less discernible without such aids.[21] There is a countervailing principle, however, that may be applied in cases of the latter type, particularly where more sophisticated mechanical or electronic de-

18. Code of Ala., tit. 15, Sec. 118(1) & (2); Ark. Stats., Secs. 43-427 to 43-435; Fla. Stats. Ann., Sec. 901.151; 725 ILCS Sec. 5/108-1.01; Ind. Stats. Ann., Secs. 9-1048, 9-1049; La. Stats. Ann., Code of Criminal Pro., Art. 215.1; Nev. Rev. Stats., Sec. 171.123; Nebr. Rev. Stats., Sec. 29.828; N.H. Rev. Stats. Ann., Secs. 594.2, 594.3; N.Y. C.P. L., Sec. 140.50; Gen. Law of R.I., Secs. 12-7-1 & 2; Utah Code Ann., Sec. 77-13-33; Code of Va., Sec. 19.1-100.2; Wisc. Stats. Ann., Secs. 968.24 & 968.25.

19. *See* Warden v. Hayden, 387 U.S. 294 (1967); Horton v. California, 496 U.S. 128 (1990); People v. Sprovieri, 43 Ill. 2d 223, 252 N.E.2d 591 (1969).

20. James v. United States, 418 F.2d 1150 (D.C. Cir. 1969); People v. Wright, 41 Ill. 2d 170, 242 N.E.2d 180 (1968).

21. Commonwealth v. Hernley, 216 Pa. Super. 177, 263 A.2d 904 (1970); Walker v. Beto, 437 F.2d 1018 (5th Cir. 1971); Wright v. United States, 449 F.2d 1355 (D.C. Cir. 1971).

vices are employed, particularly those not readily available to the average private person. That is the principle of a "reasonable expectation of privacy."[22]

Abandoned Property Seizures

Although abandoned property may be the subject of a "plain view" seizure, the mere fact of abandonment itself may remove all doubt as to the legality of the recovery of the property by the police. Questions may arise, however, as to whether there was actually an intent to part with the object, or whether it was in fact no longer possessed. One of the most interesting cases in point is that involving a householder who placed some marijuana in a trash barrel and set the barrel out on a sidewalk for garbage collection. The contraband was recovered from the trash barrel by the police, and it formed the basis for a criminal charge against the householder. A majority of the California Supreme Court held the seizure to be illegal and suppressed the evidence; the theory being that in placing the contraband in the barrel the householder had a "reasonable expectation of privacy" until the trash became commingled with that of others in the garbage collection vehicle. Most courts, however, have rejected the viewpoint enunciated by the California Court, on the ground that there is no expectation of privacy in garbage left for a trash collector.[23]

22. The "reasonable expectation of privacy" concept was used by the Supreme Court in a case where a public telephone booth was "bugged" by federal officers investigating a particular telephone user's illegal gambling activities. Katz v. United States, 389 U.S. 347 (1967). For an application of this principle to aerial overflights of property, see Florida v. Riley, 488 U.S. 445 (1989). It should also be noted that even the use of highly sophisticated technical equipment may be supported in some cases, on the basis of a court's finding that there is no intrusion into privacy. In U.S. v. Penny-Feeney, 773 F. Supp. 220 (D. Hawaii 1991), for instance, the court approved the use of a thermal imaging device without a warrant to detect waste heat emanating from the surface of a building.

23. The Cal. case is People v. Krivda, 96 Cal. Rptr. 62, 486 P.2d 1262 (1971), vacated and remanded by the United States Supreme Court in 409 U.S. 33 (1972), but affirmed by the California Supreme Court on the basis of its interpretation of California's own constitution, 105 Cal. Rptr. 521, 504 P.2d 457 (1973). However, in a subsequent case, People v. Sirhan, 102 Cal. Rptr. 385, 497 P.2d 1121 (1972), the California Supreme Court ruled that items on top of the trash pile could be considered as not within the expectation of privacy and therefore were properly seized. In California, a more recently adopted provision of the state Constitution, article I, section 28, subdivision (d), now requires that questions about the exclusion of evidence be resolved under federal rather than state law.

Among the courts rejecting the Krivda doctrine are United States v. Alden, 576 F.2d 772 (8th Cir. 1978), and United States v. Shelby, 573 F.2d 971 (7th Cir. 1978).

Also consider, with regard to the abandonment issue, Abel v. United States, 362 U.S. 217 (1960), where objects belonging to the famous Russian spy were seized in a hotel room he had occupied, but from which he had checked out as he departed with the arresting federal officers. In United States v. Ramos, 12 F.3d 1019 (11th Cir. 1994), the court ruled that a half-locked briefcase left in a condo unit after the lease expired had not been abandoned because the former tenant had a reasonable expectation of privacy that he could have more than a few hours to get his personal property off the premises. Additionally, based on his prior experience with the condo management, he had a reasonable expectation that his personal property would be gathered up and put in storage, not searched. Accordingly, a search of the briefcase by an officer called to the premises by cleaners who thought the briefcase was "suspicious" was improper, despite the fact that the condo management, and even the officer, had a right to be on the premises after the lease expired.

In 1988, addressing a similar issue, the U.S. Supreme Court ruled that defendants did not have a reasonable expectation of privacy protected by the Fourth Amendment in garbage which they placed in opaque bags outside their house for collection by the trash collector.[24] The Court noted that it is "common knowledge" that plastic garbage bags left along a public street are readily accessible to animals, children, scavengers, snoops, and other members of the public. By placing their refuse at the curb for the express purpose of conveying it to a third party, the trash collector, the Court reasoned, who might himself have sorted through it, they could not reasonably object to a police search of it. The police, the Court concluded, cannot reasonably be expected to avert their eyes from evidence of criminal activity that could have been observed by any member of the public.

Ordinarily, the issue of abandonment arises in cases where a criminal discards contraband as she is approached by the police or is fleeing from the police who were seeking to question or arrest her.

EXAMPLE

Officer Burns observed Watson walking down the street. Watson, aware that she was being observed, threw away a package. Burns retrieved the package. It contained some jewelry that had been reported as stolen. The package and its contents are admissible into evidence at Watson's trial for possession of stolen property, because the package had been abandoned.

Consent Searches

A police search may be rendered valid by the consent of the person whom it is to affect, or by someone authorized to act in her stead, such as a joint tenant or a relative or friend who may have an equal right to use or possession of the premises.[25]

EXAMPLE

Wallace, in custody after his arrest for burglary, gave an indication to the police that the loot of the burglary was in his home. Wallace's wife met the police at the door of their home and consented to the search. The search for and seizure of the loot were with consent and therefore valid.

24. California v. Greenwood, 486 U.S. 35 (1988).

25. United States v. Cataldo, 433 F.2d 38 (2nd Cir. 1970). On the other hand, see Minnesota v. Olson, 495 U.S. 91 (1990), in which the U.S. Supreme Court ruled that an overnight guest in another person's home had standing to object to a search by police. The Court rejected the argument that the guest must demonstrate that he had "complete dominion and control" over his person and personal property in order to acquire Fourth Amendment standing, in favor of a reasonable expectation of privacy rationale.

   In Illinois v. Rodriguez, 497 U.S. 177 (1990), the U.S. Supreme Court ruled that police may enter a home and search it if the person on the premises has "apparent authority" to grant consent to a search, even if he did not really have that authority. However, in People v. Keith, 625 N.E.2d 980 (Ill. App. 1994), the court invalidated the search of the defendant's home based upon the consent given by a babysitter who had been hired to provide child care while the defendant was at work, when the officers knew that the babysitter was neither a resident nor a co-tenant of the home and the babysitter had no independent right, aside from her employment, to be on the premises.

EXAMPLE

Garland's girlfriend, who occasionally spent the night in his apartment, consented to a search of the apartment in Garland's absence. There was no evidence of conduct on the part of either Garland or the woman suggesting that they had equal rights to the apartment nor joint control over it; there was no proof that she had a key to the apartment or that she either brought her friends into it or had authority to invite them; nor was there proof that she shared his board as well as his bed, or that she resided with him in the apartment. Her permission for the search, therefore, was invalid.

Under most circumstances, a hotel keeper or landlord may not validly consent to a police search of the room or residence of the guest or tenant.[26] Likewise, university or other school officials generally do not have the right to consent to a search of a student's dormitory room for police investigative purposes. Some courts hold, however, that a search is permissible for the institution's own supervisory purposes, and particularly where a regulation to that effect is made known to the students.[27]

A parent in control of premises where her son or daughter resides may consent to a police search, thereby rendering admissible the incriminating evidence obtained from the search.[28] A minor child's consent to a search, however, is not valid as against the parent. Also, a parent is unable to give an effective consent to search areas within a child's exclusive use; for example, if a child has left home, locked the door of her room, and instructed her parents not to let anyone into it, the parents cannot consent to a search of the room.[29]

26. Chapman v. United States, 365 U.S. 610 (1961). A landlord, however, may consent to a search of common areas. Gillars v. United States, 182 F.2d 962 (D.C. Cir. 1950). *But see* People v. Garriga, 596 N.Y.S.2d 25 (N.Y. App. 1993) (holding that the tenants of a rooming house had a constitutionally protected "expectation of privacy" in the common hallway of a rooming house; court found that the fact that tenants shared the common areas with each other did not make them "public" vis-a-vis the police).

27. In general, see United States v. Kress, 446 F.2d 358 (9th Cir. 1971). Educational institutions sometimes follow the practice of notifying students of a regulation whereby the right is reserved to inspect rooms and lockers. Such a regulation was considered valid in Piazzola v. Watkins, 442 F.2d 284 (5th Cir. 1971), insofar as it was limited in its application "to further [the institution's] function," but it "cannot be construed or applied so as to give consent to a search for the primary purpose of a criminal prosecution." *Compare* People v. Overton, 24 N.Y.2d 522, 249 N.E.2d 366 (1969), *but see,* as to the seizure of drugs from a high school student's wallet by a teacher who also served as a security coordinator, People v. Scott D., 34 N.Y.2d 483, 315 N.E.2d 466 (1974). The teacher was considered an agent of the state and the student was accorded the Fourth Amendment's protection against illegal searches and seizures. *See also,* for a case upholding the right of school officials to inspect student lockers, *In re W.,* 105 Cal. Rptr. 775 (Cal. App. 1973) and State v. Wingerd, 318 N.E.2d 866 (Ohio App. 1974).

In New Jersey v. T.L.O., 469 U.S. 325 (1985), the U.S. Supreme Court held that under the Fourth Amendment a school administrators' search of a locker need only be reasonable under the circumstances, and need not be supported by probable cause to search, a warrant, or exigent circumstances.

28. United States v. Stone, 401 F.2d 32 (7th Cir. 1968). Some courts hold, however, that when a son or daughter has exclusive use of a particular room, a parent cannot validly consent to a search. Reeves v. Warden, 346 F.2d 915 (4th Cir. 1965).

29. People v. Nunn, 288 N.E.2d 88 (Ill. App. 1972). Nor can a parent validly consent to the search of a locked toolbox belonging to a seventeen-year-old son. *In Re* Scott K., 155 Cal. Rptr. 671, 595 P.2d 105 (1979).

The legality of an employer's consent to a police search of lockers, desks, cars, or other things belonging to the employer, but used by an employee, is not well settled. For instance, one case held as invalid the employer's consent to a police search of a desk used by the employee, whereas another validated a consent with regard to a truck used by the employee.[30]

Although decided in the context of public employers and employees (as opposed to private), the decision of the United States Supreme Court in *O'Connor v. Ortega,*[31] is instructive in this regard. The Court rejected the argument that public employees have no right of privacy or protection under the Fourth Amendment against unreasonable searches and seizures in the workplace context. However, those rights can be clearly limited in several ways, including the

---

30. United States v. Blok, 188 F.2d 1019 (D.C. Cir. 1959) (desk); Braddock v. State, 127 Ga. App. 313, 194 S.E.2d 317 (1972) (truck). *See also* People v. Smith, 204 N.W.2d 308 (Mich. App. 1972) (invalid inspection of a calculator); United States v. Bunkers, 521 F.2d 1217 (9th Cir. 1975) (locker search valid). If police are given consent by an employer to search the workplace premises, because of information concerning employee at-work drug use, do police thereby also gain authority to detain other employees for investigation, even in the absence of particularized suspicion as to those employees? "No" was the answer one court gave, stating that an employer is not able to grant consent to the detention of an employee on its premises in the absence of reasonable suspicion that the employee has committed or is committing a crime. The situation, the court said, is not like that involving the execution of a search warrant for the employer's premises, where a judge has made a probable cause finding that someone on the premises has committed a crime; in such a case employees on the premises may logically be detained while the warrant is executed. Here, the employer told the police that some of his employees had been coming to work on drugs, but the particular employee had not been in the group singled out by the employer. Evidence of the employee's cocaine use that resulted from his unfounded detention was ordered suppressed. People v. Shields, 252 Cal. Rptr. 849 (Cal. App. 1988).

31. O'Connor v. Ortega, 480 U.S. 709 (1987). *See also* Thorton v. University Civil Service Merit Board, 507 N.E.2d 1262 (Ill. App. 1987), in which a court upheld the videotaping of a campus police officer's gambling while on duty in a nonprivate office during his on-duty hours. The court found that the very fact that the gambling took place in an office used by all university police officers to do business and that the officer invited others to come to the building to gamble "belies his claim of a reasonable expectation of privacy." Actual office practices and procedures or legitimate regulation may reduce employees' expectations of privacy in their offices, desks and file cabinets. *See also* Gamble v. State, 552 A.2d 928 (Md. App. 1989) (no warrant required to search a police cruiser since it was police property, but officer had a legitimate expectation of privacy in a closed zippered gym bag which was not the department's property; such expectation was waived by the officer consenting to a search of the trunk of the vehicle, which the court ruled consented to the search of "any and all unlocked or unsealed packages, bags, or containers found within the trunk.") A case-by-case analysis must be made to see if the expectation of privacy is "reasonable" under the circumstances. *In* Moore v. Constantine, 594 N.Y.S.2d 395 (A.D. 1993), a search of a state trooper's locker by the superintendent of the state police did not violate the Fourth Amendment. The court found that the special needs associated with public employment permitted searches of public employees' offices, desks, and effects. *See also* Williams v. Philadelphia Housing Auth., 826 F. Supp. 952 (S.D. Pa. 1993) (upholding the right of a supervisor to load and read a computer disk found in an unlocked drawer of a desk assigned to a subordinate; the employee lacked a reasonable expectation of privacy). For a more detailed discussion of this issue, see DANIEL L. SCHOFIELD, *Fourth Amendment Rights of Law Enforcement Employees Against Searches of Their Workspace,* FBI LAW ENFORCEMENT BULLETIN 24 (July 1987).

usual access which supervisors or other personnel have to offices, departmental vehicles, etc. for work related purposes—in fact, for purposes which are necessary to get the job done.

One important consent problem resolved in 1973 by the United States Supreme Court was whether a warning of constitutional rights as to searches and seizures, similar to the *Miranda* rule regarding confessions, must first be given in order to obtain a valid consent to search. The Court held that such a warning was not a prerequisite to a consensual search, although the lack of a warning might be considered in assessing the voluntariness of the consent.[32]

Permissible Nonconsensual Entries upon Private Areas

Although a nonconsensual warrantless entry on a private area will ordinarily render illegal the seizure of incriminating evidence, two general exceptions exist: a seizure following the "hot pursuit" of a criminal offender, and an "emergency search."

The rationale of the hot pursuit doctrine is that if there is a right to arrest someone, there is a right to pursue her if she flees, and that if she enters a private area the police have a lawful right to enter in order to apprehend her.[33]

An emergency search is one involving facts such as these: (a) the police are called to a residence where a bludgeoned body was found by a private citizen, and the police uncover incriminating evidence against the resident;[34] (b) a person is found unconscious on a public street, and while searching for identification papers the police discover narcotics.[35]

Although an emergency may justify a warrantless search by governmental agents such as health and building inspectors, the general rule is that absent an emergency, an inspector must obtain a search warrant, even though such a war-

---

32. Schnickloth v. Bustamente, 412 U.S. 218 (1973). An interesting issue was considered in People v. Milton, 862 P.2d 1282 (Colo. 1992): does consent have to be explicit consent for a search, or is it sufficient that an officer receive consent to enter a dwelling, whereupon she can seize evidence seen in plain view. In this case, the defendant freely granted permission for the officers to enter to discuss a crime report, and while inside the officers saw evidence in plain view linking the defendant to a crime, which they seized. The court found that consent to *enter* a house is a sufficient foundation for a plain view seizure of evidence once inside the house, since it supplies the vital element of a plain view seizure, i.e., being in a place where the viewing officer has a right to be. It rejected the defendant's argument that he had to explicitly consent to a *search* before the officers could seize the evidence.

33. *See* Warden v. Hayden, 387 U.S. 294 (1967); People v. Bradford, 104 Cal. Rptr. 852 (Cal. App. 1972).

34. Patrick v. State, 227 A.2d 486 (Del. 1967).

35. Vauss v. United States, 370 F.2d 250 (D.C. Cir. 1966).

rant may be issued upon less than the general "reasonable grounds" standard required for the customary search for criminally incriminating evidence.[36]

Automobile Searches

A warrantless search may be made of an automobile in a public place, or at a police station lot to which it has been lawfully taken, provided reasonable grounds exist to believe it contains evidence of a crime. The justification for this is the great mobility of the vehicle.[37] If, however, the car is in a private area, there must be "exigent circumstances" for a search without a warrant; in other words, the circumstances must clearly indicate the need for immediate action. The following example illustrates such circumstances:

EXAMPLE

A police officer had reasonable grounds to believe that a large quantity of stolen shoes was stored in a trailer parked in a private parking lot. A reliable informant had told the officer that the trailer would soon be moved to another location. The warrantless search of the trailer and the seizure of the shoes were legal.[38]

One issue that was once shrouded with uncertainty by several United States Supreme Court decisions concerns the extent of and limitations upon police searches into containers within an automobile when there already exists probable cause to search the vehicle itself. Distinctions between types of containers were made on the basis of whether the occupant of the car harbored an "expectation of

---

36. Camera v. Municipal Court of San Francisco, 387 U.S. 523 (1967) (city housing code inspection); *See* v. Seattle, 387 U.S. 541 (1967) (commercial warehouse inspection). *Compare,* however, United States v. Biswell, 406 U.S. 311 (1972), in which the Court approved a warrantless inspection of a federally licensed gun dealer's storeroom. *See also* Steigler v. Anderson, 496 F.2d 793 (3rd Cir. 1974), holding admissible incriminating evidence obtained by a fire marshal who responded to a fire in the defendant's home, in which several relatives died and for whose deaths the defendant was prosecuted.

    Warrantless surprise inspections may be made of highly regulated businesses and industries, when the purpose of such inspections is to enforce the regulatory scheme rather than to search for evidence based on direct suspicion of criminal activity, which would require a warrant. The U.S. Supreme Court has explicitly recognized an exception to the Fourth Amendment warrant requirement for "highly regulated" businesses, such as auto junkyards. New York v. Burger, 482 U.S. 691 (1987). And the fact that, in the regulatory scheme in Burger, it was police officers rather than other governmental personnel who were empowered to conduct the warrantless inspections did not alter the results, or prevent the officers from seizing evidence or making arrests when such inspections did uncover crimes. *See also* S & S Pawn Shop Incorporated v. City of Del City, 947 F.2d 432 (10th Cir. 1991) and United States v. Branson, 21 F.3d 113 (6th Cir. 1994).

    Regarding the general issue of the search privileges of fire inspectors, consider the three categories set forth in Michigan v. Tyler, 436 U.S. 488 (1978).

37. Chambers v. Maroney, 399 U.S. 42 (1970).

38. United States v. Bozada, 473 F.2d 389 (9th Cir. 1973). The utilization of informer tips was discussed previously in Chapter 1.

privacy" with respect to the container that is the object of the search. In other words, is there a difference between a paper bag and a leather pouch, insofar as expectation of privacy is concerned? In 1982 the Supreme Court itself seemed to recognize the dilemma it had created and clarified the issue.[39] The Court abandoned such esoteric distinctions and established an understandable, clear-cut rule: once there is probable cause to search an automobile, the police may search any receptacle suspected of containing the object of the search. "When a legitimate search is under way, and when its purpose and its limits have been precisely defined, nice distinctions between closets, drawers, and containers, in the case of a home, or between glove compartments, upholstered seats, trunks, and wrapped packages, in the case of a vehicle, must give way to the interest in the prompt and efficient completion of the task at hand."[40]

SEARCHES AND SEIZURES BY PRIVATE CITIZENS

Search of Arrestees

Although arrest statutes may be quite explicit regarding a private citizen's right to arrest (including that of a nondeputized or noncommissioned security officer's), they are generally silent as to the search that may be made incident to such an arrest. Common sense dictates, however, that at least a search for weapons should be permitted for the arrester's protection. Moreover, there are cases (both federal and state) that have upheld the right of a private citizen to search the person she has arrested for stolen objects as well as weapons.[41] In one such case, after a security guard had made an arrest for shoplifting, he requested the arrestee to

---

39. See Robbins v. California, 453 U.S. 420 (1981), and New York v. Belton, 453 U.S. 454 (1981).

40. United States v. Ross, 456 U.S. 798 (1982). The adoption of this rule was suggested to the Court in the "friend of the court" (*amicus curiae*) brief filed by Americans for Effective Law Enforcement, Inc. *See also* California v. Carney, 471 U.S. 396 (1985) (warrant not required for car search when there is probable cause to believe that a car contains evidence of a crime). For an application of this principle, see U.S. v. Cooper, 949 F.2d 737 (5th Cir. 1991). Officers also may conduct "inventory" searches of vehicles which are impounded, including opening closed containers, provided that their department has a regular "policy or practice" designed to produce an inventory. In Florida v. Wells, 495 U.S. 1 (1990), the court found that a state trooper could not open a locked suitcase found in the trunk of a car under the rationale of an "inventory" search, when his department did not have such a policy. *See also* State v. Hathman, 65 Ohio St. 3d 403, 604 N.E.2d 743 (1992) and People v. Williamson, 608 N.E.2d 943 (Ill. App. 1993).

41. United States v. Viale, 312 F.2d 595 (2nd Cir. 1963), where the court said: "The rationale that justifies searches incident to lawful arrests would seem to apply with equal force whether the arrest is made by an officer or a private citizen." In this case the arrest was made by federal officers who had not been accorded a federal right to arrest for the offense, but under the state law they were privileged to do so as private citizens. The fact that they were federal officers did not deprive them of the rights accorded ordinary citizens of the state. *Accord,* as to searches incident to citizen arrests: Montgomery v. United States, 403 F.2d 605 (8th Cir. 1968); Galbraith v. State, 184 So. 2d 633 (Miss. 1966).

For a statutory provision permitting the search for offensive weapons incident to an arrest made by "any person," *see* Cal. Penal Code, Sec. 846.

empty his coat and jacket, and the stolen merchandise was produced. The arrestee was then requested to remove the coat and jacket, and in them the security officer found a loaded pistol. Upon a prosecution for unlawful possession of the weapon, the court held the search to be legal.[42]

Presumably, the citizen's search is not restricted to the person of the arrestee, but may include the immediate vicinity of the arrest. Moreover, in one case in which a gas station attendant observed a person carrying to a car what the attendant reasonably believed to be cases of cigarettes belonging to the gas station owner, a search of the car, after a detention of the driver, was held to be lawful.[43]

Security Officer's Search of Nonemployees Absent an Arrest

A person who is invited on another person's premises makes no automatic surrender of her general right to privacy of her person or possessions. Consequently, neither she nor her possessions can be searched at the whim of the inviter or her security officer or other agent—unless, of course, the invitation is clearly coupled with a condition by which the inviter is accorded that privilege. Absent such a waiver, or the explicit consent of the visitor, or a legislative grant of some reasonable and limited privileges of that nature to the inviter, the only search and seizure right possessed by the inviter or her security officer or other agent is that accorded any other private citizen who has made an actual arrest.[44]

A Security Officer's Search of Employees and Their Possessions

As with a nonemployee invitee, an employee does not automatically surrender her general right to privacy even while on the employer's premises. Neither the employee nor her possessions can be searched at the whim of the employer or one of her security officers. A reasonable limited search privilege may be obtained by an employer, however, as a condition to the employment.

---

42. People v. Santiago, 278 N.Y.S.2d 260 (App. Div. 1967).

43. Patrick v. State, 301 S.W.2d 138 (Tex. Crim. App. 1957).

44. A visitor's consent must be of her own free will and not coerced. For a case where a search was held to be without consent because a security guard directed a suspicious person to empty his pockets, see People v. Matera, 258 N.Y.S.2d 2 (1965). The court also rejected the argument that the search was incident to a valid arrest, because the arrest itself was dependent upon the contraband (syringes and needles) produced by the unreasonable search.

Oklahoma, in its detention statute, specifically permits "a reasonable search of a detained person and his belongings when it appears that the merchandise or money may be lost." (See statute in the Appendix.)

In Kentucky, a private citizen can search a person she has arrested only when the search is for the arrester's own property or where it is property over which she has a custodial responsibility. Thacker v. Comm., 221 S.W.2d 682 (Ky. App. 1949).

Preemployment Consent to Search.   Where merchandise or equipment belonging to an employer may be readily concealed on an employee's person, or in a lunch pail or other container, an employer may prescribe, as a condition to the employment, the right to search an employee when she is about to leave the premises, or even at other times. Such a condition could also be imposed with respect to lockers, desks, or even employees' cars parked on the employer's premises. Thereafter, an employee's refusal to permit a search would be grounds for dismissal from employment. If an employer adopts this preemployment consent practice, it is advisable that the consent form be in writing and signed by the prospective employee.

Postemployment Consent to Search.   Even in the absence of any preemployment consent to search, if a request is made to search an employee or any of her possessions, and she consents, then the employer is absolved of any liability, provided, of course, the search is reasonably conducted, and the employee has not been coerced or intimidated into consenting. Experience has indicated that a polite request made in private for permission to search an employee or her possessions will usually result in a grant of consent. This procedure, obviously, is the correct one to follow.

It is very important, for legal reasons, that a search request be made out of the presence of other persons; otherwise, the request itself may be viewed as the equivalent of an accusation of wrongdoing, thereby subjecting the requester and her employer to an action for slander.

Searches Without Employee's Consent.   A limited power to search exists in situations where the employee has little or no reasonable expectations of privacy. An example of this privilege is the case of a Customs Department employee whose jacket was reasonably searched while it was hanging in the outer office of his supervisor.[45] This was considered to be a public area, not shown to be segregated for private purposes from other work areas. The court held that the search was within the power of the government as an employer to supervise and investigate the performance of the employee's duties.

When wrongdoing is suspected, an employer, security officer, or other agent need not close her eyes when evidence of the crime is clearly visible. Thus, the previously discussed "plain view" doctrine would apply, for example, in a situation where a guard investigating a suspected theft observes burglar tools in the open trunk of an automobile parked alongside the employer's building.[46]

---

45. United States v. Collins, 349 F.2d 863 (2nd Cir. 1965), *rehearing denied,* 384 U.S. 947 (1966). For a similar holding, see Quaglione v. State, 292 A.2d 785 (Md. App. 1972), in which a shoeshine employee stored illegal drugs in a shoebox in the establishment's storage area (a place not set aside for employee use or privacy); a police search on the authority of the store manager was therefore permissible.

46. People v. Moulton, 27 Cal. Rptr. 132 (Cal. App. 1962). Although this case did not involve an employee, the principle would apply in that situation as well.

Legal Status of Lockers and Desks Provided by Employer.   When an employee is provided a locker, but the employer retains a duplicate or master key, and this is known to the employee, the employer may be considered as reserving the right to enter the locker at will.[47] If, on the other hand, an employee uses her own lock and key, the locker will in all probability be considered the equivalent of her own property and not subject to invasion without her consent. Once again, however, an employer is privileged to attach, as a condition to supplying the locker accommodation, the right to inspection without consent, using a key or even forcible means applied to the locker door. Moreover, there is a case that holds that even if an employee does not know that her employer (in this instance, the government) has reserved the right of inspection, no right of privacy exists beyond that granted by the employer.[48]

The degree of privacy accorded to desks depends upon whether the employee has exclusive use and control. In a case where the desk was assigned to be exclusively used by one employee, it was held that a supervisor had no legal authority to authorize a search of the desk by law enforcement officers.[49] However, in a situation where other employees have access to the desk to obtain paper clips and pencils, for example, or where the desk is not permanently assigned to the employee, the right of privacy does not exist.[50]

---

47. State v. Robinson, 86 N.J. Super. 308, 206 A.2d 779 (1965). However, in the case of United States v. Speights, 557 F.2d 596 (3d Cir. 1977), a police department supervisor, suspecting that a certain police officer illegally possessed a sawed-off shotgun, used a master key to open the officer's police station locker. The gun was found in the locker, and the officer was prosecuted for its unlawful possession. His conviction was reversed upon appeal because the court found that he had a "reasonable expectation of privacy," and consequently the gun's seizure was violative of the Fourth Amendment's protection against unreasonable searches and seizures.

The court in the *Speights* case observed that the police department did not post a notice or have any regulation indicating that assigned lockers might be inspected, in which event the officer's expectation of privacy would have been eroded.

A Cal. statute, known as a Public Safety Officers Procedural Bill of Rights Act, contains a section that provides that "No public safety officer [which includes "all peace officers"] shall have his locker, or other space for storage that may be assigned to him searched except in his presence, or with his consent, or unless a valid search warrant has been obtained or where he has been notified that a search will be conducted." Ch. 9.7, Division 4 of Title 1 of the Government Code, Sec. 3309.

48. United States v. Donato, 379 F.2d 288 (3rd Cir. 1968) (affirming lower court, without opinion). The Third Circuit Court of Appeals in the foregoing Speights case expressed approval of Donato, but observed that in Speights there was no notice of inspection and that the defendant had an expectation of privacy, especially since he had his own lock on the locker.

49. United States v. Blok, *supra* note 30.

50. Freeman v. United States, 201 A.2d 22 (D.C. Ct. App. 1964). It is questionable, however, whether an employee can give valid consent to search a co-worker's desk. In People v. Smith, 204 N.W.2d 308 (Mich. App. 1972), the court held that a secretary could not effectively consent to a search of her boss's desk.

Stop-and-Frisk Privileges of Security Officers

As already mentioned, a public police officer, under certain conditions, may stop a suspected person in order to make reasonable inquiries of her. Along with the stop, if the officer has a reasonable fear for her own safety or that of other persons, she may conduct "a carefully limited search" of the detained person to discover whether she possesses a weapon. This police practice of "stop-and-frisk" is not dependent on any legislative grant. In fact, there was no statute involved in the Supreme Court case that decided that the practice did not involve a violation of the Fourth Amendment prohibitions against unreasonable searches and seizures.

As pointed out in the preceding chapter, many state statutes grant to private security officers, or at least to those who are uniformed, the same on-the-premises arrest powers possessed by regular police officers in public places. Where this is so, it appears that private security officers should possess the same stop-and-frisk privileges as well, because it is essential that they employ protective crime prevention measures on behalf of the company or institution they serve, and that they should also be accorded the right to protect themselves from the use of weapons by the persons they stop for questioning.

In addition to the fact that a public police officer is entitled to stop-and-frisk privileges even without statutory authorization, and that there is authority for a private citizen to make an actual search of the person she arrests, there seems to be no reason to deny stop-and-frisk privileges to private security officers who have been accorded by law the same powers as public police officers. It would also seem that even when a security officer has not been empowered with official arrest powers, she should possess stop-and-frisk privileges if he is in uniform at the time. This is subject to the obvious limitation that the privilege be exercised only on the premises of the employer.

SEARCH WARRANTS

The Fourth Amendment to the United States Constitution, in addition to the general guarantee of "the right of the people to be secure in their persons, houses, papers, and effects, against unreasonable searches and seizures," prescribes that "no warrants shall issue, but upon probable cause, supported by oath or affirmation, and particularly describing the place to be searched, and the persons or things to be seized." Basically, what this Amendment means is that a search is invalid unless it is made upon "reasonable grounds." As previously discussed, there are many situations where warrantless searches are permissible; there are others, however, where the courts have considered searches to be unreasonable unless they are made pursuant to a warrant. The search of a home, for instance, is generally considered impermissible in the absence of a warrant. Moreover, as the Fourth Amendment clearly indicates, the warrant can be issued only upon information supplied under oath or affirmation, and the warrant itself must be specific as to "place," "persons," or "things" toward which the search is to be directed.

Nature and Form of "Complaint" for a Search Warrant

An application for a search warrant must be supported by oath or affirmation by either a police officer or a private citizen.[51] Although some states require a written affidavit, others permit a warrant to be issued upon oral testimony.[52] The person making the complaint is called the *affiant* or *complainant*.[53]

The complaint must state facts (not mere conclusions) to establish reasonable grounds (probable cause) that the person or place to be searched and the things to be seized will be found as stated in the complaint. A warrant issued upon mere information and belief of the affiant or applicant without adequate recitation of facts and the underlying circumstances forming the basis for such belief is void.[54] Reasonable grounds simply means that the facts and circumstances within the knowledge of the affiant, or of which she had reasonably trustworthy information, based on the totality of the circumstances recited in the application for the search warrant, were sufficient in themselves to warrant a person of reasonable caution to believe that the law was violated and that evidence of it was on the person or in the premises or vehicle to be searched. Although the required reasonable grounds must be based on more than mere suspicion, there need not be a showing of guilt beyond a reasonable doubt. That degree of proof is required only to es-

---

51. For an example of the statutory requirements, see the Ill. Code of Criminal Procedure, 725 ILCS Sec. 5/108-3, which provides that a judge may issue a search warrant "upon the written complaint of any person under oath or affirmation which states facts sufficient to show probable cause and which particularly describes the place or person, or both, to be searched and the things to be seized. . . ."

    Even where the law permits search warrants to be issued upon a private citizen's request, courts are disinclined to do so unless the citizen has the cooperation of the police. Moreover, as a practical matter, a citizen search warrant would not be of much value because of the execution problem.

52. Moreover, as earlier stated (in note 4), two states (Ariz. and Cal.) have statutes that authorize the issuance of telephonic search warrants in response to sworn telephonic complaints. Additionally, the issuance of search warrants on the basis of sworn telephonic complaint is now authorized under Fed. Rule Crim. Proc. 41(c)(2)(A).

53. The complaint may not be signed with a fictitious signature in an effort to protect an informant. United States *ex rel.* Pugh v. Pate, 401 F.2d 6 (7th Cir. 1968).

54. Aguilar v. Texas, 378 U.S. 108 (1964); Spinelli v. United States, 393 U.S. 410 (1969). Courts developed a "two-pronged" test to determine the reliability of information supplied by informants—particularly anonymous informants—supporting an application for a search warrant. First, the informant's report as supplemented by the affidavit for the search warrant had to reveal the "basis of knowledge of the informant"—the particular means by which she came by the information. Second, it had to provide facts sufficiently establishing either the "veracity" of the affiant's informant, or alternatively, the "reliability" of the informant's report in this particular case. This could be done by an officer independently corroborating some of the facts in the informant's report, and the amount of detail in the informant's report or tip was often of concern. In Illinois v. Gates, 412 U.S. 213 (1983), the U.S. Supreme Court overturned Aguilar and Spinelli's "two-pronged test" as too complex and mechanical, replacing it with a "totality of the circumstances" test. Under this test, the task of the magistrate issuing a warrant in reviewing an application for one is "simply to make a practical, common-sense decision whether, given all the circumstances set forth in the affidavit before him, including the 'veracity' and 'basis of knowledge' of persons supplying hearsay information, there is a fair probability that contraband or evidence of a crime will be found in a particular place."

tablish guilt. Moreover, the requirement may be met by evidence that would be inadmissible in court. Thus, even though there is a general rule prohibiting the use of hearsay evidence in court, a complaint for a search warrant may be based on hearsay evidence if there is "a substantial basis for crediting the hearsay."[55] This substantial basis may be found where information has been relayed to the affiant by a previously reliable informant and where facts are related that corroborate the word of the informant.

EXAMPLE

Jones told police officer Brown that a gambling operation was being operated at a company warehouse. Jones showed Brown betting slips which he said he himself had purchased in the place within the past week. Jones had given Brown reliable information about gambling activities on previous occasions. Brown's complaint should be adequate for a search warrant.[56] (In such a case, however, the police should seek additional corroboration, such as their own observation of known gamblers going in and out of the warehouse. Some courts may require further corroboration of this nature.)

In contrast to the extent of corroboration needed to support the word of an informant who is an associate of criminals, greater credence is placed on the word of an ordinary citizen, particularly if she is the crime victim.[57] A similar rule prevails with regard to an undercover police officer.[58]

The complaint must describe with particularity what is to be seized; general and broad descriptions are inadequate.[59] Particularity is especially important with respect to the seizure of evidence for the prosecution of obscenity cases.[60] Where the search warrant is for the purpose of searching an individual, that person must be named or described in detail both in the complaint and in the warrant. Although the warrant may be sufficient even when the name of the person to be searched is unknown, she must be described in enough detail to permit an accurate identification; for instance, the person's physical appearance, nickname, and the place or places she frequents may be sufficient to satisfy the specificity requirement.[61]

If a search warrant is used to search a building or other place, there must also be a particularized description.[62] The premises must be described with such detail as to exclude any other premises. For example, a warrant describing an entire apartment house, hotel, or rooming house, issued on probable cause for search of

---

55. Jones v. United States, 362 U.S. 257 (1960); United States v. Ventresca, 380 U.S. 102 (1965).

56. People v. McNeil, 52 Ill. 2d 187, 290 N.E.2d 602 (1972). *See also* United States v. Harris, 403 U.S. 573 (1971).

57. United States v. Mahler, 442 F.2d 1172 (9th Cir. 1971).

58. Brooks v. United States, 416 F.2d 1044 (5th Cir. 1969).

59. Stanford v. Texas, 379 U.S. 476 (1965).

60. Marcus v. Search Warrant, 367 U.S. 717 (1961).

61. United States v. Ferrone, 438 F.2d 381 (3d Cir. 1971).

62. *See* United States v. Ortiz, 311 F. Supp. 880 (D. Colo. 1970); People v. Avery, 173 Colo. 315, 478 P.2d 310 (1970); United States v. Higgins, 428 F.2d 232 (7th Cir. 1970).

only one room therein, would typically be held void. The address, apartment number, apartment location, and any other descriptive data should be detailed. There is no need, however, to identify the person in charge of the premises, to name the person in possession of the things to be seized, or to give the name of any person as a particular offender.[63]

In the event an address or name given in the search warrant is incorrect, the officer executing it may not legally alter or amend it; only the issuing judicial officer has the authority to make such alteration.[64]

The search warrant must state the time and date of issuance. It must be executed by a designated police officer, or by members of a law enforcement agency, or perhaps even by a named private individual.

Most of the descriptive data of the complaint must be repeated in the warrant. If the warrant does not adequately describe the person or premises to be searched, the fact that the complaint itself detailed such information does not cure the defect in the search warrant.[65] However, a search warrant will not usually be quashed (nor evidence suppressed) because of technical irregularities not affecting the substantive rights of the accused.[66]

The warrant and complaint are generally interpreted by the courts in a "common-sense and realistic fashion."[67]

EXAMPLE

The warrant listed the person to be searched as "Charles F. Smith" in three out of the four places where his name was mentioned. In the fourth place in the warrant, his name was inadvertently stated as "Charlie Smith." The warrant will not be quashed.

EXAMPLE

The complaint described the premises as Apartment 2-B in a three-story red brick building with the address of 2300 S. State Street. This description was correct, except for the fact that the correct address was 2310 S. State Street. However, there was only one building (the subject premises) on the 2300 block of South State Street. The description is adequate.[68]

Major defects will, of course, render the warrant or complaint void, and this will require the suppression at trial of the seized items. For instance, if the complaint is unsworn, or if the magistrate failed to sign the warrant, or if she did not have the authority to issue it, then all of the seized evidence is subject to suppression.

---

63. Wangrow v. United States, 399 F.2d 106 (8th Cir. 1968). *See also* 47 A.L.R.2d 1444 (1956).

64. State v. Buchanan, 432 S.W.2d 342 (Mo. 1968).

65. O'Brien v. State, 158 Tenn. 400, 14 S.W.2d 51 (1929).

66. People v. Harrison, 226 N.E.2d 418 (Ill. App. 1967).

67. United States v. Ventresca, *supra* note 53.

68. People v. Watson, 26 Ill. 2d 203, 186 N.E.2d 326 (1962).

Things Subject to Seizure

At one time, the things that could be ordered seized in a search warrant were very limited—generally limited to the instrumentalities of the crime (e.g., burglars' tools) or the fruits of the crime (e.g., the stolen property). Modern-day statutes and court discussions, however, have realistically enlarged the kind of things subject to seizure. For instance, the Federal Rules of Criminal Procedure contains the following enumeration of objects to be searched for and seized:[69]

1. property that constitutes evidence of the commission of a criminal offense; or
2. contraband, the fruits of crime, or things otherwise criminally possessed; or
3. property designed or intended for use or which is or has been used as the means of committing a criminal offense; or
4. person for whose arrest there is probable cause, or who is unlawfully restrained.

If, in a search for the articles named in the search warrant, contraband or other articles not lawfully possessed, are discovered, they too are subject to seizure.[70]

Execution of the Search Warrant

The time period within which a warrant must be executed—that is, served, and the search made—is usually governed by statute or court rule.[71] Where no statutory period is specified, the test is whether it is reasonable to believe that the probable cause upon which the warrant issued has not been dissipated.

---

69. Federal Rule of Criminal Procedure 41(b). *See also* the Illinois Code of Criminal Procedure, 725 ILCS Sec. 5/108-3, which contains the following enumeration:

> 1. Any instruments, articles or things used in the commission of an offense; for example, a revolver used in a murder.
> 2. Any instruments, articles or things which may constitute evidence of an offense, or contraband, the possession of which is an offense, or property which the officer knows or has probable cause to believe is stolen; for example, a blood or semen-stained undergarment worn by a rapist.
> 3. A kidnap victim.
> 4. A human fetus—for example, in an abortion investigation.
> 5. A human corpse—for example, in a murder investigation.

> The constitutionality of such an extension of things subject to seizure was raised in the Supreme Court case of Warden v. Hayden, *supra* note 33, the contention being that "mere evidence" of a crime, in contrast to the instrumentalities or fruits of a crime, was beyond the scope of lawful seizure. The Court, however, rejected this argument; hence statutory provisions such as the Ill. one are constitutionally valid.

> The same scope of items subject to seizure with a warrant prevails in Illinois and many other states with respect to searches incident to a lawful arrest. *See, e.g.,* 725 ILCS Sec. 5/108-1.

70. Warden v. Hayden, *supra* note 33.

71. *See, e.g.,* 725 ILCS Sec. 5/108-6 (96 hours); FED. R. CRIM. PROC., 41(c)(1) (10 days).

Many statutes distinguish between day and night searches, and some statutes require positive information and necessity in order to search at night; others permit searches during either day or night.[72]

The validity of the execution of a search warrant will not be affected by an invalid search without warrant made contemporaneously with the search based upon the valid warrant.

EXAMPLE

Police officers obtained a valid search warrant to search Apartment 25 of the Jet Hotel. They proceeded to the Jet Hotel and searched Apartment 25. While they were at the hotel, they also searched Apartment 26, without lawful authority. The unlawful search of Apartment 26 does not affect the validity of the search of Apartment 25 pursuant to the warrant.[73]

Statutes typically require an officer seeking to execute a search warrant to announce her authority and purpose in seeking access to the premises. If admittance is refused, the officer may use reasonable force to enter.[74]

When executing a search warrant, a police officer may reasonably detain and search any person in the place at the time, in order to: (1) protect herself from attack, or (2) prevent the disposal or concealment of any instruments, articles, or things particularly described in the search warrant.[75]

All the objects seized must be brought before the judge who issued the warrant, or another judge with competent jurisdiction. An inventory of the things seized must be presented to the judge at that time, and the judge must enter an order providing for their custody pending further proceedings.[76]

In most states the complaint for search warrant and the search warrant itself need not be filed with the clerk of the court until *after* the warrant has been executed or has been returned "Not Executed."

If a person hinders, delays, or prevents the officer from executing a valid warrant by means such as refusing entry into the described premises on proper announcement, or hiding or destroying the items the officer is authorized to search

---

72. *See, e.g.*, 725 ILCS Sec. 5/108-13 ("The warrant may be executed at any time of any day or night"); Fed. R. Crim. Proc., 41(c) ("The warrant shall be served in the daytime, unless the issuing authority, by appropriate provision in the warrant, and for reasonable cause shown, authorizes its execution at times other than daytime. . . . The term 'daytime' is used in this rule to mean the hours from 6:00 A.M. to 10:00 P.M. according to local time"). Regarding the daytime/nighttime rule in general, see 26 A.L.R.3d 951 (1969).

73. People v. Serrano, 32 Ill. 2d 84, 203 N.E.2d 885 (1965).

74. White v. United States, 346 F.2d 800 (D.C. Cir. 1965). For a statutory authorization of the use of force, see 725 ILCS Sec. 5/108-8. In the application of this statutory authority, however, forced entries may not be made "without a prior announcement of authority and purpose, unless at the time of entry there exist circumstances which excuse compliance with this requirement." People v. Stephens, 310 N.E.2d 755 (Ill. App. 1974).

75. For a statutory enactment of this rule, see 725 ILCS, Sec. 5/108-9.

76. For an example of a statutory provision, see 725 ILCS Secs. 5/108-10, 11.

for, penalties may be imposed for contempt of court because of interference with the judicial process or obstruction of justice.

Fourth Amendment Constitutional Right Not Generally Applicable to Private Actions

The Fourth Amendment to the U.S. Constitution prohibits unreasonable searches and seizures but protects only against governmental action. Searches by private individuals, including private security personnel, even if "unreasonable," are therefore not "unconstitutional," and the exclusionary rule barring the evidence uncovered by such searches does not apply.[77] This does not mean, however, that such unreasonable searches are tolerated under the general law. Private security personnel who engage in certain searches and seizures may find themselves embroiled in civil lawsuits for anything from assault and battery to invasion of privacy. (For a further discussion of this, see Chapter 10 of this text.)

EXAMPLE

A security employee of an express package service conducted a visual inspection of some packages and detected an odor of laundry soap emanating from one of the boxes. Knowing that cocaine is often packed in laundry products to mask its smell, he decided to investigate further. He checked a telephone directory and found no listing of the shipper's name, and he further learned that the address given for the shipper was fictitious. He then proceeded to open the package, whereupon he found cocaine. He contacted law enforcement authorities and their investigation resulted in a criminal prosecution of the intended recipient of the package. The court rejected the defendant's contention that the evidence seized was the result of an illegal search, since the Fourth Amendment does not apply to searches by private persons. [78]

In that case, the court also rejected the argument that the security officer was acting as a "de facto government agent" when he opened the package, since he was following the company's own policy, which allowed searches of suspicious packages to protect itself and its employees. The fact that the company had historically maintained good relations with law enforcement officials did not alter the result, nor did the fact that this employee had cooperated in the past with law enforcement officials. In order to transform a private search into one governed by the Fourth Amendment, the court stated, a defendant must "prove some exercise of governmental power over the private entity, such that the private entity may be said to have acted on behalf of the government rather than for its own private purposes."

---

77. Burdeau v. McDowell, 256 U.S. 465 (1921).

78. United States v. Koenig, 856 F.2d 843 (7th Cir. 1988). *See* People v. Ornelas, 253 Cal. Rptr. 165 (Cal. App. 1988) in which the court expressed the view that a "civil remedy available to the victims of . . . wrongful conduct against the offenders and their employees should provide a greater and more equitable deterrent than exclusion of the evidence."

The case clearly indicates that, in order for the employer to protect herself and her employees from harm she may pursue a policy regarding the opening and inspecting of packages on a random and periodic basis when there is suspicion concerning some specific package. Additionally, a private company, the court concluded, "may conduct a search for security reasons or simply out of its own interest in combatting crime," and the restrictions of the Fourth Amendment will not apply unless the search was conducted at the behest of the government.

Accordingly, since private employers may serve an important role in combatting criminal activity in ways in which governmental entities may be limited, the authors of this book encourage private entities to carefully explore, with their own legal counsel, the adoption of well-thought-out policies similar to that described above, utilizing to the fullest extent legally allowable the advantage that private security has in combatting crime and gathering evidence to bring offenders to justice. At the same time, caution must be exercised so that such searches do not break state or local laws.

THE BASIC RIGHT OF AN OWNER TO REGAIN PERSONAL PROPERTY

When a person is observed carrying away the personal property of another without authorization, the owner of the property may demand its return, and if return is refused she may obtain the property by the use of reasonable force.[79] Under this accepted principle, a security officer (or other agent) is justified in retaking store merchandise or other company property that someone is carrying away without excuse or jurisdiction.[80] The proof, however, must be forthcoming that the person involved had no right to possession of the goods.

Although under this theory an unlawful intent on the part of the person carrying away the property would not be required to justify the forcible retaking of the merchandise—as would be necessary in justification of an arrest—the fact remains that it would be extremely risky to attempt a forcible retaking except in a

---

79. Winter v. Atkinson, 92 Ill. App. 162 (1900); Donel v. United States, 299 F. 948 (7th Cir. 1924). The right to retake is limited, however, by the condition that it be done in "fresh pursuit" of the taker. PROSSER AND KEETON, LAW OF TORTS, ch. 4, Sec. 22 (5th ed. 1984).

The Wisconsin Criminal Code, Sec. 939.49 provides that "A person is privileged to threaten or intentionally use force against another for the purpose of preventing or terminating what he reasonably believes to be an unlawful interference with his property." However, "only such degree of force or threat thereof may intentionally be used as the actor reasonably believes is necessary to prevent or terminate the interference." But no force is permissible that is "likely to cause death or great bodily harm for the sole purpose of defense of one's property."

80. Kroger Grocery & Baking Co. v. Waller, 208 Ark. 1063, 189 S.W.2d 361 (1945); Collyer v. S.H. Kress & Co., 5 Cal. 2d 175, 54 P.2d 20 (1936); Prieto v. May Dept. Stores Co., 216 A.2d 577 (D.C. Ct. App. 1966); Lopez v. Wigwam Dept. Stores, 49 Hawaii 416, 421 P.2d 289 (1966); Sima v. Skaggs Payless Drugs Center, 82 Idaho 387, 353 P.2d 1085 (1960); Teel v. May Dept. Stores Co., 348 Mo. 696, 155 S.W.2d 74 (1941); Swafford v. Vermillion, 261 P.2d 187 (Okla. 1953); Cohen v. Lit. Bros., 166 Pa. Super. 206, 70 A.2d 419 (1950); Little Stores v. Isenberg, 172 S.W.2d 13 (Tenn. App. 1943).

situation where the security officer (or other agent) feels certain that the taker intended to steal the goods. In that event, of course, the agent might just as well make an arrest.

There is one type of situation when retaking possession of store merchandise is definitely in order; that is when merchandise that had been stolen or lost has been brought to the exchange counter for refund. This involves no force for its retaking, since the store employee will already have physical possession of the property. The risk here is negligible and the justification absolute.

In refund cases the security officer should play the role of an adjuster or section manager. She should set aside such outer clothing as her hat and top coat, and approach the customer for information as to her name, address, telephone number, and so forth. After receiving the item in question, the officer should advise the person that the matter will be checked into and that the store will communicate with her later. This will usually end the whole matter. However, where the security officer sees someone take merchandise and carry it to the refund desk, she is privileged to make an arrest. Moreover, in such instances it might be advisable to let the thief commit the additional offense of cashing the refund slip.

3

Temporary Detention and Inquiries of Detained Persons

DETENTION AND INQUIRIES OF CUSTOMERS AND OTHER NONEMPLOYEES

Many court decisions hold, based on a well-established common law concept, that a merchant or one of his agents, such as a security guard, who reasonably believes that someone on the premises is in wrongful possession of the merchant's property may detain that person in order to ascertain the facts. This right is conditioned, of course, based on the factor of reasonableness with respect to both the manner and the period of detention.[1] The practical justification for allowing such detentions is that a person's right to protect his own property supersedes the general right of an individual to move about free from restraint by another private citizen.[2]

---

1. Kroger Grocery & Baking Co. v. Waller, 189 S.W.2d 361 (Ark. 1945); Collyer v. S. H. Kress & Co., 5 Cal. 2d 175, 54 P.2d 20 (1936); Prieto v. May Dept. Stores Co., 216 A.2d 577 (D.C. Ct. App. 1966); Lopez v. Wigwam Dept. Stores, 49 Hawaii 416, 421 P.2d 289 (1966); Sima v. Skaggs Payless Drug Center, 82 Idaho 387, 353 P.2d 1085 (1960); Teel v. May Dept. Stores Co., 348 Mo. 696, 155 S.W.2d 74 (1941); Swafford v. Vermillion, 261 P.2d 187 (Okla. 1953); Cohen v. Lit. Bros., 166 Pa. Super. 206, 70 A.2d 419 (1950); Little Stores v. Isenberg, 172 S.W.2d 13 (Tenn. App. 1943).

   A detention of the same type is also permissible for a customer's nonpayment for food consumed or services rendered on the premises. In both instances, though, the merchant may detain only to investigate whether payment was in fact made. He has, for example, no right to hold a customer captive in order to coerce payment. If he holds a customer beyond the investigatory stage, he makes an arrest and assumes the possible liabilities that may accompany an unauthorized arrest.

2. On the general subject of protective property detention, *see* PROSSER AND KEETON, HANDBOOK OF THE LAW OF TORTS, ch. 4, Sec. 22 (5th ed. 1984), and Appendix to the SECOND RESTATEMENT OF THE LAW OF TORTS, Sec. 120A. The Restatement recognizes the right of temporary detention without arrest by one who reasonably believes that another has tortiously taken a chattel, provided that the detention is solely for reasonable investigative purposes and is carried out only on the premises of the detaining party. Comment (a) of that section makes the rule specifically available to shopkeepers in shoplifting situations. No position is taken, however, in the Restatement regarding whether the privilege extends to the situation where the suspect has left the premises but is still in the immediate vicinity. (The statutory law on off-premises detention will be subsequently discussed in this chapter.)

Almost all states now have legislative enactments, known as temporary detention statutes, the objective of which has been to alleviate the shoplifting problems that merchants are encountering with increasing frequency. (The various statutes are reproduced in the Appendix of this text.) The primary legal necessity for such legislation is the generally prevailing viewpoint that private citizens should not be empowered to make *arrests* except for serious crimes (felonies) or where there is a "breach of the peace."[3] Even in other states with more liberal citizen arrest powers, detention statutes are considered helpful adjuncts to citizen arrest statutes, for reasons that will become evident in the ensuing analyses of the various detention statutes.[4]

Detention statutes usually provide that merchants or their agents who have "probable cause" or "reasonable grounds" to believe that merchandise is unlawfully possessed may detain the suspected person "in a reasonable manner" and for a "reasonable time" to investigate the matter. Some of the statutes, however, do employ different kinds of phraseology. The language of the Colorado statute is of considerable interest, both to members of the legal profession and private security personnel. It permits detention and questioning when the detainer acts "in good faith and *upon probable cause based upon reasonable grounds*" (emphasis added). This phraseology appears to impose a greater burden on the detainer than most state laws which use *either* the phrase probable cause *or* the phrase reasonable grounds. Because the two terms are generally considered synonymous, compounding one upon the other, as does the Colorado statute, is superfluous, if not meaningless.[5]

An example of noncompliance with the requirement of reasonable grounds or probable cause for a detention is a case in which the detainer had observed noth-

---

3. The limitations on private citizen arrest powers were discussed in Chapter 1.

  It is of interest to note at this point the unique provision of the West Virginia detention statute that placed reliance on this early "breach of the peace" concept as the basis for its detention statute by declaring shoplifting to constitute a "breach of the peace." This represents a considerable departure from the original meaning, although a legislature is not legally inhibited from pursuing this approach. W. Va. Code, Sec. 61-3A-4.

4. Consider Ill., for instance, where a private citizen may make an arrest when he has "reasonable grounds to believe that an offense other than an ordinance violation is being committed." Even though this constitutes authorization to *arrest* persons believed to be shoplifting, which is an "offense" under the Ill. Criminal Code; nevertheless, Ill. has a comprehensive detention provision in its criminal code. (Both the arrest and detention provisions are reproduced in the Appendix of this text.)

5. Illustrative of this is the case of J. S. Dillon & Sons Co. v. Carrington, 169 Colo. 242, 455 P.2d 201 (1969), which involved the following circumstances:

  A drugstore's security officer saw a shopper walk past him with a prescription drug in his shopping cart. When the officer saw the shopper pass a second time, the officer did not see the package in the cart. He then went to the druggist in the back of the store and to the cashier in the front and ascertained that a prescription had been filled by the shopper and that he had not paid for it. As the shopper left the store, the security officer stopped him and required him to empty his grocery bag in the presence of several people. No evidence of stolen merchandise was found. The Colorado Supreme Court decided that the security officer's stopping and questioning of the shopper was in good faith and "upon probable cause based upon reasonable grounds," which was in effect a finding that the detainer's actions were "reasonable."

ing more than a bulge in a man's coat pocket. Another example, and a very obvious one, is a case where the manager of a store followed a policy of selecting at random persons at a checkout counter and then questioning them on the assumption they had stolen cigarettes—a commonly pilfered item. The manager stepped in front of the plaintiff, whom he had observed looking at a carton of cigarettes, and forcefully told her to follow him to a back room, where she was interrogated in the presence of a cashier for about twenty minutes. She had not, in fact, taken any cigarettes. Her suit for false arrest and false imprisonment was successful.[6]

A good statement of what the prerequisites to detention are was made by one court, which pointed out that the test is not whether the detained person is actually guilty of shoplifting, but whether the known facts and circumstances are such to justify a person of "prudence and caution in believing that the offense has been committed."[7]

The fact that a person who was observed doing suspicious actions suggestive of shoplifting had actually shoplifted in the store on a recent prior occasion may be a factor that will escalate mere suspicion into reasonable grounds for a detention. There can be no detention, however, for the purpose of investigating

The case was decided under an earlier Colo. statute, but the language quoted in the above text was the same in the earlier one. In the prior statute, however, there was an ambiguity in another part that the Supreme Court should have clarified by an instruction from the judge to the jury, and for that reason the case was reversed for a new trial. The opinion of the court in this Colo. case will be of interest to lawyers with respect to the difference between issues of law (to be decided by the trial judge) and issues of fact (to be decided by the jury).

6. The first example is Isaiah v. Great A. & P. Tea Co., 174 N.E.2d 128 (Ohio App. 1959); the second is Clark v. Kroger Co., 382 F.2d 562 (7th Cir. 1967).

The distinction between false arrest and false imprisonment is that the former applies when the action is performed by a person who has or pretends to have the authority to take a person into custody on a criminal charge; the latter may be committed by anyone who restrains or confines another person without legal justification. *See* Alsup v. Skaggs Drug Center, 203 Okla. 525, 223 P.2d 530 (1950).

7. Doyle v. Douglas, 390 P.2d 871 (Okla. 1964). *See also* Guion v. Associate Dry Goods Co., 395 N.Y.S.2d 8 (App. Div. 1977); Simmons v. J.C. Penney Co., 186 So. 2d 358 (La. App. 1966).

The evidence on which detention is based need not be of the same "degree or conclusiveness" as that required for an arrest. People v. Rivera, 14 N.Y.2d 441, 445, 201 N.E.2d 32, 34, *cert. denied,* 379 U.S. 978 (1965). An example of a failure to meet the "reasonable cause" test as used in one detention statute is the La. case of Levy v. Duclaux, 324 So. 2d 1 (La. App. 1976), which involved the detention of a female customer during a dress sale where customers who bought two dresses would receive one free. According to the plaintiff, she told an employee, who was checking the number of dresses taken into a try-on room by a customer against the number taken out, that she had five dresses. However, the checker jotted down six. Instead of the checker's stopping and questioning the customer as she left the try-on room, the stopping and detention occurred as the customer was about to leave the store. She then became hysterical and pulled down her trousers to demonstrate that she was not concealing an unpaid-for-dress. The trial judge's finding of no "reasonable cause" was sustained on appeal. *See also* Chretien v. F.W. Woolworth Co., 160 So. 2d 854 (La. App. 1964).

Under a detention provision of the La. Code of Criminal Procedure (art. 215), if a merchant uses electrical devices designed to detect the unauthorized removal of marked merchandise, a signal from such a device constitutes "a sufficient basis for reasonable cause to detain." There is a requirement, however, to post a notice indicating the utilization of this equipment.

the earlier suspected offense itself; in other words, the detention is permissible only as incidental to the presently observed occurrence.[8] Likewise, a person's mere reputation as a shoplifter will not in and of itself meet the reasonable grounds requirement for a detention. Nevertheless, as will be discussed in Chapter 7, a merchant or security officer may, in discrete circumstances, request that the person leave the premises, and he may even be compelled to leave by the exercise of reasonable force. This merchant's privilege is based on the legal principle that persons who come into a store or a mercantile establishment occupy the status of invitees, and the invitation is subject to revocation at the will of the invitor.

In any detention situation, the merchant or his agent may use only reasonable force; he cannot use force that is likely to cause serious bodily harm. He may, for example, stand in the exit doorway to prevent a departure; however, he cannot put an armlock on the suspect to detain him, unless he is willing to forego his protection under the special statute and take the risk of liability attending an actual arrest.[9] However, if the customer initiates violence in response to a request to stay for investigation, the merchant may use violent force to protect himself or others.

The language used in many detention statutes, such as "effecting a recovery" of merchandise or "investigating its ownership," or "to determine whether the person detained has in his possession unpurchased merchandise," may suggest that a reasonable *search* of the person may be made. However, only Oklahoma's statute specifically authorizes "a search of the detainee person and his belongings."[10] The California detention statute, as amended in 1981, permits "a limited and reasonable search" but only of "packages, shopping bags, handbags, or other property in the immediate possession of the person detained." There is, however, no privilege under this statute to search "clothing worn by the person."[11]

Most legislatures appear to deliberately avoid authorizing a search. Traditionally, of course, a search without a warrant is usually allowable only when incidental to an actual arrest. Absent specific statutory authorization, it is inadvisable, therefore, to undertake a search. In most instances, of course, a tactful request of a person to empty a pocket or permit a look into a handbag or other container will permit an investigation opportunity.

With respect to the permissible detention time, some state statutes specify a maximum period, such as thirty or sixty minutes, instead of relying on the general

---

8. J.C. Penney Co. v. Cox, 148 So. 2d 679 (Miss. 1963).

9. Jefferson Stores v. Caudell, 228 So. 2d 99 (Fla. 1969). The La. Code of Criminal Procedure (art. 215) specifically permits the use of "reasonable force to detain."

10. See Okla. statute in the Appendix. It permits "a reasonable search of the detained person and his belongings when it appears the merchandise or money may otherwise be lost."

11. Cal. Pen. Code, Sec. 490.5(4). This section also provides that upon surrender or discovery of the suspected item, the person detained may be "requested, but may not be required, to provide adequate proof of his or her true identity."

guidelines of a "reasonable time."[12] However, Montana's Supreme Court held unconstitutional a part of its detention statute allowing detention for thirty minutes.[13] The amount of detention time was viewed as a violation of a unique provision in Montana's constitution that "the right of individual privacy is essential to the well-being of a free society and shall not be infringed without the showing of a compelling state interest." The court made clear, however, that its holding did not nullify the state's grant of authority to merchants to stop, detain, question, or recover merchandise when their efforts were conducted in a reasonable manner and for a reasonable time. The court only nullified the allocation of the thirty-minute period of detention specified in the statute.

In contrast to the Montana Supreme Court's decision, the Wisconsin Supreme Court declared that a twenty-minute detention period in the Wisconsin statute is reasonable.[14] This was held even in a case where a woman was detained for the purpose of investigating whether she had paid for an infant seat occupied by her child. The seat bore a price tag, and this fact gave rise to the suspicion that the mother was leaving the store without having paid for it. She actually had purchased it at an earlier date and showed the investigator food particles on the seat, evidencing its prior usage. The decision is an excellent example of the value to merchants of a detention statute, because in its absence the appellate court may have sustained the trial court's award of damages.

Regardless of whether a state statutory provision permits a detention for a specified time, and irrespective of the fact that such a specification is permissible under the state's own constitution, the prudent practice is to use no more time than is necessary by the circumstances of the particular case.

Most detention statutes make no mention of the permitted place of detention, but the assumption is that the detention must occur "on the premises," and some

---

12. In Ind. and La. the maximum detention time is sixty minutes; in Me., Mont., and W. Va., thirty minutes. New York and Wash. statutes provide that the detention time may not exceed the time needed for the customer to make or to refuse to make a statement and for the merchant to question employees and examine store records in an attempt to determine ownership of the merchandise.

If no time limit is set by statute, the issue of what is a "reasonable" time is to be decided in court, and this determination, of course, depends on the facts and circumstances of each case. An example of "reasonable" time as decided by one court is Delp v. Zapp's Drug & Variety Stores, 238 Ore. 538, 395 P.2d 137 (1964). In this case, a woman shopper who refused to identify herself was detained for thirty minutes in the investigation of a package of dye which a security officer had seen her put in her pocket as she was walking about the store with a large turkey and a half gallon of milk she had bought elsewhere. The thirty-minute period of detention was considered reasonable by the Supreme Court of Oregon.

It has been held that during a period of authorized detention, the defendant may be asked to sign a voluntary confession, on the theory that such a request is consistent with mere investigation, and that the request does not turn the investigation into an arrest. Collyer v. S.H. Kress & Co., 5 Cal. 2d 175, 54 P.2d 20 (1936). In no event, however, may a detainee be told he has to sign a confession before he will be permitted to leave the premises. Wilde v. Schwegman Bros. Giant Supermarkets, 160 So. 2d 839 (La. App. 1964).

13. Duran v. Buttrey, 616 P.2d 327 (Mont. 1980).

14. Johnson v. K-Mart Enterprises, 98 Wis. 2d 533, 297 N.W.2d 74 (1980).

statutes are specific in that respect.[15] Others, however, permit the detention to be made either "in the immediate vicinity" or "off" the premises.[16]

Several states have statutes that not only permit detaining suspected shoplifters, but also provide immunity from civil and criminal liability to detainers.[17] This immunity, of course, is conditioned on the factors of reasonable grounds (probable

15. *See* the statutes of Idaho, La., Me., Nev., and Ohio, in the Appendix. *See also* the provision in Del.'s shoplifting statute.

Although the La. Code of Criminal Procedure (art. 215) uses the term "on the premises," in *Durand v. United Dollar Store of Hammond*, 242 So. 2d 635 (La. App. 1970), the court held that detention on the sidewalk immediately in front of the defendant store could reasonably be encompassed within the phrase "on the merchant's premises."

16. *See* statutes of Alaska, Haw., Ill., Kan., Mass., Minn., N.Y., N.D., Pa., S.C., and S.D. The Ill. statute defines "premises of a retail mercantile establishment" as including "any common use areas in shopping centers and all parking areas set aside . . . for the parking of vehicles for the convenience of the patrons. . . ." The Minn. statute specifically covers any vehicles or premises under the control of the mercantile establishment. North Dakota specifically refers to parking areas. Illinois and Va. permit "off the premises" detention where it occurs in close pursuit of a suspected shoplifter.

The Michigan Court of Appeals has held that on common law principles a detention is permissible outside as well as on the premises. *Bomkowski v. Arlan's Dept. Store*, 162 N.W.2d 347 (Mich. App. 1968). *See also People v. Hasty*, 262 N.E.2d 292 (Ill. App. 1970), in which the defendant had already left the store when he was stopped by a security officer who testified that he had seen the defendant place some phonograph records in the shopping bag of a companion, who departed with them and was not caught. The court said that "the testimony of a single witness [the security officer], where credible, will be sufficient to sustain a conviction, although the testimony is contradicted by the accused." (Even though this was actually an arrest situation, the court decided the case on the basis of the state's detention statute.)

17. The following states have detention statutes with immunity provisions that are quite similar: Ala., Alaska, Del., Fla., Ga., Haw., Idaho, Ill., Ind., Iowa, Kan., Ky., Md., Mass., Mich., Minn., Miss., Mo., Mont., Neb., Nev., N.J., N.M., N.Y., N.D., Okla., Or., Pa., S.C., Tenn., Utah, Wash., W.V., Wis., and Wyo. The Wis. statute "entitles the merchant or his employee . . . to the same defense . . . as is available to a peace officer making an arrest in the line of duty."

In Ark., Colo., and S.D., a merchant is accorded immunity only when the detained person has actually concealed unpurchased merchandise, and in the last named state the immunity is lost if the merchant refuses to sign a complaint and testify in court if requested to do so by the prosecuting attorney. In Va., immunity applies only when an arrest, rather than a mere detention, is made.

Although Ariz. has no immunity labeled as such, there is a statutory provision that "reasonable grounds" constitute a defense to an action for "wrongful detention."

In a very unusual case situation, N.Y.'s highest court has held that the immunity granted by its detention statute extended to the following actions of a security officer. The officer saw a customer place some merchandise in his pants pocket and leave the store without paying for the articles, whereupon the officer stopped him, told him he was "under arrest," and escorted him to the store's security office. He was detained there until the police arrived (about twenty minutes later) and took him to police headquarters. Although the arrestee admitted to the security officer that he took the articles and was "sorry," and even though he also made the same admission to the judge, the judge refused to accept his guilty plea without a lawyer. The charge was later dismissed at the request of an assistant district attorney "because of lack of proof of intent." The arrestee then sued the store and the security officer. Although the jury found, in answer to a specific interrogatory, that the arrestee was "detained for a reasonable time" at the store and that there were "reasonable grounds to detain him," it nevertheless returned a verdict awarding him $1,600. When the case reached the New York Court of Appeals, the contention was made by the plaintiff that the term "detention" in the statute did not encompass an "arrest," that it did not provide a defense for a "reasonable" arrest, and consequently the "reasonable detention for questioning would not provide

cause) and a reasonable manner of the detention.[18] In Nevada, a merchant is accorded immunity only if a notice of his detention privilege is "displayed in a conspicuous place."

Although the detention statutes discussed thus far confer significant protection to merchants, two aspects of the detention problem have received scant legislative attention or judicial guidance. First of all, with few exceptions, the statutes refer only to "merchandise," thereby seemingly narrowing down the traditional common law judicial rule, so that only persons suspected of being shoplifters of merchandise may be detained for investigation.[19] This does not, however, foreclose an owner of other kinds of property from the exercise of other legal rights, such as

immunity for an arrest not resulting in conviction." The court held that the legislative history of the N.Y. statute indicated "a purpose to protect merchants even where criminal actions are eventually dismissed." The court said that "reasonable detention," within the language of the detention immunity statute, "included a full-fledged arrest as well as temporary detention." Jacques v. Sears, Roebuck & Co., 30 N.Y.2d 466, 285 N.E.2d 871 (1972).

18. An example of the failure of statutory compliance is the Neb. case of Schmidt and Clifton v. Richmond Gordon, Inc., 191 Neb. 345, 215 N.W.2d 105 (1974). In this case, two shoppers covered a shirt on a hanger with a vest, then proceeded to pay only for the vest and leave the store. The shoppers were detained for forty-five minutes by the merchant, who called the police and had both shoppers arrested. The shoppers were found not guilty of shoplifting after testifying that they thought they had paid for the shirt, having left the store without counting their change. Thereafter, they instituted an action for false arrest, slander, and malicious prosecution against the merchant and recovered $10,000. The Supreme Court of Nebraska upheld this verdict despite Neb.'s merchant detention statute, holding that the merchant arrested the shoppers without probable cause.

Another example of consequences of protective action that was subsequently viewed to be unwarranted is May Department Store v. Devercelli, 314 A.2d 767 (D.C. 1974). In this case a man was awarded $155,000 in compensatory and punitive damages for false imprisonment despite the D.C.'s judicially recognized right of a merchant to detain. Store police had stopped Devercelli after he had placed items of merchandise in a shopping bag and moved away from the counter. His demeanor appeared to be that of a drug addict, but testimony at trial revealed that the needle tracks in his arms and his nervous gait were due to a kidney condition. He was held incommunicado by store police for one and one-half hours and was also apparently subjected to verbal abuse. He finally signed a liability release form and was released without charge. At trial, the store's release form was circumvented by Devercelli's testimony that the store refused to release him until he agreed to sign it. (The legal significance of a release is discussed in Chapter 10.)

19. The exceptions, in varying degrees, are the following:

Minnesota ("any article of value"); N.D. (where the statute uses the word "merchandise," but defines merchandise to mean "any item of tangible personal property," and specifically includes shopping carts); and Okla. ("money" as well as "merchandise").

North Carolina has a generally worded statute on "detention of offenders by private persons." It permits a private person "to detain" another person when the detainer has probable cause to believe that "the person detained has committed in his presence . . . a crime involving theft. . . ."

Massachusetts has an immunity statute that covers not only merchandise but also property of employees, customers, and other persons, but the detention may be made only by "persons authorized to make arrests" (Mass. Ann. Laws, ch. 231, 94-B).

An illustration of the effects of limiting the detention privilege to merchandise is the case of Washington Kennel Club v. Edge, 216 So. 2d 512 (Fla. App. 1968), *cert. denied,* 255 So. 2d 522 (Fla. 1969), in which the court held that a merchandise detention statute did not afford protection to a race track whose agent thought the plaintiff obtained wrongful payment on a parimutuel ticket.

the previously discussed rights of arrest, search, and seizure, or the common law right to regain property unlawfully possessed by another person.[20]

Secondly, immunity statutes (except for those in a very few states), afford relief only in lawsuits for false arrest or false imprisonment; they do not afford similar protection against allegations of slander or defamation attending an act of detention.[21] In other words, no immunity is conferred on a merchant or security officer in cases where the person detained claims that the detention was conducted in the presence of other persons in such a manner as to amount to an alleged accusation of criminal conduct. The defense of such a suit becomes very difficult when the assertion is made that "other persons" witnessed the occurrence, whereas it may not have been witnessed, and the detainer may in fact have acted in a very unobtrusive and proper manner. In such situations an immunity provision could be very helpful to the defense, especially if the plaintiff's complaint charges false arrest, false imprisonment, *and* slander or defamation. Regardless, however, of the existence or nonexistence of immunity from slander or defamation, any detention should be conducted as discreetly as circumstances permit. Moreover, apart from the accrued legal advantage, a shoplifter handled in such a manner is more likely to surrender whatever objects were concealed, and is more likely to admit to a theft attempt.

In regard to the immunity provision in detention statutes, consideration should be accorded the interpretation given the Nebraska statute's provision by the state's supreme court in a case involving a suit against the merchant as well as the

As may be expected, not only must the objects be merchandise, but the usual statutory language covers only a store, so that the detention privilege would not apply to a bank, a school, or a church. State v. Worten, 197 S.E.2d 614 (N.C. App. 1973). *See also* Wolin v. Abraham and Straus, 316 N.Y.S.2d 377 (1970).

For a recent case illustrating the exclusion of "nonshoplifting" offenses from the protection of such "merchant's privilege" statutes, *see* Taylor v. Super Discount Market, Inc., 441 S.E.2d 433 (Ga. App. 1994), in which the court ruled that a grocery store was not protected by a merchant's privilege statute in allegedly detaining customers on suspicion of passing counterfeit currency, since no "shoplifting" by the customers was suspected. In this case, however, the court nevertheless found the store not liable for false imprisonment based on other circumstances.

20. The legal requirements for arrest, search, and seizure are, of course, more stringent than the conditions prescribed for a mere detention; consequently, merchants generally seek to avoid arrest, search, and seizure situations, because the liability damage risks are greater than when mere detention is involved, particularly when the detention is discreetly conducted. The common law right to regain property was discussed in Chapter 2. In an interesting decision, a Wisconsin appellate court ruled that a store could recover actual and punitive damages from a convicted shoplifter even though the merchandise taken was recovered undamaged and unused. Shopko Stores, Inc. v. Kujak, 433 N.W.2d 618 (Wis. App. 1988). In those instances where a convicted shoplifter has assets, a merchant might, under the rationale of this case, seek to recover damages suffered despite the recovery of stolen merchandise, possibly including the costs of the store's investigation, employee's lost time, and "punitive" damages simply intended to punish the shoplifter for his intentional wrongdoing against the merchant.

21. Apparently there are only a few state detention immunity statutes (e.g., those of Colo., Md., and Neb.) that confer slander or libel protection.

Regarding the merchant's defamation problem generally, *see* Southwest Drug Stores v. Gamen, 195 So. 2d 837 (Miss. 1967); Eason v. J. Weingarten, Inc., 219 So. 2d 516 (La. 1969); Williams v. F.W. Woolworth Co., 242 So. 2d 16 (La. 1970); Tip Top Grocery Co. v. Wellnes, 135 Fla. 518, 186 So. 219 (1938); American Stores Co. v. Byrd, 229 Md. 5, 181 A.2d 333 (1962); Lily v. Belk's Dept. Store, 178

independent contractor who supplied the security service.[22] Because the immunity provision of the statute used the term "merchant or employee of the merchant," the security contractor was deprived of the immunity protection that had been granted to the merchant's employees, because the independent contractor's agents were not within that category.

The privilege accorded by detention statutes is used to a limited extent by merchants. They still harbor fears of civil suits for unlawful restraint or false arrest, despite the qualified immunity the particular statute may create. Their principal concerns are that in a jury trial the conduct of the detainer may be viewed as "unreasonable," and it is a fact that juries are generally more sympathetic to the detained person than to the merchant.[23]

The following is a good example of the risk that remains even under statutory detention authorization that may be rather broad in scope. The Massachusetts detention statute authorizes detention "for questioning on or in the immediate vicinity of the premises of a merchant" if there are "reasonable grounds" to believe the person detained has stolen or was attempting to steal the merchant's goods. A security officer observed the plaintiff, an elderly man, pull an ascot out of his pocket and put it around his neck, underneath his topcoat, just as he was leaving the store. The officer approached him outside the store and said, "Stop. Where did you get that scarf?" to which the plaintiff said, "Why?" The officer then grasped his arm and said, "You better go back and see the manager." Present at the scene was another employee and ten other persons. The plaintiff agreed to reenter the store. As he was being escorted up the stairs to the second floor, he developed chest pains which later were determined to be the result of a heart attack. An investigation disclosed that the plaintiff lawfully owned the scarf before he entered the store, where he had just purchased a sport coat and left it for alterations. A jury found the security officer and the store civilly liable, and the jury's verdict was sustained by the Supreme Judicial Court of Massachusetts. The court held that the objective standard of a "reasonably prudent man" was properly utilized by the jury in determining the absence of reasonable grounds for believing a larceny had been committed.[24]

S.C. 278, 182 S.E. 889 (1935); Little Stores v. Isenberg, 172 S.W.2d 13 (Tenn. App. 1943); Camp v. Maddox, 92 S.E.2d 581 (Ga. App. 1956); Hart v. Coy, 40 Ind. 553 (1872). *See also Defamation: Actionability of Accusation or Imputation of Shoplifting,* 29 A.L.R.3d 961.

For a case dealing extensively with the problem of when a detention may or may not constitute a defamation, *see* Durand v. United Dollar Store of Hamond, 242 So. 2d 635 (La. App. 1970).

Since truth is a complete defense to a slander or defamation suit, a person actually guilty of shoplifting obviously has no legitimate cause of action against a detainer. A more complete discussion of defamation is subsequently presented in Chapter 10.

22. Bishop v. Bockhoven, Inc., 199 Neb. 613, 260 N.W.2d 488 (1977). The statute was Sec. 29-402.01.

23. *See, e.g.,* Weingarten v. Halfpenny Auto Parts, Inc., 525 N.Y.S.2d 657 (A.D. 1988), in which an employee, whose own testimony in his false imprisonment suit confirmed that he had stolen cash from his employer, was initially awarded $140,000 in damages, but the award was overturned on appeal.

24. Coblyn v. Kennedy's, 359 Mass. 319, 268 N.E.2d (1971).

Once a plaintiff makes a prima facie case of unlawful detention, the burden shifts to the merchant to show that reasonable grounds did indeed exist for the detention. Isaiah v. Great A. & P. Tea Co., 174 N.E.2d 128 (Ohio App. 1959).Temporary detention statutes in false imprisonment suits are discussed in 86 A.L.R.2d 435 and 47 A.L.R.3d 991.

Although the appellate process can, and does, serve as a check on jury verdicts not supportable by the facts adduced at the trial, the cost of an appeal serves as a deterrent to going beyond a trial court determination.

As a result of the prevailing cautious attitude by merchants, many of them view detention statutes to be of limited value, except for the psychological effect they have on potential shoplifters who may have heard about them or perhaps have seen notices or reproductions of the detention privileges posted somewhere within the store. This overly cautious policy apparently accounts for significant pilferage losses.

DETENTION AND INQUIRIES OF EMPLOYEES

An employer obviously has a right to conduct a reasonable investigation of employee thievery. Consequently, an employee may be requested to discuss such matters as shortages in cash register receipts, missing merchandise, and the disappearance or loss of money or other articles of value belonging to the employer or fellow employees and other persons on the premises. If an employer requested an employee to go to a security office or other place in the establishment for questioning, compliance would not constitute a restraint for which the employer would be liable, even though the consequence of noncompliance may be termination of the employment.[25] Any such request, of course, should be made in a calm, tactful manner and, whenever possible, out of the presence or hearing of other people. A request made under such circumstances will minimize the risk of legal liability for slander.[26] It will also be conducive to a more effective investigation.

What is not altogether clear is the right to detain an employee during the investigative process. One reasonable assumption is that nonforcible detention is permissible during the work hours of the employee.[27] However, if physical force, or the threat of such force, is used, or if the detention, even though not actually in-

---

25. In regard to the right of an employee in a unionized establishment to have a union representative present during any such questioning, see *infra,* Chapter 4.

Union contracts may, of course, contain various restrictive conditions, but in this text we can discuss only the general law regarding the investigative rights of the employer.

26. For a person to recover in a suit for slander, the words spoken must be reasonably and fairly susceptible of a defamatory meaning, and they must be uttered within the hearing of other persons. Summers v. W. T. Grant Co., 178 F.2d 916 (5th Cir. 1950); Great Atlantic & Pacific Tea Co. v. Paul, 256 Md. 643, 261 A.2d 731 (1970); Terwilligen v. Wands, 17 N.Y. 54, 72 Am. Dec. 420 (1858).

To be classified within the required category, the words, according to one state supreme court, must expose their object to public hatred, shame, or ridicule in the eyes of "right-thinking" people. Kimmerle v. New York Evening Journal, 262 N.Y. 99, 186 N.E.217 (1933). (If words of the foregoing character are put into writing and distributed in that form, the wrong is known as *libel.*)

27. Landsburgh's Inc. v. Ruffin, 372 A.2d 561 (D.C. Ct. App. 1977). In this case, the court upheld the right to detain an employee for about two hours for questioning about the failure to record the receipt of money for the sale of boots. The incident was discovered when the customer returned to exchange the boots. The detention was held to be on reasonable grounds and for a reasonable time. *See also* Harrison v. Phillips, 539 So. 2d 911 (La. App. 1989), in which the court ruled that the mere fear of an employee that he would cast further suspicion on himself by leaving his employer's officer after the employer called the police did not constitute a detention.

volving force, is utilized after work hours, the liability risk of the employer could be considerable.[28]

The distinction between an employee's compliance with a security officer's request and coercive detention is illustrated by a Texas case involving the following facts. A shopper service agent observed a clerk in a large grocery store taking some of the store's money. The clerk was asked by the store manager to come to a secluded area of the store—"the most private place available," an aisle with about a four- to six-foot clear passage at all times. While there, he was questioned for about half an hour during the period of his working day, after which he admitted taking a total of $500. He also signed a statement to that effect. In a suit for false imprisonment, the employee received a substantial judgment in the trial court, but the case was reversed on appeal. The appellate court said that "an employer is entitled to discuss with an employee matters relevant to his employment and particularly where he has information touching upon the fidelity of the employee." The court further commented that "the logical place for the conference would be the establishment where the employee was hired to work."[29]

Although, as already pointed out, there are numerous detention statutes that deal with situations involving nonemployee shoplifting of merchandise, there are very few that cover the detention of employees suspected of stealing merchandise or other property belonging to the employers, fellow employees, or other persons.[30] New Jersey's detention statute defines the term "any person," as used in the statute, to include employees, but the articles referred to are of a merchandise nature.[31] The Illinois statute, which is very comprehensive, defines "any person" to mean "any natural person or individual" (obviously including employees), and "merchandise" means "any item of tangible personal property,"[32] although as to the latter the title of the particular statute is "retail theft" and the legislative intent is stated to be the prevention of "retail theft." One section of the statute, however, that certainly is directed to employee thievery is labeled "underrings," meaning "to cause the cash register or other sales recording device to reflect less than the full value of the merchandise."[33]

28. An employer or his agent who forcibly detains an employee may be liable criminally as well as civilly for assault and battery. Moreover, consideration should be given to actions available under the Federal Civil Rights Act. *See* Chapter 10 for further discussion of criminal and civil liability arising out of temporary detention and inquiries.

29. Safeway Stores v. Amburn, 388 S.W.2d 443, 446 (Tex. Civ. App. 1965). Other cases in accord are: Roberts v. Coleman, 228 Ore. 286, 365 P.2d 79 (1961); Weiler v. Herzfeld-Phillipson Co., 189 Wis. 554, 208 N.W. 599 (1926).

30. *See* De Angelis v. Jamesway Dept. Store, 501 A.2d 561 (N.J. Super. A.D. 1985) (merchant's privilege statute allowing detainment for possession of stolen goods was not applicable to employees suspected of stealing money from employer).

31. N.J. Stats., Sec. 2C:20:11(5).

32. Ill. Comp. Stats., ch. 720 Sec. 5/16A-2.6, 5/16A-2.3.

33. Ill. Comp. Stats., ch. 720, Sec. 5/16A-2.11. It should also be noted, however, that the switching of price tags by shoplifters is another way in which this offense is committed. *See* State v. Kirksey, 727 S.W.2d 201 (Mo. App. 1987) (security guard's testimony that suspect switched price tags on merchandise and that she refunded suspect's money was properly admitted in criminal prosecution).

One basic consideration in respect to an employer's right under any detention statute that does not specifically cover employees is the fiduciary relationship between employers and employees. In either the application of common law principles or in the interpretation of any statute, unless the statutory language is specifically restricted, the fiduciary relationship should give an employer detention rights at least comparable to those accorded him with respect to nonemployees. Another important consideration is that merchants incur far greater losses due to stealing by employees than those attributable to ordinary shoplifting.[34]

Irrespective of the law pertaining to the detention of employees suspected of thievery, a merchant can provide, in the contract of employment, that reasonable detentions are permissible, that reasonable searches may be made of employees to safeguard against the loss of property, and that searches may be made at any time of employees' desks or lockers, and of lunch boxes or other containers that are being carried off the premises. Union contracts, however, may either preclude or specifically permit such practices.

34. Employee theft has been estimated to cost employers more than $50 billion in stolen merchandise every year, *Los Angeles Daily Journal,* p. B1, col. 3 (Jan. 2, 1986). In Meerbrey v. Marshall Field & Co., 524 N.E.2d 228 (Ill. App. 1988), a court upheld as legally enforceable a store's decision to bar a former employee from its premises who was discharged after money on the premises was missing.

4

The Interrogation
of Suspected Persons

In order for a security officer or business person to adequately understand her rights and responsibilities when interrogating an individual suspected of thievery or some other criminal offense, she must be familiar with the rules governing interrogations by the police themselves.*

POLICE INTERROGATIONS

Avoidance of Coercive Tactics

The principal legal requirement for a confession to be usable as evidence against a confessor is that it must be *voluntary*. This long time legal principle was established for *the protection of the innocent*. It was not created as a prophylactic rule for keeping the police in line, or for respecting a legal rule unrelated to the issue of guilt or innocence. There can be no valid objection, therefore, to the continued existence of the voluntariness test.

The best example of an interrogation practice that will void a confession is the infliction of physical force or pain upon the person under interrogation, because it is an incontestable fact that a practice of this nature may produce a confession of guilt from an innocent person. This is also true as regards indirect physical harm, e.g., an unduly prolonged continuous interrogation (especially by two or more interrogators working in relays), or the deprivation of food, water, or access to toilet facilities for an unreasonable period of time.

A threat of physical harm may also have a similar effect on the extraction of confessions from innocent persons. Likewise, an interrogator's promise to a suspect that if she confesses she will go free, or receive a lenient penalty, may also induce

---

* For a text on the permissable tactics and techniques for the effective interrogation of criminal suspects by security officers and the police, consult F.E. INBAU, J.E. REID, AND J.P. BUCKLEY, CRIMINAL INTERROGATION AND CONFESSIONS (3d ed. 1986).

an innocent person to confess rather than risk being convicted and severely punished. This is particularly true of suspects caught in a strong web of circumstantial evidence, or mistakenly identified as the offender by a crime victim or an alleged witness. An acceptance of a promise of freedom, or of a light sentence, may be an appealing alternative.

A law enforcement officer who employs physical force to obtain a confession from a suspect not only risks having it rejected as evidence, but may also expose herself to a criminal prosecution or a civil lawsuit, particularly in the federal courts.[1]

The contrast to these coercive interrogation practices is the use of trickery and deceit by the interrogator to obtain a truthful admission of guilt. The difference between the two is that the latter does not present the hazard of procuring incriminations from the innocent. A tacit recognition of this fact appears in a 1969 opinion by the United States Supreme Court in the case of *Frazier v. Cupp*,[2] where the Court upheld a criminal conviction based on a confession obtained by a substantial degree of trickery and deceit. The defendant, while being interrogated as a murder suspect, was falsely told that a suspected accomplice had confessed and implicated him. The Court considered the misrepresentation "insufficient... to make this otherwise voluntary confession inadmissible" as evidence.

An authoritative text on criminal interrogation techniques recommends that interrogators use the following test to ascertain the validity of a contemplated tactic of deceit and trickery: "Is what I am about to say or do apt to make an innocent person confess?" If the objective answer is no, the interrogator should say or do what she had in mind. If, however, the answer is that it might produce an incrimination from an innocent suspect, the interrogator should refrain.[3]

Some academics have castigated the police for using trickery or deceit during their interrogations of criminal suspects. From their "ivory tower" viewpoint, such tactics are unfair and immoral, and any lying to suspects also has a demoralizing effect on the police themselves. Apart from the unreality consideration, these critics overlook the fact that by their standards *all* interrogations of criminal suspects are unfair and immoral unless they are told, before an interrogation begins, that, "Sir, I want you to know that my reason for talking to you is to find out from you if you committed this crime, and if so, I want to obtain a confession from you so that it can be used to convict you in order to send you to prison (or be sentenced to death). So, you see, I want to be fair with you and not deceive you into thinking that this interrogation is for your benefit. I also want you to know that you may now have the advice of a lawyer, and you are entitled to one as a matter of law. Knowing all this, are you willing to talk to me about this crime?"

1. *See,* on the federal level, 42 U.S.C. § 1983 and 18 U.S.C. § 242, and the case of Cooper v. Dupnik, 963 F. 2d 1220 (9th Cir. 1992), *certdenied,* 113 S. Ct. 407 (1992); Johnson v. Cheyenne (1993) WL335802. Flanigan v. Kent City Sheriff's Dept., 817 F. Supp. 660 (W.D., Mich. 1993). For an example of state law, see Ill. Rev. Stats., 720 ILCS 5/12-7; 7 N.Y. Consal. Laws, art. 60, §6C.45.

2. 394 U.S. 731 (1969).

3. *See* F.E. INBAU, J.E. REID, AND J.P. BUCKLEY, CRIMINAL INTERROGATION AND CONFESSIONS, 217 (3d ed. 1986).

Requirement of Lawful Custody

In addition to the voluntariness requirement, the courts have established other rules to protect certain values derived from interpretations of various provisions of the federal or state constitutions. One such rule—the exclusion of illegally seized evidence—has been applied to confessions obtained by the police from persons who have been illegally arrested. Regardless of the confession's otherwise voluntary nature, an illegal arrest will nullify its use as evidence.[4]

Required Warnings of Constitutional Rights

Another court-established rule, and one familiar to many lay persons as well as to the police and security officers, was mandated by the United States Supreme Court's 5 to 4 decision in the 1966 case of *Miranda v. Arizona*.[5] It prescribed the requirement that before *the police* interrogate a person they have taken into *custody,* or deprived her of her freedom "in any significant way," she must be given the following warnings: (1) you have a right to remain silent; (2) whatever you say may be used against you; (3) you have a right to a lawyer; and (4) if you cannot afford a lawyer, one will be provided to you free.

The interrogation may proceed only after the suspect makes a "knowing and intelligent" waiver of the prescribed warnings. Moreover, if at any time the suspect declines to talk or requests a lawyer, the interrogation must cease. The Court also added that any statement made without the warnings or a waiver of those rights is not usable as evidence.

The rationale for the *Miranda* decision was that the rich, the educated, or the intelligent person who has been taken into custody probably knows at the outset that she has the right to remain silent and the right to consult with a lawyer, whereas the less fortunate person does not. Consequently, reasoned the Court, in fairness to all, every custodial suspect must be advised of her right to silence; and to ensure that she is aware of it, she is entitled to the presence of a lawyer who can so advise her. In actuality, however, the usual lawyer advice to the suspect is to refuse to answer any questions.[6]

Among the unfortunate consequences of the *Miranda* mandate is the overreaction to it by many police legal advisors and prosecuting attorneys. Because of their concern regarding the possible court rejection of a confession due to noncompliance with *Miranda,* the warnings are often given when not required, or else they are embellished with additional warnings that were not prescribed by the Supreme Court.[7]

---

4. Dunaway v. New York, 442 U.S. 200 (1979); United States v. Clark, 822 F. Supp. 990 (W.D. NY. 1993).

5. 384 U.S. 436 (1966).

6. For a critical view of the *Miranda* mandate, see F.E. INBAU AND J.P. MANAK, *Miranda v. Arizona—Is It Worth the Cost?,* 24 CAL. W. L. REV. 185–201 (1987). With regard to the above statement, see p.196.

7. An outstanding example is the interrogation of John W. Hinckley, Jr. regarding the attempted assisination of President Ronald Reagan. The full details are in F.E. INBAU, *OverReaction—The Mischief of Miranda v. Arizona,* 73 J. CRIM. L. & CRIMINOL. 797–810 (1982).

SECURITY OFFICER INTERROGATIONS

Prohibition of Coercive Tactics

The legal requirement that confessions must be voluntary as a condition for admissibility as evidence was established to protect the innocent. It still prevails for all confessions, regardless of whether they have been obtained by the police, by security officers, or by other private citizens. A case example of private citizen conduct that will nullify a confession on the grounds of involuntariness is one in which the husband of a woman who had undergone an illegal abortion kidnapped the alleged abortionist, beat him, and threatened him with further harm. After being rescued by the police, he confessed. However, an appellate court held that the husband's conduct rendered the confession inadmissible as evidence.[8]

An unduly prolonged interrogation constitutes coercive conduct that can nullify an otherwise valid confession. Less obvious as a nullifying factor, however, is the making of a promise of leniency on the part of a security officer or a crime victim. In former times such a promise would only nullify a confession's admissibility if the promise came from a person in authority, i.e., someone in a position to fulfill the promise. That qualification may no longer prevail, so the better practice is to avoid making a promise unless there is no intention on the part of the security officer or the crime victim to pursue a prosecution.

A test that can help security officers determine whether a contemplated tactic crosses the voluntary/involuntary line is the previously discussed one for police: Is what is intended apt to induce an innocent person to confess?

Exemption from Miranda Requirements

As earlier stated, the Supreme Court's decision in *Miranda*[9] was directed at police interrogations. In that case, the Supreme Court was not concerned with the questioning or interrogation of suspects conducted by nonlaw enforcement officers; its mandate was directed only at the *police* in *custodial interrogation situations*. In other words, private persons, including security personnel and such other persons as insurance company investigators, do not need to give the warnings to suspected employees, customers, or others, even when the suspected person has been subjected to a citizen arrest.

There are many court decisions holding that private security officers are not required to give the *Miranda* warnings before interrogating a person they have

---

8. People v. Bowe, 51 Cal. 2d 286, 322 P. 2d 97 (1958). *See also* State v. Atkins, 251 Ore. 485, 446 P. 2d 660 (1968).

   A provision in a New York statute specifically declares as inadmissible a confession involuntarily made to *any* person who obtained it by the use or threatened use of force. Section 60.45, N.Y. Crim. Proc. Law.

9. *Supra* note 5.

taken into custody pursuant to citizen arrest powers. A most noteworthy case for security officers, and particularly those in mercantile stores, is *People v. Deborah C., a Minor*, decided by the Supreme Court of California in 1981.[10] A store's security officer arrested a fifteen-year-old girl whom he had seen put some costume jewelry in her pocket and walk out without paying for it. When the officer questioned her in the security office, without issuing the *Miranda* warnings, she was asked why she had taken the jewelry. The girl replied that her girlfriend companion told her "it was easy to steal, so she thought she would." The jewelry and her incriminating statement were admitted in evidence, and she was found guilty at a hearing on a "wardship petition" charging her with petty theft. On appeal, Deborah's counsel argued that the statement she made should not have been used against her, because of the security officer's failure to give the *Miranda* warnings. In a unanimous opinion, the California Supreme Court rejected that contention, holding that the security officer was not required to give the warnings, even though Deborah was in his custody at the time.

Although the California court referred to prior decisions in California to the effect that *Miranda* applied only to police interrogations, and also to decisions of other courts to the same effect, the court relied heavily on some special considerations with respect to security officers' procedures in shoplifting situations. They warrant the following quotation from the court's opinion:

> There is evidence that retailers exercise restraint; more than half the store representatives contacted in a national study said that store policy was to release most shoplifters without police involvement.[11] Thus, though detentions by store personnel may at times seem frightening, the "compelling atmosphere" that *Miranda* deemed inherent in a custodial interrogation by police and other government personnel appears diminished.
>
> *Miranda* criticized police preference for confessions over independent investigation, but [in California] citizens may not arrest for misdemeanors not committed in their presence. The study referred to above indicated that stores discourage detention and arrest of suspects not actually seen by store employees leaving the premises with unbought merchandise. That procedure was followed here. Before detaining Deborah, [the security officer] saw her conceal several items and then watched until she left the store without paying.
>
> Thus it appears that shoplifting convictions routinely may depend more on eyewitness testimony and physical evidence than on the suspect's inculpatory statements. Store detectives' incentive to extract confessions is diminished even when the basic intention is to prosecute. Should psychological or physical abuse produce a confession, the exclusionary remedy is of course available.

Another important case to security officers is *People v. Ray*, decided in 1985 by New York's Supreme Court.[12] In *Ray* a clothing store detective arrested and ques-

---

10. 177 Cal. Rptr. 852, 635 P. 2d 446 (1981). The case also carries the title of "*In Re* Deborah C., a Person Coming under the Juvenile Court Law."

11. The study to which the court referred is *Merchants' Responses to Shoplifting: An Empirical Study*, 28 STAN. L. REV. 589, 604 (1976).

12. 65 N.Y. 2d 282, 480 N.E. 2d 1065 (1985). *See also* People v. Dunnigan, 592 N.Y. S. 2d 207 (1992).

tioned a suspected shoplifter, to whom the arrestee confessed and signed a statement of guilt. At trial, a challenge was made to the admissibility of the statement because the arrestee had not received the *Miranda* warnings.

In support of his claim, the defendant established that a "special police officer" had been regularly assigned to the store to process security officer prosecution charges. This was alleged to be "governmental participation" and consequently required issuance of the *Miranda* warnings. Although an intermediate appellate court accepted that contention, the higher court reversed, holding that the mere presence on the premises of a regular police officer, who did not participate in the arrest or in the questioning of the arrestee, did not mandate the warnings.

The conclusion that private security officers are not obligated to abide by the requirements of *Miranda* presupposes that the security officer is not an actual police officer working part-time in that capacity during off-duty hours (i.e., moonlighting). It also presupposes that the security officer is acting independently of the police in the investigation up to and including the interrogation of the apprehended suspect. In either of these situations, *Miranda* warnings are required. The rationale with respect to the moonlighting police officer, as stated in a concurring opinion in the previously discussed California case of *Deborah C.,* is that "a police officer is under a continuing duty to protect the public" and she is not to be relieved of the *Miranda* mandate merely because she happens to be working in private security at the time she interrogates the apprehended person. As to the security officer who acts for or with the police, the general principle of agency law equates her position to that of a police officer.

Coming within the ambit of security personnel who may be required to administer *Miranda* warnings are the campus police at state or private universities and colleges who are given powers similar to those possessed by conventional police officers.[13] This also may be true of persons who have been "commissioned" by a public official (pursuant to legislative authorization) to act in a law enforcement capacity for a limited purpose. However, the mere legislative requirement of the "licensing" of private security officers does not transform the licensee into a police officer for *Miranda* purposes[14]; nor does the legislative authorization of the right of a private security officer to temporarily detain suspected employees or customers; that, too, has been held to fall short of the Supreme Court's contemplated purpose in its *Miranda* decision.[15]

---

13. *See, e.g.,* the California Education Code, § 89560, and California Penal Code, § 830.2. *See also* People v. Dickson, 154 Cal. Rptr. 116 (Cal. App. 3d 1979), in which the warnings were required.

    Other examples are Ill. statutes 110 I.L.C.S. 805/3 42.1, and 110 I.L.C.S. 305/7, and Illinois ordinances in the Municipal Codes of Chicago, § 173, and of Evanston, § 99-0-71.

    The broader subject of campus police, covering arrest, search and seizure, was discussed in the earlier Chapters 1 and 2.

14. For a general discussion of this issue see the rather unusual case situation in Pratt v. State, 263 A. 2d 247 (Md. App. 1970). *See also* art. 41, §64 of Md. Ann. Code, and tit.18, § 18.185 (30), Mich. Stats. Ann.

15. State v. Bolan, 271 N.E. 2d 839 (Ohio 1971); People v. Raitano, 401 N. E. 2d 278 (Ill. App. 1980); and People v. Deborah C, *supra* note 10.

The mere fact that a security officer works at a government owned or operated facility, such as a hospital, does not require her to issue the warnings.[16]

Although the *Miranda* rule was developed to benefit persons taken into custody for a criminal offense, some state legislatures have extended that concept to include police officers who are under investigation by their commanding officers or by members of a public safety department. The legislation, usually described as the "Police Officers Bill of Rights," requires a department's investigator or board to advise an officer of the right to counsel before interrogation about a matter that may result in a suspension beyond fifteen days, or a dismissal.[17] When an infraction is sufficiently serious to result in a possible criminal prosecution, one state requires that the interrogator immediately inform the officer of her full constitutional rights.[18]

Security officers, as well as regular police officers, should avoid administering *Miranda* warning when not legally required to do so. In addition to cutting off the opportunity to interrogate a suspect who might otherwise be willing to talk, another unfavorable consequence may result: if, after receiving the warnings, a suspect remains silent, that silence cannot be used as a tacit admission of guilt, as might be permissible if she had not been admonished of her right to remain silent.[19]

Privacy in Interrogations

For psychological reasons, a suspected person should be questioned by only one interrogator, and in a quiet room where an uninterrupted interview will be possible. However, in instances where the suspect is a female and the interrogator a male, it is advisable to have another woman placed in a position where she can see and hear all that transpires. This will afford considerable protection against the possibility of unfounded charges of impropriety.[20]

The interrogation room should be devoid of a door lock and any other physical impediment to an exit by the suspect if she should want to leave.

There is an important legal issue that may frustrate the desire for privacy in conducting interviews with employees suspected of thievery or some other offense. The United States Supreme Court, in the 1975 case of *National Labor Relations Board v. Weingarten*, upheld a National Labor Relations Board ruling that a denial of an employee's request to have a union representative present at

---

16. People v. Wright, 57 Cal. Rptr. 781 (Cal. App. 1967).

17. For example, the Cal. Gov't. Code, ch 9.7, Division 4, tit.1, § 3303–3311. This seems comparable to the "focus of suspicion" test that a few states had erroneously applied in criminal cases. The Supreme Court rectified this in Beckwith v. United States, 425 U.S. 341 (1976), which held that "custody" rather than "focus of suspicion" was the required test. *See also* Md. Code, art. 27, § 728 (b).

18. *Supra* note 17, §3303 (g).

19. People v. Givens, 220 Cal. Rptr. 756 (Cal. App. 1985).

20. For further comments on the general desirability of interrogation privacy, see *supra* note 3, at 24–28, 310.

an "investigatory interview," which the employee reasonably believed might result in disciplinary action, constitutes an unfair labor practice.[21] The ruling of the Board was based on a provision in the National Labor Relations Act that protects the right of employees "to engage in . . . . concerted activities for . . . mutual aid or protection." In this particular case an employee, working as a cashier at a lunch counter, was suspected of placing only $1 in the cash register for a personal purchase of a box of chicken worth $2.98. She was summoned for an investigative interview and requested that a union representative be present, which was refused. As a result of the interview she was found to be innocent of any wrongdoing. The interviewer apologized and told her the matter was closed, whereupon she began to cry and "blurted out that the only thing she had ever gotten from the store without paying for it was her free lunch." This revelation surprised the interviewer, but a check into the matter disclosed that the practice had been tolerated with regard to all employees in her department. All of them, including the manager, were receiving free lunches. The employee was asked to consider the entire interview a private matter between her and the store. She nevertheless reported it to the union, which proceeded to file a grievance charge.

Three Supreme Court justices dissented in the *Weingarten* case on the grounds that (a) the incident did not involve "concerted activity," and (b) no discipline or discharge had resulted. The dissenting justices noted that the Board's ruling in this case was a reversal of the position the Board had followed for many years, and that there was no explanation for any change in viewpoint. The dissenters thought that "union representation at investigatory interview is a matter that Congress left to the bargaining process" and that the type of personalized interview in this case "is simply not 'concerted activity' within the meaning of the National Labor Relations Act."

Although there is no requirement that employees be advised of their right to have a union representative present at a Board hearing, two federal appellate courts have held that a union representative may participate in the hearing.[22] Several Labor Board decisions have held, however, that the *Weingarten* decision is not applicable to nonunion employees.[23]

---

21. 420 U.S. 251, 95 S. Ct. 959 (1975). *See also* the companion case, decided the same day as *Weingarten*, International Ladies Government Workers Union v. Quality Mgf. Co., 420 U.S. 276 (1975). The Court has stated that the rule applies only when the employee makes a request for a representative to be present. A federal court of appeals case has specifically held that the right to have a union representative at an interview is conditioned upon a request to that effect by the employee. It also discusses limitations on a representative's participation. Climax Molybdenum Co. v. N.L.R.B., 584 F. 2d 360 (10th Cir. 1978). As to the effect of an annual notice to employees of this right, see Sears v. Department of the Navy, 680 F.2d 863 (1st Cir. 1982).

22. Montgomery Ward and United Food and Commercial Workers Union Local 770, 269 NLRB 598 (1984). N.L.R.B. v. Southwestern Bell Tel. Co., 730 F. 2d 166 (5th Cir. 1984).

23. *See* DuPont de Nemours, 289 N.L.R.B. 627 (1988) holding that nonunion employees do not have a right to a representative present at a hearing. *See also* Slaughter v. N.L.R.B., 876 F. 2d 11 (3rd Cir. 1989); DuPont v. N.L.R.B. 707 F. 2d 1076 (9th Cir. 1983); and Lighting Fixtures v. N.L.R.B. 719 F. 2d 851 (6th Cir. 1983).

Slander/Defamation Issue in Interrogation Situation[24]

The law is absolutely clear that no slander or other form of defamation occurs when an interrogator directly accuses a suspect of committing a criminal offense, even though it later develops that she is completely innocent. Either of two conditions must prevail, however. First, the accusation must be made under conditions of privacy—in other words, outside the presence or hearing of a third person or persons. There can be no slander or other defamation without a "publication," which, in the legal sense, means letting another person hear or know what has been said.[25] Under the privacy setting recommended for interrogations, there will be no publication.

Second, if a third party is to be present or within hearing, there must exist what is legally known as a "qualified privilege" with respect to her awareness of what is being said. An example of this is an interrogation conducted in the presence or within the hearing of a fellow interrogator or supervisor, or of someone else who has a legitimate common interest in the subject being investigated, such as the suspect's employer in an embezzlement case. Other examples are instances where the presence of a female police officer or female private security officer is considered necessary during a male's interrogation of a female suspect; or an interpreter's presence because of a suspect's language difficulty. As to the presence of a fellow union member employee requested by the suspect, which must, by law, be honored by the interrogator, this should be considered a waiver as regards slander or other defamation.[26]

Interrogation Stress Issue[27]

Although a suspect whom the interrogator accuses will probably be upset and incur hurt feelings if actually innocent, that fact alone will not provide the basis for legal action against the accuser. The general rule of law is that the First Amendment right to "free speech" renders permissive the utterance of derogatory, or even rude or insulting remarks, subject, however, to the conditions of privacy or qualified privilege. A cause of action arises only when the statements are made for the *intended purpose of inflicting severe emotional distress.*[28] That element

24. This section is a reproduction from INBAU, REID, AND BUCKLEY, *supra* note 3, at 218.

25. PROSSER, W., ET AL., THE LAW OF TORTS, § 111 (5th ed. 1984).

26. With regard to the general law on the subject, consult KEETON ET AL., *supra* note 25, at §115.

27. This section is a reproduction from INBAU, REID, AND BUCKLEY, *supra* note 3, at 219.

28. RESTATEMENT OF THE LAW ON TORTS, §§ 46, 312, 313, 436 A. Section 313 provides that a person who unintentionally causes emotional distress is liable for resulting illness or bodily harm if she should have realized that the conduct involved an unreasonable risk of causing the distress and, according to PROSSER, W., ET AL., *supra* note 25, at § 12, for liability to result the conduct must "exceed all bounds usually tolerated by decent society, of a nature which is especially calculated to cause, and does cause, mental distress of a very serious kind." The authors also state that "the emotional distress must in fact exist, and it must be severe." For a case dealing with many aspects of the stress issues, see Hall v. May Dept., 292 or 131, 637 P. 2d 126 (1982). *See also* Kiphart v. Community Federal Savings, 729 S.W. 2d 510 (Mo. App. 1987).

is obviously lacking in a case situation where, in an effort to solve a criminal offense, a police interrogator, acting in the public interest, or a private security interrogator, seeking to protect an employer's legitimate interest, uses an accusatory confrontation while interrogating a suspect. There is the understandable limitation, of course, that the confrontation must not extend beyond the point where severe mental distress becomes a probability.

Preserving Confessions

The Written Confession

Once an oral confession is obtained by either a security officer or a law enforcement officer, it should be preserved in writing and signed by the confessor as soon as possible. A delay could result in a change of mind.

The writing need only record the essential aspects of the offense; thereafter, if deemed advisable, a more detailed statement may be obtained, perhaps in a question and answer form, recorded and typed by a stenotypist or shorthand reporter, or electronically recorded.

When recording confessions, one should avoid asking leading questions. In other words, the interrogator should let the confessor supply details rather than recite them to the confessor and then merely ask for a yes or no answer. The confession must speak for itself when read later to or by a court or jury, because at that time explanatory remarks by the interrogator may not be permitted.

As a practical matter, and particularly with regard to security officers, with limited available facilities and time, the interrogator herself may write out a brief statement, in ink, as though dictated by the confessor, to be read and signed by her. It should be somewhat as follows: "I [Jane Doe] state on my own free will, and without any threats or promises having been made to me, that, on [date or dates] I [here relate the admitted offense]." The confessor's signature should appear immediately after the last word in the statement.

At the writing and signing of a confession there is no legal requirement that it be witnessed, so the element of privacy should continue to prevail. It is advisable, however, to have the confessor confirm that she made the confession and signed the written one.

It is a good practice to arrange, whenever possible, to include within the written confession, one or two intentional errors such as the wrong spelling of a person's name, or a wrong street address. Then, when the confession is read by or to the subject, she should be instructed to write in the necessary correction. Later on, the subject will have considerable difficulty in claiming that the confession was signed without a reading.

The Electronic Confession

If an electronic recording is contemplated, someone should check to determine whether there are any state legal prohibitions or restrictions upon its usage. Consideration should also be given to the applicability of federal law.

Contrary to common belief, an oral confession is just as admissible as a written or electronically recorded one. The advantage to the latter forms, of course, is that they serve to verify an interrogator's testimony that there was, indeed, a confession.[29]

Interrogation of Juveniles

In the absence of a statutory provision regarding youthful suspects, the same basic legal rules usually apply to them as to adults. There are several jurisdictions, however, that prescribe some restrictions. For instance, one state requires that a juvenile's parent, guardian, or lawyer be present to advise her of her rights, and also be present during the interrogation itself.[30]

Security officers should, therefore, acquaint themselves with the prescribed law that may prevail in their own jurisdiction regarding the interrogation of juveniles.[31]

29. For further details regarding the preservation of a confession, consult test, *supra* note 3 at 180–182.

30. *See* Colo. Rev. Stats., § 19-2-102 (3) (c) (I). For a recent Colorado Supreme Court case interpreting the statute's application (favorable to the prosecution) see People v. S.M.D., 864 P. 2d 1103 (1994).

31. Following are a few recent cases dealing with such subjects as the competency to waive the *Miranda* rights, and other issues: *In re* W.C. (State of Illinois) v. W.C. 633 N. E. 2d 956 (Ill. App. 1994); Rhoades v. State, 869 S.W. 2d 698 (Ark. 1994); In the Interest of Shawn B.N. v. State, 497 N.W. 2d 141 (Wis. 1992); People v. Aven, 1 Cal. Rptr. 2d 655 (1992).

5

Scientific Investigations

A. DRUG TESTING

Understandably, many employers are increasingly concerned about the illegal use of drugs by employees. Substance abuse has a detrimental impact on work performance; and in safety sensitive positions it can endanger the lives of co-workers and the general public, as well as the substance-abusing employees themselves. Such substance abuse, whether on or off the job, also poses a threat to, and significantly increases, the security risks of private businesses.

Employees who use illegal drugs may resort to theft in order to financially support their habits. They also tend to have high absenteeism and high accident rates. In response to this, thousands of private businesses across the country, as well as federal, state, and local governmental employers, have implemented drug screening programs. Many others, however, still hesitate because of concern about lawsuits by employees or applicants for employment.

Federal Laws Mandating Drug-Free Workplaces

Companies that are defense contractors, or the recipients of federal contracts or grants, have a legal obligation to address the problem of employee drug abuse, as mandated by new federal statutes and regulations. The law with the most wide-spread effect is the Drug Free Workplace Act of 1988 (DFWA), which covers all business recipients of federal contracts for the procurement of goods or services of $25,000 or more.[1] The law also includes any individual entering into a contract with a federal agency (regardless of the amount of money involved), and any federal grant recipient (regardless of the size of the grant).

Under DFWA, no company is considered a "responsible source" eligible for a procurement contract over $25,000 if it fails to certify that it will provide a drug-

---

1. 41 U.S.C. Secs. 701–707, effective March 18, 1989.

free workplace.[2] While drug testing is not required, the company must (1) publish a statement notifying employees that the unlawful manufacture, distribution, dispensation, possession, or use of a controlled substance is prohibited in the workplace, and specify actions that will be taken against employees for violations of such prohibitions; (2) establish a drug-free awareness program to inform employees about the dangers of drug abuse in the workplace, the company policy of maintaining a drug-free workplace, and of any available drug counseling, rehabilitation, and employee assistance programs, and also of the penalties that may be imposed on employees for drug abuse violations; and (3) require that each employee involved in the performance of the contract be given a copy of the employer's policy statement on a drug-free workplace. Further, employees must be told that, as a condition of employment under the contract, they will abide by the drug-free policy and notify their employer of any criminal drug conviction for a violation occurring in the workplace no later than five days after it occurs. The employer then must notify the contracting federal agency no later than ten days after receiving notice of the conviction and either impose a sanction on the employee or require his satisfactory participation in a drug abuse assistance or rehabilitation program. Similar requirements are imposed on companies receiving federal grants.[3]

Individuals receiving federal contracts or grants of any size must certify that they will not engage in the "unlawful manufacture, distribution, dispensation, possession, or use of a controlled substance in the performance of a contract."[4] Companies and individuals who do not comply may be suspended or disbarred from receiving contracts or grants. Disbarment by any one agency under the DFWA will render the company or individual ineligible for any future contract or grant by any Federal agency, for a period up to five years.[5] Among the grounds for disbarment are circumstances in which "such number of employees" of the company have been convicted of violations of criminal drug statutes for violations occurring in the workplace "as to indicate that the contractor has failed to make a good faith effort to provide a drug-free workplace . . ."[6]

The DFWA does not require drug screening, but prudent steps are necessary to prevent disbarment from government contract and grant eligibility. Likewise, although the Act does not require an employer to provide drug counseling, treatment, or employee assistance programs, employees must be informed about any such programs that are provided.

Federal defense contractors face similar legal obligations under the "Fiscal 1989 Defense Funding Law,"[7] but this statute does require drug testing of all employees in sensitive positions. If an employee tests positive, he cannot stay in his position until certified as fit and drug free by medical personnel. There are some excep-

2. 41 U.S.C. Sec. 701 (a) (1).
3. 41 U.S.C. Sec. 702 (a) (1).
4. 41 U.S.C. Sec. 701 (a) (2) and 702 (a) (2).
5. 41 U.S.C. Sec. 701 (b) (2), (3), 702 (b) (2) (3).
6. 41 U.S.C. Sec. 701 (b) (1), 702 (b) (1).
7. Public Law 100–400.

tions to this law if the implementation of drug screening is inconsistent with an existing collective bargaining agreement; however, the company is required to make drug screening a subject of bargaining at the time of union contract renewal. Regulations promulgated by the Department of Defense provide that such programs must also apply to employees with access to classified information, and that sanctions for drug use shall not be limited to on the job use or problems.[8]

General Case Law

Most legal challenges to drug screening programs have occurred in the public sector, where they have focused on whether such screening is an unlawful search under the Fourth Amendment. In two 1989 cases, the United States Supreme Court addressed for the first time the constitutionality of mandatory workplace drug testing. In both cases, mandatory drug testing without "particularized" individual suspicion of drug use was upheld. It should be noted, however, that in neither case did the Court consider the issue of random drug testing.

In *Skinner v. Railway Labor Executives*,[9] the Court examined a 1985 Federal Railroad Administration regulation which required blood and urine tests for drug use of all crew members of trains involved in serious or major accidents. Although the Court's opinion acknowledged that the screening tests were "searches," it found nothing unreasonable about them, since the "diminished" privacy interests of workers involved in a "highly regulated industry" like railroads were outbalanced by a "compelling" governmental interest to protect public safety by deterring and detecting drug abuse by rail employees.

In the second case, *National Treasury Employees v. Von Raab*,[10] the Court upheld, by a 5 to 4 decision, a 1986 Customs Service program making mandatory drug testing a condition of placement or employment in three job categories. Employees directly involved in intercepting drugs, carrying firearms, or handling classified material were required to submit to urine tests with five days' notice without any requirement of individualized suspicion of drug use. In a later case, the Supreme Court also upheld Conrail's unilateral imposition of drug screening as part of all periodic physical examinations which employees must take.[11]

Fourth Amendment protection against unreasonable search and seizure does not generally apply to employees of private companies,[12] because that amendment only limits *governmental* action. However, several states have a "right to privacy" provision in their state constitutions which may also limit activities by private

---

8. Department of Defense Drug Rules, 53 F.R. 37763-65.

9. 489 U.S. 602 (1989).

10. 489 U.S. 656 (1989).

11. Consolidated Rail v. Railway Labor Exec. Assn., 491 U.S. 299 (1989).

12. *See, e.g.,* United States v. McGreevy, 652 F.2d 849 (9th Cir. 1981) (private security guard is not a state actor); United States v. Gumerlock, 590 F.2d 794 (9th Cir. 1979) (Fourth Amendment does not apply if government is not connected with or involved in the search).

employers. A series of recent decisions seems to indicate that private employers, not surprisingly, may have even a broader right than governmental employers to require widespread drug and alcohol screening. One decision even upheld a program of completely random testing of current employees—without even a requirement of reasonable suspicion that a particular employee was engaged in drug use.

An important question for private employers is to what extent such privacy rights limit drug testing of job applicants. A California appeals court[13] has upheld compulsory drug screening of all job applicants by a private employer against just such a state constitutional privacy challenge. Three job applicants filed a lawsuit against the policy.

In issuing its ruling, the court did find that the right to privacy contained in Article I, Section 1, of the California Constitution limits the action of private parties, not just the actions of government. It also found, however, that this privacy right can be overcome by something less than a compelling interest. "Instead, the operative question is whether the challenged conduct is reasonable." In this case, applicants for positions at a private publishing company knew that they had to submit to a physical examination and that a urine test was a routine part of the exam. "Thus subjecting urine samples to analysis for alcohol or drugs is only slightly more intrusive than the procedures which plaintiffs already reasonably had to expect as job seekers with private business."

13. Wilkinson v. Times Mirror Corp., 264 Cal. Rptr. 194 (Cal. App. 1989). But *see* Semore v. Pool, 266 Cal. Rptr. 280 (Cal. App. 1990) (when private employee is terminated for refusing to take random drug test, he may evoke public policy exception to the employment at will doctrine to assert a violation of his state constitutional right to privacy). This court agreed with *Wilkinson,* however, that the right to privacy under the California constitution limits action by private employers as well as public agencies. It also held, citing Foley v. Interactive Data Corp., 47 Cal. 3d 654, 254 Cal. Rptr. 211, 765 P.2d 373 (1988), that an employee who alleged that taking a random drug test violated his right to privacy could bring a tort cause of action based on a discharge in violation of public policy. The test in question was a pupillary reaction test to determine whether the employee was using drugs. The court rejected the employer's argument that a contractual agreement to such test would bar such a claim. While the employee "could contractually agree not to assert his right to privacy," the court said, "we think it clear that the employer could not use such an agreement to circumvent the public policy favoring privacy," and therefore, the provision would not be enforceable if a court found that it intruded on the right to privacy. The court remanded for further proceedings to determine whether the provision of the test or manner of its implementation violated the employee's privacy right. The employer had also argued that the observation of the eyes of an employee, as used in the test, was nonintrusive because it is lawful "sensory surveillance" and is not a search in the criminal law context [People v. Snider, 78 Cal. App. 3d 560, 142 Cal. Rptr. 900 (1978)]. The court first noted that the United States Supreme Court had recently granted review of a case relied on for the proposition that the type of observation utilized was not a search, Brotherhood of Locomotive Eng. v. Burlington Northern (9th Cir. 1988), 858 F.2d 1087, *cert. granted and judgment vacated,* 492 U.S. 901 (1989). It then agreed, however, that "if an employee appears to be under the influence of alcohol or drugs, an employer can take appropriate action." Such "sensory surveillance is nonintrusive" because the employer "is only observing what anybody can see." But the test used here might impinge upon privacy because the employee must be "detained" for the observation to take place. The court recognized that the test utilized here was "far less intrusive and burdensome" than the blood, urine, or breath tests that were approved by the U.S. Supreme Court in *Skinner,* but found that further hearings were needed to address the nature of the test, the equipment used, the manner of administration, the test's reliability, the handling of test results, and "similar concerns."

"Perhaps the most important factor in our analysis," the court said, "is that plaintiffs are applicants for employment, not employees, either public or private. Any individual who chooses to seek employment necessarily also chooses to disclose certain personal information to prospective employers, such as employment and educational history, and to allow the prospective employer to verify that information." As applicants for employment, "when plaintiffs were asked to consent to drug and alcohol screening as a condition of an offer of employment, they were in effect asked to disclose voluntarily the personal information which might be revealed by that screening."

The court noted that the employer did take steps to ensure that the intrusion into privacy was minimal. Applicants were not watched while providing urine samples and the company was not given the specific results of the test, but rather only a numeric score which indicates whether or not an applicant is recommended for employment. A negative score can result from other factors besides a positive drug test.

In conclusion, the court stated that a private employer "unquestionably has a legitimate interest in a drug- and alcohol-free environment, and in excluding from employment those individuals whose drug and alcohol use may affect their job performance or threaten harm to themselves."[14]

This California decision seems to be in the mainstream of recent trends regarding private employer drug screening programs. In *Ditomaso v. Electronic Data Systems*,[15] for instance, the court held that the Michigan constitution guarantees against unreasonable search and seizure do not prohibit drug screening by private employer and that security guards given urine tests by their employer could not recover for emotional distress. In this case, four security guards sued their private employer after they were discharged because they failed urinalysis tests for marijuana use.

The claims made by the guards almost constitute a checklist of challenges made by private employees to drug screening programs. Their lawsuit claimed that the employer, in taking this action: (1) breached a covenant of good faith and fair dealing; (2) discharged them in violation of public policy; (3) intentionally inflicted emotional distress upon them; (4) was negligent; (5) discriminated against them in violation of Michigan handicap discrimination laws; (6) invaded their right to privacy; and (7) defamed their character. The federal court, applying Michigan state law, rejected all these claims and granted the defendant employer's motion to dismiss the suit. In Michigan, the court concluded, there is no implied covenant to act in good faith in an at-will employment contract, and these guards were at-will employees with no contractual guarantee of continued employment. The court also found that the Michigan constitutional prohibitions of unreasonable search and seizure do not apply to private employers and this defeated the "public policy" argument.

---

14. A subsequent California appellate court decision set a higher standard (compelling interest v. reasonableness) for justifying privacy invasions under the California constitution. Soroka v. Dayton Hudson, 225 Cal. App. 3d 654 (1991). However, the standard was recently lowered by the Supreme Court of California in Hill v. NCAA, 865 P.2d 633 (1994).

15. U.S. Dist. Ct. E.D. Mich., 3 I.E.R. Cases (BNA) 1700 (October 5, 1988).

A claim for emotional distress, the court noted, is normally entertained only where the distress inflicted "is so severe that no reasonable man could be expected to endure it." In this case, however, three of the four guards admitted to smoking marijuana. "It is ironic," the court asserted, "that individuals who admit being illegal drug users now come before this Court contending that this label has inflicted distress which is so severe that no reasonable man could be expected to endure it." In any event, no evidence showing such distress was presented.

The court found that the employer had a significant interest in ensuring that its security guards were free from drug use "prior to the formation of any reasonable suspicion," since they handled firearms. "In fact," the court noted, "had an incident occurred which one plaintiff was unable to handle resulting in an injury to another, [the employer] would likely be liable for failing to test its security personnel for potential drug use."

The manner in which the urine samples were taken was not overly intrusive, since it was extracted in private with two male managers from the security department outside the bathroom stall to maintain the chain of custody of each sample. The court found the claim of handicap discrimination contradicted by the plaintiffs' deposition testimony denying that they suffered any impairment from the drug use.

Also of interest is *Jennings v. Minco Technology Labs, Inc.*,[16] in which the employer's plan to test an at-will employee, with her consent, by urinalysis, to determine whether she had recently consumed illegal drugs was held to be lawful and enforceable under Texas law. The employer threatened no act contrary to the public policy underlying the common law right of privacy, the court noted, in that the plan contemplated that the employee's urine would be taken and tested only if she consented. The fact that the failure to consent was grounds for dismissal from employment did not vary the result, as she had no right to continued employment.

The existence of her privacy right, the court noted, did not enlarge her contract rights and diminish those of the company. The plan at issue involved asking employees—at random—to consent to give a sample of their urine, together with written consent to its analysis. A reliable testing method would be employed. If the test revealed evidence of illegal drug consumption, the company would ask the employee to participate in a rehabilitation program at company expense. An employee might be denied continued employment, however, if he declined to give a urine sample or to participate in a rehabilitation program should that be required of him. The plan, the court further noted, contains "various safeguards for accuracy, confidentiality, and modesty." In addition to holding in favor of the employer, the court awarded it $45,000 in attorneys' fees from the employee to compensate it for the cost of having to defend the suit.

In *Monroe v. Consolidated Freightways, Inc.*,[17] a federal district court rejected contentions that a private employer's drug testing policy violated the Fourth Amendment, employees' rights under the Missouri constitution, or the public pol-

16. 765 S.W.2d 497 (Tex. App. 1989).

17. 654 F. Supp. 661 (E.D. Mo. 1987).

icy of Missouri. The suit was brought by several supervisors at Consolidated Freightways, Inc. against their employer when they were terminated for refusing to submit to drug tests. The court refused their claims on the basis that both the Fourth Amendment and the provisions of the state constitution prohibition on unreasonable searches apply exclusively to governmental searches and not to private ones.

The court further rejected the petitioners' contentions that the drug testing policy was against public policy. It said: "Missouri does not recognize 'violation of public policy' as an independent cause of action. Neither does Missouri recognize a cause of action for wrongful discharge based on a violation of public policy. Furthermore, this Court would be reluctant to find that efforts to assure a drug-free environment contravened the public policy of the State of Missouri."[18]

State Statutory Restrictions

Several states have passed statutes regulating drug testing of employees and prospective employees. Montana limits preemployment testing to certain types of employment (hazardous work environments or in "jobs the primary responsibility of which is security, public safety, or fiduciary responsibility").[19] Other states,

18. Other cases supporting private employer drug screening programs either directly or by implication include: Luedtke v. Nabors Alaska Drilling, Inc., 768 P.2d 1123 (Alaska 1989) (discharge of employees by private employer for refusing to submit to urine drug test did not violate the Alaska constitutional right of privacy); Jackson v. Liquid Carbonic Corp., 863 F.2d 111 (1st Cir. 1988) (no federal or state privacy bar to firing truck driver for refusal to submit to drug testing; employee must file grievance under labor contract); Fremont Hotel v. Esposito, 760 P.2d 122 (Nev. 1988) (employer was entitled to terminate employee for misconduct for refusal to take drug and alcohol tests; discharged employee was not entitled to unemployment benefits; union contract allowed the employer to subject employees to the tests and the employer had reasonable suspicion of the employee's drug or alcohol use); and Tex. Emp. Com'n v. Hughes Drill Fluids, 746 S.W.2d 796 (Tex. App. 1988) (employee discharged for refusing to submit a urine sample for drug screening program could be denied unemployment benefits). See also O'Halloran v. Louisiana General Services, Inc., 531 So. 2d 554 (La. 1988) (privacy rights not violated because of absence of state action and the subject had consented; also, those engaged in hazardous employment have a serious interest in a drug-free workplace); Greco v. Halliburton Co., 674 F. Supp. 1447 (Wyo. 1987) (proper to fire employees for refusing to submit to drug test since attempts to maintain a drug-free workplace do not violate public policy); and Bally v. Northeastern University, 532 N.E.2d 49 (Mass. 1989) (random testing by private organization does not implicate government or any governmental interest).

In three other recent decisions, courts have upheld denials of unemployment compensation benefits because of: (1) refusal to participate in a random drug screening program of a private employer who terminated the refusing employee, Chiles Offshore, Inc. v. Adm'r Dept. of Employment Security, 551 So. 2d 849 (La. App. 1989); (2) criminal charges pending against an employee for possession of drugs in his home, after which the employer suspended the employee until the determination of the outcome of these charges, Sensley v. Adm'r Office of Employment Security, 552 So. 2d 787 (La. 1989); and (3) a positive drug test revealing marijuana metabolites in the employee's blood, for which the employer terminated the employee, Johnson v. Dept. of Employment Sec., 782 P.2d 965 (Utah App. 1989).

19. Mont. Code Ann. Sec. 39-2-304 (1987).

while not limiting the type of jobs in which such testing can be conducted, set forth certain requirements, such as written notification to prospective employees of test requirements, confidentiality of results, or conducting of tests according to certain procedures.[20] This is a highly volatile area and no employer should implement a drug testing program without first seeking competent legal counsel as to the requirements, if any, under state law.

Implementation of Testing Program

Even if a drug screening program is upheld in general, of course, there may still be liability for the way in which it is carried out. In *Kelley v. Schlumberger Technology Corp.*,[21] a federal appeals court upheld a $125,001 award to an employee who although testing positive for marijuana, suffered emotional distress after being watched while urinating. He had been fired from his job after two of his urinalysis tests proved positive. There was no dispute that the employee had, in fact, used the drugs. The focus of the lawsuit was on the "disgust" the employee had at the "whole idea of someone being paid to look at [his] penis while [he] urinated." The company had required another employee to watch the plaintiff as he provided a sample to make sure he did not "cheat" by switching samples or diluting his sample with water.

Although the case was tried in federal court, it was based on Louisiana law, with $1 being awarded for violation of a right to privacy guaranteed by the state constitution and $125,000 awarded for negligent infliction of emotional distress. Louisiana allows recovery for negligent infliction of emotional distress without physical impact or resulting physical impairment, so long as the emotional injuries were reasonably foreseeable and constitute serious mental distress rather than transitory unpleasantness.

The lesson learned from this Louisiana case is that giving a sample under observation can potentially be held to be embarrassing and a humiliating experience. The collection procedure needs to accommodate both the integrity (chain of custody) of the sample and the personal privacy interests of the individual employee. In collecting urine samples for drug testing, both interests can be accommodated (1) by providing a secured restroom; (2) by inspecting the restroom before each employee enters to provide the sample; (3) by providing a monitor of the same sex who does not enter the stall or directly observe the process of producing the sample; and (4) by procedures designed to prevent employees from bringing in "clean" urine.

---

20. *See* Gen. Stats. of Conn. Secs. 31-51t to 31-51bb, Iowa Code Ann. Sec. 730.5; 13A Minn. Stats. Ann. Sec. 181.950–181.957; Utah Code Ann. Sec. 34-38-1; tit. 21 Vt. Stats. Ann. Secs. 511–520.

21. 849 F.2d 41 (1st Cir. 1988).

It is also suggested that when a positive test result is returned, a second confirmatory test be ordered. Since the purpose of drug screening is to identify employees engaged in substance abuse, in fairness, every reasonable safeguard should be used to prevent mistakenly identifying and sanctioning an individual not engaged in substance abuse. At least one court has also held that an employer has a duty to preserve a urine specimen, especially when the employee so requests, to allow the employee to subject it to another test at his own expense, etc.[22]

Sanctions for drug, as well as alcohol abuse, should be fairly and equitably applied to all employees. An increasingly common ground for legal action is an allegation that such sanctions are imposed in a discriminatory fashion, as on racial lines. In one such case, the employer successfully rebutted racial discrimination claims for firing black employees who tested positive for drug use by showing that similar white employees who had not been fired had undergone a voluntary rehabilitation treatment program.[23] Employers implementing drug screening programs, therefore, should keep clear and detailed records of the results of the tests and actions taken after positive results are obtained.

Employers who are covered by the Federal Rehabilitation Act,[24] and by the Americans With Disabilities Act,[25] which prohibit discrimination against "otherwise qualified" disabled individuals, or by one of the many state laws similarly prohibiting disability discrimination may find that their possible range of sanctions immediately following a positive test is limited by a duty to "reasonably accommodate" an employee who claims disability on the basis of drug or alcohol addiction. Federal statutes do not, however, protect any employee whose drug use is current.[26] However, both statutes do provide protection for current alcoholics.

Employers must be very careful with regard to their drug and alcohol screening policies, in order to avoid some of the pitfalls which have led to lawsuits and liability. However, the benefits to both the security of the employer's business and the safety and morale of the employees are well worth the cost and planning required.[27]

22. Feguson v. Meehan, 529 N.Y.S.2d 525 (A.D. 1988).

23. Anderson v. Lewis Rail Service Co., 868 F.2d 774 (5th Cir. 1989).

24. 29 U.S.C. Sec. 791, et seq. See Hazlett v. Martin Chevrolet, Inc., 25 Ohio St. 3d 279, 496 N.E.2d 478 (1986) (court holds that alcoholism and drug addiction are handicaps under Ohio state law; discharge of alcoholic who also used cocaine was unlawful handicap discrimination).

25. U.S.C. Sec. 12101 et seq.

26. 29 U.S.C. Sec. 706. See also Casse v. Louisiana General Services, Inc., 531 So. 2d 554 (La. App. 1988) (employees fired after they voluntarily submitted to drug testing and tested positive were not "handicapped" persons entitled to protection).

27. This is a highly volatile area of law, subject to rapid change. A monthly journal which summarizes recent cases in this area is EMPLOYMENT HEALTH LAW & BENEFITS, 5519 N. Cumberland, #1008, Chicago, Illinois 60656.

B. THE POLYGRAPH TECHNIQUE[28]

It would not be possible in the space of a section of this book to adequately explain the intricacies of the polygraph technique, nor to fully cover the attending legal issues. The objective is only to accommodate the general interests and ordinary needs of security officers and legal counsel.

As will be subsequently discussed, a 1988 federal law has severely restricted the opportunity of private employers to avail themselves of the polygraph technique to protect against employee thievery and other criminal conduct. Nevertheless, there are certain circumstances under which use of the technique is permissible on behalf of private employers, and for that reason we will briefly discuss the technique itself. This discussion will be followed by an analysis of the legal issues.

The Instruments for Diagnosis of Truth or Deception

To many persons the polygraph is thought of as a "lie-detector," and all too often they perceive it to be a mechanical device that will somehow alert the operator whenever a question is answered untruthfully. Or they may have an entirely different viewpoint and discount altogether the notion that deception can be detected with the aid of any kind of instrumentation. Both positions are unsupportable.

Although no mechanical device exists that will, in and of itself, detect deception, it is a demonstrable fact that there are instruments capable of recording physiological changes that may serve as the basis for a reliable *diagnosis* of truth or deception, provided certain procedures are followed. The instruments are technically known as polygraphs, and the procedure by which they are used for diagnostic purposes is known as the polygraph technique.

The standard polygraph instrument is designed to make a permanent and simultaneous recording of a subject's respiratory rate and volume, changes in blood pressure and heart rate, and relative changes in electrodermal resistance (the ability of the skin to conduct electricity). These physiological systems have been selected for monitoring because they each reflect activity within the subject's autonomic nervous system. While some instruments may make additional recordings (muscle movement recorder, cardio tachometer, cardio activity monitor), any instrument that does not record, at a minimum, the three aforementioned physiological systems is inadequate for actual case testing.

The body attachments by which respiration, pulse, blood pressure, and electro-

---

28. This section on the polygraph technique is an abstract of the discussion of that subject which the present senior author prepared for his contribution to Chapter 20 of the 1995 edition of SCIENTIFIC EVIDENCE IN CIVIL AND CRIMINAL CASES, by A.A. MOENSSENS, J.E. STARRS, C.E. HENDERSON, AND F.E. INBAU.

dermal resistance are recorded are as follows:

1. Pneumograph tubes, with the aid of beaded chains, are fastened around the chest and abdomen of the person being tested.
2. A blood pressure cuff, of the type used by physicians, is fastened around the subject's upper arm.
3. Two electrodes are affixed to the subject's fingers, and an imperceptible amount of electric current is passed from one to the other for the purpose of measuring electrodermal resistance.

Examiner Qualifications and Training

Because the polygraph technique involves a diagnostic procedure rather than the mere mechanical operation of an instrument, a prime requisite to its effectiveness and reliability is examiner competence.

An examiner must be a person of intelligence, with a good educational background—preferably a college degree. Since the examiner will be dealing with persons in delicate situations from a myriad of different backgrounds, he must also possess suitable personality characteristics, which might be summarized as the ability "to get along" well with others and to be confident and persuasive during interpersonal relationships.

Adequate training for a polygraph examiner should consist of both classroom instruction as well as an internship conducted under the guidance of a competent, experienced examiner. During training the student should be exposed to a sufficient volume of actual cases to permit frequent observations of polygraph examinations. Classroom instruction should include lectures relating to polygraph instrumentation and procedures as well as the relevant areas within psychology, psychopathology, physiology, pharmacology, and law. Attention must also have been given to the detailed study and analysis of a considerable number of polygraph test records in actual cases in which the true facts of truthfulness or deception were later established by corroborating evidence. Supplementing this, there should be a period of approximately one hundred hours of supervised internship with a competent, experienced examiner.

There are, unfortunately, relatively few persons holding themselves out as polygraph examiners who have received this recommended level of training, particularly with respect to the fully supervised internship during which the trainee examines subjects in actual case situations.

Examination Room Requirements

The examinations must be conducted in a quiet, private room. Extraneous noises, or the presence of a third party, except for an interpreter when needed, would produce distractions that could seriously affect the examination and diagnosis.

Test Procedure

Case Issue Selection for Pretest Interview and for Examination

A polygraph examination consists of three separate phases: (1) a pretest interview with the person to be examined, (2) a chart recording phase, and (3) the diagnosis of truth or deception.

Prior to the examination, the examiner must be advised of all relevant facts regarding the matter being investigated. This is essential for both the pretest interview and for a determination of the specific issue for which the test questions are to be formulated.

The polygraph technique is most valued when a single issue or incident is addressed, such as the theft of a specific sum of money, or a specific act. It is not suitable for ascertaining a person's true opinions, beliefs, or interpretations. Such general issues are too nebulous for test purposes.

Pretest Interview

There are several reasons for conducting a pretest interview. They include discussing with the subject and defining the issue of the examination, explaining the instrument and test procedures, and developing the test questions. During this period, a determination may be made of the subject's physical and emotional suitability for the examination. The examiner will also seek to alleviate the subject's apprehensions, and to present assurance of the objectivity of the diagnostic process. The control questions that will be asked are developed during this session.

Under no circumstances should the examiner indulge in an interrogation during a pretest interview. To do so could seriously impair the validity of the subject's subsequent responses to test questions.

Control Questions   The development and use of proper control questions is indispensable to a valid polygraph examination. A control question is one that is unrelated to the issue under investigation, but it nevertheless addresses a behavior or motivation similar to that concerning the matter under investigation. Of utmost importance, the control question must be one to which the subject will either lie or be uncertain of his answer. An example is an embezzlement case in which the subject is asked "Have you ever stolen anything?" The response on the recorded chart, or the lack of one, is compared to what appears when a relevant question is asked about the matter under investigation.

Irrelevant Questions   An irrelevant question is one that has no bearing whatsoever on the issue under investigation and also one to which the subject will be answering truthfully. An example of such a question is one regarding the place where the examination is being conducted—for instance, "Are you in Chicago right now?" Irrelevant questions serve primarily to acclimate the subject to the testing procedure so that normal physiology can be recorded.

Prior to a test the subject is told precisely, word for word, what questions will be asked. Assurance is also given that no questions will be asked that have not been specifically reviewed. Surprise has no role in a properly conducted polygraph examination.

Relevant Questions   Relevant questions should be worded in simple language and be as succinct and direct as possible. They must not address multiple conduct.

Required Chart Recordings   A single polygraph test consists of the examiner asking each of the 9 or 10 prepared test questions. About 10 seconds should elapse after each irrelevant question, and 15 to 20 seconds following a relevant or control question.

One such test does not constitute a polygraph examination; a minimum of three is considered standard before a diagnosis can be attempted. Depending on the technique utilized, there could be as many as five separate tests conducted during an examination. There are several different tests designs that an examiner can use, depending upon the specific circumstances of the case.

The Diagnosis of Truth or Deception

At the risk of oversimplification, it may be said that a subject who is telling the truth about the offense under investigation will focus emotional attention (as identified through chart responses) toward the control questions and away from relevant questions. Conversely, a deceptive subject's focus of emotional attention will be directed toward relevant questions and away from control questions.

The nature of the polygraph technique and the inherent difficulty of evaluation of the results in actual cases do not afford a reliable means to ascertain the degree of accuracy. What can be stated, however, is that when the examination is made by a competent examiner, the results are very reliable. This assessment takes into account, of course, that competent examiners are not reluctant to report that in about ten percent of their cases the results are inconclusive as to truthfulness or deception. This allowance for inconclusiveness greatly reduces the risk of actual error.

LEGAL STATUS OF THE POLYGRAPH TECHNIQUE

A fundamental change in the legal status of the polygraph technique occurred in the 1988 when Congress enacted the Employee Polygraph Protection Act.[29] It significantly restricted the opportunity of private employers to avail themselves of the technique in their efforts to protect against employee thievery and other criminal actions committed against them.

Although the title of the Act uses the word "polygraph," it is also directed at "lie-detectors," which, by the Act's definition, includes "polygraph, deceptograph,

---

29. 29 U.S.C. § 2001 etc. It was enacted on June 27, 1988, and became law 90 days thereafter.

voice stress analyzer, psychological stress evaluator, or any other similar device . . . that is used . . . for the purpose of rendering a diagnostic opinion regarding the honesty or dishonesty of an individual." "Polygraph" itself is separately defined as an instrument that "records continuously, visually, permanently, and simultaneously changes in cardiovascular, respiratory, and electrodermal patterns as minimum instrumentation standards . . ."

With certain exceptions specified in the Act, it is "unlawful for any employer engaged in or affecting commerce or in the production of goods for commerce . . ." to "require, request, suggest, or cause any employee or prospective employee to take or submit to any lie detector test . . . " Any auxiliary use of any test, or of its results or refusals to take a test, is also specifically prohibited.

An employer who violates any provision of the Act is subject to a civil penalty up to $10,000. Additionally, the Secretary of Labor is empowered to impose injunctive action. Also, a violator may be sued either in the federal or state courts by employees or applicants, and a class action is also available on behalf of persons similarly situated. The rights and procedures provided by the Act "may not be waived by contract or otherwise."

Despite the condemnation of the polygraph technique (along with all other "lie detector" implements and procedures referred to in the Act), Congress provided a number of important exceptions to the prohibitions. A major one, insofar as criminal investigators are concerned, is testing by "the United States Government, any state, or local government, or any political subdivision of a state or local government." Police use, therefore, is permissible.

Among other exceptions from the Act's coverage are experts or consultants under contract with the various national intelligence agencies, or with the FBI.

With respect to nongovernmental, private employers, exceptions are made for those whose primary business purpose consists of providing security systems or services, and whose functions include protection of public transportation, facilities such as electric or nuclear power plants, and authorized drug manufacturers, suppliers, and dispensers of controlled substances.

Upon compliance with the requirements of two specified sections of the Act, private employers may have polygraph tests conducted for "an ongoing investigation involving economic loss or injury to the employers' business . . . " provided the employee to be tested had access to the missing property and against whom there is reasonable suspicion of involvement. This is conditioned, however, upon the employer providing the employee with a written statement revealing such facts and suspicion.

One polygraph testing firm, John E. Reid and Associates, will conduct a test on a private employee *only* if the following conditions are met:

1. The employer has suffered a *specific economic loss*;
2. The employer can establish that the employee in question had *access* to the missing property;
3. The employer can articulate in a written statement that there is a *reasonable basis to suspect* that the employee in question may have been involved in the theft; and,

4. The employer provides the employee a *written statement* detailing the nature of the economic loss, the access that the employee had to the missing property, and the basis for the employer's suspicion that the employee may have been involved in the theft. This statement must be given to the employee at least 48 hours before a polygraph test can be administered.

Because of the complexity of meeting the rigid requirements for any attempted use of the Act's exceptions and prescribed conditions, private employers are advised by the authors of this text to obtain the advice of legal counsel who may examine the Act, and possibly contact a polygraph examiner or firm to avail himself of the various forms and documents that have already been used to guard against inadvertent noncompliance. Some states have their own laws upon the polygraph technique, including examiner licensing, which also may require attention.

Admissibility of Test Results as Evidence

Assuming the legality of a polygraph test in a particular case, civil or criminal, the issue may then arise as to the admissibility of the test results as courtroom evidence. The prevailing judicial attitude is a general unwillingness, in both civil and criminal cases, to admit polygraph test results in evidence. Some courts, however, will admit the evidence upon the condition that opposing counsel and the parties agree to have the examination conducted and stipulate that the results may be admissible.[30]

---

30. For an extensive discussion of the case law prior to 1977, consult J.E. REID AND F.E. INBAU, TRUTH AND DECEPTION (2d ed. 1977). Updated material appears in Chapter 20 of the 1995 edition of MOENSSENS ET AL., SCIENTIFIC EVIDENCE IN CIVIL AND CRIMINAL CASES.

6

Security Surveillance of Customers and Employees

In most stores and industrial plants, it is absolutely essential to conduct some type of surveillance of customers and, in many circumstances, of employees as well. Neglecting to do so may amount to a tacit invitation to thievery and other offenses. This chapter discusses the privileges and limitations with respect to surveillance.

As we have attempted to do in some of the preceding chapters, in order to adequately understand the legal issues with respect to concealed surveillance by private security officers, it is necessary to ascertain the permissible bounds and restrictions on police activities of this nature.

CONCEALED SURVEILLANCE

Generally, a store owner can conduct surveillance on individuals in public areas because individuals in the plain view of others discard any shield of privacy. Therefore, a person who commits a theft or other offense within a public access area in plain view of persons lawfully occupying their vantage point has no legal grounds to object to the results of those observations being used against her.

"Peeking"

Sometimes police or private security guards conduct surveillance of an individual who is not necessarily in "plain view." For example, police or private security guards may attempt to combat illegal conduct in washrooms or fitting rooms.

The controlling principle regarding this issue was developed in the landmark opinion of the Supreme Court of the United States in the 1967 case of *Katz v. United States*.[1] It established that a "reasonable expectation of privacy" is the key

---

1. 389 U.S. 347 (1967).

factor in deciding whether a police officer or a private citizen violated the prohibition on warrantless searches is whether or not an objectively reasonable expectation of privacy has been invaded. In *Katz*, FBI agents engaged in electronic eavesdropping of a suspected gambler's conversation in a public telephone booth and subsequently attempted to use the overheard evidence against him. The Court held that the agents' actions violated the individual's reasonable expectation of privacy. Consequently, any such actions by the FBI required a court warrant, despite the fact that the agents possessed information about the gambler's prior illegal transactions over the telephone, and that they had taken ample precautions to safeguard the privacy of other persons using the booth.

The *Katz* decision, however, has not completely cleared up the problem of what the police are permitted to do when confronted with complaints of illegal washroom activities. In situations like *Katz,* obtaining a warrant may be feasible because the investigators are able to acquire detailed evidence of prior illegal conduct as well as fairly specific information regarding when and where it may reoccur. However, warrants are often not feasible in washroom situations. It appears, therefore, that action without a warrant may be taken only in washrooms when the circumstances clearly indicate that no reasonable expectation of privacy exists, or when there is an exigent circumstance.[2]

In determining whether individuals in different washroom cases possess a reasonable expectation of privacy, most courts seek to determine whether the illegal activity occurred in a place visible to another person. Thus, surveillance may not violate a privacy right in common areas such as open stalls or stalls with open portions in the doors, or with space between the bottom of the door and the floor sufficient to permit an individual to be observed. Similarly, courts have approved the use of visual observation and films taken through a false mirror when the mirror view was at the same eye level as other individuals within the washroom itself.[3]

2. For examples: United States v. White, 890 F.2d 1012 (8th Cir. 1989) (no reasonable expectation of privacy when police officer looked through a gap between stall door and did not position herself in any way unexpected by someone using the washroom); United States v. Billings, 858 F.2d at 618 (10th Cir. 1988) (no reasonable expectation of privacy in open area of stall where any patron of public washroom could see drugs taped to defendant's leg through visible gap between the washroom stall and floor); Barron v. State, 823 P.2d 17 (Alaska Ct. App. 1992) (no reasonable expectation of privacy where two pairs of feet were visible in space between floor and door); United States v. Tanner, 537 N.E.2d 702 (Ohio Ct. App. 1988).

   The Oregon Court of Appeals has taken a different approach. In State v. Casconi, 766 P.2d 397 (Or. Ct. App. 1988), the court held that the warrantless use by police of a hidden video camera to record a man masturbating inside a doorless stall in a public washroom violated his right to privacy under the Oregon Constitution. The court determined that the surveillance technique impaired the right to be free from government scrutiny. In this case, "allowing the police to conduct hidden surveillance of a doorless toilet stall significantly impair[ed] freedom from scrutiny." The court took a similar approach in State v. Owczarzak, 766 P.2d 399 (Or. Ct. App. 1988). There, a majority held that video surveillance that captured a defendant masturbating in the common area while standing in front of a stall occupied by another man was also unlawful under the state privacy guarantee.

3. *See, e.g.,* Young v. State, 849 P.2d 336 (Nev. 1993) (no reasonable expectation of privacy when sheriff's department captured defendants' sexual acts in a public washroom on video through a hole about eye level to person seated on a commode). Some other courts, albeit prior to *Katz,* have further limited the reasonable expectation of privacy in public washrooms, finding that even ceiling

On the other hand, courts often find that closed stalls, impervious to observation by the other individuals in the area, constitute a zone of privacy sought by the user when she closes the door, and, consequently, afford legal protection against intrusions upon that privacy.[4] In one case, the Minnesota Supreme Court held, by a 4-to-3 margin, that a closed toilet stall in a department store washroom was a privately protected area.[5] Therefore, police observations and pictures taken through a ceiling ventilator could not be used as evidence in the prosecution of an offender.

Another type of washroom case where police action is justified without a warrant is where reasonable grounds and an exigent situation exist. For example, where individuals, in one case, entered a gas station washroom together and remained there for thirty minutes, a court upheld a subsequent warrantless police search. The court held that the right of privacy within a washroom is not of indefinite duration but rather limited in time to that which is "reasonable and justifiable."[6]

Some cases have suggested that the legal impediment to surveillance can be avoided by posting signs stating that the washroom is under surveillance.[7] Even if posting signs serves as a privacy waiver, however, the consideration of customer relations probably reasons against using such a measure in washroom situations.[8]

Many of the same considerations and concerns of washroom surveillance situations occur in the surveillance of fitting rooms, a paramount responsibility of security officers in retail establishments. Individuals in fitting rooms can place clothing underneath their own garments and thereby steal from the store. Of assistance with respect to the measures that may be lawfully employed to prevent thievery is the opinion of the California Supreme Court in the previously discussed case of *People v. Deborah C.*[9]

cameras above closed stalls do not constitute a violation of a reasonable expectation of privacy. One federal circuit court of appeals declared admissible a surveillance of closed toilet stalls from a camouflaged hole in the washroom ceiling, even though the officers did not have any prior suspicion that the defendant entering the washroom was one of the offenders. Smayda v. United States, 352 F.2d 251 (9th Cir. 1965), *cert. denied*, 382 U.S. 981 (1966). *See also* Poore v. Ohio, 243 F. Supp. 777 (N.D. Ohio 1965), *aff'd sub nom* Townsend v. Ohio, 366 F.2d 33 (6th Cir. 1966); State v. Coyle, 181 So.2d 671 (Fla. Dist. Ct. App. 1966).

4. *See, e.g.,* People v. Kalchik, 407 N.W.2d 627 (Mich. Ct. App. 1987); State v. Limberhand, 788 P.2d 857 (Idaho Ct. App. 1990)

5. State v. Bryant, 177 N.W. 2d 800 (Minn. 1970). Cases in accord with the majority opinion in *Bryant* are: Buchanan v. State, 471 S.W.2d 401 (Tex. Ct. App. 1971) and Kroehler v. Scott, 391 F. Supp. 1114 (E.D. Pa. 1975).

6. Kirsch v. State, 271 A.2d 770 (Md. 1970). *See also* People v. Douglas, 244 Cal. Rptr. 854 (Cal. Ct. App. 3d 1988) (police entry legal when man and women entered men's room at gas station together and stayed in there twenty minutes).

7. State v. Bryant, *supra* note 5.

8. Regarding the legal validity of notices of surveillance, *see* Lucas v. United States, 411 A.2d 360 (D.C. 1980).

9. 177 Cal. Rptr. 852, 635 P.2d 446 (Cal. 1981).

The principal holding in *Deborah C.* was that security officers are not required to give the *Miranda* warnings prior to interrogating suspects. The court, however, also wrestled with the issue of whether the evidence of shoplifting obtained by fitting room surveillance should have been suppressed as a violation of the prohibition against unreasonable searches and seizures. The court, in dealing with this issue, decided that the surveillance procedures used by the store were reasonable.[10] Therefore, the court found no need to decide whether California should deviate from the practically unanimous viewpoint of the courts that the exclusionary rule does not apply to the conduct of private security officers.[11]

Generally, so long as store owners post a notice that the fitting rooms are under same-sex surveillance, the courts will uphold the surveillance. For example, in one case, a store security guard, looking through a "peep hole," noticed that a customer in the fitting room was carrying a concealed weapon. The guard detained the man, who turned out to be an undercover police officer. The police officer brought suit, alleging that the practice of watching people in fitting rooms was a violation of privacy. The court ruled that since signs were posted, warning of such observation, the security guard was free to peer inside fitting rooms that were occupied by the same sex as the guard.[12]

Following

Following a suspected person while she is in a public place, often referred to as "shadowing" or "tailing," is a well-accepted and legally permissible police practice. It is a tactic to which an employer or private security officer may resort, especially

10. In the *Deborah C.* case, the store's fitting rooms opened "off a three-foot-wide corridor," and the individual rooms were "about four by five feet square in area." The door was "about three feet high from the bottom edge to top edge, with approximately two foot gaps above and below," thus allowing "substantial portions of the small room's interior to be seen from the corridor." A female security officer suspected the defendant Deborah, a minor, of being a shoplifter. The officer followed Deborah into the fitting room corridor, saw her enter a room, close the door, place her purse-shopping bag on the floor, and begin to stuff it with clothing taken from the store's display racks. The court considered the security officer's action reasonable and held that the actions did not violate privacy.

11. With respect to the decisions holding that only the actions of law enforcement officers are affected by the exclusionary rule, *see*, in addition to the cases cited in Chapter 2, the Ohio case of State v. McDaniel, et al., 337 N.E.2d 173 (Ohio Ct. App. 1975), which involved a ladies' fitting room observation situation. The court held that even though the female defendants in the room may have had a reasonable expectation of privacy while using the store's fitting rooms, the exclusionary rule was inapplicable where the observations were made by a private security officer acting solely on behalf of and for the benefit of the store. *See also* City of Grand Rapids v. Impens, 327 N.W.2d 278 (Mich. 1982) (statements made by defendant to store security person admissible); In Re O.R., 447 N.W.2d 922 (S.D. 1989) (confession made to private security official admissible).

12. Lewis v. Dayton Hudson Corp., 339 N.W.2d 857 (Mich. Ct. App. 1983). *See also* Gillett v. State, 588 S.W.2d 361, 362-63 (Tex. Crim. App. 1979) (court held the Fourth Amendment was not violated when a private security officer observed customer stealing goods because notice on wall warned of same-sex surveillance).

in regard to employees suspected of transporting stolen property from the employer's premises. The general case law clearly indicates that so long as this type of surveillance is conducted in a reasonable manner and for legitimate purposes, there is no liability on the basis of a claim of invasion of privacy.[13]

Surveillance Photography

Persons in a public place are aware, of course, that they may be visually observed. They may even be photographed, either to preserve the visual image or because they happen to be in a scene being photographed. As long as observation is permissible, so is photography.[14] Some limitations prevail, however, upon the usage of the photographs themselves. A clear example would be the publication or distribution of photographs of identified persons for commercial advertisements.

Because individuals in a public area possess no shield of privacy, employers or private security officers may generally surreptitiously photograph a "public" area of the premises in the course of an investigation of employee thefts or other criminal conduct.[15]

Selective photographing of suspected persons or groups based upon racial or ethnic factors is prohibited. For instance, a state police agency, in one case, directed banks to photograph any blacks entering the bank who looked or acted suspiciously. A federal circuit court of appeals held that this practice violated civil rights.[16] The court indicated that it was not condemning all photographing of suspicious persons, only the practice of selecting persons to be photographed because of their racial characteristics.

Employers need to be prudent when instituting surveillance photography in areas where employees likely possess a reasonable expectation of privacy, like washrooms, locker rooms, fitting rooms, and recreational ("break room") areas. In a 1993 decision by the Supreme Court of Hawaii, United States postal inspectors, while conducting an investigation into employee gambling within a post office, conducted a covert video surveillance of an employee recreational ("break room") area. This was held to constitute an illegal search within the meaning of Hawaii's search and seizure constituitional provision similar to the one in the

---

13. For case illustrations of the legal permissibility of such surveillance, *see* Johnson v. Corporate Special Services, Inc., 602 So.2d 385 (Ala. 1992); Tucker v. American Employers' Ins. Co., 171 So.2d 437 (Fla. Dist. Ct. App. 1965); Nader v. General Motors Corp., 25 N.Y. 2d 560, 255 N.E. 2d 765 (1970).

14. *See* Donohue v. Duling, 465 F.2d 196 (4th Cir. 1972), which involved police filming of a group of demonstrators. *See also* Aisenson v. ABC, 269 Cal. Rptr. 379, 387 (Cal. Ct. App. 1990); Laird v. Tatum, 408 U.S. 1 (1972). However, the sharing of photographs with private (nonpolice) individuals or organizations (e.g., television stations) has been held impermissible by a federal circuit court of appeals. Philadelphia Yearly Meeting of the Religious Society of Friends, 519 F.2d 1335 (3d Cir. 1975).

15. *See* McLain v. Boise Cascade Co., 533 P.2d 343 (Or. 1975) (holding that secret video surveillance of a worker's compensation claimant while he was outdoors exposed to public view did not violate his right to privacy).

16. Hall v. Pennsylvania State Police, et al., 570 F.2d 86 (3d Cir. 1978).

Fourth Amendment. The employees were found to be protected from governmental intrusion into their legitimate expectations of privacy.[17]

One course for an employer to pursue is to post notices in such places stating that the area is an open one subject to inspection at any time.[18] However, if any such plan is contemplated, employees should be given thorough consideration in order to guard against employee resentment or possible violations of union contracts or, perhaps, even some local law.[19]

Employers should remain alert regarding the efforts that have been made, and may continue to be made, in Congress to practically bar any type of electronic monitoring within the workplace. (The National Association of Manufacturers has established a task force to learn of future developments of that nature.)

Electronic Eavesdropping

Eavesdropping without the aid of artificial, mechanical, or electronic devices, in areas where no reasonable expectation of privacy exists, generally does not violate the prohibition of the Fourth Amendment.[20] An entirely different issue arises, however, if the eavesdropping on a conversation is augmented by any electronic device.

Tapping telephone lines and, recently, computer screens provides a way for employers to monitor employees' work without their knowledge. Whenever a business person or security officer contemplates using any form of electronic eavesdropping, consideration must be given to the possible legal prohibitions or restrictions upon such practices, by either state or federal law.

Several state statutes absolutely ban all electronic eavesdropping, authorizing no exception even for law enforcement officers.[21] On the other hand, some states

17. State v. Bonnell, 856 P.2d 1265 (Hawaii, 1993).

18. Beyond the scope of the present text are cases pertaining to the photographing (by means of a visible closed-circuit television) of employees on the job for purposes of evaluating their work performance in order to increase efficiency or promote safety, or the photographing of employees engaging in picketing and other union activities. In regard to the former, see Caprico, Inc. v. Upholsterers Union of North America, Local 25, 71-1 ARB ¶ 18127 (1971); Thomas v. General Electric Co., 207 F. Supp. 792 (D.C. Ky. 1962); and EICO, Inc., 44 L.A. 563 (1965). See also Cooper Carton Co., 61 Lab. Arb. 697 (1973), and FMC Corp., 46 Lab. Arb. 335 (1966). With repect to photographing union member activities, see the comprehensive survey of the law in 45 A.L.R. Fed. 148 (1979).

19. For an excellent discussion of the difficulty of reaching an agreement between employers and employees regarding surreptitious surveillance and the current attempts by arbitrators to balance the need for industrial security and efficiency against the intrusiveness of the security measure and the probative value of the evidence obtained, see Carver, *The Inquisitional Process in Private Employment*, 63 CORNELL L. REV. 1, 51-65 (1977). See also Robert G. Boehmer, *Artificial Monitoring And Surveillance Of Employees: The Fine Line Dividing The Prudently Managed Enterprises From The Sweatshop*, 41 DEPAUL L. REV. 739 (1992).

20. See, e.g., United States v. Agapito, 620 F.2d 324 (2d Cir 1980), cert. denied, 449 U.S. 834 (1980); United States v. Mankani, 738 F.2d 538, 543 (2d Cir. 1984); United States v. Hessling, 845 F.2d 617 (6th Cir. 1988).

21. Ala. Code, § 13A-11-31; Idaho Code, § 18-6705; Iowa Code Ann., § 727.8; Ky. Rev. Stat. § 176.2.14; N.D. Cent. Code, § 12.1-15-02; Wyo. Stat., § 37-12-122.

have no statutory provisions at all concerning the subject.[22] Between these two extremes are states that permit electronic eavesdropping without a court order, but only when *all* parties to the conversation have given their consent,[23] or when merely *one* party has consented.[24] Many state statutes provide exceptions whereby law enforcement officers may employ electronic surveillance, although some circumstances may require court authorization.[25]

In addition to the legislative prohibitions upon electronic eavesdropping, and the criminal penalties that are prescribed, a number of statutes provide that civil suits may be filed against the eavesdroppers by the aggrieved persons.[26] Some of the statutes even provide specific recoverable amounts regardless of actual damages;[27] others provide for punitive or treble damages;[28] and at least one state allows recovery for the mental "pain and suffering" sustained by the aggrieved parties.[29]

22. Arkansas, Ind., Mo., Miss., Tex., Vt., and W. Va. (Employers or their attorneys should always check for the current status of the law.)

23. Del. Code Ann., tit. 11, §§ 1335-1336; Fla. Stat. Ann., §934.03 (where, however, the police make the interception, there need be the consent of only one of the parties); Kan. Stat. Ann., 21-4001; N.C. Stat., §14-227.1 (which pertains only to communications between a person in police custody and her attorney); Pa. Stats. Ann., tit. 18, § 5701-C; Wash. Rev. Code Ann., § 9.73.030-.040.

The Cal. Penal Code (§ 632) prohibits electronic eavesdropping on "confidential" communications "without the consent of all parties." A confession to a police interrogator, however, is not treated as a "confidential" communication except in certain very unusual situations.

The Ga. Criminal Code (§26-3001) contains this interesting provision: "It shall be unlawful for . . . any person in a clandestine manner to intentionally overhear . . . or attempt to overhear . . . the private conversation of another which shall originate in any private place."

The Illinois Criminal Code (720 ILCS 5/14-1-5 and 725 5/108A-1) makes it a criminal offense to use an "eavesdropping device" to hear or record any part of a conversation unless it is done with the consent of all of the parties, or with the consent of one party and the authorization of the prosecuting attorney *and* pursuant to a court order.

24. Alaska Stat., § 42.20.310; Ariz. Rev. Stat. Ann., § 13-3005; Colo. Rev. Stat. Ann. 16-15-101; Conn. Gen. Stat. Ann., §§ 53a-187, 188, 189; Fla. Stat. Ann. § 934.03 [but, according to (2)(c), only when law enforcement officers are the interceptors; otherwise, according to (2)(d), the consent of all is required]; Haw. Rev. Stat. §803-41 to 50; La. Rev. Stat. Ann., § 14:322; Me. Rev. Stat. Ann., tit. 15, §§ 709-712; Mass. Ann. Laws, ch. 272, § 99; Minn. Code Ann., § 626A.02; Neb. Rev. Stat., § 86-702; Nev. Rev. Stat., § 200.620; N.J. Stat. Ann., § 2A:156A-4; N.Y. Penal Law, § 250.00; Ohio Rev. Code Ann., §2933.58 (allowance only "to prevent crime or bring the offender to justice"); Okla. Stat. Ann., tit. 13, § 176.2.14; R.I. Gen. Laws, § 11-35-21; Va. Code Ann., § 19.2.62; Wis. Stat. Ann., § 968.31.

Maine's provision is unique in that it permits a law enforcement officer to intercept electronically a conversation where one party consents, but evidence thus obtained cannot be used in court. Me. Rev. Stat., tit. 15, § 712.

25. For example, Ga. Code Ann., § 26-3004; Minn. Stat. Ann., § 626A.02; N.H. Rev. Stat. Ann. 570-A-1-11; Or. Rev. Stat., § 165-540 (5); S.D. Codified Laws Ann. § 23A-35-A-1-21.

26. *See, e.g.,* Cal. Pen. Code, § 637.2; 720 ILCS 5/14-6; Kans. Stat. Ann., §22-2518; Me. Rev. Stat. Ann., tit. 15, §711; Mich. Stat. Ann., § 28-867(8); Minn. Stat. Ann., § 626 A.13; Nev. Rev. Stat., §200.690; N.H. Stat. Ann., §570-A:11; N.J. Stats. Ann., § 2A:156A-24; Pa. Stats. Ann., tit. 18, §5704; Va. Code Ann., § 19.2-69; Wash. Rev. Code, § 9.73.060; Wis. Stat. Ann., § 968.31 (2)(d).

27. *See* the statutes of Nev., N.J., Va., and Wis., cited in *supra* note 26.

28. *See* the statutes of Cal., Ill., Minn., and Pa., cited *supra* notes 25-26.

29. Wash. Rev. Code, § 9.73.060.

In 1968, Congress made it an offense—and also the basis for a civil suit—for anyone, without proper authorization, to employ an electronic, mechanical, or other device to: (a) tap a telephone or intercept any other wire communication; (b) intercept other oral conversations that occur on the premises of any business or other commercial establishment engaged in interstate or foreign commerce, or; (c) intercept elsewhere than on such premises where the purpose is to obtain information relating to the operation of any business or other commercial establishment whose operations affect interstate or foreign commerce.[30]

The term "interstate commerce," as used in the statute, has been broadly construed by the courts to include practically all business and commercial operations. In other words, any business transaction is likely to require, or to have required, some form of interstate activity. "Proper authorization," as we have used the term, refers to court-authorized interceptions, national security interceptions, and certain others not relevant to the subject matter of this text.

An exception to the federal prohibitions against electronic surveillance occurs when one party to the conversation has consented to the interception.[31] Courts have held that this consent may be implied.[32] Employers can also avoid liability under the "telephone extension" exception which provides that the use of an extension telephone by the employer to monitor employee calls "in the ordinary course of business" is not a violation.[33] Courts have found that, under this language, businesses may monitor phone conversation in any way related to the business,[34] but may not monitor personal phone calls.[35]

A court order is required, unless the interceptions fall within one of the few statutory exceptions. Although the statutory law does not specifically permit a business owner or a private security officer to obtain a court order for electronic eavesdropping, the federal statute, and most of the state statutes, do permit them to engage in that activity. They may do so, however, only when one party to the conversation consents, and with the further qualification that the interceptor must not have a criminal, tortious, or injurious intent.[36] We caution, how-

---

30. Title III of the Omnibus Crime Bill of 1968, 18 U.S.C. §§ 2510-2520. Note that some circuits have held that Title III does not cover the use of video cameras that record only images and not aural communication. *See* United States v. Mesa-Rincon, 911 F.2d 1433, 1436-37 (10th Cir. 1990).

31. § 2511(2)(d). *See* James v. Newspaper Agency Corp., 591 F.2d 579 (10th Cir. 1979).

32. *See* Griggs-Ryan v. Smith, 904 F.2d 112 (1st Cir. 1990).

33. §2510(5)(a). *See also* Burnett v. Texas, 789 S.W.2d 376 (Tex. App. 1990).

34. *See* Briggs v. American Air Filter Co., 630 F.2d 414 (5th Cir. 1980) (allowing supervisor to listen in on phone conversations of competitor and employee under suspicion of divulging confidential information); Epps v. St. Mary's Hospital of Athens, Inc., 802 F.2d 412 (11th Cir. 1986) (allowing monitoring calls between co-workers).

35. *See* Walkins v. L.M. Berry & Co., 704 F.2d 577 (11th Cir. 1983) (finding that employers may not monitor personal calls except to determine whether or not they are business-related).

36. An illustration of the meaning of the latter restriction is a 1971 federal case in which an insurance company claims a manager and his employer were sued for civil damages when they disclosed in a workmen's compensation hearing that a tape that had been made of a telephone conversation with the plaintiff contained an admission which rendered the claim noncompensable. It was held that the

ever, that the interceptor should determine in advance that there is no prohibition or restriction upon such an activity in her particular state. It is the right of any state to enact a statute more restrictive than the federal one, and some of the statutes cited in this chapter serve as examples that a number of states have already done so.[37]

Electronic Theft Detection

Retail merchants have employed the usage of special sensitized tags on merchandise that will set off an alarm if such objects are being moved without a desensitizing of the tags upon payments for the cost of the merchandise. Such an alarm will serve as probable cause for the detention, questioning, and arrest of the possessor of the object.[38]

Ultraviolet Light Search of a Suspect's Hands for Powder Planted on Objects of Thefts

As a means for investigating thefts by employees and other persons, fluorescent powder has been placed upon a targeted object and when a suspect is detected her hands are subjected to an ultraviolet light examination. When the revealed incriminating evidence is being offered at the trial, the contention has been made that the procedure constitutes an illegal search. The Colorado Supreme Court,

---

use of the tape to protect the company's rights was not the "injurious" type of conduct contemplated by the federal wiretap statute. Meredith v. Gavin, 446 F.2d 794 (8th Cir. 1971). *See also* Holmes v. Burr, 486 F.2d 55 (9th Cir. 1973), *cert. denied*, 414 U.S. 1116 (1973). And in United States v. White, 401 U.S. 745, 91 S. Ct. 1122 (1971), the Supreme Court held admissible the testimony of a third party regarding the electronically intercepted conversation between a police informant and a criminal suspect. The Court found no violation of the principles of Fourth Amendment privacy it had established in Katz v. United States, *supra* note 1.

37. At least one federal court has said that Congress intended that Title III of the Omnibus Crime Bill of 1968 be as pervasive as the Fourth Amendment constitutional standards. *See* Kinoy v. Mitchell, 331 F. Supp. 379 (S.D. N.Y. 1971). But Congress has allowed concurrent state regulation of wiretapping and electronic surveillance, subject, at a minimum, to the requirements of the federal regulations. *See* Commonwealth v. Vitello, 327 N.E. 2d 819 (Mass. 1975), and United States v. Upton, 502 F. Supp. 1193 (D.N.H. 1980). Although a state may not adopt standards that are less restrictive than federal requirements, some state wiretapping and eavesdropping laws protect individuals' rights to privacy to a greater degree than the Federal Constitution for the federal wiretapping statute. *See* State v. Ayres, 383 A. 2d 87 (N.H. 1978), and also United States v. Keen, 58 F.2d 986 (9th Cir. 1974).

38. Dent v. May Dept. Stores, 419 Atl. 2d 1042 (D.C. Ct. App. 1982).
       See also Nored v. State, 875 S.W. 2d 392 (Tex. Ct. App. 1994), affirming a conviction for theft of a privately owned bicycle that had been traced by means of a planted "beeper." Dye had also been placed on the bicycle and traces of it were found on the hands of the suspect. That evidence was also held to be admissible as evidence.

with three dissents, sustained that objection, but the decision represents a minority viewpoint of the courts.[39] In one of the decisions the Michigan Court of Appeals made the observation that "Even though the powder could not be detected with the naked eye, neither may a fingerprint be examined without the application of ink."[40]

39. People v. Santistevan, 715 P.2d 792 (Colo. 1986).

40. People v. Hulsey, 440 N.W. 2d 59 (Mich. App. 1989). It references the general case law upholding the majority view.

7

Property Owners' Protection
Against Intrusion

PERSONS WHO ABUSE THEIR PRIVILEGES
AS INVITEES

Although a store is obviously a place where merchants invite the public, it is still considered private property, as are other mercantile establishments to which customers and other persons are invited. Therefore, an owner or occupant retains the right to revoke his invitation to anyone who conducts himself in a manner not consistent with the purposes of that invitation.[1]

The action to be taken by a security officer or other authorized person when he sees someone abuse his privilege as an invitee will depend on the kind and degree of misconduct. In most instances, of course, a suggestion or warning to behave properly will suffice to protect the business interests, and the rights of other persons on the premises. In some instances, however, it may be necessary to ask the invitee to leave, or to eject him forcibly if he refuses to depart voluntarily.

The best way to eject a person who has indicated his unwillingness to leave voluntarily is to place a hand around one of his arms and seek thereby to lead him off the premises. If that proves ineffective, there may be recourse to stronger measures, provided the force used does not exceed that which is reasonably necessary to accomplish the objective.[2] For example, although pushing a person toward an exit might be permissible, punching him would not. Certainly, force should not be employed to merely expedite a departure or to punish the ejectee for his unwillingness to leave voluntarily.[3]

---

1. For a succinct presentation of this legal principle, see Ramirez v. Chavez, 71 Ariz. 239, 226 P.2d 143 (1951); Rodgers v. Bryan, 82 Ariz. 143, 309 P.2d 776 (1957).

2. Shranek v. Walker, 152 S.C. 88, 149 S.E. 331 (1929); Brookside-Pratt Mining Co. v. Booth, 211 Ala. 268, 100 So. 240 (1924); Noonan v. Luther, 206 N.Y. 105 (1912).

3. A clear example of unreasonable force is the case of Symalla v. Dusenka, 206 Minn. 280, 288, N.W. 385 (1939), in which a patron of a tavern was beaten up because of his reluctance to leave.

Once a person has been asked or forced to leave the premises, no further action should be taken except to prevent a reentry, destruction of property, or physical harm to some person on the premises. Insults or curses that may be uttered by the ejected person should be ignored. If, however, the ejected person persists in his misconduct, the police may be called and the matter reported to them for whatever action they may deem appropriate.[4]

In the event the ejector himself is attacked, he may, of course, use whatever force is reasonably necessary in self-defense.[5]

A security officer or other authorized person who is involved in the ejection of an unruly person should be careful not to injure innocent bystanders in the store. If the unruly ejectee injures a third party, it is unlikely that the injured person would have a claim against the ejector.[6] If the ejector himself carelessly injures an innocent bystander in any scuffle with the person being ejected, however, he may be liable for damages to the injured person.[7] Furthermore, if the ejector injures a bystander while using excessive force on the ejectee, there may be liability even though all possible care was used to confine the force used to eject the person.[8]

In some states, whenever an invitee is ordered to leave the premises and refuses to do so, he thereby commits the offense of trespass,[9] an offense for which a few states permit an arrest by a private citizen.[10] In some states, trespass also occurs when an ejectee reenters the premises after being ordered not to return.

In most instances where a discharged employee refuses to leave his place of employment, the matter can be handled satisfactorily by using quiet persuasion on the part of the security officer or other agent of the employer; nevertheless, forcible ejection is permissible as a last resort.

As stated earlier, under certain circumstances an employer may be held liable for an assault and battery committed by his employee if the acts of the employee were in furtherance of the business's interest and within the scope of the em-

---

4. In such a situation the call itself is not a direction to the police to make an arrest; consequently, the caller does not subject himself to liability for the action taken by the police. *See* Lemel v. Smith, 64 Nev. 545, 187 P.2d 169 (1947). The same legal principle would apply to calls to the police regarding the initial behavior of an unruly person while on the premises.

5. Penn v. Henderson, 174 Oreg. 1, 146 P.2d 760 (1944).

6. Polando v. Vizzini, 97 N.E.2d 59 (Ohio App. 1949).

7. Morris v. Plat, 32 Conn. 75 (1864); Paxton v. Boyer, 67 Ill. 132 (1873). *See also* W. PROSSER, *Transferred Intent*, 45 TEX. L. REV. 650 (1967).

8. Bannester v. Mitchell, 127 Va. 575, 104 S.E. 800 (1920).

9. *See, e.g.,* the Ill. Criminal Code, 720 ILCS Sec. 5/21-3; Md. Ann. Stats., art. 27, § 577; Miss. Stats., § 97-17-97. Of particular interest, perhaps, is the following portion of a Mo. statute: "A person who, regardless of his purpose, enters or remains in or upon premises which are at the time open to the public does so with license and privilege unless he defies a lawful order not to enter or remain, personally communicated to him by the owner of such premises or by other authorized person. . . . " Mo. Ann. Stats., tit. 38 § 569.010(8). *See also* W. PROSSER AND W. KEETON, LAW OF TORTS, 43 (1984), and 75 Am. Jur. (2d, Trespass), § 86 et seq.

10. *See, e.g.,* in Illinois (725 ILCS Sec. 5/107-3) offense means a violation of a state penal statute, which, in this instance, covers the offense of trespass as specified in § 21-3.

ployment. Thus, in one case the court determined that responsibility can be fixed upon the employer if at the time of performing wrongful acts the employee was acting on behalf of the employer and not on his own account. The court noted that it is not necessary that the employer expressly authorize the employee to commit the tortious act; it need only be committed in the course of a transaction of the employer's business.[11] Similarly, in another case, a corporation operating a bar was held liable for injuries to a patron whom the night manager struck with a heavy blunt instrument while ejecting him from the premises.[12] No justification or provocation was found for such excessive force and violence. The court held that the employer was responsible for his employee's acts, because they were within the scope of his employment and in furtherance of business entrusted to the employee. Consequently, the employer must answer for the unlawful manner in which such acts were performed. An employer will not be considered responsible, however, for an assault made by an employee who abandons a business purpose to effect a purpose of his own.[13]

THE RIGHT TO UNIONIZE, PICKET, AND PROTEST AT OR UPON BUSINESS ESTABLISHMENTS

Labor Management Issues

Employees and union representatives have a well-recognized right to use public property adjoining an employer's premises to conduct a picket or to urge nonpatronage of the business, provided the activity is directed toward a lawful objective and conducted in a peaceful and orderly manner. Such picketing is disallowed, however, where union pickets try to induce a company to refuse to sell to nonunion retailers, and where the objective is to restrain trade or is otherwise in violation of state or federal antitrust laws. In these types of cases there is no federal constitutional prohibition against a state court enjoining picketing for the particular unlawful purpose, because it is within the state's power to regulate and govern the manner in which certain trade practices shall be conducted.[14] In a case where picketing was aimed at compelling an employer to sign a union contract that

---

11. McChristian v. Popkin, 75 Cal. 2d 249, 171 P.2d 85 (1946). *See also* Canon v. United States, 111 F. Supp. 162 (D.C. Cal. 1953), *aff'd*, 217 F.2d 70 (9th Cir. 1954), holding that an act complained of does not transcend the scope of employment just because it benefits the employee as a third person if it also serves the employer's business and promotes the object of employment. This case offers a good discussion of the different factors that need to be considered in determining whether the act of the employee is within the scope of employment.

12. Westerland v. Argonaut, 185 Wash. 411, 55 P.2d 819 (1936).

13. *See supra* note 12. *See also* Titus v. Tacoma Smeltermen's Union, 383 P.2d 504 (1963), where the Supreme Court of Washington held that "a union may be liable for assaults committed by its members while picketing, providing it is done in the furtherance of the union's business and within the scope of the employment."

14. Giboney v. Empire Storage Co., 336 U.S. 490, 69 S. Ct. 684 (1949).

would have had the effect of coercing the employees to designate the union as their bargaining representative, the picketing was enjoined.[15]

Even where the objective of picketing is lawful and the picketing is peaceful, it may be enjoined if it is "so enmeshed with and set in such a background of violence that it [is] a part of a pattern of violence."[16]

Product picketing (against a specific product) is permissible so long as its foreseeable effect is not to completely stop trade against a neutral third party or secondary employer with whom the union has no dispute. Picketing against a specific product may be prohibited, however, if it reasonably appears that such picketing will induce customers to boycott the neutral party's business.[17] This occurs, for example, when the designated product is the sole product marketed by the picketed party (in which case, as the Supreme Court recently said, the party will have to choose between survival and the severance of its ties with the manufacturer of the product). It also occurs when the picket signs do not specify that the strike is directed at an easily identifiable product sold by the neutral party, rather than the neutral party itself.[18]

Difficult problems have arisen with respect to the delineation between public and private property, and the extent to which traditional property rights may be overridden or diluted by considerations of social interests and values. One example is a case involving migrant farm workers housed on private farm property. Representatives of two nonprofit federally funded organizations sought to render legal advice, economic aid, health services, and other governmental services available to the workers, but the property owner refused them access to the camp quarters. The New Jersey Supreme Court held that ownership of the real property could not bar entry for the intended purposes.[19] The court attempted to balance the rights and needs of the parties in light of the realities of their relationship. In its opinion, the court also stated that "the migrant worker must be allowed to receive visitors there of his own choice, so long as there is no behavior hurtful to others," and added that "members of the press may not be denied reasonable access to workers who do not object to seeing them."

The public–private delineation has been featured in supermarket type case situations. These situations present many interesting questions of law. For instance, what is the status of that portion of a privately owned supermarket complex used as a parking area? A somewhat analogous situation is that of defining the limitations upon union picketing of a business located in a high-rise building.

For privately owned property to be treated in any way comparable to public property, it must, as the United States Supreme Court has stated, "assume to some significant degree the functional attributes of public property devoted to public

15. Building Service Employees International Union v. Gazzam, 339 U.S. 532 (1950).

16. Milk Wagon Drivers Union v. Meadowmoor Dairies, 312 U.S. 287 (1941).

17. NLRB v. Retail Store Employees Union, Local 1001, 447 U.S. 607 (1980).

18. Kaynard v. Independent Routemen's Association, 479 F.2d 1070 (1973). *See also supra* note 17.

19. State v. Shack and Tejeras, 58 N.J. 297, 277 A.2d 369 (1971). *See also* Baer v. Sarbello, 177 N.J. Super. 1982, 425 A.2d 1089 (1981), *pet. for cert. denied,* 434 A.2d 1070.

use."[20] As the Court explained in another case, however, property does not "lose its private character merely because the public is generally invited to use it for designated purposes," and it added that "[t]he essential private character of a store and its privately owned abutting property does not change by virtue of being large or clustered with other stores in a modern shopping center."[21]

The United States Supreme Court, in a 1976 case, held that union pickets have no legal right to enter a privately owned shopping center to advertise their strike against one of the retail stores leased from the owner of the center.[22] However, a United States Circuit Court of Appeals held, in 1980, that a union could picket against a restaurant on the forty-sixth floor of an office building, so long as it remained orderly and did not impede the use of the other facilities on that floor.[23] The court reasoned that the owner of the building, technically considered an employer of the restaurant workers for the purposes of the National Labor

20. Central Hardware Co. v. NLRB, 407 U.S. 539 at 547 (1972). *See also* HENELY, *Property Rights and First Amendment Rights: Balance and Conflict,* 62 A.B.A.J. 77 (1976).

21. Lloyd Corp. v. Tanner, 407 U.S. 551 (1972). In Pruneyard Shopping Center v. Robins, 447 U.S. 74 (1980), the Supreme Court explained the holding in Lloyd, saying that "when a shopping center owner opens his private property to the public for the purpose of shopping, the First Amendment to the United States Constitution does not thereby create individual rights in expression beyond those already existing under applicable law."

It should be noted that in *Pruneyard,* the U.S. Supreme Court held that a state may constitutionally require the owner of a private shopping center to permit the exercise of free speech on the shopping center property, pursuant to a state constitutional provision or statute. For a more detailed discussion of this, see Comment, *Pruneyard Progeny: State-Created Free Speech Access to Quasi-Public Property,* 1984 ANN. SURV. AM. L. 121 (1985).

In a recent decision, relying on the free speech provisions of the New Jersey State Constitution, the New Jersey Supreme Court ruled that owners and managers of large shopping centers in that state have to allow the distribution of leaflets on political issues. The court believed that such shopping centers today have replaced downtown business districts as the area where the public gathers. New Jersey Coalition Against War v. J.M.B. Realty Corp., 650 A.2d 757 N.J., (1994). The Colorado Supreme Court has also ruled that the Colorado State Constitution prevents the owner of an enclosed private shopping mall from excluding a political group from passing out literature and gathering petition signatures in mall common areas. Bock v. Westminister Mall Co., 819 P.2d 55 (Colo. 1991). For decisions upholding the prohibition of distribution of literature in private shopping malls, see Cologne v. Westfarms Associates, 469 A.2d 1201 (Conn. 1984), and Alliance v. Smith Haven Mall, 498 N.Y.S.2d 99 (N.Y. 1985). *See also* Geibels v. City of Cape Coral, 861 F. Supp. 1049 (M.D. Fla. 1994) (arrest of man circulating petitions for signatures on private property did not violate his free speech rights when owner asked him to leave before he was placed under arrest).

In Citizens to End Animal Suffering and Exploitation, Inc. v. Faneuil Hall Marketplace, 745 F. Supp. 65 (D. Mass. 1990), a federal court ruled that a privately run marketplace had taken on a "traditional public function" and also had a "symbiotic" relationship with the city, making its actions state action. As a result, animal rights protesters had a constitutional right to hand out leaflets in lanes between buildings at the marketplace.

22. Hudgens v. NLRB, 424 U.S. 507 (1976).

23. Seattle First National Bank v. NLRB, 651 F.2d 1272 (9th Cir. 1980). *Compare,* however, Silverman v. 40-41 Realty Associates, 668 F.2d 678 (2nd Cir. 1982), in which the Second Circuit Court of Appeals vacated an injunction issued by a federal district court permitting picketing in the corridors of an office building outside of the employer's premises. The court rejected as novel the contention that the area inside a building ought to be considered the functional equivalent of the traditional picket site, a public sidewalk. Although it refrained from passing judgment as to the wisdom of the Seattle First

Relations Act, had sanctioned an invitation to the public to patronize the restaurant. Apparently, the court understood that because most of the restaurant's lunchtime patrons worked in the building where the restaurant was located, if the union were forced to picket on the street below it would be unable to reach those persons. Thus, the court seemed to have considered the area inside of the building as the functional equivalent of the traditional public forum—the public sidewalk.

A recent NLRB ruling held that if pickets do not actually enter the complex of a targeted tenant, the picketers may urge customers not to patronize any of the businesses in that mall,[24] at least in situations where there is a mutually dependent and beneficial relationship between the mall owner and the tenants. In this circumstance the hand-billing, requesting a total consumer boycott, is considered to be protected by the publicity provision of the National Labor Relations Act.[25]

An employer cannot prohibit employees from striking or picketing outside of the employer's premises during an employee-management dispute. An employer may, however, place a number of restrictions upon activities occurring on his property. For instance, he may forcibly eject and even fire any employee who conducts a sit-down strike on his premises.[26]

Employees may engage in attempts at self-organization on their employer's premises provided they do so in a manner that does not disrupt the normal operation of the employer's business.[27] Generally, then, the employer cannot complain if his employees spend coffee-break or lunch-hour time forming a union. On the other hand, nonemployee organizers may not enter the premises (including a factory parking lot) to organize the workers, unless the employer has allowed other outsiders to distribute literature to his workers, or if attempts by organizers to contact workers off the plant's grounds would be unreasonably burdensome upon the union.[28] The same restrictions apply to off-duty employees, who, in cases involving employer rules forbidding them from entering or remaining on the premises.[29] have been treated by the NLRB as analogous to nonemployees.

Union activities involving hospitals may not be prohibited except in immediate patient-care areas.[30]

National Bank decision, the court in Silverman went on to say that "neither the [National Labor Relations] Board nor any court has ever construed the [National Labor Relations] Act to permit interior picketing in the corridors of an office building."

24. Florida Gulf Coast Building Trades Council, 252 NLRB #99, 1980, CCH NLRB ¶ 17452 (1980).

25. Section 8(b)(4)(ii)(B). For National Labor Relations Act as amended, see 29 U.S.C. §§ 151-168.

26. NLRB v. Fansteel Metallurgical Corp., 306 U.S. 240 (1939).

27. Republic Aviation Corp. v. NLRB, 324 U.S. 793 (1945).

28. NLRB v. Babcock & Wilcox Co., 351 U.S. 105 (1956).

29. G.T.E. Lenkurt, 204 NLRB #75 (1973); Tri-County Medical Center, 222 NLRB #174, 91 LRRM 1323 (1976).

30. NLRB v. Baptist Hospital, 442 U.S. 773 (1979).

NONUNION PROTEST ACTIVITIES AT OR UPON BUSINESS PREMISES

When persons conduct group activities at or on a business premise in support of a nonlabor-related grievance, they must operate within somewhat different rules than those previously discussed. Once again, though, the precise nature of the property (i.e., private or public) and the way it is used will significantly shape the rights and liabilities of persons involved in the activities. A good illustration is the landmark United States Supreme Court case that held that the First Amendment rights of a Jehovah's Witness to distribute religious literature outweighed the property rights of the owner of a company-owned town with a shopping area open to the general public.[31]

As previously discussed, a merchant has the right to rescind the invitations extended to patrons, because the premise retains its character as private property. Thus, an owner is justified in asserting his property rights against persons engaged in activities that have no overriding social value. For instance, a tavern keeper may oust a drunk from his bar if the individual refuses to leave peacefully, or a department store may banish shoplifters. This right does not apply, however, where persons come on the premises for a valid social protest, for example, against racial discrimination, sex discrimination, or unethical credit practices. One very specialized group of cases holds that a commercial property owner or operator may not thwart social protest, even though it occurs on his private property or during the conduct of his business. Specifically, the courts have ruled that blacks may conduct sit-in demonstrations in business establishments that refuse service or give unequal service along racial lines. Even before the Supreme Court of the United States considered this problem,[32] an Illinois appellate court foreshadowed the Supreme Court's holding by ruling that a restaurant owner could not have the police arrest blacks who peacefully conducted a sit-in at a bar and refused to leave until they were served.[33] The patrons, said the Illinois court, were entitled to remain and to be served in the same manner as whites were being served. This right was considered superior to the bar owner's property right.[34]

Does this group of cases mean, then, that anyone with an armload of political or religious tracts may peaceably invade the owner's premises against his will? May

---

31. Marsh v. Alabama, 326 U.S. 501 (1946). Although in *Marsh* the Supreme Court followed a strict test, the *Marsh* rationale was subsequently extended to shopping centers in Amalgamated Food Employees Union v. Logan Valley Plaza, 391 U.S. 308 (1968). Four years later, in Lloyd Corp. v. Tanner (*supra* note 21), the Court began to cut short Logan Valley until, finally, expressly overruling it two years later, in Hudgens v. NLRB (*supra* note 22). Some questions remain, however, as to the possibility of a First Amendment right of access to privately owned property when no other "avenues of communication" are available. *See* Cape Cod Nursing Home v. Rambling Rose Rest Home, 667 F.2d 238 (1st Cir. 1981).

32. Hamm v. City of Rock Hill, 379 U.S. (1964); Garner v. Louisiana, 368 U.S. 157 (1961).

33. City of Chicago v. Corney, 13 Ill. App. 2d 396, 142 N.E.2d 160 (1957).

34. The Ill. Human Rights Act, 775 ILCS, §§ 5/1-101 to 5/1-103, dealing with public accommodations covers this type of situation.

any group sit in to protest an owner–employer's job discrimination along lines of race or sex? It is unlikely that courts will go so far as to say that an owner must open his doors to (or else allow in) any and all protestors, social prophets, and critics just because they claim to carry a message of overriding social import. For example, persons who pass out antiwar pamphlets have no greater right to enter a grocery store than, say, those who enter with pamphlets advertising a beauty shop down the street. A war protest bears no reasonable relationship to the business of the grocer, just as the promotion of another store does not relate to the grocer's business. In both instances the grocer has a legal right to bar the pamphleteers.[35] Suppose, however, that demonstrators enter a grocery store to discourage shoppers from buying grapes or other produce because of the low quality of the living conditions of the migrant workers harvesting these products. Unlike the racial discrimination of patrons in a restaurant, the activity protested against in this case, the selling of grapes or other products, is lawful and violates no law. Consequently, independent of the truth or falsity of the protestors' claims, they do not have a right to use or remain upon the private premises.

The sit-in cases raise the greatest difficulties for merchants in those instances where the protest involves an issue of social importance in which the business's policies are claimed to violate the law—for example, discriminatory hiring practices. As a practical matter, the invasion of an employer's premises in opposition to job discrimination is quite different from a sit-in at a lunch counter to protest discriminatory service. In the latter case, the restaurant owner can easily remedy the wrong by serving lunch to the patrons. On the other hand, the storeowner in the former case probably cannot remedy the grievance by hiring the crowd of protestors on the spot.

When demonstrations or politicking regarding a nonlabor-related issue occur on privately owned but publicly used property outside the actual business premises, an employer's property rights may be tempered by the free speech protection of the First Amendment.[36] It was held, for instance, that a citizen environmental group had the right to solicit promotional or protest signatures on the private sidewalk property of a shopping center, even without the consent of the owner. This right is subject, however, to reasonable regulations by the owners to prevent "undue interference" with other members of the public who have an equal right to the sidewalks.[37]

Simply because the general public is invited to use privately owned property for a designated purpose, the property does not automatically lose its private character. Without proof that the demonstration, picketing, handbilling, or whatever ac-

---

35. Lloyd Corp. v. Tanner, *supra* note 21.

36. For a comprehensive analysis of federal and state constitutional protections of freedom of speech vis-a-vis the rights of private property owners, see State v. Schmid, 84 N.J. 535, 423 A.2d 615 (1980), *appeal dismissed*, 455 U.S. 100. In that case the Supreme Court of New Jersey recognized that, in the appropriate situation, the state constitution may independently provide a basis for protecting personal rights when it is not clear that the guarantees of the federal constitution would serve to grant the same level of protection. *See* State v. Alston, 88 N.J. 211, 440 A.2d 1318 (1981).

37. Sutherland v. Southcenter Shopping Center, 3 Wash. App. 833, 448 P.2d 792 (1970).

tivity has a rational relation to the purpose to which the property has been put, or without proof that alternative means of demonstration or distribution are unavailable or extremely burdensome, the owner's right to ban the demonstrators will be sustained.[38]

As in the labor dispute cases, protestors or pickets in support of nonlabor causes have fairly broad rights to express themselves so long as they do so on public property and in a peaceful manner. For example, neighborhood residents have been allowed to picket and urge a boycott of a tavern that attracted undesirable persons to the neighborhood; the neighbors had a right to express their concern about matters affecting their welfare as members of the public.[39]

38. Lloyd Corp. v. Tanner, *supra* note 21.

39. 1621, Inc. v. Wilson, 402 Pa. 94, 166 A.2d 271 (1960). An excellent discussion of this general problem appears in 92 A.L.R.2d 1284. *See also* 10 A.L.R. 3d 846, and 62 A.L.R. 3d 227.

8

The Procurement of Information Regarding the Dishonesty/ Criminality of Job Applicants, Employees, and Customers

CRIMINAL HISTORY INFORMATION ON APPLICANTS AND EMPLOYEES

The protective security of a business usually warrants background checks on the honesty of applicants for employment and, in some instances, checks on presently employed persons as well. In this regard, information from criminal history records would obviously be very helpful. This chapter discusses the extent to which such information is accessible to employers.

Public Records

The English common law did not recognize a general right of all citizens to inspect public records. Instead, under the English rule, the individual seeking access had to prove a particularized interest.[1] Because proving such an interest was so difficult, the word *public* was rather meaningless, in that few individuals believed they were qualified for access. The particularized interest requirement, though adopted at one time by American courts, has been largely aban-

---

1. The common law doctrine has been formulated as follows: Every person is entitled to the inspection either personally or by his agent, of public records, including legislative, executive, and judicial records, provided he has an interest therein which is such as would enable him to maintain or defend an action for which the document or record sought can furnish evidence on necessary information. 66 Am. Jr. 2d, RECORDS AND RECORDING LAWS, §15.

doned.[2] Today, interest as a citizen or taxpayer is sufficient to satisfy the vestiges of the common law rule.[3] Accordingly, many current statutes explicitly grant the right to all members of the public to inspect public records.

Although the right of inspection is now well established, usually by state statutes, some uncertainty exists as to what actually constitutes a public record. At times litigation is required to resolve the issue.

The courts usually find the elements of a public record to be a written memorial, made by a public officer, who is authorized by law to make it.[4] Some states, however, have tried to remove uncertainty by enacting statutes that specifically define a public record. For example, in Kentucky, the phrase "public records" includes all documentary materials that are prepared, owned, used, or retained by a public agency.[5]

The general rule is that all people should be afforded the right to inspect public records. A few courts have held, however, that a legitimate and reasonable purpose for the inspection must be shown; the right must not be used merely to satisfy one's curiosity, or to meddle with or harass public officials.[6] It is generally recognized, nevertheless, that citizens do have a common interest in good government and consequently should be accorded the right to inspect. Therefore, a general citizen interest will suffice.[7]

Under certain exceptional circumstances, the right to inspect may be denied, after applying a balancing test to determine whether the citizen's interest and needs outweigh the government's interest in nondisclosure.[8]

---

2. For instance, in City of St. Matthews v. Voice of St. Matthews, Inc., 519 S.W. 2d 811, 815 (Ky. 1974), the court found the common law requirement "to be an unwarranted impediment to the right of people generally to acquire information concerning the operation of their government" and held that "the right to demand inspection of public records must be premised upon a purpose which tends to advance or further a wholesome public interest or a legitimate private interest."

3. Forum Publishing Co. v. City of Fargo, 391 N.W. 2d 169, 172 (N.D. 1986). The court found that the citizens and taxpayers should have the right to examine public records "to determine whether public money is being properly spent, or for the purpose of bringing to the attention of the public irregularities in the handling of public matters."

4. South Jersey Publishing Co., Inc. v. New Jersey Expressway Authority, 124 N.J. 478, 591 A.2d 921 (1991).

5. Ky. R.S. 61.870 (2) (1986).

6. Blankenship v. City of Hoover, 590 So. 2d 245 (Ala. 1991): "Right of free examination is the rule, and the inhibition of such privilege, when the purpose is speculative, or from idle curiosity, is the exception." In addition, the right of inspection must not unduly interfere or hinder the discharge of public officials' duties.

7. South Jersey Publishing Co. v. N.J. Expressway Authority, *supra* note 4.

8. Estate of Hearst, 67 Cal. App. 3d 777, 136 Cal. Rptr. 821 (1977); Craemer v. Superior Court for the County of Marin, 265 Cal. App. 2d 216, 71 Cal. Rptr. 193 (1968). Cases such as these two establish that, if a countervailing public policy is found to exist, the court has a right to limit access to its court records (usually classified as "public records") for temporary periods. Countervailing public policy, as the court in *Craemer* suggested, might come into play as a result of events that tend to undermine individual security, personal liberty, or private property, or that are injurious to the public.

The statutory right to inspect public records was established in 1966 when Congress enacted, and later augmented, the Freedom of Information Act.[9] Its purpose was to afford the public an opportunity to scrutinize the actions of administrative agencies and, consequently, to hold the agencies accountable for their actions. The underlying principle was that all members of the public should have access to public records, regardless of the purpose for which they are sought. Nevertheless, Congress did create certain exceptions and restrictions. Among them was the provision that "records or information compiled for law enforcement purposes," would not be available if they "(a) could reasonably be expected to interfere with enforcement proceedings, (b) would deprive a person of a right to a fair trial or impartial adjudication, (c) could reasonably be expected to constitute an unwarranted invasion of personal privacy, (d) could reasonably be expected to disclose the identity of a confidential source, . . . (e) would disclose techniques and procedures for law enforcement investigations or prosecution . . . if such disclosure could reasonably be expected to risk circumvention of the law, or (f) could reasonably be expected to endanger the life or physical safety of any individual."[10]

Criminal History Records

The principal repository of criminal history records is the Federal Bureau of Investigation (FBI). Its duties and responsibilities are governed by federal statutes and federal regulations. (As defined by statute, a regulation is a document of a governmental agency that has general applicability and legal effect on its publication, with the approval of the President, in either the Federal Registry or by filing with the Administrative Committee of the Federal Registrar.)[11]

A federal statute[12] provides that:

(a) The Attorney General shall (1) acquire, collect, classify, and preserve identification, criminal identification, crime, and other records; and exchange such records and information with authorized officials of the Federal Government, the states, cities, penal, and other institutions.

(b) The exchange of records . . . is subject to cancellation if dissemination is made outside the receiving departments or related agencies.

(c) The Attorney General may appoint officials to perform the [authorized] functions.

(d) For purposes of this section, the term "other institutions" includes:

(1) railroad police departments which perform the administration of criminal justice . . . ; and

(2) police departments of private colleges or universities which perform the administration of criminal justice . . .

9. 5 U.S.C. § 552.

10. 5 U.S.C. § 552 (b)(2).

11. 44 U.S.C. § 1510 (a)(1988).

12. 28 U.S.C. § 534 (1988).

In accordance with the authority delegated to the Attorney General [in (c) above], the Director of the FBI has been empowered, by a federal regulation, to "conduct the acquisition, collection, exchange, classification and preservation of fingerprint cards and identification records from criminal justice and other governmental agencies, including fingerprint cards voluntarily submitted by individuals for personal identification purposes . . ."[13]

The Director of the FBI may also "approve and conduct exchanges of identification records with officials of federally chartered or insured banking institutions to promote or maintain the security of those institutions and, if authorized by State statute and approved by the Attorney General, to officials of State and local governments for purposes of employment and licensing . . . [and] . . . approve and conduct exchanges of identification records with certain segments of the securities industry and the Commodity Futures Trading Commission . . ."[14]

By February 1995, the Identification Division of the FBI contained 208,601,523 sets of fingerprints on file for both criminal justice and civilian purposes. It receives thousands of fingerprint cards a day, not only from law enforcement agencies, but also from the military and other contributing sources, including voluntary submissions.

More than 7,000 federal, state, and local agencies supply criminal history information to the FBI. The FBI's system is a mutual one whereby contributing agencies voluntarily submit information and, in turn, are entitled to receive information upon request for authorized purposes.

As part of its record-keeping task, the FBI also regulates the availability and dissemination of criminal record information. When a fingerprint card arrives for an identification check, the FBI searches its records and either reports to the inquirer that no prior arrest appeared, or else forwards a copy of the individual's criminal history record—the so-called "rap sheet." It is also disseminated upon request to other authorized agencies, such as court officers and probationary authorities.[15]

Because the FBI has little control over the criminal history information it disseminates, a 1974 federal court decision imposed on the FBI a duty to take reasonable precautions to avoid inaccuracies.[16] For instance, the FBI has a responsibility to forward to state or local departments any challenges that are made to a subject's record.[17] An example of this type of violation occurs if the FBI neglects to update its own records after receiving a correction notice from an agency.[18] However, the FBI is not obligated to determine the accuracy of the

---

13. 28 CFR § 0.85 (b) at 47 (1991).

14. 28 CFR § 0.85 (j) 1991 at 47.

15. For the general regulatory provisions regarding federal, state, and local criminal records information systems, consult 28 CFR, § 20.1–38 at 325–338 (1991).

16. Tarlton v. Saxbe, Attorney General, 507 F.2d 1116 (D.C. Cir. 1974); on remand, 407 F. Supp. 1083 (D.D.C. 1976). One of three judges dissented to the judicial oversight power his two colleagues created upon operations of the FBI.

17. 28 CFR § 20.34 (b) at 333 (1991).

18. See Pruett v. Levi, Attorney General, 622 F. 2d 256 (6th Cir. 1980).

criminal history it receives before entering it in its files.[19] The FBI may also be faulted if it fails to follow its own regulations.

Disputes over alleged inaccuracies in criminal history records must be resolved by the subject of the information and the agency supplying the data.[20] For this reason, a party claiming a grievance over inaccuracy in a criminal history record must exhaust all other administrative remedies before a suit may be brought against the FBI itself.[21]

Access to Criminal History Records—Federal and State

A criminal history record may be in the form of a conviction for a criminal offense, an arrest, or another kind of police detention. Although a conviction is clearly identifiable as a public record and therefore is subject to the right of access and inspection by members of the public, that is not intrinsically so with regard to nonconviction police data. The main distinction is that a conviction signifies proof of guilt beyond a reasonable doubt, whereas nonconviction data in police files do not carry any such assurance. Nevertheless, a trend has emerged within the courts and legislatures to render *all* criminal history records open to public inspection, under certain circumstances.[22] The primary motivation for this trend is an increasing awareness of the public's need to know "what the police are up to."[23] Otherwise, a person might be subjected to secret detention without relatives or friends knowing about it. Therefore, the public's "right to know" transcends the protection of the privacy interests of the affected individual. There is also a need to provide employers some protection from hiring a person whose criminal record may evidence a high risk of the commission by her of physical or severe financial harm to the employer, fellow employees, or other persons.[24]

According to a 1990 report of the Bureau of Standards of the United States Department of Justice, the laws of the various jurisdictions governing access to criminal history records for noncriminal justice purposes "are so varied as to defy classification." As a result, it is obviously impractical in this text to do more than discuss the subject generally, with references to a few statutes or regulations and to the Bureau's 155 page report for the full details. The report, entitled

---

19. Crow v. Kelley, 512 F. 2d 752 (8th Cir. 1975).

20. Alexander v. U.S., 787 F. 2d 1349 (9th Cir. 1986).

21. Allen v. Webster, 742 F. 2d 153 (4th Cir. 1984). *See also* Pruett v. Levi, *supra* note 18.

22. *See Compendium* referred to in text at *infra* note 25, at 6.

23. Newspapers, Inc. v. Breir, Chief of Police, 89 Wis. 2d 417, 279 N.W. 2d 179 (1979).

24. An employer may be found guilty of negligent hiring if the employer acted unreasonably when she allowed the employee to perform her job in light of the information the employer should have known about the employee. Tallahassee Furniture, Inc. v. Harrison, 583 So. 2d 744 (Fla. App. 1991). In this case, the employer should have foreseen the employee's dangerousness based on his history of unlawful and violent behavior, drug abuse, and mental illness.

A Compendium of State Privacy and Security Legislation—A 1989 Review of Privacy and Security of Criminal History Information, lists all state statutes as well as the governmental regulations—federal and state.[25] The preface to the Compendium states that a "full text (1497 pages) of legislation is available free in microfiche . . . "[26]

Anyone searching for the law or criminal history information in a particular jurisdiction should be aware that the law may be in the form of an official regulation, federal or state, rather than in a legislative enactment.[27]

By way of a brief summary of access rights, the Bureau of Standards' *Compendium* reports that a few states allow only for the inspection of criminal convictions,[28] and that certain others do not allow for any criminal history access at all.[29] Most states, the Bureau reports, permit access to all criminal history record data by at least some types of noncriminal justice agencies and private entities.[30]

The subject of a record may obtain a copy of it, by sending a written request to the FBI or by applying in person at the FBI headquarters.[31]

The only records kept by the FBI are those involving serious offenses. They do not include such "nonserious" ones as "drunkness, vagrancy, disturbing the peace, curfew violation . . . "[32] They also exclude offenses committed by juveniles, unless the juvenile has been tried in court as an adult.[33]

On occasions, court decisions are required to clarify constitutional inquiries regarding statutory provisions or governmental regulations. One example is the immunity accorded access to police records in a situation involving an ongoing investigation.[34]

---

25. Publication source: Office of Criminal Justice Statistics (NCJ-121157) April 1990 Dept. of Justice, Washington, D.C. 20531.

26. Source for obtaining copy: Order No. NCJ-113021, Justice Statistics Clearinghouse, National Criminal Justice Reference Service, P.O. Box 6000, Rockville, MD 20850. Later editions may be obtained from the same agency.

27. Examples contained in the *Compendium*: Alas, S.C., and Va. (For definiiton of "regulation," refer to text *supra* note 11.)

28. *Compendium* examples: Idaho, Ill., Ind., La., Miss., and N.D. The Ill. statute, known as the Illinois Uniform Conviction Information Act, 20 1LC 263514, provides that "all conviction information . . . shall be open to public inspection . . ."

29. *Compendium* examples: Tenn., Tex., Vt, and V.I.

30. *Compendium*, p. 6. For example, private employers screening applicants for sensitive positions, such as ones involving children, valuable property, or public safety, are allowed access to this information.

   For a listing, state by state, of the statutes and regulations governing access to CHR, *see Compendium*, 50–155.

31. 28 CFR § 16.32. *See also* § 20.34.

32. 28 CFR § 20.32 (1991).

33. Id.

34. State *ex rel* NBC v. City of Cleveland, 57 Ohio State 3d 77, 566 N. E. 2d 146 (1991). The court formulated a two-fold test: (1) whether the desired information involved a confidential law enforcement investigatory record, and (2) whether inspection would create a high probability of disclosing specific investigatory work product data.

It is generally required that a set of the subject's fingerprints must accompany requests made to a governmental agency for a criminal history record, and a federal regulation requires submission of fingerprints even when the subjects themselves are the requesters.[35] The purpose is to insure a positive identification of the subject of the inquiry. It is suggested, therefore, that this requirement be transmitted by an employer to applicants who may harbor some sensitivity by submitting to a practice they associate with the process of fingerprinting criminals following an arrest.

Usually, an employer, or anyone else seeking a criminal history record, must contact a state control facility (e.g., the state police) rather than a local police agency, the identity of which can be obtained, however, from the local one. In some jurisdictions a local agency itself might have been designated by the central facility as its point of contact.

It is inadvisable for an employer to simply require an applicant to obtain a copy from a criminal justice agency of a criminal history record or to certify that no such record is on file. Advisable, however, is the procurement from an applicant, or employee, of written consent to the employer to make a criminal history search.

Access to criminal history records may be unavailable as a result of expungment of the record by court order based on several possible reasons. In the federal system, expungment is much more restricted than in the states, where a more liberal policy prevails. Federal courts usually require "exceptional circumstances," as when, for instance, mass arrests have been made without probable cause, or when an arrest has been made under a statute later declared unconstitutional. Lesser reasons may suffice under state law. We here wish only to alert the reader that criminal history records may be eradicated by the expungment process. A listing of the state statutes and regulations regarding the expungment of both nonconviction and conviction records appears in the aforementioned compendium.[36]

In addition to expungments of records of adults, the records of juveniles may be unavailable, either by statutory provisions, or by court considerations of the broad sociological principles of giving youthful offenders "a fresh start, free from the stain of a criminal conviction, and an opportunity to clean their slates to afford them a second chance, in terms of both jobs and standing in the community."[37]

With regard to inspection rights generally, note should be made that at least one state, Illinois, has enacted a statute that gives *employees* the right "to inspect any personal documents which are, have been or are intended to be used in determining qualifications for employment, promotion, transfer, additional compensation, discharge or other disciplinary action," subject to certain exceptions.[38] Among the exceptions are letters of reference for the employee, any portion of a test document, but with the right to see a cumulative test score of

35. *See* 28 CFR, §§ 16.32 (1991).

36. *See Compendium* (note 25), at 26–27.

37. *See* Doe v. Webster, 606 F. 2d 1226, at 1234 (1979).

38. Ill. Comp. Stats. § 820, 4012 (1992).

either an entire test or a section of it. Also excepted are "investigatory or security records maintained . . . to investigate criminal conduct by an employee or other activity by the employee which could reasonably be expected to harm the employer's property, operations, or business or could . . . cause the employer financial liability . . . "

Inquiries of Applicants and Employees About Criminal History

Because arrest records may be viewed as an unfair hindrance to employment, many states prohibit employers from inquiring of applicants or employees about arrests that have not resulted in convictions.[39]

California provides that "no employer whether a public agency or private individual or corporation shall ask an applicant for employment to disclose, through any written form or verbally, information concerning an arrest or detention which did not result in conviction . . . "[40] It further prohibits any employer from seeking or using, as a condition of employment or promotion or termination, any such record of arrest or detention not resulting in a conviction. However, exceptions are made (1) for persons arrested for a sex offense who will have "regular access" to patients in a health care facility, and (2) for persons with access to drugs and medication who have been arrested for a controlled substance offense.

A former Illinois statute, which was repealed in 1991, seemed to strike a balance between the privacy rights of an applicant and an employer's right to hire trustworthy persons.[41] It prohibited only *written* inquiries about nonconviction arrests. The rationale for the distinction between a written and an oral inquiry was that during an oral interview the applicant could explain the arrest experience and its attending circumstances. In this way an employer might learn of the arrest, while at the same time the applicant would receive some protection by virtue of the explanation opportunity.

Several courts have ruled that arrests for certain offenses may constitute grounds for discharging an employee. In one case, a federal circuit court of appeals upheld the discharge by an international airline of two employees who had been arrested for conspiracy to distribute cocaine.[42] The court stated that the discharge was not based on the mere fact of the arrest but rather on "the perception that the employee was involved in drug related activity, which could harm the company's reputation."

39. Examples: Mass. Ann. Laws, ch. 151B, § 4 (9) (1989); Va. Code Ann., § 19.2–392 (1990 & Supp. 1992).

40. Cal. Lab. Code, § 432.7 (1992).

41. Ill. Rev. Stats., Ch. 68, § 2–103 (Human Rights Act; replaced by 6 Ill. Comp. Stats. (1992), ch. 775-5/2-103.

42. Kinoshita v. Canadian Pacific Airlines, 803 F. 2d 471, 475 9th Cir. 1986).

Even with regard to actual convictions, New York, in its Correction Code, prohibits rejection on that basis, unless "(1) there is a direct relationship between one or more of the previous criminal offenses and the specific license or employment sought; or (2) the issuance of the license or the granting of the employment would involve an unreasonable risk to property, or to the safety and welfare of specific individuals, or to the general public."[43] In determining whether these statutory conditions have been met, the following factors must be considered: the elapsed time between the conviction and the employment application, applicant's age at the time the offense occurred, the relevance of the conviction upon fitness to perform in the job, and the legitimate interest of the employer in protecting property and the welfare of the general public. Also, in making the determination of fitness, the employer must give consideration to "a certificate of good conduct issued to the applicant, which certificate shall create a presumption of rehabilitation . . . "[44]

With regard to an applicant whose criminal record has been expunged, some state statutes have resolved the applicant's dilemma when asked about the offense. They provide that the applicant may answer "no record." Some states (such as New Hampshire), go even further by prescribing the exact language that must be used on an application form—"Have you ever been arrested or convicted for a crime that has not been annulled by a court?"[45]

In the absence of a governing statute on expunged or protected records, the courts generally hold that the employer's inquiry must be answered in the affirmative.[46]

Employers should be aware that the Equal Employment Opportunity Commission (EEOC) and several courts have found that the use of criminal history information in employment decisions may violate the Civil Rights Act.[47] One EEOC decision has held that the use of arrest records in determining employment is a violation of the act since it will hurt a disproportionate number of blacks because they are arrested much more frequently than whites.[48] In addition, one court has held that an employer who inquired about arrest records in the hiring process was guilty of racial discrimination, because the selection procedures had a disparate impact on blacks, and the employer could not justify the request of information as job related.[49]

43. New York Correction Law, § 752 (1987).

44. Id. § 753.

45. N.H. Rev. Stats. Ann. § 651:5 (1991).

46. *See* Spock v. Dist. of Columbia, 283 A. 2d 14, 20 (D.C. Cir. 1971); Cissel v. Brostron, 395 S.W. 2d 322 (Mo. App. 1965).

47. 42 U.S.C.A. § 2000e, Equal Employment Opportunities (1991).

48. CCH/EEOC Decisions #6564, Dec. #770-9 (1977).

49. Reynolds v. Sheet Metal Workers, 498 F. Supp. 952 (1980), *aff'd.* 702 F. 2d 221 (1981).
    An early case on disparate impact is Griggs v. Duke Power Co., 401 U.S. 424 (1971), in which the Supreme Court held that neither a general intelligence test nor a high school education could be a condition of employment when neither was shown to be related to a successful job performance, and both disqualified blacks at a substantially higher rate than whites.

An employer may also be guilty of violating the act if the employer uses conviction records alone in making employment decisions. This practice is considered to have a disproportionate effect on blacks and will therefore be unlawful unless the rejection falls within the "business necessity."[50] In order to do so, the employer must prove that the criminal conviction will prevent the applicant from performing the job in an acceptable business-like manner. Moreover, the employer must have taken into consideration the nature and gravity of the offense, the time that has passed since the crime was committed, and the requirements of the job for which the applicant is applying.[51]

An employer must also be concerned about the consequences of discharging employees who have lied either on their applications, or during their interviews, about not having a criminal history. To establish racial discrimination under these circumstances, an employee would have to show that black employees had been discharged for lying about their past criminal records at a higher rate than white employees who also made misstatements about not having prior arrest or conviction records.[52] One court found that when an employer's established termination policy is discretionary, an employee cannot prove racial discrimination by showing that others who also lied were not discharged.[53] In this case, the discharged employee was unable to demonstrate a racial intent by the employer, since none of the employees (white or black) who had previously lied about their criminal pasts were fired. The court also found that the employer had a legitimate reason for the discharge, since the conviction of sexual procurement made the employee unsuitable to care for psychiatric patients.

(The general subject of civil rights in the context of applicant questioning is further discussed in Chapter 10.)

INTERBUSINESS EXCHANGE OF INFORMATION REGARDING APPLICANTS, EMPLOYEES, AND CUSTOMERS

Although significant protective security information is available through the previously described processes, a source of additional material is the interbusiness exchange provided by businesses themselves. This exchange also helps to make available information on customers and other persons such as shoplifters.

---

50. EEOC Dec. 81-7 (Nov. 1980), 33 ALR Fed. 263, § 7-(b) Supp. (1991).

51. Green v. Missouri Pacific Railroad, 549 F. 2d 1158 (1977), in which an injunction was issued against the defendant from using conviction records as an absolute bar to employment.

   The subject of the utilization of criminal history information in applicant questioning is subsequently discussed in Chapter 10.

52. Jimerson v. Kisco, 542 F. 2d 1008 (1976).

53. Osborne v. Cleland, 620 F. 2d 195 (8th Cir. 1980).

Information on Applicants and Employees

Interbusiness exchange of information about applicants and employees can be very helpful, not only as a protection against internal theft and other criminal conduct, but also as a protection to others who come into contact with employees in the transaction of the employer's business. Certain legal risks, however, attend such exchange of information.

Employers are most commonly sued for defamation (libel or slander) when they provide, usually at the request of a prospective employer, derogatory information about a present or former employee. Truth of the supplied information is usually a complete defense to any defamatory action when the protected interest is a personal reputation.[54]

Statements that cannot reasonably be interpreted as containing "facts" about an individual are not defamatory.[55] A liability is incurred, however, when the disclosed information consists of statements of facts that are false; and if that information concerns a criminal offense, the accusation may result in a monetary award without proof of actual damages.[56]

Even with regard to truthful disclosures, there are some qualifications. Employers are usually protected by a qualified privilege when they make statements to another person who has an interest or a duty regarding the subject matter, such as security personnel or personnel managers.[57] However, this privilege requires that such statements be made in good faith. Consequently, maliciousness or recklessness will defeat the privilege.

Several states have enacted statutes granting immunity for good faith disclosures of job performance information.[58]

Dissemination of information outside the employer–employee community may give rise to another form of action by employees, one based on a violation of the right to privacy.[59] Such an action has considerable limitations, however, by reason of the First Amendment right to free speech.[59]

In a situation where an employee is discharged for what the employer considers dishonest conduct, consideration should be given to a recent case law development on defamation. It is exemplified by a Minnesota Supreme Court decision regarding the tort liability requirement of a "publication" of the alleged defamation.[60] The case involved the following facts: Several employees were fired because they

---

54. In Cox Broadcasting Corp. v. Cohn, 420 U.S. 469, 489 (1975), the Court distinguishes between an injury to someone's personal reputation and an invasion of privacy.

55. Milkovich v. Lorain Journal Co., 497 U.S. 1 (1990).

56. Barlow v. International Harvester Co., 95 Idaho 881, 522 P. 2d 1102 (1974); Babb v. Minder, 806 F. 2d 749 (7th Cir. 1986).

57. *See* Curtis Publishing Co. v. Butts, 388 U.S. 130 (1967); Austin v. Torrington Co., 810 F. 2d 416 (4th Cir. 1987), *cert. denied*, 484 U.S. 977 (1987), Chamber v. Am. Trans. Air, 577 N. E. 2d 612 (Ind. App. 1991).

58. *See, e.g.,* Alas. Stats., § 9.65.160 (1993); Ga. Code, § 54–1104 (1993).

59. Briscoe v. Readers Digest Assoc. 93 Cal. Rptr. 866, 483 P. 2d 34, 42–43 (1971).

60. Lewis v. Equitable Life Assurance Soc., 389 N.W. 2d 876 (Minn. 1986).

had refused to revise their expense reports involving expenses incurred while working out-of-town on behalf of the employer. The reason given to them, *and to them alone*, for their discharge was "gross insubordination." When they were seeking other employment some of them, in response to questions regarding their previous employment, revealed to prospective employers the stated reason for their dismissal—"gross insubordination."

As to whether the disclosure by the employees themselves—and not by the employer—constituted a "publication," the Minnesota court concluded that "the plaintiffs were compelled to repeat the alleged defamatory statement" and "the company knew plaintiffs would be so compelled." Thus the required test of a "publication" was met. In other words, the employees thought they were required to disclose the "gross insubordination" reason for their discharge. The court let stand the jury's finding that the employer acted "with actual malice which defeated the employer's qualified privilege." It added that the employer's stated reasons "went beyond accusations and were conclusory statements." The court also upheld the jury's finding that the charge of "gross insubordination" was false.

A dissenting opinion in the foregoing case expressed the view that under the majority's reasoning "the only way an employer can avoid litigation and possible liability for substantial damages is to cease communicating the reason it felt justified the termination, not only to third persons, but even to the employee . . . "[61]

Information on Customers and Other Persons

The tremendous financial losses incurred by businesses from shoplifting and other criminal conduct by customers and others who enter on the premises necessitate the lawful procurement of whatever information is available regarding potential offenders. Merchants also have an interest in knowing whether their patrons are credit worthy. Consequently, businesses are permitted to exchange information of that type among themselves. They must be aware, however, of the attending risk of being held liable for defamation.

Imputing criminal behavior to an individual may be considered defamatory per se and actionable without proof of actual damage. However, a merchant may avoid liability if she can prove that the derogatory information is true, or that she possesses a "qualified privilege," often referred to as a "common interest privilege," to disclose to other merchants criminal behavior of customers.

To exercise the qualified privilege the business must be able to prove that untrue information (1) was communicated in good faith; (2) was on a subject in which the business had an interest, or there was a public or private duty to communicate it; and (3) was communicated to someone with a corresponding

---

61. For a recent case rejecting the "self-compelled" defamation principle, see Layne v. Builders Plumbing Co., 210 Ill. App. 3d 966, 569 N.E. 2d 1104 (1991). *See also* annots. in 62 A.L.R. 4th 581, at 632 (1988).

interest.[62] Understandably, the privilege becomes unavailable if the disclosure extends beyond the interbusiness interests, or if the information is given to persons who have no legitimate use for it.[63]

The following two cases illustrate situations in which the qualified privilege is available and when it is not. In one case, information about a suspected shoplifter was transmitted from a security officer in one store to a security officer in another store; in the other case the derogatory information was communicated from a store manager to nonsecurity personnel at a different store. The privilege doctrine prevailed in the first case, but was held inapplicable in the second.[64]

Creditors who submit erroneous reports to a credit reporting agency are usually protected by the privilege, absent actual malice or reckless disregard for the truth.[65]

62. Boydston v. Chrysler, 511 N.E. 2d 318 (Ind. App. 1987).

63. Shallenberger v. Scoggins-Tomlinson, 439 N.E. 2d 699 (Ind. App. 1982).

64. Danberg v. Sears Roebuck & Co., 198 Neb. 234, 252 N.W. 2d 168 (1977) (privilege allowed); Brown v. P.N. Hirsch, 661 S.W. 2d 587 (Mo. App. 1983) (privilege disallowed).

65. Boydston v. Chrysler, *supra* note 62. For the requirement that in order for a credit report to come within the qualified privilege, it must involve matters of public concern and the free flow of commercial information, *see* Dun & Bradstreet v. Greenmoss Builders, 472 U.S. 749 (1985).

9

Laws and Governmental Regulations Regarding Psychological Testing for Dishonesty Among Applicants

The present chapter is devoted to the usage of psychological tests by employers to ascertain employee proclivity toward dishonesty.

For many years, psychologists, sociologists, and criminologists have attempted to predict delinquent behavior on the basis of psychological tests. In the past, the tests were usually used primarily for diagnostic and treatment purposes, but recently they have been used for the prediction of one specific kind of delinquent behavior—theft. The potential value of this type of test to employers is readily apparent, in view of the extensive losses sustained by business and industry from employee thievery.

Currently, the form of psychological test most widely used in employment situations is a "pencil-and-paper" questionnaire. For illustrative purposes we shall describe the first one ever used, and a leading one in the field, the Reid Report.

The Reid Report, developed by John E. Reid, became available to the business community in 1951. Its appearance was followed by other tests that were more or less modeled after the Reid prototype. All of them, including the Reid test, are known in the testing field as proprietary tests, because the publisher does not release the scoring key to the employer.[1]

This text focuses on the Reid report because, in addition to that test being the pioneer, it is highly rated in a significant number of business, psychological, and

---

1. The three largest testing companies are Reid Psychological Systems (Chicago, Illinois); London House (Rosemont, Illinois); and Stanton Corporation (Charlotte, North Carolina).

criminological publications,[2] and it has survived the scrutiny of civil rights commissions.[3]

Following our discussion of the nature and operation of the test is an analysis of the various legal issues presented by it and, indeed, by any other psychological testing procedure that may be used for a similar purpose.

The Reid Report, as an applicant test, consists essentially of a questionnaire with approximately 80 yes/no questions, accompanied by biographical data questions, and by a list of thefts or theft-related acts which the examinee may have committed. It consists of four parts.

In Part 1, trustworthiness is determined mainly by the examinee's yes/no answers which reveal (a) his concept of punitiveness, as reflected in his answers to such questions as "Do you believe a person should be fired by a company if it is found that he helped another employee take a little merchandise from the company?"; and (b) his projective appraisal of his own trustworthiness, as disclosed in his answers to such questions as "Did you ever think about committing a burglary?"

No one answer, or even several answers, can determine trustworthiness. Reliance is placed only upon a total score, for which the answers are keyed toward one conclusion or the other.

Part 2 is a criminal admissions questionnaire which inquires about the examinee's possible commission and/or conviction for various illegal activities. Incredible as it may seem, many examinees admit to committing not only minor thefts but also serious crimes, such as burglaries and robberies. The presumed reason for this phenomenon is that a person making the admissions views their conduct to be within the "normal" category.

Part 3 is an illegal drug usage questionnaire which inquires about the frequency of recent drug use, which in many instances is a factor involved in theft. Here again, a surprising number of examinees admit to recently using illegal drugs during or just before going to work.

Part 4 is the work history questionnaire. This part is similar to many job applications in the information it provides; however, test administrators have found this part extremely useful in detecting inconsistencies in the examinee's job history.

---

2. The following general evaluation by Stanley L. Brodsky, Professor of Psychology, University of Alabama, appears in the 1978 (Eighth) *Mental Measurements Yearbook*, edited by Oscar Kresen Buros: "The overall assessment [of the Reid Report] is that it is a straightforward, meaningful, and useful test. Much more information on reliability has been gathered than on most such instruments ... [It is] a solid and useful measure of potential employee dishonesty." *See also* M.R. CUNNINGHAM AND P. ASH, *The Structure of Honesty: Factor Analysis of the Reid Report*, 3 J. BUS. PSYCHOL. 54–66 (1987); P. ASH, *Screening Employment Applicants for Attitudes Toward Theft*, 55 J. APPL. PSYCHOL. 161–164 (1971); M.R. CUNNINGHAM, D.T. WONG, AND BARBEE, *Self Presentation Dynamics on Overt Integrity Test: Experimental Studies of the Reid Report*, 79 J. APPL. PSYCHOL. 643–658 (1994).

3. *See* Equal Employment Opportunity Commission, charge #31A920266, 11/30/92 (Dallas, Texas); Illinois Dept. of Human Rights, charge #1989 C.F. 2327, 319192 (Chicago, IL); Equal Employment Opportunity Commission, charge #28191099, 9/20/91 (Kansas City, MO); Equal Employment Opportunity Commission, charge #104850357, 12/18/85 (San Francisco, CA); Equal Employment Opportunity Commission, charge #033850205, 6128185 (Baltimore, MD).

The Reid Report can be scored by the employer in a variety of ways, the most common of which is communication by telephone or by computer software with the test suppplier. Regardless of the procedure used, however, the scoring key is not released to the employer or to anyone else.

Although the Reid Report was designed explicitly to identify employment applicants who have unfavorable attitudes toward honesty, some research has demonstrated that it can also predict other employment related behaviors such as productivity, time theft, absenteeism, turnover, and even positive aspects of personality.[4]

RELIABILITY OF PENCIL-AND-PAPER HONESTY TESTS

Reid Psychological Systems accords to its tests a high degree of reliability, based upon its many years of administering them to over seven million examinees since 1964. This claim of reliability is also shared by the other major publishers. All test manuals recommend, nevertheless, that test scores should not be used solely to determine eligibility for employment.

Three studies, reported in 1990–1992, have been conducted by nonproducers of the tests regarding their validity and reliability. One was by a task force of the American Psychological Association (APA), which is comprised of 108,000 psychologists; another by the Office of Technology Assessment (OTA) of the United States Congress; and a third by researchers at the University of Iowa.

The APA issued its report in 1991 under the title of The Prediction of Trustworthiness in Pre-Employment Selection Decisions.[5] The guideline for any such study, as urged in the report, was stated as follows:

> . . . the [tests] should not be evaluated against absolute levels of validity; rather they must be evaluated comparatively against the validities of other procedures that would inevitably be used in their stead . . . For any potential problem with honesty tests, one must determine the extent to which alternative procedures used for the same purpose would be similarly indicted.[6]

The task force report stated that the error problem regarding pencil-and-paper tests is not dissimilar from that of any other selection instrument, such as aptitude testing, interviews, or educational requirements—"all of which are fallible to some degree."

After having considered the various available data regarding the reliability of pencil-and-paper tests, and other relevant factors, the APA task force concluded that "there is no sound basis for prohibiting [their] development and

---

4. *See* S. KOCHKIN, *Personality Correlates of a Measure of Honesty*, 1 J. BUS. & PSYCHOL. 236–247 (1987); R.C. HOLLINGER AND J.P. CLARK, THEFT BY EMPLOYEES 240 (1983).

5. *Science Directorate*, American Psychological Association (1991), 1200 Seventeenth St., N.W. Washington, D.C. 20036.

6. APA Report, note 2 at 7.

use."[7] To do so, stated the report, would only invite alternative forms of pre-employment screening that would be less reliable and less controllable.

The Office of Technology Assessment (OTA) issued its report in 1990 under the title of *The Use of Integrity Test for Employment Screening.*[8] At the time of the study and the report, the OTA was a unit of a Congressional Board comprised of six senators and six members of the House of Representatives. A co-chairman of the Board was Senator Edward M. Kennedy, who had been a prime mover in the passage of Congress' antipolygraph act in 1988. That act practically eliminated the usage of the polygraph technique by private employers.

The OTA report was generally critical of pencil-and-paper tests, but it ultimately concluded that "The research on integrity tests has not produced data that clearly supports or dismisses the assertion that these tests can predict dishonest behavior."[9]

Although the report stated that in order to ascertain integrity test reliability, "sophisticated analytical methods" had to be applied, the OTA itself relied primarily on a single experiment and set of data. They were described as follows:

> A total of 3,790 employees were given the test and hired regardless of their test performance. Subsequent investigations by management revealed that 91 employees had committed some type of theft. Among these 91, 75 had failed the integrity test and 16 had passed. Among the 3,699 for whom the investigation did not reveal any theft, 2,145 had failed the test and 1,554 passed. Thus, 75 of those taking the test (2 percent of the total 3,790) are known to have been characterized correctly by the test, and 16 are known to have been characterized incorrectly. But what about the rest?
>
> If those 3,699 not detected as thieves are assumed to be honest, then 2,145 (58 percent) were misclassified; if a substantial number of them were indeed thieves, the observed correlation between the test and the outcome measure could be higher, lower, or equal to the actual correlation.[10]

Considerable criticism has been expressed about the OTA study, regarding both its methodology and its inferences from the resulting data. Moreover, in the Report itself reference is made in the following terms to the view of one of the OTA's own five contractors, Dr. Robert M. Guion, "a prominent personnel psychologist," who believes that "while integrity tests are far from perfect, they are better than any available alternative for screening and selecting honest job applicants."[11]

---

7. APA Report, at 26.

8. The report is obtainable, on purchase, as OTA-SET-442 [Order processing code 6889], from U.S. Government Printing Office, Washington, D.C. 20402-9325. [Telephone: (202) 783-3238] [$4.00 MC/Visa].

9. OTA Report p. 8.

10. OTA Report p. 54.

11. OTA Report p. 9.

Additional criticism of the OTA Report appears in the 1992 Annual Review of Psychology. In its section on personnel selection, it labels the OTA report as "superficial and in part clearly erroneous."[12]

The most recent, and by far the most extensive appraisal of integrity tests, was conducted by researchers at the University of Iowa.[13] They analyzed 665 studies from a database of 576,460 test takers. The results disclosed that the test validities are positive, and in many instances substantial for predicting job performance, as well as various forms of counterproductive behavior (theft, disciplinary problems, absenteeism, etc.).

LEGAL ISSUES

The Civil Rights Act of 1964 as Amended in 1991

An important legal issue regarding integrity testing, or any other test of a similar nature, is compliance with the requirements of the 1964 Civil Rights Act, as amended in 1991,[14] and comparable fair employment laws on the state level.[15] Specifically, the issue is whether such testing involves discrimination or other illegal employment practices.

The underlying purpose of the Civil Rights Act is "to achieve equality of employment opportunities,"[16] and to provide victims of employment discrimination with "substantive rights and a federal forum for their vindication."[17]

The federal statute only applies to employers of fifteen or more employees who are engaged in an industry affecting interstate commerce,[18] but some state laws apply to employers of a fewer number.[19]

---

12. See F.L. SCHMIDT, D.S. ONES, AND J.E. HUNTER, *Personnel Selection*, 1992 ANNU. REV. PSYCHOL. 627–70 (1992).

13. See D.S. ONES, C. VISWESVARAN, AND F.L. SCHMIDT, *Meta-Analysis of Integrity Test Validities: Findings and Implications for Personnel Selection and Theories of Job Performance*, J. APPL. PSYCHOL. (1993).

14. 42 U.S.C. 2000 (1988).

15. States *without* such statues are Alabama and Arkansas. Louisiana requires "intentional discrimination." The laws in Georgia and Mississippi do not apply to private employers. In these various states, however, their courts invoke the federal law.

16. Griggs v. Duke Power Co., 401 U.S. 424, 429-30 (1971).

17. Dubnick v. Firestone Tire & Rubber Co. of California, 355 F. Supp. 138, 141-42 (E.D.N.Y. 1973), *quoting* Pure Oil Co. v. Suarez, 384 U.S. 202, 206 (1966). Note must be made, however, that "initial resort to state and local remedies is mandated, and resort to the federal forum is appropriate only when the state does not provide prompt or complete relief." New York Gaslight Club, Inc. v. Carey, 447 U.S. 54, 65 (1980).

18. 42 U.S.C. 2000 (e) (1988).

19. See, e.g., Pa. Stats. Ann., 43:954 (West Supp. 1993) (anyone employing four or more individuals); R. I. Gen. Laws, 28-5-6 (West Supp. 1992) (four or more); and Iowa Code Ann., 216.2 (West Supp. 1993) (every person employing anyone within the state).

With regard to federal employers there also exists a Presidential Executive Order directed toward the same objective as the Civil Rights Act—the elimination of discriminatory employment practices.[20] All contractors with the federal government are also covered by the executive order.[21]

The most relevant portion of the Civil Rights Act makes it an unlawful employment practice for an employer "to fail or refuse to hire or to discharge any individual, or otherwise to discriminate against any individual with respect to his compensation, terms, conditions, or privileges of employment, because of such individual's race, color, religion, sex, or national origin . . . "[22] The Act provides, however, that "it shall not be an unlawful employment practice for an employer . . . to give and to act on the results of any professionally developed ability test provided that such test, its administration or action upon the results is not designed, intended or used to discriminate because of race, color, religion, sex or national origin."[23]

The implementation of the federal civil rights legislation is the responsibility of the Equal Employment Opportunity Commission (EEOC), which was established by Congress in the Civil Rights Act.[24] On the state level there are agencies comparable to EEOC, known by various names, such as commission for human rights, civil rights commission, fair employment practices commission, and department of fair employment.[25]

Regulations and guidelines are promulgated by both federal and state commissions. They will be discussed later in this chapter.

TESTS FOR ASCERTAINING DISCRIMINATORY EMPLOYMENT PRACTICES

The following discussion of the legal tests for discrimatory practices presents issues that pertain primarily to ordinary employment situations rather than to psychological testing for dishonesty; however, the same basic principles are applicable.

In attempting to prove discrimination in violation of the Civil Rights Act (or a comparable state statute), the plaintiff has two separate but related paths to pursue: a showing of either "disparate treatment" or "disparate impact."

---

20. Presidential Executive Order No. 11,478, 3 C.F.R. 207 (1974) *reprinted* in 42 U.S.C. app. at 402 (1988).

21. Presidential Executive Order No. 11,246, 3 C.F.R. 169 (1974), *reprinted* in 42 U.S.C., app. at 398 (1988).

22. 42 U.S.C. § 2000e-2(a)(1)(1988).

23. 42 U.S.C. § 2000e-2(h)(1988).

24. 42 U.S.C. § 2000e-4(1988).

25. Illustrative are: Alas. Commission for Human Rights; Ill. Human Rights Commission; Iowa Civil Rights Commission; and Wyo. Fair Employment Commission. As stated in note 19, *supra,* some laws apply to employers of a lesser number of employees than does the federal statute.

"Disparate treatment" occurs when some employees or applicants are treated less favorably than others, based on race, color, religion, sex or national origin; "disparate impact" occurs when an employer's practices, though facially neutral, fall more harshly on one group or another, without a justification of business necessity.[26] Both shall be discussed separately.

Disparate Treatment Test

The Supreme Court has outlined procedures to be followed in cases with respect to burden of proof and the presentation of evidence.[27] First, the plaintiff has the burden of proving by a preponderance of the evidence a prima facie case of discrimination.[28] If the prima facie case is established, the burden shifts to the defendant to show that "the plaintiff was rejected, or someone else was preferred for a legitimate, nondiscriminatory reason."[29] However, the defendant need not persuade the court that it was actually motivated by the proffered reasons. It is sufficient if the evidence raises a genuine issue of fact as to whether there was discrimination against the plaintiff. To accomplish this, the defendant must clearly set forth, through the introduction of admissible evidence, the reasons for rejection.[30]

If the defendant's burden is met, the plaintiff has the opportunity to prove by a preponderance of the evidence that the legitimate reasons offered by the defendant were not its true reasons, but were a pretext for discrimination. Basically, in disparate treatment cases, "proof of a discriminatory motive is critical"; and motive can be established either by an outward intent to discriminate or by inference based on the mere fact of differences in treatment.[31]

26. For definitions and comparison between disparate treatment and disparate impact, see Chrisner v. Complete Auto Transit, Inc., 645 F.2d 1251, 1257 (6th Cir. 1981). *See also* the *1978 Uniform Guidelines on Employee Selection Procedures*, 8 LABOR REL. REP. (BNA) (403 Fair Employment Practice Manual) § 1607.11 (1990) which states: "Disparate treatment occurs where members of a race, sex, or ethnic group have been denied the same employment, promotion, membership, or other employment opportunities as have been available to other employees or applicants."

"Disparate impact involves facially neutral practices that are not intended to be discriminatory, but are discriminatory in effect." *Fair Employment Rules,* 1 EMPLOYMENT PRACTICES GUIDE (CCH) TT 252 (1992).

27. McDonnell Douglas Co. v. Green, 411 U.S. 792, 802 (1973).

28. The applicant for employment can establish a prima facie case of discrimination by showing: (a) that he belongs to a racial minority; (b) that he applied and was qualified for a job for which the employer was seeking applicants; (c) that, despite his qualifications, he was rejected; and (d) that, after his rejection, the position remained open and the employer continued to seek applicants from persons of complainant's qualifications. *Supra* note 27 at 802, 1824. *See also* EEOC v. Chicago Miniature Lamp Works, 947 F.2d 292, 299 (7th Cir. 1991) (a prima facie case of disparate treatment can be established by using statistical evidence to demonstrate substantial disparities in minority employment if there is also evidence of general policies or specific instances of discrimination).

29. Texas Dep't. of Community Affairs v. Burdine, 450 U.S. 248, 254 (1981).

30. Johnson v. Bunny Bread Co., 646 F. 2d 1250, 1254 (8th Cir. 1981).

31. International Brhd. of Teamsters v. United States, 431 U.S. 324, 335 note 15 (1977).

Disparate Impact Test

The focus of inquiry in disparate impact cases begins with the burden on the plaintiff to show that the employment practice selects applicants for employment or promotion in a pattern significantly different from that within the pool of applicants or employees,[32] even though the practice may be facially neutral and unintentional.[33]

As analyzed in an excellent article published in 1980, there are three general approaches that have been used to establish a prima facie case of disparate impact with regard to applicants for employment.[34] Only two of them, however, need be mentioned as relevant to psychological testing. The first approach is the "applicant statistics" approach, which involves "a comparison of the percentage of minority applicants successfully passing the test with the percentage of majority applicants successfully passing the test."[35] Several courts have expressed a preference for this approach.[36]

32. *See* Johnson v. Bunny Bread Co., *supra* note 30, where the plaintiff relied on generalized statistics to persuade the trial court that an inference of a particular discriminatory intent should be drawn. The court of appeals held, however, that statistical evidence that the employer's work force was 2.7% black, whereas the surrounding city was 4.1% black and the surrounding country was 3.0% black was insufficient to establish a pretext for firing the black employee. This does not mean, however, that generalized statistics can never be used to raise an inference of discriminatory intent.

33. Albemarle Paper Co. v. Moody, 422 U.S. 405, 425 (1975). *See also* Connecticut v. Teal, 457 U.S. 440 (1982), where the court found that a prima facie case of disparate impact could be established, based on a written promotional exam that allegedly discriminated against minorities, even though the "bottom line" result of the promotional process was an appropriate racial balance. The court stated, "Congress never intended to give an employer license to discriminate against some employees on the basis of race or sex merely because he favorably treats other members of the employee's group." *Id.* at 454, 2534.

34. The authors of the article are DEAN BOOTH and JAMES L. MACKAY of the Georgia Bar. It is entitled *Legal Constraints on Employment Testing and Evolving Trends in the Law,* and appears in 29 EMORY L. J. 121–94 (1980). The article is an invaluable source of information for lawyers confronted with any of the many problems suggested by the title.
    The authors state at 142, note 102 that the three approaches are discussed in Green v. Missouri Pac. R.R. Co., 523 F. 2d 1290, 1293–94 (8th Cir. 1975) and in League of United Latin Am. Citizens v. City of Santa Ana, 410 F. Supp. 873, 891–92 (C.D. Cal. 1976).

35. Booth and Mackay, *supra* note 34, at 142.

36. Hester v. Southern Ry Co., 497 F.2d 1374, 1379 (5th Cir. 1977) (noting that the initial inquiry courts must make in evaluating employee testing is whether the tests "operate to disqualify Negroes at a substantially higher rate than whites.") [*Quoting* Griggs v. Duke Power Co. 401 U.S. 424, 426 (1971)].
    Applicant statistics, however, may not be persuasive when the applicant pool is atypical or otherwise suspect, or there is a history of prior discrimination by the employer and it is reasonable to expect a chilling effect on potential minority applicants. Rodriguez v. East Tex. Motor Freight Sys., Inc., 505 F.2d 40, 55–56 (5th Cir. 1974), vacated and remanded on other grounds, 431 U.S. 395 (1977). Similarly, the *Uniform Guidelines on Employee Selection Procedures* also recognizes that "Greater differences in selection rate may not constitute adverse impact . . . where special recruiting or other programs cause the pool of minority or female candidates to be atypical of the normal pool of applicants from that group." 29 C.F.R. § 1607.4(D)(1992).

The second approach involves "a comparison of the percentage of minority persons employed in the specific job or jobs for which the test is required with the percentage of minority persons in the relevant geographic labor market."[37] Although this "population statistics" approach has been used by many courts,[38] most are reluctant to find that these statistics are sufficient to establish adverse impact in the absence of either "gross" disparities[39] or strong corroborating evidence of discrimination.[40] In other words, most courts recognize that differences in employment levels relative to the population can result from many reasons other than discrimination.[41]

Some decisions, though approving the use of population statistics, have narrowed their application; the relevant labor pool must be based both on the geographical area from which the employer draws its labor force and on those persons in the pool who are qualified for the job.[42] However, in the 1989 case of *Wards Cove Packing Co. v. Atonio*, the Supreme Court made more difficult the burden and standard of proof that plaintiffs had to meet.[43] Then, in the 1991 amend-

---

37. Booth and Mackay, *supra* note 34, at 142.

38. *See, e.g.*, International Bhd. of Teamsters v. United States, *supra* note 31, at 337, where the court noted that there were terminals in areas of substantial minority populations, but that all of the company's line drivers in these areas were white. *See*, however, Hazelwood Sch. Dist. v. United States, 433 U.S. 299, 308 (1977), which distinguishes between skilled and unskilled jobs. The Court held that the "population statistics" approach is appropriate only when unskilled jobs are at issue. When special skills are required to fill certain positions, the Court found the comparison should be between the percentage of minority persons employed in the jobs and the racial composition of the *qualified* population in the relevant labor market.

39. Waisome v. Port Authority of N.Y. & N.J., 948 F.2d 1370 (2d Cir. 1991) ("Statistical evidence may be probative where it reveals a disparity so great that it cannot be accounted for by chance.").

40. For example, in Watson v. Fort Worth, *supra* note 30, at 994, 2788–2789, the court held that the plaintiff must show more than statistical disparities. The plaintiff must be able to identify the specific employment practice that is being challenged and must then prove that this practice causes the disparity.

41. For example, the court in EEOC v. Chicago Miniature Lamps, *supra* note 28, at 302, found that people will not commute very far for economic reasons when the jobs are low-paying. Perhaps, therefore, only smaller geographic areas should be analyzed for unskilled jobs. In addition, the sample size can have the effect, as one court noted, that "the smaller the sample size, the greater the likelihood that the underrepresentation reflects chance rather than discriminatory practices." Williams v. Tallahassee Motors, Inc., 607 F.2d 689, 693 (5th Cir. 1979).

42. *See, e.g.*, Gilmore v. Kansas City Terminal Ry. Co., 509 F.2d 48, 52 (8th Cir. 1975) (court required data from the "relevant market area"); Hazelwood Sch. Dist. v. United States *supra* note 38. *See also* Johnson v. Uncle Ben's Inc., 965 F.2d 1363 (5th Cir. 1992) (where the court compared the percentage of Black employees at the company with the percentage of Blacks in the pool of qualified applicants), and Chrisner v. Complete Auto Transit, Inc., *supra* note 26, at 1258 (when special skills are required for certain positions, comparisons to the general population may have little probative valve).

43. 490 U.S. 642 (1989). For example, the Court found that once the plaintiff had proved a prima facie case of disparate impact by identifying a specific employment practice that caused a significant disparity, the burden shifted to the defendant to show business necessity. However, the defendant's burden was found to be one of production only, with the ultimate burden of persuasion resting upon the plaintiff at all times.

ment to the Civil Rights Act, Congress stated in its "findings" that the *Wards Cove* decision had "weakened the scope and effectiveness of Federal civil rights protections," and that legislation was necessary "to provide additional protection against unlawful discrimination in employment."[44] Consequently, an amendment codified the concepts of "business necessity" and "job related" that the Supreme Court had enunciated in its decisions prior to *Wards Cove*. The result was that the majority of disparate impact decisions subsequent to *Wards Cove* became no longer applicable.

Although litigation will probably be required to determine the ultimate impact of the Civil Rights Act of 1991, the statute generally[45] states that the following process shall be adhered to in disparate impact cases:

1. The complaining party must demonstrate a prima facie case of discrimination by showing that the employer uses a selection process significantly adverse to a protected minority group in the relevant labor pool;
2. Once a prima facie case is established, the burden shifts to the employer to either demonstrate that the specific practice does not cause the alleged impact, or that the practice is job related for the available position, and consistent with business necessity;
3. If the test is job related, the complainant may still prevail if proof is offered that other available tests would not produce a similar disproportionate effect while at the same time serving the employer's legitimate interests.

THE EQUAL EMPLOYMENT OPPORTUNITY COMMISSION (EEOC) GUIDELINES

In its 1966 Guidelines, the EEOC sought, among other objectives, to establish a "job-related" requirement for preemployment testing.[46] It allowed for the usage of a "professionally developed ability test," which was interpreted as follows: "It means," said the Commission, "a test which fairly measures ... the applicant's ability to perform a particular job or class of jobs." Then, in 1970, a new set of regulations was issued by the Commission which greatly expanded the earlier regulations and specified certain technical requirements for test validation. This revised set proved to be so restrictive, however, that the regulations were viewed as effectively precluding almost all usage of employment testing.[47] Nevertheless, the Supreme Court in two subsequent decisions accorded considerable deference to the 1970 Guidelines.

---

44. Civil Rights Act, 42 U.S.C.A. § 1981, app. at 89 (Supp. 1992).

45. Civil Rights Act, 42 U.S.C.A. § 2000e-2 (K) (l) (a) (West Supp. 1993).

46. 29 C.F.R. § 1607. The guidelines were entitled *Guidelines on Employment Selection Procedures* (Aug. 1966).

47. *See* Booth and Mackey, *supra* note 34, at 125.

In the 1971 case of *Griggs v. Duke Power Co.*,[48] the Court faulted an intelligence test on the grounds that its use had a disproportionate impact on job-transfer applicants and that the employer had failed to demonstrate "business necessity" sufficient to justify the test usage. The relevant significance of the decision is that it accorded "great deference" to the EEOC "job-relatedness" requirement. According to the Court, not only overt discrimination is proscribed, but also practices that although fair in form are discriminatory in operation. The "touchstone is business necessity," said the Court, and "[i]f an employment practice which operates to exclude Negroes cannot be shown to be related to job performance, the practice is prohibited."[49] What this means is that if a given employment selection technique has a disproportionate impact upon one race or one suspect class, and the employer cannot show that the requirement has a manifest relationship to the employment in question, the selection technique is prohibited.

The Supreme Court next considered the force and effect of the 1970 Guidelines in *Albemarle Paper Co. v. Moody*.[50] That decision, however, represents the high point in the Court's deference to the Guidelines. Although it was there held that the validation study was insufficient to demonstrate job relatedness, the Court stated that "discriminatory tests are impermissible unless shown, by professionally acceptable methods, to be predictive of or significantly correlated with important elements of work behavior which comprise or are relevant to the job or jobs for which candidates are being evaluated."[51] The Court seemed to suggest that the question of whether an employment test was "job related" was determined by the employer's adherence to the Guidelines. Both Justices Burger and Blackmun, in opinions dissenting in part from that of the majority, argued vigorously against the majority's deference to the Guidelines.

One year after the decision in *Albemarle*, the Court decided *Washington v. Davis*,[52] a decision that led the way toward a de-emphasis of the 1970 Guidelines. The Court modified its *Albemarle* position in two ways. First, it held that, although disproportionate impact was not irrelevant, "it is not the sole touchstone of an invidious racial discrimination forbidden by the Constitution."[53] The Court appeared to suggest that intent to discriminate is the important factor. Second, in contrast to what was previously presumed, a training-course performance, and not just job performance, could be utilized in validating promotion testing procedures. This placed a less burdensome task upon employers than did the 1970 Guidelines.

In 1976, in realization of the Supreme Court's reluctance to fully accept the 1970 Guidelines, the Departments of Justice and Labor, and the Civil Service Commission, proposed the "Federal Executive Agency Guidelines on Employment

48. 401 U.S. 424 (1971).

49. *Id.* at 431.

50. 422 U.S. 405 (1975).

51. *Id.* at 431.

52. 426 U.S. 229 (1976).

53. *Id.* at 244.

Selection Procedures."[54] Declining to adopt them, EEOC proceeded to republish its 1970 Guidelines in substantially unaltered form.[55] Then, in 1978, EEOC agreed to the drafting of a set of uniform guidelines which, when drafted and adopted, were very similar to the ones that had been proposed by the Justice and Labor Departments and the Civil Service Commission. The guidelines are now entitled "Uniform Guidelines on Employee Selection Procedures."[56] Although they purport to incorporate "a single set of principles . . . to assist employers [and others] to comply with requirements of Federal law . . . [and] provide a framework for determining the proper use of tests and other selection procedures," the court decisions do not seem to accord them much weight.

The procedural posture of an employment discrimination claim is as follows: Before a charging party can file a civil rights suit in a federal court, a charge must first be filed with the EEOC or a comparable state agency. In fact, if the state has such an agency, which is considered a "deferral" agency of EEOC, the charges must be filed with it before any can be filed with EEOC itself.[57] After the agency process has been pursued, a complainant who wishes further consideration may file a complaint with the EEOC.[58] Only after a disposition by EEOC may suit be filed in the federal court.[59]

Although the Civil Rights Act itself prescribes procedures, EEOC Guidelines deal with such substantive matters as the validity of tests used for employment and promotion. In other words, the act governs exclusively the procedures for bringing suit, but the EEOC Guidelines may be applied to testing procedures. Any testing technique that is used as a basis for an employment decision should first be validated to avoid the consequences of a selection procedure being ultimately considered discriminatory because of an adverse impact. It is important to note, however, that an employer has no legal obligation, at the outset, to validate a selection procedure if the test itself does not appear to have a significant impact on a protected group.

Enforcement action will be taken, however, if one component is discriminatory, even if the overall selection process is not.

PROHIBITED INQUIRIES

As discussed in Chapter 8, there are restrictions in some jurisdictions upon employer access to the criminal history records of applicants and employees. Where access is curtailed as, for instance, with nonconviction arrests, it is reasonable to

54. 41 Fed. Reg. 51734 (1976).
55. 41 Fed. Reg. 51984 (1976).
56. 29 C.F.R. § 1607 (1979).
57. 42 U.S.C. § 2000e-5 (c) (1988).
58. 42 U.S.C. § 2000e-5 (d) (1988).
59. 42 U.S.C. § 2000e-5 (f) (1988).

assume that test questions about the protected information would also be restricted. In that eventuality we recommend that the test questions be confined to criminal acts the subject may have *committed,* or about *convictions* that had been incurred. This practice is pursued by Reid Psychological Systems, which also limits, in deference to certain state laws, inquiries about convictions within a period of five years prior to the testing.[60]

A shorter version of this chapter, prepared by the senior author, was published under the title of "Integrity Tests and the Law" in the January, 1994 issue of *Security Magazine,* a publication of the American Society for Industrial Security.

---

60. The subject of access to criminal records is fully discussed in Chapter 8.

10

Legal Consequences of Impermissible Investigative Conduct

LEGAL CONSEQUENCES OF AN ILLEGAL ARREST

Although the invalidity of an arrest will not deprive the state of an opportunity to prosecute the arrestee,[1] there are restrictions on the use of evidence obtained as a result of such an arrest. Moreover, the person who makes an illegal warrantless arrest may incur some personal liability, either civilly or criminally, or both.

Civil and Criminal Liability of Police Officers

A police officer's statutory power to make a warrantless arrest is no shield against either civil or criminal liability in the event she acts illegally. Moreover, liability may be imposed by either the federal or state courts, or by both. In federal courts a state or local police officer may be sued for damages by reason of the Civil Rights Act of 1871,[2] or may be prosecuted criminally under a 1948 statute in those instances

---

1. This is so even though the arrestee is a fugitive who was kidnapped in one state for return to the state where the crime was committed. Frisbie v. Collins, 342 U.S. 519 (1952); United States v. Sobel, 142 F. Supp. 515 (D.C.N.Y. 1956); People v. Griffith, 130 Colo. 475, 276 P.2d 599 (1954). However, a few more recent cases have held that when a suspect is returned to a jurisdiction by flagrantly unlawful means, due process requires that she be released, although the refiling of charges is not necessarily barred. United States v. Toseanino, 500 F.2d 267 (2d Cir. 1974); Bennally v. Marcum, 89 N.M. 463, 553 P.2d 1270 (1976).

   In the case of Adolph Eichmann, the chief executioner of millions of Jews and other concentration camp victims during the Nazi regime in Germany, the Supreme Court of Israel relied heavily on American case law to justify its right to try and execute Eichmann, who had been kidnapped in Argentina and flown to Israel for trial.

2. This Act (42 U.S.C. Sec. 1983), now a section of the Public Health and Welfare Act, provides as follows:

where she acts willfully.[3] She may also be prosecuted criminally if she conspires with others to deprive a person of her constitutional rights.[4] In the state courts, a police officer who acts illegally may be sued under the tort (civil wrong) law of the state,[5] and, under certain conditions, she may also be prosecuted criminally.[6]

Although a federal officer may not be sued under the Federal Civil Rights Act,[7] nor even prosecuted, except when she acts as a conspirator to violate a federal constitutional right,[8] she may be sued in a federal court on a tort (civil wrong) theory based on a constitutional rights violation.[9] Her employer, the federal government, may also be found liable, under the Federal Tort Claim Act,[10] for conduct of hers which would result in liability for the negligence of state or local law enforcement officers.

Every person who, under color of any statute, ordinance, regulation, custom, or usage, of any State or Territory or the District of Columbia, subjects, or causes to be subjected, any citizen of the United States or other person within the jurisdiction thereof to the deprivation of any rights, privileges, or immunities secured by the Constitution and laws, shall be liable to the party injured in an action at law, suit in equity, or other proper proceeding for redress. For the purposes of this section, any Act of Congress applicable exclusively to the District of Columbia shall be considered to be a statute of the District of Columbia.

The key phrases that have the effect of restricting the statute's application to agents of state and local governments are "under color of" and "of any State or Territory or the District of Columbia."

3. The statute (18 U.S.C. Sec. 242) provides:

Whoever, under color of any law, statute, ordinance, regulation, or custom, willfully subjects any inhabitant of any State, Territory, or District to the deprivation of any rights, privileges, or immunities secured or protected by the Constitution or laws of the United States, or to different punishments, pains, or penalties, on account of such inhabitant being an alien, or by reason of his color, or race, than are prescribed for the punishment of citizens, shall be fined not more than $1,000 or imprisoned not more than one year, or both; and if death results shall be subject to imprisonment for any term of years or for life.

The key phrases in this penal statute are the same as in the civil remedy statute quoted in the preceding footnote.

Because of their historical backgrounds, as well as the wording, neither of the foregoing statutes can be invoked against federal law enforcement officers (except those in the District of Columbia, where they may be prosecuted under Sec. 242, and subjected to civil liability under Sec. 1983).

4. 18 U.S.C. Sec. 241, reproduced *infra* note 18.

5. 5 Am. Jur. 2d, *Arrest*, Sec. 114 (1962); 80 C.J.S., *Sheriffs and Constables*, Sec. 52 et seq. (1953).

6. For example, in Illinois there is a provision of the criminal code that states that it is an offense to "knowingly without authority" detain another person. 720 ILCS Sec. 5/10-3. In any prosecution, of course, it must be proved "beyond a reasonable doubt" that the arrester acted in the prohibited manner. Moreover, it is very unlikely that there would be any prosecution except in a case involving rather flagrant conduct.

7. *See* note 3.

8. *See* note 3.

9. Bivens v. Six Unknown Agents of Federal Bureau of Narcotics, 403 U.S. 388, 91 S. Ct. 1999 (1971).

10. 28 U.S.C. Sec. 2675.

When an arrest is made pursuant to an illegal warrant, a police officer is relieved of liability so long as she acted in good faith in the procurement and execution of the warrant. Recent court decisions have made it clear, however, that the issuance of a warrant by a magistrate will not immunize the officer from liability if no objectively reasonable officer could think that the warrant was supported by probable cause.[11] Additionally, as previously stated with regard to an arrest without a warrant, the officer will subject herself to liability if she uses excessive force in executing an arrest pursuant to a warrant.

Finally, a police officer can generally be held personally liable for negligent, needless, or wrongful acts causing personal injury or death in effecting or attempting to effect an arrest. This liability can include both civil liability for damages[12] and criminal liability for assault, battery, or even homicide.

Civil and Criminal Liability of Security Officers and Other Private Citizens

Under state laws, private citizens, including security officers, who make an illegal warrantless arrest are liable in damages to the arrestee. If, in making the arrest, the arrestor acts within the scope of her employment, her employer may also be liable.

EXAMPLE

Harris entered into a department store where Dickerson was a security officer. To Dickerson, Harris "looked like a crook." As Harris picked up a necktie, Dickerson arrested him. Subsequently, Dickerson ascertained that Harris was an honest citizen. Dickerson and the store are liable in damages for false arrest.

EXAMPLE

In the foregoing example, assume that it was a janitor who arrested Harris. Although the janitor would be liable, the store probably would not be, because in making the arrest the janitor was not within the scope of his employment.[13]

---

11. Malley v. Briggs, 475 U.S. 335 (1986). *See also* 60 A.L.R.2d 873, 879–883 (1958).

12. Chaudoin v. Fuller, 67 Ariz. 144, 192 P.2d 243 (1948).

13. A principal's liability in false arrest and false imprisonment suits is discussed in 92 A.L.R.2d 15 (1963). False arrest and wrongful imprisonment damages are dealt with in 35 A.L.R.2d 273 (1954). An employer's liability in malicious prosecution suits is discussed in 18 A.L.R.2d 402 (1951). For a collection of cases with regard to the admissibility of the employer's rules or instructions for dealing with shoplifters in actions for false imprisonment or malicious prosecution, see 31 A.L.R.3d 705 (1970).

What is the liability situation when a company employs a moonlighting police officer for security purposes? In Dillard Dept. Stores v. Stuckey, 511 S.W.2d 154 (Ark. 1944), it was held that a store cannot thereby immunize itself from false arrest liability; the officer acts as an agent of the store. *Compare,* however, an earlier case decided by the same court, where a railroad was considered not liable for the actions of a police officer assigned by the police department to one of the company's depots, even though the railroad paid one-half of his salary as an inducement to

If, in making an illegal arrest, a private citizen acts in good faith while rendering assistance to and obeying the directions of a police officer, many jurisdictions will not hold the citizen liable even though the police officer may have exceeded her authority and may be liable personally.[14] However, there is authority to the effect that a private person is not protected if the illegal arrest was made by the officer at the citizen's instigation,[15] or if she acts in a wanton and unreasonable manner or goes beyond what she was summoned to do.[16]

A security officer or any other private citizen who reports to the police the details of a presumed offense, which report leads to the arrest of a person who is unsuccessfully prosecuted, will not be subject to civil liability in the absence of malicious intent. The following example is based on an actual case:

EXAMPLE

The manager of an ice cream company store heard, along with other persons within the store, a citizen band radio broadcast of obscene and derogatory remarks about the company's products. The manager immediately went to a window and looked into the store's parking lot, from which she saw a "white Chevrolet" leaving the vicinity of the store and being driven by a man holding a "C.B." radio mike to his face. She ran down the street and observed the license number of the car. All of this information was supplied to the police. Also, in her signed complaint against the car owner, she stated that she recognized his voice from having heard it about two months earlier in the store's parking lot. Also, at the car driver's trial, the store manager identified him as the man transmitting the messages heard within the store.

Following the accused's acquittal for the criminal offense of disorderly conduct, he sued the store manager and the company. In this he was unsucessful.[17]

Whenever time and circumstances permit, the best course to follow in arrest situations is to file a sworn complaint with a judicial magistrate for the issuance of an

---

the police department to have an officer on such an assignment. Chicago, R.I. & P. Ry. v. Nelson, 87 Ark. 524, 113 S.W. 44 (1908). *See also* Glenmar Cinestate, Inc. v. Farrell, 292 S.E.2d 366 (Va. 1982) (theater hires off-duty officer to direct traffic; theater was not liable when such officer negligently directed traffic which resulted in a death); and Dinmark v. Farrier, 510 So. 2d 819 (Ala. 1987) (off-duty police officer working as security guard was acting as police officer when he made arrest; store not liable). *See* Annot., *Actions of Off-Duty Policeman Acting as Private Security Guard as Actions 'Under Color of State Law' Actionable Under Civil Rights Act of 1871 (42 U.S.C. Sec. 1983)*, 56 A.L.R. Fed. 895 (1994).

14. Kagel v. Brugger, 119 N.W.2d 395 (Wis. 1963); Moyer v. Meier, 205 Okla. 405, 238 P.2d 338 (1951); Firestone v. Rice, 71 Mich. 377, 38 N.W. 885 (1888).

   An example of a state statutory exemption in such instances is the following Illinois Code of Criminal Procedure provision [725 ILCS Sec. 5/107-8(c)]: "A person commanded to aid a peace officer shall not be civilly liable for any reasonable conduct in aid of the officer." *See also* 35 C.J.S., *False Imprisonment* Sec. 43 (1960).

15. Kearley v. Cowan, 217 Ala. 295, 116 So. 145 (1928); Reichneder v. Skaggs Drug Center, 421 F.2d 307 (5th Cir. 1970).

16. Moyer v. Meier, 205 Okla. 405, 238 P.2d 338 (1951); Note, *Criminal Law—Requiring Citizens to Aid a Police Officer*, 14 De Paul L. Rev. 159 (1964).

17. Mangus v. Cock Robin Ice Cream Co., 52 Ill. App. 3d 110, 367 N.E.2d 203 (1977).

arrest warrant. In other words, the decision regarding whether an arrest is justi-fied will then be made by an impartial person—a judicial officer—and that factor serves as the basis for relieving the complainant of any liability by reason of a mis-taken accusation. Malicious intent, of course, will offset the protection otherwise afforded by a warrant.

The possible risks to a security officer of violating federal law in the course of her activities must be considered in light of the federal civil rights statutes en-acted by Congress. A security officer may be subjected to a federal prosecution if she is involved in a conspiracy to violate a person's constitutional rights. This is due to a provision in the law stating that *anyone* who participates in such a con-spiracy commits a federal offense.[18] What is not clear, however, is whether the se-curity officer comes within the coverage of those statutory provisions affixing civil or criminal liability upon someone who, while acting under "color of law," vi-olates a person's constitutional rights.[19] Obviously, a police officer acts under color of law, but what is the status of a security officer who is commissioned or li-censed under state or local law? Then, too, even where she does not function under any commission or license, is she brought within the color of law coverage

---

18. The provision, 18 U.S.C. Sec. 241, reads as follows:

If two of more persons conspire to injure, oppress, threaten, or intimidate any citizen in the free ex-ercise or enjoyment of any right or privilege secured to him by the Constitution or laws of the United States, or because of his having so exercised the same; or

If two or more persons go in disguise on the highway, or on the premises of another, with intent to prevent or hinder his free exercise or enjoyment of any right or privilege so secured—They shall be fined not more than $10,000 or imprisoned not more than ten years, or both; and if death results, they shall be subject to imprisonment for any term of years or for life.

The key word in the statute is "conspire." It clearly applies to a private security officer involved in any such conduct. However, with respect to the other federal civil rights legislation (42 U.S.C. Sec. 1983; 18 U.S.C. Sec. 242—reproduced *supra* notes 2 and 3), the issue has arisen as to whether a li-censed or deputized private security officer falls within the coverage of acting under color of state law. That issue will be discussed subsequently in this chapter. *See also* S., NAHMOD, CIVIL RIGHTS & CIVIL LIBERTIES LITIGATION: THE LAW OF SECTION 1983, Sec. 2.08 (3d ed. 1991).

In a case involving a Section 1983 civil suit filed against police officers *by an off-duty security offi-cer*, he alleged a violation under the following circumstances. He was observed gazing in a window of a clothing store (presumably at night). Police officers approached him and inquired if he had a handgun. He acknowledged that he had one, whereupon he was arrested. His lawsuit was to no avail, because while off the employer's premises he had no legal right to carry a handgun and his arrest was valid. Evans v. Reivers, 595 F.2d 372 (7th Cir. 1979).

For a case holding a private citizen liable under the above Section 242, see Griffin v. Breckenridge, 403 U.S. 88 (1971).

See also Annot., *Actionability, Under 42 U.S.C. Sec. 1983, of Claims Against Persons other than Police Officers for Unlawful Arrest or Imprisonment*, 44 A.L.R. FED. 225 (1994) and Annot., "Supreme Court's Views as to when person is acting 'under color of' state law, within meaning of civil rights statute (42 U.S.C. Sec. 1983) providing private right of action for violation of federal rights," 101 L.Ed. 2d 987 (1993).

19. The statutes containing the phrase under color of law are the ones previously reproduced in notes 2 and 3. The former deals with civil liability, the latter with criminal liability.

A law review article dealing with a security officer's liability under one of these two statutes ap-pears under the title *Liability of Private Police Under Sec. 1983,* in U. ILL. L. FOR. 1185 (1976).

when making an arrest or detaining someone pursuant to a statute or ordinance specifically permitting such action?

In a 1951 case, the Supreme Court held that a security officer's actions came within the coverage of color of law on the basis that he had met the qualifications prescribed by city ordinance, had taken an oath of office, and had received a card identifying him as a "special policeman." He was prosecuted for participating, along with regular city police officers, in the beating of persons suspected of thievery for the purpose of obtaining their confessions.[20] Even in the absence of a combination of circumstances such as those in the foregoing case, several lower federal appellate courts have reached similar conclusions in finding color of law applicable regarding the actions of security officers. In one case, the court ruled that the actions of ordinary security officers, who do not function under specially conferred governmental privileges, may nevertheless take on a color of law label whenever they act "in concert with police officers pursuant to customary procedures agreed to by police departments, particularly when a state statute authorizes merchants to detain suspected shoplifters."[21]

In another federal case, a majority of a three-judge panel of a circuit court of appeals found the element of color of law because there existed between a store, its security officers, and the local police what the court labeled a "preconceived plan" whereby a person arrested by a security officer for shoplifting would be turned over to the police.[22] The dissenting judge expressed the view that the mere practice of security officers delivering arrestees to the police pursuant to authorization in a suspected shoplifter detention statute did not satisfy the required element of action under color of law. He also expressed the view that the detention statute was of a "self-interest" nature to merchants and not based on "broad public interest," which difference he considered significant in ascertaining whether color of law was involved.

The self-interest factor discussed by the dissenting judge in the foregoing case featured in the reasoning in support of four federal district court decisions. One judge held that no color of law was created merely because of two statutes, one of

20. Williams v. United States, 341 U.S. 97 (1951). The prosecution was for a violation of 18 U.S.C. Sec. 242, appearing in *supra* note 3. The defendant Williams was the operator of a private detective agency which had been employed by a company to investigate thievery. Three Justices dissented, on the basis of views expressed in the dissent to the effect that under color of law meant actions *authorized* by state law, so that crimes such as the one in the earlier case, the killing of a young black arrestee by Georgia police, and the offense committed by Williams in the present case, should be punishable only by the state upon the basis of specific state law violations. However, the majority holding in the earlier case, Screws v. United States, 355 U.S. 91 (1944), still prevails.

21. The quotation is from El Fundi v. Deroche, 625 F.2d 195 (8th Cir. 1980), in which the appellate court reversed a district judge's dismissal of a Sec. 1983 filed by the complainants personally. Although the allegations were "crudely drafted," the appellate court held that they adequately stated a cause of action. Since this was the limited extent of the decision, the quoted language might not have been as extensive as it seems if the court had been confronted with a factual situation developed at an actual trial, accompanied by arguments of opposing counsel.

22. Smith v. Bookshire Bros., 519 F.2d 93 (5th Cir. 1975). *See also* a similar holding by another three-judge panel of the same court in the latter case of Duriso v. K-Mart, 559 F.2d 1274 (1977).

which licensed private detectives and the other of which permitted store security officers to briefly detain suspected shoplifters.[23] Two other cases held that no color of law existed where there was only a detention statute and a general right of private persons to make arrests for offenses committed in their presence.[24] A fourth case rejected the color of law contention based on a statute providing a legal defense to merchants who exercised their right to detain suspected shoplifters. The opinion of the judge stated that such a statute was "not sufficient to bridge the gap between private and state action."[25]

However, the language of the Federal Civil Rights statute, while requiring that the action must have been taken "under color of law" for liability to be imposed, does not require that the actor be a governmental employee. In a 1982 case, the U.S. Supreme Court[26] noted that a private party might be deemed to be a state actor "because he has acted together with or has obtained significant aid from state officials, or because his conduct is otherwise chargeable to the state." The test for liability also requires that a federally protected right be violated.

Similarly, the Supreme Court of the United States held that a private person can be liable under the United States Code (42 U.S.C. Sec. 1983) as a result of a willful participation in joint activity with the state or its agents which results in a deprivation of constitutional rights.[27] The case involved a restaurant that refused to serve the plaintiff, a white individual, because she was in the company of blacks. The plaintiff was then arrested for vagrancy immediately after she was refused service.

The Court noted that if this plaintiff could show that the arresting police and the restaurant had reached an understanding to this effect or were otherwise involved in a conspiracy to violate the plaintiff's rights, then the refusal of service, together

---

23. Weyandt v. Mason's Stores, 279 F. Supp. 283 (W.D. Pa. 1968). As to the general private citizen arrest right involved in this case, the court found that it was distinguishable from an arrest right specifically conferred upon a security officer by statute, as was true in an earlier case in the same federal district, De Carlo v. Joseph Horne and Co., 251 F. Supp. 935 (W.D. Pa. 1966), in which the "Professional Thieves Act" of Pennsylvania had been interpreted by the state court as a specific grant of such a right.

24. Warren v. Cummings, 303 F. Supp. 803 (D. Colo. 1969); Battle v. Dayton-Hudson Corp., 399 F. Supp. 900 (D. Minn. 1975).

25. Iodice v. Gimbels, Inc., 416 F. Supp. 1054 (E.D. N.Y. 1976); Klein v. Alexander's Dept. Store, 75 Civ. 6024 (S.D.N.Y. 1977) (unreported).

With respect to this "bridging of the gap" in another case context, see Pratt v. State, 9 Md. App. 220, 263 A.2d 247 (1970), in which the court held that the *Miranda* warnings (discussed in Chapter 4) were required before a "special policeman," who was clothed with full police powers, could interrogate an arrestee. *See also* State v. Muegge, 360 S.E.2d 216 (W.Va. 1987), earlier discussed in Chapter 4. (West Virginia Supreme Court holds that state law applies *Miranda*-like requirements to interrogation of suspected shoplifter by security guard; state prohibition of unreasonable searches also applies); and Glean v. State, 397 S.E.2d 459 (Ga. App. 1990) (store clerk did not need to give suspected shoplifter *Miranda* warnings before questioning her).

26. Lugar v. Edmonson Oil Co., 457 U.S. 922 (1982).

27. Adickes v. Kress & Co., 398 U.S. 144 (1970).

with the later arrest would constitute sufficient state involvement to warrant a finding of state action.[28]

There is at least some case authority, however, for the proposition that a private corporation cannot be held *vicariously* liable for its employees' deprivation of the constitutional rights of others under Section 1983. In one case[29], for instance, the former managers of a mobile home park brought a federal civil rights action against the park's owners and employees, as well as against two police officers. They claimed that their civil rights had been violated and they had been deprived of their property when they were ejected from a mobile home on the premises.

The court found that there were sufficient allegations to state a claim against individual employees of the mobile home park owners under the civil rights statute. The complaint stated that they acted jointly with two police officers in conducting a search of a mobile home that the plaintiffs occupied, and removed their property. In response to their request for proof of authorization for the search, the plaintiffs had been told that they would not be arrested if they left peaceably. The court held, as a matter of law, that a private corporation could not be held vicariously liable for its employees' actions under Section 1983.

It has long been clear that merely reporting alleged criminal behavior to the police does not convert the action of a private security guard into action under color of law. In a South Carolina case,[30] for instance, a security guard reported to police that he had observed two men driving through a company parking lot, with one man getting out of the vehicle and appearing to tamper with a vehicle in the lot. He furnished officers with the license plate of their vehicle. When they were later arrested, they sued the security guard and the company which supplied him. The court rejected the claim. It noted that the guard, in reporting the information to the police, had not "acted jointly" with them, and the mere fact that the police based their decision to arrest the alleged auto tamperer solely on the guard's accusation did not establish "joint action," which requires a "conspiracy or meeting of the minds" or "prearranged plan."

The court also rejected the argument that because the security guard was licensed by the state this rendered his actions state action. While the state licensing statute did grant the guard the power to arrest and detain persons on

---

28. *See also* Dennis v. Sparks, 499 U.S. 24 (1980) (private defendant who conspires with an absolutely immune state judge acts under color of law). A more recent case, Wyatt v. Cole, 112 S. Ct. 1827 (1992), provided that private party defendants sued under 42 U.S.C. Sec. 1983 for violation of federal civil rights are also not entitled to assert qualified immunity defenses available to individual government employee defendants in such suits. Another important case in this area is Rojas v. Alexander's Department Store, Inc., 924 F.2d 406 (2nd Cir.), *cert. denied*, 112 S. Ct. 52 (1991), in which the U.S. Supreme Court declined to review a federal appeals court decision holding that a private department store could not be held liable under the federal civil rights statute for an unlawful arrest, absent a store policy of such arrests. Generally, there is no *respondeat superior* vicarious liability under 42 U.S.C. Sec. 1983, and this decision seems to indicate that this general principle applies in the context of private employers as well as municipalities.

29. Fraser v. Schultze, 663 F. Supp. 512 (N.D. Ill. 1987).

30. Chiles v. Crooks, 708 F. Supp. 127 (D.S.C. 1989).

property they are hired to protect, in this instance, the guard did not exercise that authority.[31]

Similarly, a federal appeals court[32] held that shopping mall security guards did not act under color of law in requesting arrest of patrons. The plaintiffs, several shopping mall patrons arrested by sheriffs' deputies for creating a disturbance, argued that the mall's security guards acted "in concert" with the deputies, so that their actions constituted those of the state. Such a theory of recovery was upheld earlier.[33] Crucial to establishing such a theory, however, the court noted, is a finding that "the state police acted according to a preconceived plan and on the say-so of the private actor, not on the basis of their own investigation." In the earlier case, the court continued, there was testimony stating that store officials knew they could have people detained "merely by calling the police and designating the detainee." In the instant case, by contrast, no evidence existed of any such customary or preconceived plan. The plaintiffs had alleged that they were arrested "in part for the incident in the mall and at the request of the security personnel, and not *wholly* based on any independent observations of the officers." The arresting officer testified that she made the arrest on the basis of what she observed. Whether an additional basis for the arrest was the statements and request of the mall security personnel was not certain, but reliance on such statements and requests does not render private parties state actors, as long as the police officer makes her "own determination of cause to arrest." As the court noted: "Unless he were an eye-witness, a police officer could not make any arrest if he could not rely on information provided by citizens who witnessed the events. Such reliance does not convert the informing party into a state actor."

What about detaining a store customer under a "merchant's privilege" statute, or making a citizen's arrest of a shoplifter once merchandise is found? Simply because a statute allows a merchant to detain suspected shoplifters, does not mean the merchant is acting under color of law.[34] Her ability to detain is to recover her stolen property, not for any state benefit; the state statute merely permits but does not mandate detention of suspected shoplifters.[35] However, where the state licensed individuals who were authorized to make detentions, and the right was not conferred directly on the merchant by virtue of her ownership of the goods, the court held that sufficient state action was alleged.[36]

31. *See also* Khadijah v. Conrail Rail Road, 711 F. Supp. 930 (N.D. Ill. 1989) (private parties who acted as complainants in criminal prosecution were not liable in federal civil rights action).

32. Bartholomew v. Lee, 889 F.2d 62 (5th Cir. 1989).

33. Smith v. Brookshire Brothers, Inc., 519 F.2d 93 (5th Cir. 1975).

34. Moher v. Stop and Shop Companies, Inc., 580 F. Supp. 723 (D. Conn. 1984).

35. *See also* Hut v. G.C. Murphy Co., 624 F. Supp. 512 (S.D. W.Va. 1986) and Estate of Iodice v. Gimbels, Inc., 416 F. Supp. 1054 (E.D. N.Y. 1976) (same results). However, in Thompson v. McCoy, 425 F. Supp. 407 (D.S.C. 1976), where the state licensed individuals who were authorized to make detentions, and the right was not conferred directly on the merchant by virtue of his ownership of the goods, the court held that sufficient state action was alleged.

36. Thompson v. McCoy, 425 F. Supp. 407 (D.S.C. 1976).

In one recent case,[37] a federal appeals court held that making a "citizen's arrest" is not "state action" for purposes of federal civil rights liability. This case involved citizen arrests made by employees of a women's health service facility of anti-abortion picketeers who were violating a court injunction prohibiting picketing on the same side of the street as the facility. The court noted that there was no joint action with a police officer who was on the scene actually attempting to "discourage" the making of the arrests by warning of the danger of civil liability. Additionally, there was no allegation that the prosecutor failed to exercise independent judgment in prosecuting the charges.

Although the Supreme Court has never decided whether a citizen's arrest would qualify as state action or action under color of state law for purposes of federal civil rights liability, all existing federal court decisions on the subject have held that a citizen's arrest can not form the basis of such liability.[38]

Beyond the "merchant's privilege" statutes allowing temporary detention to investigate suspected shoplifters, many states also have statutory provisions allowing private persons to make "citizen arrests," especially for felonies committed in the presence of the arresting citizen. Although security guards and their employers making such arrests without probable cause may be subject to liability under state law for false arrest or imprisonment, these cases seem to indicate that they cannot, when acting alone without the participation of law enforcement officials, face civil rights liability for such actions.

By way of contrast, in a lawsuit in which store employees were found to have acted in concert with police officers in detaining a customer suspected of shoplifting, they were found to have therefore acted under color of law.[39] Three reasons for this conclusion were stated as follows:

1. The store manager stated during his testimony that it is the practice of the store to work with the police department in prosecuting shoplifters. The store security guard had telephoned the police after an unfruitful search of the customer's purse and requested the "assistance of an officer" because she had "detained a shoplifter." The police responded, taking the customer into custody.

2. The security guard was also an employee of the police department "and has a close relationship with the prosecuting attorney, who apparently made his recommendation to prosecute based on [the officer's] word, not upon an independent investigation of the facts." The security guard's "incomplete versions of the facts" were used by the police and prosecutor to justify detaining, searching, and prosecuting the customer.

3. The court noted that the state law specifically authorizes merchants and their employees to detain suspected shoplifters to recover unpurchased goods.

37. Collins v. Womancare, 878 F.2d 1145 (9th Cir. 1989).

38. *See* Carey v. Continental Airlines, Inc., 823 F.2d 1402 (10th Cir. 1987); Lee v. Town of Estates Park, 820 F.2d 1112 (10th Cir. 1987); Warren v. Cummings, 303 F. Supp. 803 (D. Colo. 1969); Shakespeare v. Wilson, 40 F.R.D. 500 (S.D. Cal. 1966); Bryant v. Donnell, 239 F. Supp. 681 (W.D. Tenn. 1965).

39. Murray v. Wal-Mart, Inc., 874 F.2d 555 (8th Cir. 1989).

The court found that the state statute, combined with the "concerted efforts" of the store and local police department, "afford[ed] ample evidence of willful, joint activity" supporting a federal civil rights claim against the store. A total of $15,000 in compensatory and $10,000 in punitive damages, as well as $7,850 in attorneys' fees, were awarded against the store.[40]

Simply acting on the basis of information obtained from the police will not be sufficient to convert private action into under color of law. In one case with such facts,[41] a paper mill was cooperating with a police department's undercover investigation of the possession and use of illegal drugs on the job site. A police officer reported to his superiors that he had observed an employee drinking on the job. When the employee was fired, he filed a federal civil rights lawsuit against his employer, claiming he had been deprived of a property interest in continued employment without due process (a hearing). The court noted that the firing was not caused "by the exercise of some right or privilege created by the State"; nor did the cooperation between the employer and the police in the investigation lead to liability.

The mere fact that a business is licensed by the state does not convert its private action into state action. In an Ohio case,[42] the fact that a bar was licensed to sell alcohol to the public was not held to be sufficient basis to claim state action for the bar's serving a patron liquor until he became intoxicated. The patron claimed that the bar failed to stop serving him liquor after he became intoxicated and thereafter shot the bar owner, for no apparent reason. He was subsequently arrested for attempted murder, pleaded guilty to the charge, and was sentenced to 5–25 years. As if he hadn't already done enough damage to the bar owner, he now filed a federal civil rights claim against him, claiming that the result of the shooting incident violated his civil rights due to his subsequent loss of liberty! The court quickly dismissed this claim.

When liability is established under Section 1983, the court may also award attorneys' fees pursuant to Section 1988. In one case,[43] a court held that a verdict against a private business on a state law false arrest claim was sufficient to make the restaurant jointly liable with an off-duty police officer for attorneys' fees under Section 1988. The restaurant unsuccessfully argued that it was not responsible for the fees because only the officer was sued under the federal civil rights statute and they were sued only for state law claims.

In addition to federal civil rights statutes, several states have their own—often unique—civil rights statutes which may apply to private parties. California, in particular, has the Unruh Civil Rights Act, which is designed to prohibit all businesses from engaging in arbitrary or stereotypical discrimination. In one case

---

40. *See also* Lusby v. T.G.&Y. Stores, Inc., 796 F.2d 1307 (10th Cir. 1986), *cert. denied,* 106 S. Ct. 65 (1985) (store and security guard liable for arrest of three brothers who had shoplifting charges dropped; police acted on basis of judgment of merchant and its guard rather than conducting independent investigation).

41. *See* Hudson v. S.D. Warren Co., 665 F. Supp. 937 (D. Me. 1987).

42. Harrison v. Malchom, 664 F. Supp. 1110 (N.D. Ohio 1987).

43. Woodard v. Hardee's Restaurant, 643 F. Supp. 691 (W.D. Mo. 1986).

interpreting this statute,[44] the court found violative of this law a policy adopted by five topless bars of denying admission to patrons wearing clothing with motorcycle club insignia. The bars argued that the policy was not designed to exclude motorcycle club members as such, but merely adopted to better exercise control over patrons and help prevent fights and other disturbances. The court held that it was stereotypical discrimination to believe that members of motorcycle clubs are more likely to commit misconduct. It therefore enjoined enforcement of the policies.[45]

This example is only one of many state statutes dealing with civil rights violations subject to adjudication.[46] Other state remedies are also available, of course, for false arrest or false imprisonment suits. Later, we will examine some cases imposing such remedies. In most instances, it is the state remedy, rather than liability under federal statutes, that is imposed in instances of impermissible arrests or detentions by private security personnel.

Vicarious Liability of Employer for Wrongful Actions of Security Officers

Under a well-established legal principle, not only is an employee civilly liable for her wrongful conduct, but her employer is also liable if the wrongfulness occurred while the employee was acting within the scope of her employment. Because a security officer is employed to protect the business of the employer, an arrest of a suspect or offender is clearly within the scope of the officer's employment.[47]

An interesting and unique case involving an employer's vicarious liability for a security officer's conduct is a 1980 one in which a bank participated in a local police department's "secondary hiring" program, whereby certain off-duty police officers worked as "security tellers." If a crime occurred in the bank, the primary function of such a teller was to take appropriate action with respect to the offender. The officer in this case was found to have acted illegally in detaining a suspected customer. The bank was held liable in tort under the state law. The "good faith" and "probable cause" defenses that might have been available in the civil rights

---

44. The Unruh Civil Rights Act is Cal. Civ. Code Sec. 51. The case discussed in the text is Renteria v. Dirty Dan's Inc., 244 Cal. Rptr. 423 (Cal. App. 1988).

45. *See also* Hernandez v. Six Flags Magic Mountain Inc., 688 F. Supp. 560 (C.D. Cal. 1988), in which Latino youths sued an amusement park for alleged violations of civil rights for the practice of stopping and searching patrons on suspicion of their being gang members.

46. *See, e.g.,* Cal. Civ. Code, Secs. 51, 52; N.Y. Civil Rights Law, Sec. 1 et seq.

47. If, however, the arrest by a security officer is in violation of specific authorizations, guidelines, or procedures prescribed by the employer, there may arise a question of whether the officer was within permissible legal bounds. For a discussion of the admissibility of manuals of instruction to employees, and their significance regarding liability pro and con, see Peak v. W.T. Grant Co., 386 S.W.2d 685 (Mo. App. 1964) (used to show a store's floor manager was acting within the scope of employment); Brown v. Great Atlantic & Pacific Tea Co., 89 N.Y. Supp. 2d 244 (App. Div. 1949) (used to show arrester acted outside scope); but *compare* J.J. Newberry v. Judd, 259 Ky. 309, 82 S.W.2d 359 (1935). *See also* 31 A.L.R.3d 705 (1970).

part of the customer's allegations were considered unavailable to the officer, said the court, because of his "off-duty" private employee status.[48]

In addition to an employer's liability for compensatory damages occasioned by an employee's wrongful conduct, an additional award for punitive damages may be granted by a court or jury for what occurred. Ordinarily, however, this additional amount is permitted only in situations where the employer condoned or suggested prior wrongful acts of a similar nature, or where the employer hired or retained as an employee a person known to have a proclivity for such conduct.[49]

The best way for an employer to avoid liability due to a security officer's illegal detention or arrest conduct, as well as any other illegal investigative or protective procedure, is the proper selection of personnel coupled with appropriate training. This is especially so for security officers, and, most certainly, for security guards equipped with firearms. The training should encompass an understandable explanation of the legal rights and limitations concerning arrests, searches and seizures, detentions, the use of force, the questioning of suspected persons, and all other relevant procedures. This type of explanation is one of the primary goals of this book.

Some businesses seek to avoid liability arising out of the wrongful action of security personnel by hiring an outside security agency (an "independent contractor") to provide such services.[50] This attempt at liability avoidance, however, is a tenuous one. First of all, in almost all types of protective security situations the hirer or one of her employees will inevitably become a participant in certain aspects of the activities of the independent contractor's agents—for instance, calling attention to the suspicious conduct of a customer or some other person, assisting in identifying a stolen item, providing a place for detention or interrogation, or filing a criminal complaint. Such participation will negate the avoidance principle based on the independent contractor's independent "right to control" the activities of its own agents. Then, too, some courts will view as nondelegable the highly sensitive or "inherently dangerous" functions of a security officer, and especially an armed guard.[51] These considerations and others are good reasons, therefore, to

---

48. Traver v. Meshriy, 627 F.2d 934 (9th Cir. 1980).

49. For cases specifically involving punitive damages, see Dart Drug Co. v. Lithicum, 300 A.2d 442 (D.C. Ct. App. 1973), and 93 A.L.R.3d 826 (1979). *See also* Moore's Inc. v. Garcia, 604 S.W.2d 261 (Tex. Cir. App. 1980).

50. *See, e.g.,* Adams v. F.W. Woolworth Co., 144 Misc. 27, 257 N.Y. Supp. 776 (1932); and Malvo v. J.C. Penney Co., 512 P. 2d 575 (Alas. 1973). Also consider Bishop v. Bockoven, Inc., 199 Neb. 613, 260 N.W.2d 488 (1977), in which a mistake was made by an independent security company's employee in arresting a suspected shoplifter. The merchant was held not liable, but the security company was. The court reasoned that only the merchant or its own employees were entitled to the privileges and immunity of the state shoplifting statute.

51. The opinion of the court in the case of Dupree v. Piggly Wiggly Store Rite Foods, 542 S.W.2d 882 (Tex. Civ. App. 1976), contains an extensive, case-documented discussion of the merchant-independent contractor issue in protective security cases. The case involved a false imprisonment, malicious prosecution suit, in which the court held that (a) protection from shoplifting was "an inherently dangerous" undertaking, and (b) it constituted a "personal character duty," both of which factors rendered the matter nondelegable.

exercise considerable caution when selecting the independent contractor—one who has competent security personnel. Consideration should also be given to the advisability of an indemnity clause in the contract to cover the liability that may be incurred by the hirer due to negligence on the part of the independent contractor's agents.[52]

In many instances, security companies will enter into contracts to provide certain security services or alarm systems to businesses or private residences. Many such contracts contain limitations upon the scope of services supplied, or attempted exclusions or limitations in the area of potential liability for losses. Many reported appellate court decisions have addressed the question of whether such exclusions and limitations are legally enforceable—with some such exclusions and limitations being struck down by the courts on "public policy" grounds.

In a recent decision in New York,[53] for instance, the court held that public policy prohibited an alarm company from limiting its liability for "gross negligence" to a maximum of $250. The contract, which the alarm company entered into with a couple for a burglar alarm system in their home, explicitly excluded all liability for negligence and limited any other liability to a maximum of $250. The company was unable to attach alarm wires to windows in the couple's bedroom and agreed instead to install another device there which they said would detect vibrations and set off the alarm. Later, burglars entered through a window in the room. The burglars stole the couple's property, and assaulted their daughter.

The couple's suit against the alarm company claimed that the failure of the company to test the vibration device amounted to gross negligence. The court held that public policy in the state prohibits such an alarm company from limiting its liability for gross negligence, much less disclaiming it altogether.

Some courts have upheld contractual limitations on liability. The Tennessee Supreme Court upheld the validity of a "liquidated damages clause" limiting the company's liability to a specified amount and releasing the security company from all hazards covered by insurance.[54] The plaintiffs were homeowners who suffered burglary losses of an estimated $185,000 (of which $81,144 was covered by their insurer). The homeowners sued the security company, claiming breach of contract, breach of warranties, negligence, intentional misrepresentation, negligent misrepresentation, and deceptive trade practices. The court overturned a jury award of $100,000. It noted that greater liability protection had been available if the homeowners had chosen to purchase it, which they had declined to do. In addi-

In a case involving the employment of a moonlighting uniformed police officer as a security officer, a company unsuccessfully sought to obtain immunity from liability for a false arrest he had made; in other words, he was declared to be an agent of the company and not an independent contractor. Dillard Dept. Store v. Stuckey, 511 S.W.2d 154 (Ark. 1974).

52. See Hendricks v. Leslie Fay, Inc., 273 N.C. 59, 159 S.E.2d 362 (1968). For a general discussion, see 38 A.L.R.3d 1332 (1971).

53. Gentile v. Garden City Alarm Co., 541 N.Y.S.2d 505 (App. Div. 1989). For an earlier decision seemingly at variance, see Koos Van Den Akker Atelier v. Honeywell, 539 N.Y.S.2d 7 (A.D. 1989) (security company's written agreement limiting liability for burglary even if employee was grossly negligent in failing to investigate cause for alarm signal).

54. Houghland v. Security Alarms & Services, 755 S.W.2d 769 (Tenn. 1988).

tion, the homeowners had declined to provide the security firm with a key to their home for the purpose of making an internal inspection of the premises if an alarm sounded. The court found that the facts could not support intentional fraud, deceit, or intentional misrepresentation. In the absence of that kind of conduct, the court held that the parties were bound by their agreed on contractual limits on liability.[55]

Liability under a contractual security agreement may be limited to parties to a contract and "third party beneficiaries" of the contract. In one case,[56] for instance, a security company and a warehouse entered into a contract to install and maintain a burglar alarm system. A burglary took place at the warehouse, and another company which stored goods at the warehouse sued the security company, as well as the warehouse. The lawsuit alleged that the security company failed to repair the alarm system.

The court noted that there was no allegation in the complaint that the plaintiff was an intended third-party beneficiary of the alarm service contract between the defendants. No duty, the court concluded, was owed by the security company to the plaintiff. The purported wrong was nonfeasance (i.e., the failure to repair the alarm system) rather than misfeasance (i.e., negligent performance). Since the theory of the suit was a duty owed under the contract, rather than negligence, the security company incurred no liability to the plaintiff, which was an "unintended and incidental beneficiary of the contract."[57] This result normally happens in lawsuits filed on the basis of a purported violation of contractual duty.

In other instances, however, the existence of the contract may imply a duty to carry out its obligations in a reasonable manner, imposing a duty not to act negligently toward third parties. In one Arizona case,[58] for example, a security company which contracted to provide security for baseball games at a stadium was found to have a duty to protect underage patrons of the ball park from illegally consuming alcohol. The case involved a 16-year-old who became intoxicated at the ball game by drinking beer bought by his 17-year-old companions. The legal drinking age at the stadium was 19. The 16-year-old stumbled as he left the stadium, and was struck by an automobile.

The court found that the existence of the contract between the company and the stadium owner created a duty to protect minors such as the plaintiff from illegally consuming alcohol. "Reasonable persons," the court concluded, "would agree that

---

55. *See also* Fretwell v. Protection Alarm Co., 764 P.2d 149 (Okl. 1988) ($50 limitation of alarm company's liability for purported failure to respond to burglar alarm was enforceable because it was "unequivocally clear" in the contract.) Other similar cases include: Royal Indemnity Co. v. Baker Protective Services, Inc., 515 N.E.2d 5 (Ohio App. 1986) (clause in security contract limiting liability for burglary to $250 was enforceable), and Ostalkiewicz v. Guardian Alarm, 520 A.2d 563 (R.I. 1987) (clause in burglar alarm contract limiting liability for negligence to $360 was not unconscionable or in violation of public policy. The language was clear and the store proprietor had read the contract before signing it. The court therefore overturned a jury verdict of $491,147 against the alarm company).

56. Northbrook Property v. D.J.L. Warehouse, 536 N.Y.S.2d 179 (A.D. 1989).

57. *See also* Gerace v. Holmes Protection of Philadelphia, 516 A.2d 354 (Pa. Super. 1986) (alarm system contract does not cover third party's losses).

58. Professional Sports, Inc. v. Gillette Security, Inc., 766 P.2d 91 (Ariz. App. 1988).

security guards who undertake for hire to patrol a stadium have a duty to exercise due care for the protection not only of the stadium, but of the stadium's patrons," rejecting the argument that duties under the contract ran only to the stadium.

Some states may impose particular requirements on security contracts. One court held that New York state law requires a contract for security services to be in writing to be enforceable and that an oral contract for such services was therefore not enforceable.[59]

CONTRACTUAL RELEASE OF A FALSE ARREST CLAIM

If a storeowner or an authorized agent such as a security officer should unlawfully arrest or detain a customer or employee, she may seek to protect herself from a civil action for damages by obtaining a *release* from the arrested or detained person. A release is merely a written statement by the aggrieved person in which she agrees not to hold the alleged wrongdoer civilly liable; in other words, not to sue. In fact, some business concerns try to obtain releases from all persons who are arrested or detained, regardless of whether the arrest was legal.

A release of a person's right to sue the storeowner can, as a practical matter, be a valuable document. However, most releases signed by wrongly detained persons are of no legal signficance whatsoever. Their value is psychological only; the individual mistakenly assumes that she has relinquished her rights and does not bother to consult a lawyer.

For a contract to be binding (and a release is merely a special type of contract), the one who makes the promise—in this case the arrested person—must receive something in return for her promise. There must be what the law terms "consideration." Otherwise, having received nothing for her promise, she is free to break it; she can still proceed with a false arrest suit.

The "something given" in return for a release may be money, goods, or even a counterpromise by the other party. This being so, it might be assumed that the arrester's promise to free the arrested person or not to prosecute her would be sufficient consideration. However, if the arrester has made a false arrest, the promise is legally worthless. The arrester, by so promising, is surrendering no valuable right, but merely doing what she was legally obligated to do anyway.[60]

The arrester cannot satisfy the legal requirement of "consideration" (bargained for detriment, such as money, goods, or a counterpromise) by making a receipt or a contract that falsely recites, for example, "one dollar and other good and valuable consideration has been paid in return for this release." The arrested person can always claim that she did not actually receive the specified consideration, even though the writing states otherwise,[61] and the courts are justifiably suspicious of "one-dollar" promises. They are likely to believe the testimony that no money

---

59. Capozzella v. Waterfun Acquisition, 532 N.Y.S.2d 653 (City Ct. 1988).

60. Guilleaume v. Rowe, 94 N.Y. 268 (1883).

61. Corbin, *Contracts* Sec. 586 at 489–90 (1960).

changed hands in the bargain, and if the court believes no money changed hands, it will not enforce the promise. Hence, more than one person should witness the exchange of consideration, and it should be more substantial than the proverbial dollar if credibility is to be accorded the arrester's side of the story.

A more crushing objection to most releases is that the contract occurred under duress. Duress may be considered to be the overpowering of the will of the promisor by the other contracting party to such an extent that the promisor made a commitment she would not ordinarily have made. Certainly, a person who extracts a promise at gunpoint with threats of death receives a promise that is unenforceable because of duress, even though ordinarily adequate consideration may have been given to the promisor. Likewise, some courts have held that a person under unlawful arrest cannot give a binding release; duress is conclusively presumed.[62] If, however, a person is told that she is not under arrest, that she is free to leave the premises or to return to work and need not sign a release in order to do so, she may sign a binding release, provided, of course, she actually receives consideration. Once the arrest is terminated and the arrestee regains her freedom, she clearly may validly contract away her rights by signing a statement similar to the following:

[Date]

I, [name], release all claims, losses, damages, and causes of action I may have against [name of store, company, or person] and its [or his or her] officers, employees, or agents arising from their detention, quesstioning, or investigation of me on [date]. In return for [sum of money], receipt of which is hereby acknowledged, I freely and voluntarily waive all of my rights, claims and causes of action against [name of store, company, or person], and its [or his or her] officers, employees, or agents, having been informed that I need not enter into this agreement in order to leave the premises or to avoid prosecution.

[Signed] _____

Witnessed by: _____

If a court is about to discharge an accused person because of a willingness of the complainant to abandon prosecution or for any other reason, a form similar to the following one is often used to forestall a civil suit for false arrest or malicious prosecution.

[Date]

In consideration of the receipt of the sum of [amount], and other good and valuable consideration, I hereby fully release, discharge, and acquit in all respects whatsoever

62. Harris v. Louisville, N.O. & T. Ry., 35 F. 116 (C.C.W.D. Tenn. 1888); Groy v. City of Galesburg, 71 Mich. App. 161, 247 N.W.2d 338 (1976).
  A good case illustration of the application of the concept of inherent coercion in written releases signed by arrested persons is Boyd v. Adams, 513 F.2d 83 (7th Cir. 1975).

[name of company], its officers, directors, employees, and agents and each of them, from any and all claims or losses, damages, and causes of action on account of, or in connection with my arrest on or about [month] [date], and the filing of a complaint against me on or about said date, and the prosecution of the cause arising upon said complaint.

[Signed]_____ [63]

The difficulties that may be encountered with releases obtained when criminal charges are dismissed are illustrated in the following actual cases.

One case involved a suit by a person who was arrested by the employees of a social club, taken to court, and charged with disturbing the peace, after which he was released on a $25 bail. The next day the district attorney agreed to dismiss the charges if the accused would sign a release of any claims against the club and the governmental agencies involved. He signed a release, the charges were dismissed, and he was returned his $25 bail money.

The release was held to be invalid in a 2-to-1 decision of the appellate court, on the ground that it represented a compromise of a crime and violated a provision of the state's penal code prohibiting "compounding a crime." The dissenting judge expressed the opinion that a distinction was made between the utilization of a release by a district attorney and one by the victim of an alleged crime. He considered the release by the district attorney to be valid, even though the one by a crime victim lacked validity.[64]

In another release situation case (more relevant because it involved the action of a security officer), the plaintiff, after having bought two items and lunch in the defendant's store, left the store wearing a jacket which the arresting security officer thought the plaintiff had shoplifted. The plaintiff claimed she had bought the jacket in the same store two weeks earlier. The security officer refused to let the plaintiff phone her husband or employer so as to confirm the explanation about the coat. At the police station a charge was filed against her for theft of the jacket. She was released upon bond. When in court the plaintiff produced five witnesses to support her statement about the jacket's purchase, the store offered to drop the charge if the plaintiff would execute a release, which she refused to do. Upon a finding of innocence, the judge chastized the store's representatives for maintaining the prosecution despite the uncontradicted evidence of innocence, for the sole purpose of forcing the plaintiff to execute a release. The plaintiff won the civil suit for false arrest.[65]

---

63. Before any release forms of the type here presented are used, a check should be made to assure that they conform to the law of the particular state where the release is requested. Laws vary from state to state and even within different appellate court districts within the same state. Additionally, state laws are subject to frequent change. The forms presented above are intended as examples; they do not and can not substitute for consultation with competent legal counsel.

64. Holmes v. Barney's Club, 156 Cal. Rptr. 557 (Ct. App. 1979). The arrest was made for disturbance of the peace.

65. Gref v. McCrory Co., 368 So. 2d 1217 (La. App. 1979).
   In addition to the foregoing cases, consider State v. Devercelli, 314 A.2d 767 (D.C. 1974).

In a major 1986 decision, the Supreme Court spelled out some of the circumstances relevant to the enforceability of a release signed in exchange for the dismissal of pending criminal charges. While rejecting a *per se* rule of unenforceability initially imposed by a lower federal court, the Court ruled that a "case-by-case" analysis was required to determine whether the release was a voluntary one. Various factors may be considered, including whether the individual was in custody at the time of signing the release, whether the individual signing the release had the advice of a lawyer, and whether the release agreement was executed under judicial supervision. Although the case was decided in the context of a release of a possible federal civil rights suit against police, courts may also utilize the reasoning in the context of suits against private security in light of its focus on voluntariness of the signing of such a release.[66]

A special circumstance requiring extra care is that involving the arrest or detention of minors. First, it should be clear that minors, under ordinary circumstances, will not have the capacity to sign releases which effectively waive the right to bring a civil lawsuit on their behalf. In addition to the signature of the minor on the release, it will ordinarily be necessary to obtain signatures from the minor's parents or guardians. In one recent case, however, a court found that even this was not a legally enforceable waiver of the right to sue, when the parent or guardian had not been specifically court-appointed as the minor's legal representative for that purpose.[67] Because the laws of each of the states may vary somewhat, the advice of competent local legal counsel should be obtained regarding the wording of releases and the required signatures.

66. Town of Newton v. Rumery, 480 U.S. 386 (1987). Other recent cases interpreting the principles of *Newton* include: Vallone v. Lee, 7 F.3d 196 (11th Cir. 1993) (unenforceable when obtained prior to release from jail); Hill v. City of Cleveland, 12 F.3d 575 (6th Cir. 1993) (enforceable because voluntary); Livingstone v. North Belle Vernon Borough, 12 F.3d 1205 (3rd Cir. 1993) (unenforceable when never reduced to writing); Woods v. Rhodes, 994 F.2d 494 (8th Cir. 1993) (enforceable because voluntary); Cain v. Darby Borough, 7 F.3d 377 (3rd Cir. 1993) (unenforceable when obtained pursuant to "blanket" policy of requiring such a release from any criminal defendant asking to be placed in special case disposition program).

67. Y.W. v. National Super Markets, Inc., 876 S.W.2d 785 (Mo. App. 1994). In this case an 11-year-old girl was allegedly observed shoplifting candy by a supermarket's security personnel. They detained the girl, and, while she was still detained, her mother entered into a stipulated release agreement whereby the store agreed not to prosecute the minor in exchange for the minor's agreement not to bring civil charges against the store. Subsequently, through a duly-appointed "next friend," the minor filed a civil suit against the supermarket alleging an assault and battery upon her. The trial court granted the store's motion to dismiss the suit on the ground that the minor's right to bring the suit had been contracted away. The release had both the mother's and the minor's names signed on it. However, a Missouri appeals court overturned the dismissal of the suit, ruling that:

   a. A minor herself would not have the capacity to sign away her right to bring suit;

   b. A parent does not have the authority to sign away the minor's right to bring suit under Missouri state law, unless already duly appointed by a court as the minor's legal representative; and

   c. That the release agreement was also unenforceable as violative of public policy because a private citizen or entity may "not contract away his/her right to press criminal charges against the perpetrator of a crime."

LEGAL CONSEQUENCES OF ILLEGAL SEARCHES AND SEIZURES

As in the case of an illegal arrest, any person, including a police officer, who makes an illegal search and seizure incurs the risk of civil and criminal liability, by reason of state statutes or state court decisions. Such liability occurs even if the person affected by the search and seizure may be guilty of the relevant offense. As in arrest situations, any person acting under color of law (e.g., a police officer) who makes an illegal search and seizure may be sued civilly and prosecuted under certain federal statutes. Civilly, he may incur liability for a violation of the Civil Rights Act of 1871, discussed previously.[68] He may also be prosecuted criminally under a 1948 statute when, while acting under color of law, he "willfully" deprives a person of a constitutional right or privilege.[69] Moreover, even if not acting under color of law, he may be prosecuted if he conspires "to injure, oppress, threaten or intimidate any citizen in the free exercise or enjoyment of any right or privilege secured to him by the Constitution or laws of the United States."[70]

If a police officer or other person making an illegal search or seizure damages someone's property, she may be prosecuted in state courts for "criminal damage to property." If entry on another's land is involved, the offense may be "criminal trespass."[71]

Suppression of Evidence Illegally Seized by the Police

An illegal search and seizure, as with an illegal arrest, does not immunize a defendant from criminal prosecution, nor does it afford her any basis for postconviction relief where no evidence so procured was used against her at trial.[72] However, whenever evidence is seized *by the police* or someone acting in their behalf, pursuant to either an illegal arrest or an illegal search, the person against whom the evidence is sought to be used in a criminal prosecution may "move to suppress" it and thereby have it excluded from use at the trial.[73] This process is based on the so-called exclusionary rule, the use of which was, until 1961, left to the discretion of

68. 42 U.S.C. Sec. 1983, *supra* note 2.

69. 18 U.S.C. Sec. 242, *supra* note 3.

70. 18 U.S.C. Sec. 241, *supra* note 18.

71. *See, e.g.,* 725 ILCS Sec. 5/21-1, 3.

72. United States v. Balistrieri, 403 F.2d 472, 477 (7th Cir. 1968); State v. Baumgardner, 79 N.M. 341, 443 P.2d 511, 513 (1968).

73. As a general rule, only a person with a proprietary interest in the objects seized or in the premises or vehicle searched has the right (i.e., "standing") to file a motion to suppress evidence. Brown v. United States, 411 U.S. 223 (1973). In some limited circumstances, state law may reject the standing requirement. *See* Article 1, Sec. 5 of the Louisiana Constitution, which has been interpreted in this manner. However, the Louisiana courts have not been expansive in their interpretation of the constitutional provision.

The United States Supreme Court continues to adhere to the standing requirement. In one of the Supreme Court's 1980 cases, a defendant who was being prosecuted for falsifying his federal tax return moved to suppress documents which had been illegally seized from the briefcase of a

the various states to either adopt or reject. Then, in the famous case of *Mapp v. Ohio*, the United States Supreme Court mandated the rule's adoption by all states.[74] The avowed purpose of the rule was to discourage illegal police conduct.

In 1984, the United States Supreme Court formally adopted a "good-faith" exception to the exclusionary rule. In two cases decided on the same date, the Court held that the exclusionary rule should not be applied when a police officer conducting a search has acted in a good-faith, objectively reasonable reliance on a warrant issued by a detached and neutral magistrate that is subsequently determined to be invalid.[75]

The motion to suppress the seized evidence generally must be made before trial,[76] but if the defendant is not aware of the grounds for the motion before trial, or if the opportunity to make the motion was not present, the motion to suppress may be made during the trial when the prosecution seeks to use the evidence. If the judge sustains a pretrial motion and suppresses the evidence, in the federal system, and in many states, an appeal from this ruling may be taken immediately by the prosecutor.[77] Such an appeal does not constitute a violation of the defendant's protection against "double jeopardy," because jeopardy does not attach until the defendant is put on trial. The defendant has no such right of immediate appeal because, as to her, the order denying her motion for suppression of evidence is not a "final order." The motion to suppress evidence may be made during a civil proceeding as well as during a criminal proceeding *if* the civil proceeding is "quasi-criminal" in nature, i.e., "almost" a criminal prosecution because of a possible penalty of some sort to the defendant.

EXAMPLE

Pusher's automobile is unlawfully searched by the police. In it, they find narcotics. Although vehicles used to transport narcotics may be subject to forfeitures, in a legal proceeding to have Pusher's automobile forfeited to the state (for delivery to a local law enforcement agency for its own use), the narcotic evidence would be suppressed, just as it would be in a criminal prosecution against Pusher himself.[78]

Bahamian bank officer. The Court held that the defendant lacked standing to suppress the evidence, because the challenged seizure did not invade the defendant's own legitimate expectation of privacy. United States v. Payner, 447 U.S. 727 (1980).

74. Mapp v. Ohio, 367 U.S. 643, 81 S. Ct. 1684 (1961).

75. United States v. Leon, 468 U.S. 897, 104 S. Ct. 3405 (1984) and Massachusetts v. Sheppard, 468 U.S. 981 (1984). The good faith exception had also been adopted earlier by a federal appeals court in United States v. Williams, 622 F.2d 830 (5th Cir. 1980), and by the highest court in New York in People v. Adams, 53 N.Y.2d 1, 422 N.E.2d 537 (1981). *See also* State v. Lehneu, 403 So. 2d 683 (La. 1981). In addition, some states adopted such an exception by statute. *See* Colo. Rev. Stats., 16-3-308 (1981).

As this book goes to press, the United States Congress is considering possible legislation which would extend the good faith exception to instances of warrantless searches and seizures where the officer reasonably believed she had probable cause for the search.

76. *See, e.g.,* Fed. Rules Crim. Pro. Rule 12(b) and 725 ILCS Sec. 5/114-12. For a collection of cases, see 50 A.L.R.2d 583 and 50 A.L.R. 2d Later Case Service, 531-592, Sec. 11.

77. Ill. Sup. Ct. Rule 604; 18 U.S.C. Sec. 3731; State v. Johnson, 50 Hawaii 525, 445 P.2d 36 (1968).

78. One 1958 Plymouth Sedan v. Pennsylvania, 380 U.S. 693, 85 S. Ct. 1246 (1965); One 1963 Chevrolet Pickup Truck v. Commonwealth, 208 Va. 506, 158 S.E.2d 755 (1968).

A defendant may also move to suppress evidence seized by the police as a result of information revealed to them in an invalid confession, or during an interrogation following an illegal arrest.[79] This evidence, say the courts, is "fruit of the poisonous tree."

Civil and Criminal Liability of Security Officers and Other Private Citizens for Illegal Search and Seizure

The earlier discussion regarding the civil and criminal liability of security officers and other private citizens for illegal arrests is equally applicable to their conduct with respect to illegal searches and seizures.

Legal Status of Evidence Illegally Seized by Security Officers and Other Private Citizens

Because the purpose of the exclusionary rule was to discourage illegal *police* conduct, and because it is designed to remedy violations of the Fourth Amendment to the U.S. Constitution (which is a limitation on governmental actions alone), the rule is generally inapplicable to evidence illegally obtained by a *private citizen* while acting on her own initiative.[80]

An exception was made by the Montana Supreme Court in a 4-to-3 decision of June 4, 1981, holding that the rule applied to searches and seizures by private citizens as well as those made by police.[81] The reason for this deviation from the otherwise

---

79. Dunaway v. New York, 442 U.S. 200 (1979).

80. The first case so holding was Burdeau v. McDowell, 256 U.S. 465 (1921), cited with approval in Coolidge v. New Hampshire, 403 U.S. 443 (1971). Representative other cases to the same effect are: Barnes v. United States, 373 F.2d 517 (5th Cir. 1967); United States v. Mekjian, 505 F.2d 1320 (5th Cir. 1975); Herbert v. State, 269 A.2d 430 (Ind. App. 1970); People v. Morton, 98 Cal. Rptr. 261 (Cal. App. 1971); Stevenson v. State, 403 A.2d 812 (Md. App. 1979). *See also* Lucas v. United States, 411 A.2d 360 (D.C. Ct. App. 1980).

When, however, a private person serves as an agent of the police or acts in concert with them, her conduct is equated with that of the police. Stapleton v. Superior Court, 73 Cal. Rptr. 575, 447 P.2d 967; United States v. Davis, 482 F.2d 893 (9th Cir. 1973). But the mere calling of the police upon discovering evidence of a crime does not have that effect. For instance, in United States v. Roberts, 644 F.2d 683 (8th Cir. 1980), the discovery by a private storage company's employees of marijuana in an unlocked locker within a storage area leased to the defendant, and the calling of the police thereafter, amounted to only a private seizure. It is of interest to note, however, the case of Walter v. United States, 447 U.S. 649 (1980). A shipment of sealed cartons containing obscene films was delivered to the wrong address. Company employees there opened the cartons, found sealed film containers with explicit descriptions, and called the FBI. The FBI picked up the packages and viewed the films without obtaining a warrant. The Supreme Court held that unauthorized viewing of the films by the FBI constituted an unreasonable invasion of the owner's privacy. It was a search; there was no warrant; the owner had not consented; and there were no exigent circumstances. The fact that the boxes were opened by a private party before the FBI acquired them was held not to excuse the failure to obtain a search warrant.

81. State v. Hyem, 38 Mont. 891, 630 P.2d 202 (1981).

unanimous court rulings is the fact that, unlike other state constitutions, Montana's contains an explicit protection of privacy rights. It provides: "The right of individual privacy is essential to the well being of a free society and shall not be infringed without the showing of a compelling state interest." The majority of the court refused to make a distinction, for purposes of applying the exclusionary rule, between a police search and one made by private citizens, which, in this case, was an illegal entry by subterfuge into a home where private citizens searched for and found a pair of stolen skis. The dissenting justices were of the view that neither the history nor the purpose of the exclusionary rule justified its application to private citizens.

The conduct of an ordinary security officer falls into the private citizen category, unaffected by the exclusionary rule, since her powers of arrest are usually no greater than those of an ordinary citizen.[82] The situation is different, however, when a security officer is a moonlighting police officer,[83] or when she conducts a search at the instigation of the police or in cooperation with them.[84] This is also true in those cases where a security officer is deputized or commissioned by a governmental agency or official, or is otherwise the recipient of a grant of powers similar to those possessed by the police. In such instances, security officers are themselves considered to be governmental agents, and their illegal seizures, therefore, become subject to the exclusionary rule.[85] The mere licensing of security officers, however, does not transform them into the police category.[86]

82. State v. McDaniel, 44 Ohio App. 2d 163, 337 N.E.2d 173 (1975); People v. Toliver, 377 N.E.2d 207 (Ill. App. 1978); People v. Horman, 22 N.Y.2d 378, 239 N.E.2d 625 (1968). In the *McDaniel* case the decision was unaffected by the fact that one of the security officers had been "deputized" by a sheriff who actually did not have the legal authority to do so. In the *Horman* case, a store detective searched a suspected shoplifter and discovered a loaded revolver, which was admitted into evidence.

An extensive note on the case law is in 36 A.L.R.3d 553 (1971). For a viewpoint to the effect that the exclusionary rule should be applicable to private police as well as public police, see *Regulation of Private Police,* 40 S. Calif. L. Rev. 540, 546 (1967).

83. Upon this point, in the context of the requirements for the constitutional rights warnings to custodial suspects prior to interrogation, see the comments of Justice Bird in her concurring opinion in *In Re* Deborah C., 177 Cal. Rptr. 852, 860, 635 P.2d 446 (1981).

84. Machlin v. State, 247 Ind. 218, 225 N.E.2d 762 (1967); United States v. Newton, 510 F.2d 1149 (7th Cir. 1975). In United States v. Roberts, 644 F.2d 683 (8th Cir. 1980), the court made a distinction, as to a single defendant, between seizures made of his property by a citizen acting independently of the police and seizures from him where there was citizen-police cooperation.

85. Pratt v. State, 9 Md. App. 220, 263 A.2d 247 (1970); Shaw v. May Department Stores Co., 268 A.2d 607 (D.C. Ct. App. 1970).

Examples of statutes dealing with commissions are Ohio Stats., R.C., Sec. 737.05 (director of public safety of city as the commissioner), and R.C., Sec. 4973.17 (governor empowered to commission security officers of banks, building and loan associations, and railway police).

For an early case involving the status of a commissioned security officer, see N.Y., Chicago & St. Louis Ry. v. Fieback, 87 Ohio St. 254, 100 N.E. 899 (1912), holding that the commission of a railroad policeman transformed him into a "public officer."

For a case involving the exclusion of evidence of intoxication because of the illegality of an arrest by a college campus uniformed police officer off the campus, see Smith v. States, 510 P.2d 962 (Okla. Crim. App. 1973).

86. United States v. Lima, 424 A.2d 113 (D.C. Ct. App. 1980). The court distinguished a licensed security officer from one commissioned as a "special police officer" who is accorded the same ar-

In a 1978 case, Maryland's Court of Appeals held that so long as a special police officer (a commissioned security officer) is acting in connection with the care, custody, or protection of her employer's property and not just that for which an arrest is made, she may exercise the same power to search incident to arrest as is possessed by a regular police officer.[87]

In contrast, the West Virginia Supreme Court held that when a security guard detains a suspected shoplifter under the authority of a statute giving merchants the right to do so, the detention activated the state constitutional protections against unreasonable search and compelled self-incrimination. When the security guard ordered the suspect to empty his pockets, this was a search. Unpaid merchandise items were uncovered in the search. The court stated that the warrantless search had not been shown necessary to uncover weapons which might be used against the security guard or to prevent the destruction of evidence. The court stated that, on remand for additional proceedings, the items seized should be admitted into evidence only if the state could meet the burden of proving that the security guard's search fell within an authorized exception to the warrant requirement.[88]

A California appellate court has held that a shopping mall security guard did not assert state authority in conducting a search and that the exclusionary rule therefore did not apply.[89] The case involved a wallet which was brought by a mall patron to the security guard. He opened it, finding a partial marijuana cigarette and a paper bundle which, after being opened, yielded a powder that resembled cocaine. The sheriff was then called and a deputy dispatched, who concluded that the powder was cocaine. He arrested the owner of the wallet when she called to retrieve it. The court found that the mall security guard acted in a purely private capacity and did not assert the power of the state; thus the Fourth Amendment and the exclusionary rule did not apply. The court distinguished *People v. Zelinski*,[90] in which the court held that store detectives, when they make an arrest, do not act in a purely private capacity but "assert the power of the state."

The court noted that the California Supreme Court in *Zelinski* had limited its decision by stating that it was not deciding that "all of the varied activities of private security personnel" are governed by the restraints of the exclusionary rule. The guards in this case did not make an arrest. "They merely inspected lost property and called the police." The mere fact that security guards

---

rest powers as regular police officers, including the right to carry a firearm while on duty. It specifically noted that a licensed security officer in the D.C. is not permitted to carry either a firearm or handcuffs.

87. Gray v. State, 38 Md. App. 343, 380 A.2d 1071 (1978). The Maryland statute that affords full police powers to commissioned security officers is Art. 41 Sec. 4-905, Md. Ann. Code. By reason of this statute, however, a person arrested by a security officer is entitled to the benefit of the exclusionary rule (see *supra* note 85), and also to the warnings of her constitutional rights prior to a custodial interrogation.

88. State v. Muegge, 360 S.E.2d 216 (W. Va. 1987).

89. People v. Brouillette, 258 Cal. Rptr. 635 (Cal. App. 1989).

90. People v. Zelinski, 24 Cal. 3d 357, 594 P.2d 1000 (1979).

"dressed like police and are looked upon by others as representing police authority" did not vary the result, nor did the fact that they assisted police by calling the sheriffs' office and allowing the customer to come to the mall office to be arrested when she thought she was coming to collect her wallet. There was no showing that the guards, in inspecting the contents of the wallet, did so as agents of the state.

In another California case,[91] however, the court held that a store employee's search of a customer while detaining him for police to arrive and arrest him was illegal under state law. In this case, a store employee saw a customer remove two packs of cigarettes from a rack and put one packet in each pocket. He notified the store manager who observed the customer leaving without going through a checkout stand. The two store employees went outside and confronted the customer, who denied taking anything. One of them reached into the customer's pockets and retrieved two packs of cigarettes. They then detained the customer in the back room of the store until police arrived.

The court, citing *People v. Zelinski,* said that whether a search is illegal depends on the purpose of the search. "If the search is conducted by the merchant or his agent for the purposes of self-help, there is no state action." Self-help would include requesting a suspected shoplifter to "voluntarily surrender" the item suspected to be stolen, or conducting a "limited and reasonable search" of packages, shopping bags, handbags, or other property in order to recover the item, or requiring the person to supply identification upon finding a stolen item. State statutes in California granting merchants a privilege to conduct such searches do not include clothing worn by the person. In this case, the defendant's pockets were searched after he denied taking anything, and he was detained until police arrived. Under California law, therefore, the search was illegal and the evidence would be suppressed under the rationale of *Zelinski.*

Despite this, however, the court noted that a new provision of the California Constitution, Article I, Section 28, subdivision (d), now requires that questions about the exclusion of evidence be resolved under federal rather than state law. Federal law, the court held, does not require exclusion of evidence obtained by a search by private parties when "no official of the government, federal or state, had any connection with the wrongful seizure or any knowledge of it until after the fact." The court therefore affirmed the conviction of the defendant.

The court still found, however, that the search was illegal under California law. A civil lawsuit for damages based on unreasonable search is therefore still possible, based on these or similar facts. The court specifically noted that "an improper search by security personnel may pose a serious threat to privacy," but that the "civil remedy available to the victims of such wrongful conduct against the offenders and their employees should provide a greater and more equitable deterrent than exclusion of the evidence."

To the extent that security personnel exceed the reasonable limits and methods designed to uncover evidence of crime, there may be civil liability, and such civil liability may be imposed on the employer as well as the employee. In one Missouri

91. People v. Ornelas, 253 Cal. Rptr. 165 (Cal. App. 1988).

case,[92] for instance, an employer was held liable for $20,000 for a security guard's grabbing of a woman's breasts and squeezing them while searching her breast pockets for a stolen item. Because the guard had authority to conduct searches for the purposes of recovering stolen property, his search was within the scope of his employment, despite the fact that his actions during it were "outside the scope of dececy and good taste."

One court recently held that airport security personnel, since they act pursuant to federal aviation law and regulations in conducting searches of passengers, are engaged in governmental action, and that their activities are therefore covered by the Fourth Amendment and the exclusionary rule. At the same time, it found that a pat-down of a passenger after she activated a metal detector, and a further, more extensive body search after the pat-down revealed "something hard" under the passenger's blouse, were reasonable, since the object concealed could have been a weapon. (It turned out to be packages containing drugs.)[93]

TYPICAL CIVIL LIABILITY SITUATIONS

The remainder of this chapter examines some of the typical types of lawsuits brought against private security personnel and their employers, and some recent examples of such cases.

Assault and Battery

There are numerous cases in which employers have been held liable for assault and battery on customers or other persons by security guards or other employees. There are three major legal theories which are used to impose such liability. The first is the doctrine of *respondeat superior* (vicarious liability) which makes an employer liable for the wrongdoing of its agents or employees when carried out "within the scope" of their employment. Employers may defend against such liability by seeking to establish that the employee acted for purely personal purposes, outside the scope of their authorized duties, or while off on a "frolic of their own."

The second theory is the "complicity" theory, under which an employer is held liable for authorizing, ratifying, or approving of its employee's wrongful acts. This doctrine is often particularly important in the context of determining whether an employer may be held liable for punitive damages (intended to punish the wrongdoer), as well as compensatory damages (designed to fairly compensate the victim for injuries suffered).

The third theory is negligence and seeks to impose liability on the employer for its own purported wrongdoing, rather than vicarious liability for the wrongdoing of the employee. These cases normally focus on an allegation that the employer was negligent in hiring, training, supervising, disciplining, or retaining the employee.

---

92. Clark v. Skaggs Companies, Inc., 724 S.W.2d 545 (Mo. App. 1986).
93. State v. Baez, 530 So. 2d 405 (Fla. App. 1988).

An employee is usually within the scope of her employment when engaged in the performance of her customary duties.

EXAMPLE

A rent-a-car company employee allegedly pounded a customer on the back of the head and kicked him during an argument over the price of a deposit. The company was held liable for $350,000 in compensatory and $400,000 in punitive damages. The employee's normal duties included dealing with customers regarding the rental of cars, so this—combined with the employer's knowledge of the employee's "short temper"—was considered sufficient to impose employer liability.[94]

The question of whether the employee is on or off duty may not be as important as the nature of the act performed.

EXAMPLE

A store employee sweeping the sidewalk outside a store told two youths parking in a fire lane to move their car. They refused to do so. The employee soon after "punched out" on the store's timeclock, but returned outside with a machete which he poked in and out of the partially opened windows of the youths' car. The employer was found liable, even though the employee's shift had ended, because the incident originated from the employee performing work-related duties.[95]

By way of contrast, there have been several cases in which employers were held not vicariously liable under the doctrine of *respondeat superior* for sexual assaults by employees.

EXAMPLE

A security guard forced a 15-year-old girl who was in a shopping mall to accompany him to the mall's security office where he assaulted, raped, and sodomized her. The court granted summary judgment for the employer on the resulting lawsuit. An employer can be held vicariously liable for the wrongdoing of its employee if committed in the course of the employee's work, even if the acts are done irregularly or with disregard of instructions. But the court reasoned that there is no *respondeat superior* liability for wrongful acts committed by the employee "for personal motives unrelated to the furtherance of the employer's business." In this instance, the court found, the outrageous conduct of the guard was "in no way incidental to the furtherance" of the company's interest. His acts were committed for "personal motives and were a complete departure from the normal duties of a security guard."[96]

Another such case, in which the employer was not held liable because the employee acted for "personal motives," involved a bar being held not liable for a bouncer's assault on a customer after the customer allegedly patted the bouncer's

---

94. Greenfield v. Spectrum Inv. Corp., 219 Cal. Rptr. 805 (App. 1985).

95. Wattik v. Lewis Grocer Co., 476 So. 2d 444 (La. App. 1985).

96. Heindel v. Bowery Savings Bank, 525 N.Y.S.2d 428 (A.D. 1988).

girlfriend on the buttocks. The bouncer followed the man outside where he allegedly bit the patron's thumb, tried to gouge his eyes out, beat his head against a brick wall, and stabbed him twice with a knife. While the bouncer may have had the responsibility to remove an unruly customer from the premises, the conduct alleged to have taken place outside "exceeded reasonable bounds and was excessively violent and not to be expected by his employer; nor was it in furtherance of his employer's business," as the bouncer admitted that he had "lost complete control" and "sought revenge."[97]

In a Nevada case, the plaintiff, a woman employed by an escort service, sued a hotel after she was pushed down a flight of stairs by two security guards. The Nevada Supreme Court upheld liability of the employer on either of the two theories advanced by the plaintiff—*respondeat superior* or "complicity." Substantial evidence presented by the hotel gave its security guards wide latitude in dealing with unescorted females who were not registered guests. The jury resolved a dispute between the two parties as to how the woman fell by finding that the guards pushed the woman down the stairs while she was waiting for an elevator, having just left a client's room. The plaintiff was awarded $15,000 in compensatory damages and $10,000 in punitive damages.[98]

Damages in assault and battery cases can be very substantial. In one Connecticut case, $2 million in damages were assessed against a gas station owner solely on a theory of vicarious liability for the actions of two employees in severely beating and stabbing the plaintiff in the heart. The plaintiff was rendered comatose and suffered permanent brain damage after the employees attacked him because they suspected him of stealing a company checkbook. The court ruled that regardless of the degree of fault attributed to each employee, the employer was liable for the entire sum.[99] When injuries are slight or almost nonexistent, a court may still award "nominal" damages, such as $1, to vindicate the right of customers to be free of an offensive or potentially harmful physical contact. When a jury or judge is sufficiently offended at the conduct engaged in, punitive (or exemplary) damages may be added on, even if only nominal damages are awarded because of the slight nature of the injuries. In one Colorado case,[100] the court awarded $1 in nominal damages for an assault by an employee against a tavern patron, but $500 in exemplary damages to deter future misconduct.

In addition to liability to those directly assaulted, in some jurisdictions there is also the possibility of liability to the victim's family if they observe the assault. In a New York case,[101] for instance, the court held that the child of a store customer could recover for the emotional distress of seeing an assault on his father in the store by two men.

97. Noah v. Ziehl, 759 S.W.2d 905 (Mo. App. 1988).

98. Ramada Inns, Inc. v. Sharp., 711 P.2d 1 (Nev. 1985).

99. Reilly v. DiBianco, 507 A.2d 106 (Conn. App. 1986).

100. Carey v. After the Goldrush, 715 P.2d 803 (Colo. App. 1986).

101. DiMarco v. Supermarkets General Corp., 524 N.Y.S.2d 743 (A.D. 1988).

A pattern of employee assaults on patrons may provide the basis for holding an employer liable for ratifying such conduct. In one Texas case,[102] for instance, a nightclub patron was awarded $15,500 in actual damages and $50,000 in punitive damages for being assaulted by several club employees. Two other patrons testified that they had also been kicked and beaten by the head doorman and required hospitalization as a result. The club owner had admitted in his testimony that he knew of at least six lawsuits for assault pending against the club at the time of trial. The court said the evidence was sufficient to support the jury's finding that the club condoned violent behavior by continuing to employ the head doorman after it knew of his "excessive use of force." It also showed a "pattern of violence" the club was apparently willing to tolerate. This "conscious indifference" to customers' rights and welfare supported the award of punitive damages.

Normally, an employer will not be found liable for the actions of another employer's agents, in the absence of a right to control their actions.

EXAMPLE

A man was observed in a department store by security personnel who suspected that he might be a shoplifter. A security guard followed the man when he left the store and proceeded to a different nearby department store. In that store, the security guard from store A notified a store B security guard regarding his suspicions, and also decided to remain to assist in case the store B guard required help. The man was then observed taking items from the men's department of the store. The store A guard gave chase and ultimately apprehended him in the store parking lot. The shoplifter broke his ankle when he jumped from one level of the parking lot to another while being chased. He sued store B for his injuries, claiming that the store A guard was acting as an agent of store B and had struck him with a nightstick and beat him with his fists. The court found that the store A guard's assistance was "neither requested nor sought by [store B] or by anyone on its behalf." In the absence of a right to control the conduct of the store A guard, the court found that store B could not be held liable for the injuries he allegedly inflicted during his chase and apprehension of the shoplifter.[103]

False Arrest/False Imprisonment

Security personnel who believe that a store customer is engaged in shoplifting, or that a business patron is engaged in other criminal activity, are faced with a dilemma. If they wait until they have solid evidence of the offense before taking action, the customer may simply leave. If they take action to detain the customer or have the customer arrested before such evidence has developed, they may face a possible civil lawsuit for false imprisonment or false arrest. Many states attempt to aid security personnel in such situations by enacting "merchants' privilege" statutes. Such statutes typically allow a merchant, or her employees who have "reasonable cause" to suspect a customer of theft, to detain such customer in a

---

102. Country Roads, Inc. v. Witt, 737 S.W.2d 362 (Tex. App. 1987).
103. Mapp v. Gimbels Department Store, 540 A.2d 941 (Pa. Super. 1988).

"reasonable manner" for a "reasonable time" to conduct a "reasonable investigation" of whether such suspicion is true.[104]

Many false imprisonment/false arrest suits still result, however, from arguably exceeding the permissible bounds of the investigation permitted by such statutes, or proceeding without the initial reasonable suspicion required. Additionally, such "merchants' privilege" statutes only apply to circumstances involving alleged shoplifting.[105]

In the absence of the existence or application of such a statute, a private citizen only has a privilege to detain another person she has probable cause to believe committed a felony. She may also have a privilege to arrest for a misdemeanor if it was committed in her presence. In one case,[106] for instance, a hotel guest was awarded $3,000 in damages when she was falsely accused of theft and was detained by a hotel manager without probable cause. No one had been at the desk when she first arrived to register. The manager later arrived and, after taking her registration and payment, discovered that the day's receipts were missing from the cash drawer. He locked the lobby door, called police, and accused the woman of the theft. Police arrived and she willingly consented to a search of her purse and car, convincing them of her complete innocence. Because the hotel manager detained her without probable cause, the hotel was liable for false imprisonment.

In order for the investigatory activity of store personnel to constitute "imprisonment," there must be some confinement of the plaintiff—a detention against the will of the customer. However, by itself, merely questioning an individual will not constitute detention. As one court noted: "a police officer—or the security guard in this case—has the same right that 'every citizen' has to question another person in a public place because the other person has an 'equal right' to pay no attention to the question."[107]

Similarly, a Texas court found that a customer who voluntarily remained on the premises to clear up the matter when she was accused by a garage manager of stealing money from the cash drawer had not been falsely imprisoned.[108] The manager had not threatened her or used force. Her consenting to a search and remaining on the premises until police arrived was her decision, so she was not confined.[109]

Although the mere accusation of theft may not constitute detention, the seizure of the customer's property—such as a bag, box or purse—may do so.

---

104. Gabrou v. May Dept. Stores Co., 462 A.2d 1102 (D.C. App. 1983).

105. See De Angelis v. Jamesway Dept. Store, 501 A.2d 561 (N.J. Super. A.D. 1985) (merchant's privilege statute did not apply to detention of employees suspected of stealing money).

106. Partin v. Meyer, 639 S.W.2d 342 (Ark. 1982).

107. Cobb v. Standard Drug Co., Inc., 453 A.2d 110 (D.C. App. 1982).

108. Martinez v. Goodyear Tire & Rubber Co., 651 S.W.2d 18 (Tex. App. 1983).

109. See J.C. Penney Co. v. Romero, 318 S.W.2d 129 (Tex. App. 1958) and Walker v. Martin, 129 S.W.2d 1149 (Tex. App. 1939), both illustrating the long-established principle that a plaintiff's willingness to remain on the premises to establish her innocence does not give rise to a cause of action for false imprisonment. See also Lopez v. Winchell's Donut House, 466 N.E.2d 1309 (Ill. App. 1984).

In a Georgia case[110], a store was found liable for $25,000 for false imprisonment of a customer. The sales clerk said "I got to search your boxes" after detaining her. The act of seizing the property, the court said, resulted in her not actually having the choice to leave the store since to do so would abandon her property. The clerk's words, "now you can go," spoken after it was clear that all merchandise had been paid for, also indicated that the plaintiff was restrained against her will.

Many retailers use electronic devices to detect theft. If store personnel detain customers on the basis of such devices, but have failed to operate them properly, there still may be liability for false imprisonment. In a Louisiana case[111], a store customer was stopped and detained by store detectives when an electronic alarm was triggered by a tag on the merchandise. The clerk had neglected to remove the tag when the plaintiff made the purchase. While several people watched, she was forced to open her shopping bag and the tagged merchandise was discovered. After it had been determined that the merchandise had been paid for, she was released. The court refused to grant summary judgment for the defendant and ordered the case to go to trial.[112]

In a decision to the contrary, one court found that the sounding of such a "sensor alarm" was held to have provided a security guard with probable cause to believe that an offense was being committed.[113] The court also found that guard had not detained the customer for an unreasonable length of time, promptly investigating the customer's side of the story and letting her go shortly after he discovered that she had in fact paid for the merchandise in question.[114]

One court upheld observations made by a security guard via a video camera as sufficient to provide him with reasonable cause to detain a customer for suspected shoplifting and declined to require the defendants to produce a tape from the video camera to prove reasonable cause.[115]

Several cases have held that the concealment of merchandise, while constituting grounds for suspicion sufficient to support detainment for investigation, does not, by itself, constitute probable cause for arrest. The concealment may be inadvertent, courts reason, or the customer may place an item in a pocket or purse for

110. Burrow v. K-Mart Corp., 304 S.E.2d 460 (Ga. App. 1983).

111. Daly v. City Stores Co., 424 So. 2d 519 (La. App. 1982).

112. *See also* Fischer v. Famous-Barr Co., 646 S.W.2d 819 (Mo. App. 1982) (ordering trial on false imprisonment claim of woman customer detained after electronic device sounded because clerk failed to remove tags from purchased merchandise) and Keefe v. Gimbels, 478 N.Y.S.2d 745 (N.Y. City Civ. Ct. 1984) ($175,000 judgment against store which detained woman twice when alarm sounded as she exited store; sensormatic tag was contained in woman's pocket a second time, which the store admitted was frequently done by shoplifters to mislead security personnel).

113. Dent v. May Dept. Stores Co., 459 A.2d 1042 (D.C. App. 1982).

114. *See also* Causey v. Katz & Bestoff, Inc., 539 So. 2d 944 (La. App. 1989) (store's detention of blind suspected shoplifter for 25 minutes after antitheft buzzer sounded was reasonable) and Estes v. Jack Eckerd Corp., 360 S.E.2d 649 (Ga. App. 1987) (storekeeper not liable under Georgia law for detaining suspected shoplifter when alarm sounds, even if employee's negligence caused device to activate).

115. Townsend v. Sears, Roebuck & Co., 466 So. 2d 675 (La. App. 1985).

ease in carrying, intending to take it out at a cash register and pay for it once exiting the store.[116]

On the other hand, merchandise need not be hidden to be considered concealed. In one New Jersey case,[117] a security guard observed a customer leaving the store wearing a coat with an inspection tag fastened to the back. He stopped her and asked her to return to show she had purchased the item. She contended that she had bought the item the day before and had forgot to remove all of the tags. She was detained approximately 30–45 minutes before being allowed to leave. She argued that the merchant's privilege statute, which at the time required "concealed merchandise" before the privilege applied, was inapplicable to the situation since she had not attempted to hide the coat when she was stopped. The court ruled that the term "concealed unpurchased merchandise" applies to those items in plain view but worn or carried as though they had been purchased.

Continuing to confine a customer after a reasonable explanation of the customer's actions are given may result in liability even if the initial detention was reasonable. In one case, $10,000 (including punitive damages) was awarded for a detention which continued after the customer explained that he did not steal an item but had placed it by the cash register after deciding not to buy it. Despite the fact that the item was found where the customer said it would be, the detention continued and the customer was arrested, with one security officer allegedly saying "my shoplifters I bust, I don't let them go free. I always prosecute." The court found that the defendants' actions were not reasonable in light of the plaintiff's explanation.[118]

Firearms Related Claims

Historically, many states had a "fleeing felon" rule which allowed police officers to use deadly force to stop a felon fleeing from the scene of her crime—regardless of whether the felon was armed, had used force in commission of her offense, or was posing an immediate threat to the life or safety of the officer or others. In some states, private citizens were also allowed to use deadly force in this fashion, standing in the shoes of a police officer in stopping a fleeing felon.

In 1985, the United States Supreme Court imposed certain constitutional limitations on the ability of police officers to use deadly force in this fashion in the important case of *Tennessee v. Garner.*[119] The Court held that an officer may not use

---

116. Vogel v. Gibson's Discount Center, 681 P.2d 40 (Mont. 1984) (jury could find that a woman did not intend to steal a pair of sandals when she tucked them in her bag since the heels and price tags were exposed, she was still inside the store, and she had not yet gone through the check out counter), and Logan v. Kuhn's Big K Corp., 676 S.W.2d 948 (Tenn. 1984) (trial needed to determine customer's intentions when he asked for a shopping bag from sales clerk and placed items within bag as he shopped).

117. Henry v. Shopper's World, 490 A.2d 320 (N.J. Super. A.D. 1985).

118. Atlantic Zayre, Inc. v. Williams, 322 S.E.2d 83 (Ga. App. 1984).

119. Tennessee v. Garner, 471 U.S. 1 (1985).

deadly force to stop a fleeing felon unless there is a reasonable belief that the felon poses a threat of death or serious physical harm either to the officer or others. The Court therefore held unconstitutional, under the Fourth Amendment, as an unreasonable search and seizure, the use of deadly force against a fleeing unarmed burglar. It would seem apparent that the same limitations on the use of deadly force—in addition to whatever other limitations are imposed under state law—will apply to armed security guards.

At least one court in Michigan has explicitly held this.[120] Earlier decisions in Michigan had allowed private citizens to use deadly force to prevent any felon from escaping because "essentially, in that situation, a private citizen is playing the part of a police officer." The court concluded that since the decision in *Garner* limited when the police are allowed to use deadly force, the same limits should apply to a private citizen who "stands in the shoes of a police officer." Security agencies utilizing armed guards, therefore, should be familiar with the parameters of the rule in *Garner*, which are:

> Where the officer has probable cause to believe that the suspect poses a threat of serious physical harm, either to the officer or to others, it is not constitutionally unreasonable to prevent escape by using deadly force. Thus, if the suspect threatens the officer with a weapon or there is probable cause to believe that he has committed a crime involving the infliction or threatened infliction of serious physical harm, deadly force may be used if necessary to prevent escape, and if, where feasible, some warning has been given.

This rule would appear to preclude the use of deadly force to protect property alone where there is no threat of bodily harm or death to any person. State and local law, in many instances, may impose still other restrictions on the use of firearms, including special licensing requirements for armed security guards.[121] Additionally, to the extent that a security guard is acting within the scope of her employment, an employer may be held vicariously liable for her unjustified or negligent shooting of an individual.[122] For an employer to be held vicariously liable for the intentional wrong of an employee, the act must be motivated, at least in part, by a purpose of furthering the employer's business and must not be unexpected in view of the employee's duties. Even if the shooting is *partially* motivated by personal motive, the employer may still be liable.

If a security guard was acting in what she thought was reasonable self-defense, there will be no liability. This principle is illustrated by an Indiana case in which the appeals court overturned a $500,000 jury damage award against a store for the fatal shooting of an innocent bystander by its clerk during a robbery. The innocent bystander customer entered the liquor store at the same time that two masked armed men entered. The two robbers flanked the customer. The robbers fired

---

120. People v. Couch, No. 101936, Mich. App., April 3, 1989, 45 CrL 2179 (June 7, 1989).

121. *See* People v. Clark, 505 N.E.2d 1179 (Ill. App. 1987) and Commonwealth v. Walton, 529 A.2d 15 (Pa. Super 1987).

122. *See, e.g.,* Weinberg v. Johnson, 518 A.2d 985 (D.C. App. 1986) ($2 million judgment against employer for employee's shooting a customer during a dispute).

some shots, which were returned by store employees. The customer vaulted over a store counter to seek cover and was fired at by a part-time store clerk who thought he was one of the robbers. The court held that the clerk acted in what he believed to be reasonable self-defense under the circumstances. The clerk was not the initial aggressor and, while the results may be tragic, it was reasonable for him to believe that he was in great risk of death and that the customer might be one of the robbers.[123]

When an armed security guard acts outside the scope of her employment, such as for *purely* personal motives, the employer will not be held vicariously liable.

EXAMPLE

One of the armed guards assigned to a store conspired with an accomplice to rob it. In the course of this robbery, the guard shot and killed the store manager.[124] A lawsuit against the store was filed by the widow, child, and parents of the deceased manager. The court found that since the guard intentionally engaged in a robbery of the store he was hired to protect, there was "no question" that he turned away from his duty and engaged in "conduct contrary to the purpose of his employment." Since his actions were clearly outside the scope of his employment, the employer was not liable.[125]

Malicious Prosecution

In order to recover for malicious prosecution or even to survive a defense motion to dismiss the lawsuit, normally all of the following elements will have to be present: (1) the commencement or continuation of an original criminal or civil judicial proceeding; (2) its legal causation by the present defendant; (3) its bona fide termination in favor of the present plaintiff; (4) the absence of probable cause for initiating the original proceeding, (5) the presence of malice in initiating it; and (6) damages.

EXAMPLE

A store employee was arrested and prosecuted on theft charges. She entered a plea of guilty to misdemeanor theft and was sentenced to one year of supervised probation, as well as to pay restitution. She sued the store for malicious prosecution. However, since

---

123. Carbo, Inc. v. Lowe, 521 N.E.2d 977 (Ind. App. 1988).

124. Vallejo v. Osco Drug, 743 S.W.2d 423 (Mo. App. 1987).

125. Other claims sometimes made involving firearms include negligence in training, Hemings v. Redford Lounge, Inc., 485 N.E.2d 1378 (Ind. App. 1985) (claim that employer did not adequately train armed guard), sale of firearms or ammunition in violation of ordinance or statute, see Montgomery Ward & Co. v. Cooper, 339 S.E.2d 755 (Ga. App. 1986) (violation of ordinance prohibiting sale of pistol without police certificate, purchaser used gun to shoot his wife), negligence in sale of firearms, see Salvi v. Montgomery Ward & Co., 489 N.E.2d 394 (Ill. App. 1986) (store liable for $546,000 for sale of BB gun to 14-year-old boy; while state law prohibited sale to children under 13, many companies increased age limit to 18; child's misuse of gun to injure brother was foreseeable), and negligence in display of guns or ammunition, see Kimbler v. Stillwell, 734 P.2d 1344 (Or. 1987) (store can be sued for not securing weapons in store display; burglar stole weapons which he later used to murder plaintiff's son).

the employee had entered an unconditional plea of guilty, she could not show that the criminal proceedings had terminated in her favor. She therefore could not maintain her lawsuit for malicious prosecution, and the court dismissed it.[126]

There are often other circumstances, besides a plea or finding of guilty in the criminal trial, which will bar the bringing of a malicious prosecution suit. In a New York case,[127] for instance, an employee had been accused of attempting to steal a package of men's tee shirts valued at $6.99. As a result of the incident, he was both discharged from his job and arrested on charges of petit larceny. He was subsequently acquitted by a jury and his union submitted to arbitration the question of whether he was wrongfully discharged. After a full hearing, at which both the union and employer were allowed to present witnesses, and at which the employee testified on his own behalf, the arbitrator ruled in favor of the store, upholding the termination.

When the employee later tried to bring a malicious prosecution/false imprisonment lawsuit, the court found that the arbitrator's award barred him from doing so, since "clearly, one of the issues litigated in the prior arbitration proceeding was whether the employer had probable cause to believe that the plaintiff attempted to steal merchandise from its store." Also important to the court's barring of the malicious prosecution lawsuit was the fact that the employee had a "full and fair opportunity" at the arbitration hearing to litigate that question, so its resolution was viewed as "conclusive" on the element of whether the employer had probable cause to believe that the employee stole merchandise.

Merely giving the police a bona fide report of what a store or other business premises honestly believes to be a crime cannot be the basis for a malicious prosecution action.

EXAMPLE

A hotel reported a guest to the police after he failed to pay his hotel bill until it reached $21,097. The hotel believed that the guest might be in violation of a local statute which presumed that a guest had an intent to defraud a hotel if he obtained credit by false pretenses or neglected to pay his bill on demand. After the police arrested the guest, charges were later dropped. But the malicious prosecution action filed by the guest was dismissed because the hotel did not act maliciously, i.e., in bad faith and without reasonable basis.[128]

In order for a store to be liable for malicious prosecution, it must not only "call" police, but must also initiate the officer's arrest of the customer. In a Georgia case,[129] the court noted that the store could not be held liable for malicious prosecution of an employee suspected of theft when the police officer conducted his own independent investigation of the store's suspicions before making an arrest.

---

126. Rabalais v. Blanche, 524 So. 2d 772 (La. App. 1988).

127. Luppo v. Waldbaum, Inc., 515 N.Y.S.2d 871 (A.D. 1987).

128. Vyas Sangidas v. Holiday Inns, Inc., 660 F. Supp. 666 (D. Puerto Rico 1987).

129. Huff v. Household International, 361 S.E.2d 273 (Ga. App. 1987).

In that case, a store investigator questioned four jewelry department sales employees about missing merchandise, and two of them implicated a fifth employee in the theft. After an investigation by local police, she was subsequently arrested, but a grand jury declined to indict her and she sued for malicious prosecution.

The arresting officer had conducted an independent investigation of the employee's alleged involvment with the missing merchandise. He stated that his decision to arrest her was made on the basis of this investigation, and was not at all influenced by any representative of the store. The store manager did not "take out a warrant" for the employee's arrest, but merely reported to police that two other employees had named her as being involved. Under these circumstances, the court entered summary judgment for the store on the employee's malicious prosecution lawsuit. Similarly, in a Missouri case,[130] a hospital was not liable for simply calling police to investigate when a security guard saw an employee pushing a laundry cart in which a calculator was covered by dirty linen. The hospital had not "instigated" the criminal prosecution of the employee. The hospital's security director testified that once the police arrived, "it was out of my hands." No hospital employee signed a complaint or testified at the preliminary hearing. The court rejected the plaintiff's argument that the security guard's statement to the police pointed him out as a thief and therefore "set in motion" the prosecution. The court disagreed, distinguishing an earlier case[131] in which an employer's agent both identified the alleged thief and also indicated a desire to prosecute. No conduct tending to influence the decision to prosecute was shown in the later case, and the court noted that if "mere identification of a particular suspect exposes one to liability for malicious prosecution," the "public policy" of encouraging citizens to assist the police would be "dissipated if not totally destroyed."

However, in those circumstances where a store or its employees furnish false information to the police and the police act on that information, the fact of who "filed" the charges may not save the store from a malicious prosecution lawsuit.

EXAMPLE

A woman was arrested following an altercation in a hospital emergency room in which she allegedly obstructed the litterbearer's entrance and refused several requests to move. She sued the hospital for malicious prosecution. The hospital argued that it could not be held liable since the officer made the arrest and filed the charges. The court held that the hospital could still be liable if the arrest were based on allegedly false information supplied to the officer by a nurse. (The plaintiff claimed that the nurse falsely told the officer that she had previously been asked to move.)[132]

Failure to conduct a reasonable investigation may constitute the "malice" required for establishing "malicious prosecution." This obviously may fall somewhat short of "malice" in the sense of ill will or vindictive motive, and is more an objective standard to be measured by the court. In one case, a customer was accused of

---

130. Beard v. St. Mary's Health Center, 735 S.W.2d 27 (Mo. App. 1987).

131. Lipari v. Volume Shoe Corporation, 664 S.W.2d 953 (Mo. App. 1983).

132. Bragle v. Revell, 674 F. Supp. 13 (W.D. Pa. 1987).

stealing merchandise which he had in fact purchased from another store before entering the defendant's store. He was arrested and subsequently found not guilty of shoplifting. The court upheld an award of $20,000 in compensatory damages in the customer's malicious prosecution lawsuit, stating that the defendants had been advised of the customer's explanation before they began the prosecution. The court stated:

> They made no effort to check out his story which could have been done by simply contacting another of Sears employees. That employee in fact verified the plaintiff's story. That, coupled with the physical viewing point of the store security officer who purported to see the theft, plaintiff's payment of items worth six times the value of what he purportedly stole, the condition of the items when taken from plaintiff indicating the possibility of prior purchase, and the inflexible policy of prosecution of Sears testified to support a finding of wanton disregard of plaintiff's rights. In addition, no investigation was conducted even after plaintiff's attorney advised the company of the results of his investigation and prosecution was continued without further review.

Plainly, in this instance, the "malice" stemmed from the objective failure to conduct a reasonable investigation. The court reversed an award of $50,000 in punitive damages made by the jury, however. Under Missouri law, proof of "actual malice," which consists of ill will or vindictive motives, is required for an award of punitive damages (damages intended to punish the defendant, rather than compensate the plaintiff for injuries actually suffered), and the mere failure to conduct a reasonable investigation did not provide a showing of such ill will.[133]

Evidence of motives for calling the police to arrest a customer are clearly relevant in a malicious prosecution suit. In one Illinois case,[134] a bank teller testified that she thought it unusual for a black customer to make large deposits; the plaintiff customer claimed that the bank and its teller were prejudiced against her because she was black and therefore arrested her, believing her to be the same person as a customer who had cashed a check bearing a forged endorsement at the bank earlier.

Because the decision to call police was made on the basis of the teller's uncorroborated identification and no effort was made to have a handwriting expert compare the forged check with the customer's signature or to examine the customer's bank statement, the court found that there was a question for the jury as to whether the bank had probable cause for the charge.

Damage awards in malicious prosecution cases may be high, since they can take into account such factors as psychological injury. In one such case,[135] the jury initially awarded $1 million to a woman after she had been accused of taking a spark plug from a store. The woman had been accompanied by her husband and the store's security guard had asked the woman to accompany him back to the store's security office after observing spark plugs on the dashboard of the woman's car.

---

133. Shaffer v. Sears, Roebuck and Co., 734 S.W.2d 537 (Mo. App. 1987).

134. Mack v. First Security Bank of Chicago, 511 N.E.2d 714 (Ill. App. 1987).

135. Panas v. Harakis, 529 A.2d 976 (N.H. 1987).

The customer claimed that the spark plugs had been there for days and had been purchased at another store. The security guard who initiated the woman's detention failed to appear at her trial for shoplifting, although subpoenaed to appear as a witness.

In addition to finding for the woman on the malicious prosecution claim, the jury found that the guard had been negligent in the performance of his duties and that the store had been negligent in hiring, training, supervising, and failing to fire the guard. The security guard had a police record for impersonating a police officer and for theft by deception.

The court overturned the $1 million damage award as excessive, however, since the woman's psychiatric care bills amounted to $5,160. The court concluded that this meant that the jury had awarded $994,840 for psychological injuries. The evidence showed that she had returned to performing routine household chores and her own psychiatrists testified that her condition had improved upon taking medication which she later discontinued. The court therefore ordered a new trial limited to the question of damages alone.

Defamation/Slander

For those involved in private security, defamation lawsuits arise in a number of contexts. The principal ones are those concerning: (1) accusations of theft or other wrongdoing against business patrons; (2) statements made in the course of investigation of possible employee misconduct; and (3) statements made in the course of responding to inquiries for employment references for former employees.

Truth of the statements made will generally be a complete defense to such lawsuits. In one Alabama case,[136] a woman entered a grocery store, upset because her husband's appeal of his worker's compensation claim against the store had been denied. She then filled her cart with groceries, told many customers about the allegedly unfair incident with her husband, walked past the cashier, and told the manager she wasn't going to pay. She said, "you can deduct that from what you owe." The manager had her arrested for refusing to pay. She sued for defamation, because of his statement to the police. The court held that the truth of the manager's statements barred any liability.

Even if a statement is not "true," however, it may still be privileged, if made without malice, and for proper purposes, to persons with a direct and immediate legitimate interest in investigating a situation. "Publication" of the statement beyond such a narrow group of persons, however, may result in the privilege being lost. In a Mississippi store, a customer was detained on suspicion of stealing a hat. Several witnesses later testified that the store manager had talked very loud when he made accusations of theft against the customer, and embarrassed and humiliated him. The manager, on the other hand, claimed that he talked in a calm, low voice and was extremely courteous throughout the matter. The court held that it was

---

136. Tidwell v. Winn-Dixie, Inc., 502 So. 2d 747 (Ala. 1987).

therefore for the jury to determine whether the store and its manager were liable to the customer for defamation.[137]

Although a store security employee may legitimately confront a customer with an accusation when warranted, even if it turns out to be false, no legitimate purpose is served by communicating that accusation broadly to other customers or to persons who are not involved in the investigation.[138]

Whether liability for defamation attaches to a store manager's accusatory statements, therefore, may depend on to whom they were made and why. Statements made to an employee not involved in the matter were not privileged. When similar statements accusing her of theft were made to the plaintiff in front of her husband, the store might be liable for defamation if the statements were made with malice and bad faith. The store could not be liable, however, for statements regarding the plaintiff's supposed guilt made to her mother after the woman entered the store with the plaintiff to question the manager, since the plaintiff (and someone acting on her behalf) had thereby invited the manager to tell his side of the story.[139]

In the context of employee termination,[140] a Georgia court held that an oral announcement to higher-level employees that the plaintiff was discharged for listing more hours on his log than he actually worked was not defamation. The supervisors and management personnel were privileged by the "need to know." The allegation that co-workers who were not privileged overheard the loud verbal accusations was found not to be supported by the evidence. In summarizing the general rule concerning disclosure of termination, the court stated:

> In defamation cases involving an employer's disclosure to other employees of the reason for a plaintiff's discharge, the general rule is that a qualified privilege exists where the disclosure is limited to those employees who have a need to know by virtue of the nature of their duties (such as supervisors, management officials, union representatives, etc.) and those employees who are otherwise directly affected either by the discharged employee's termination or the investigation of the offense leading to his termination.

This privilege to communicate among superiors in the workplace was extended by one court to discussion of an anonymous letter slipped under a personnel manager's office door telling her that certain employees were selling drugs on the premises. She discussed the letter with her superiors, and then told each named employee individually about the letter, warning them that getting caught selling

---

137. McWilliams v. Watkins, 430 So. 2d 858 (Miss. 1983).

138. *See* Mains v. K-Mart Corp., 375 S.E.2d 311 (S.C. 1988) (customer publicly accused of shoplifting awarded compensatory and punitive damages for defamation; 20 minute public discussion exceeded merchant's privilege).

139. Brown v. P.N. Hirsch & Company Stores, Inc., 661 S.W.2d 587 (Mo. App. 1983). *See* Chestnet v. K-Mart Corp., 529 N.E.2d 131 (Ind. App. 1988) (store employee not liable to customer for defamation absent proof that accusation of shoplifting was made in front of public) and K-Mart Corp. v. Weston, 530 So. 2d 736 (Ala. 1988) (customer entitled to $20,000 because of store employee's statement in front of others that his wife's check would not be accepted because of outstanding bad check).

140. Hodges v. Tomberlin, 319 S.E.2d 11 (Ga. App. 1984).

drugs at work was grounds for dismissal and that she had no reason to believe the letter was true. Other than the talk with her superiors, she told them the matter would remain private. The court rejected the employee's defamation lawsuit, finding that the personnel manager had properly utilized a qualified privilege to discuss the matter with her superiors. Such qualified privilege could only be overcome by a showing that the statements were made with malice. A similar qualified privilege exists to provide information to the police, which may only be overcome by a showing of bad faith, malice, knowing falsity, etc.[141] In a Montana case,[142] the court upheld a $470,000 jury verdict for defamation and emotional distress for an employer's alleged false report to police, which resulted in the arrest of an employee for theft. The court found that there was "substantial evidence" that the employer had "waived any conditional privilege" by making the statements "without good faith."

While investigating an employee who was suspected of theft, a company official wrote in an investigation report that the employee was "suspect No. 1." The employee subsequently quit and sued for defamation. The court found that this was not grounds for liability, given that it was written with "actual belief" of the truth, was prepared by a store official within the scope of his duty, and was covered by a qualified privilege.[143] The court noted that a showing of any of the following factors will defeat a qualified privilege:

1. actual malice;
2. an intentional publication of false defamatory material;
3. a publication of false defamatory material made with reckless disregard for its truth or falsity;
4. a publication of false defamatory material made to persons who have no reason to receive the information; or
5. a publication of false defamatory material with a primary purpose unrelated to the purpose of the privilege.

The Alabama Supreme Court has held that statements made in the context of a management-union grievance adjustment hearing conducted pursuant to a collective bargaining agreement were absolutely privileged. It therefore declined to find either the company or a supervisor liable for the supervisor's calling the employee a homosexual at the hearing. The court said its ruling was in the interest of public policy to encourage the resolution of labor grievances through open discussion and conferences. Absolute privilege will also apply to statements made as a witness in court.[144]

In a Pennsylvania case,[145] the court determined that an employee was not defamed when management accused him in front of a security guard of conspiring

141. Rucker v. K-Mart Corp., 734 S.W.2d 533 (Mo. App. 1987). *See also* Kirby v. Williamson Oil Company, 510 So. 2d 176 (Ala. 1987) (security guard's comments to police during investigation of robbery were privileged; no "actual malice" shown).

142. Niles v. Big Sky Eyewear, 771 P.2d 114 (Mont. 1989).

143. McKinney v. K-Mart Corp., 649 F. Supp. 1217 (S.D.W.Va. 1986).

144. Surrency v. Harbison, 489 So. 2d 1097 (Ala. 1986).

145. Jackson v. J.C. Penney Co., Inc., 616 F. Supp. 233 (D.Pa. 1985).

to steal. The guard was entitled to participate in the matter since he was the person responsible for the initial investigation that discovered the unpaid item. "A communication is privileged," the court noted, when it is made on a proper occasion, from a proper motive, in a proper manner and based upon reasonable cause. "Furthermore, the privilege exists when the circumstances lead any one of several persons having a common interest in a particular matter to believe that another sharing such common interest is entitled to know a given fact."

The mere fact that an investigation is being conducted is not, by itself, defamatory. A New Jersey court found that a supervisor did not slander an employee by insisting on searching through his desk in front of co-workers.[146] The employee claimed that the supervisor's actions were defamatory because of his "abusive and arrogant tone of voice" when he demanded to see the employee's accident report kit and rummaged through his desk when he said he did not have one. The employee also claimed that the supervisor's insistence on searching through his desk, personal belongings, and his company car in front of other employees "unjustifiably accused plaintiff of lying and ridiculed and embarrassed" him. The court found that the statements did not rise to the level of an implication of any statement of fact that would be damaging to the plaintiff's reputation. The mere use of "foul, abusive, or vituperative language," the court said, is not in itself defamatory.[147]

While the company may only authorize certain individuals to discuss the facts of a situation such as an employee investigation, employees may nevertheless talk to others. Is the company then liable? "No," according to the Alabama Supreme Court.[148] In that case, a store manager asked both the accused employee and the accusing employee to take a polygraph test. The accused employee failed two such examinations and was fired. The store management had cautioned all involved not to talk about the incident with customers or among themselves. The accusing employee, however, telephoned a friend, who was a former employee, and told her what had been happening. As a result, the fired employee filed a lawsuit against the store for defamation.

In upholding the trial court's grant of summary judgment for the defendant store, the Alabama court noted that the employee who made the allegedly defamatory remarks was not a corporate officer of the store, nor was she serving in any managerial position. "On the contrary," the court remarked, her primary duties involved gift wrapping and there was not a "scintilla of evidence" that she was acting within the scope of authority given to her by the store when she made her remarks. Further, her employer's explicit instructions not to discuss the investigation indicated that her conversation with her friend "could not be in furtherance of any conceivable corporate business."

---

146. Schwartz v. Leasametric, Inc., 224 N.J. Super. 21, 539 A.2d 744 (1988).

147. See also Kolczynski v. Maxton Motors, Inc., 538 N.E.2d 275 (Ind. App. 1989) (employer's search of car of employee fired for concealed auto part was not defamatory) and Dubrovin v. Marshall Field's Emp. Credit Union, 536 N.E.2d 800 (Ill. App. 1989) (inspection of dismissed employee's personal belongings by security guard was not slander).

148. Walton v. Bromberg & Co., 514 So. 2d 1010 (Ala. 1987).

In another recent case, a jury awarded $1.32 million to a fired employee, after another employee of the company told his former customers that he was "in trouble." The company was a brokerage firm, and the terminated employee had agreed to sell certain partnership interests. The company later adopted a policy prohibiting such sales without prior company approval. The employee was subsequently fired. After his termination, files of his clients were distributed to other company employees, who were told to contact them to try to keep their business. One of these employees told two such clients that the fired employee would never again work as a broker, was moving to Australia, was going to lose his broker's license, and was in big trouble with the Securities and Exchange Commission. The fired employee sued the company for slander. He alleged that the statements made were false and malicious, damaging his reputation and earnings capacity and causing him mental anguish and humiliation, with resulting physical injury. A total of $1.32 million was awarded, including $1 million in punitive damages.[149]

This case illustrates the importance of a company adopting clear policies on the dissemination of information concerning the reasons for the termination of past employees, as well as adequately conveying to employees the importance of following such policies. When an employee is terminated, there is often speculation by other employees regarding the reasons for the firing, and rumors will often be spread, both among employees and from employees to members of the public, such as customers. When such rumors are brought to the attention of security managers, active steps should be taken to prevent the further communication of false information.

False statements in employment recommendations can easily lead to liability for defamation. A Pennsylvania court ruled that a company and its high-ranking executive were liable for $100,000 in compensatory damages to a former employee, $35,000 for loss of consortium to his wife, and $50,000 in punitive damages after a bad recommendation caused the former employee to be terminated from his new job. The employment reference falsely stated that the plaintiff had missed work because of his drinking and that he was still being investigated for possible forgery of checks, when in actuality the employer knew that someone else was the forger. The damages for loss of consortium stemmed from the plaintiff allegedly indulging in drink heavily and physically abusing his wife following the loss of his job.[150]

Invasion of Privacy

The various procedures for the surveillance of employees and customers, and the attending legal issues, were fully discussed in Chapter 6. With regard to impermissible investigative conduct generally, the reader is referred to the monthly newsletter *Security Legal Update*.[151]

149. Tucker v. Shearson Lehman Bros, Inc., Tex. Nueces County 148th Judicial District Court, No. 86-5251-E, June 2, 1989, 32 ATLA L. Rep. 471 (Dec. 1989).

150. Geyer v. Steinbronn, 506 A.2d 901 (Pa. Super. 1986).

151. Published by Americans for Effective Law Enforcement (AELE), 5519 N. Cumberland, #1008, Chicago, Illinois 60656.

11

Civil Liability for Inadequate Security Duties Owed to Invitees by Business Owners and Their Security Personnel

The general legal rule is that there is no duty to protect persons against criminal assault by third parties.[1] A private business is not expected to take on the public function of providing general police protection for the public against all possible harm. On the basis of this general rule, the Michigan Supreme Court has held, in the 1988 case of *Williams v. Cunningham Drug Stores, Inc.*,[2] that a merchant's duty of reasonable care does not include providing armed, visible security guards to deter criminal acts of third parties; consequently, a store was held not liable for the shooting of a patron during an armed robbery. The store's policy was that the security present should not intervene in the event of a robbery, and their primary function, in addition to protecting the assets, was to summon medical assistance if illness or injury occurred on the premises.

1. *See, e.g.,* Boyd v. Racine Currency Exchange, Inc., 56 Ill. 2d 95, 306 N.E.2d 39 (1973) (no duty to accede to criminal demand to protect business patron taken hostage). *See also* Bence v. Crawford Savings & Loan Association, 400 N.E.2d 39 (Ill. App. 1980). For discussions of this general rule and some of its exceptions in relationship to particular types of businesses, see Annots., 93 A.L.R.3d 999 (1979) (shopping centers); 75 A.L.R.3d 441 (1977) (theaters); 72 A.L.R.3d 441 (1976) (store keepers).
2. Williams v. Cunningham Drug Stores, Inc., 418 N.W.2d 381 (Mich. 1988). *See also* Milo v. Guardian Guard Services, Inc., 440 N.W.2d 5 (Mich. App. 1988) (merchant not liable for death of man shot by robber; no duty to provide armed security guards); Foster v. Colonel Sanders Kentucky Fried Chicken, Inc., 526 So. 2d 252 (La. App. 1988) (fast food restaurant not liable for failure to provide security guard to prevent shooting of customer in drive-through lane). But *see* Sharpe v. Peter Pan Bus Lines, Inc., 401 Mass. 788, 519 N.E.2d 1341 (1988) (court finds bus company and terminal company liable for failing to provide uniformed guards which might have deterred deadly attack on patron).

"Today," the court noted, "a crime may be committed anywhere and at any time," so requiring a store to supply armed uniformed guards would require them to provide a safer environment on its premises than the invitees would encounter in the community at large. The defendant simply does not have that degree of control and is not an insurer of the safety of its customers. Yet, despite this general rule, which almost all courts acknowledge as a starting point, there are literally hundreds of cases imposing liability for negligent or inadequate security.[3] What are the special conditions which allow for such exceptions to the general rule?

A business proprietor is held to have a duty to protect his business invitees (those who enter his premises on business which concerns him—such as his customers) against known dangers and also against dangers which he could discover with reasonable care.[4] It is no surprise to most business proprietors, therefore, that they may face legal liability for a customer's injury due to a slip and fall on a wet floor, injury on a defective escalator, or injury by the fall of improperly stacked mer-

---

3. *See, e.g.,* Winn-Dixie Stores, Inc. v. Johnstoneaux, 395 So. 2d 599 (Fla. App. 1981); Coath v. Jones, 277 Pa. Super. 479, 419 A.2d 1249 (1980).

4. *See* W. PROSSER and W. KEETON, THE LAW OF TORTS, Sec. 61 (5th ed., 1984). This rule is traced back to the 1866 English case of Indermaur v. Dames, L.R. 1 C.P. 274, 35 L.J.C.P. 184, affirmed L.R. 2 C.P. 311, 36 L.J.C.P. 181, which PROSSER and KEETON state was then "accepted in all common law jurisdictions." While traditionally, under this rule, there was a lower duty of care towards "licensees" (those allowed on the premises with the business owner's consent, but not for his benefit) and still less toward "trespassers" (those on the premises without consent), it must be noted that there is a strong modern trend towards abolishing these distinctions. *See* Rowland v. Christian 70 Cal. Rptr. 97, 443 P.2d 561 (1968) (abolishing these categories and replacing them with a standard of reasonable care against foreseeable risk towards anyone who might be on the premises). *See also* Packard v. City of Honolulu, 51 Hawaii 134, 452 P.2d 445 (1969); Mile High Fence Co. v. Radovich, 175 Colo. 537, 489 P.2d 308 (1971); Smith v. Arbaugh's Restaurant, Inc., 469 F.2d 97 (D.C. Cir. 1972), *cert. denied,* 412 U.S. 939 (1973); Mariorenzi v. Joseph DiPonte, Inc., 114 R.I. 294, 333 A.2d 127 (1975); Basso v. Miller, 40 N.Y.2d 233, 386 N.Y.S.2d 564, 352 N.E.2d 868 (1976); Ouellette v. Blanchard, 116 N.H. 552, 364 A.2d 631 (1976); Cates v. Beauregard Electric Coop, 328 So. 2d 367 (La.), *cert. denied,* 429 U.S. 833 (1976); Webb v. City of Sitka, 561 P.2d 731 (Alaska 1977). Still other jurisdictions have abolished the distinction between invitees and licensees in relationship to the duty owed by the business proprietor, maintaining still a lower standard of care in relationship to the trespasser (such as not "actively harming" him, etc.). *See, e.g.,* Poulin v. Colby College, 402 A.2d 846 (1979). Under the traditional rules, a proprietor, while having a duty of reasonable care to make the premises safe for invitees, had toward "licensees" the duty merely of refraining from injuring them intentionally or through "willful and wanton misconduct" (as well as warning them of "hidden dangers"). *See* Armstrong v. Sundance Entertain, Inc., 347 S.E.2d 292 (Ga. App. 1986) (no liability of business for shooting by third party of person on premises who was a licensee rather than an invitee). Toward trespassers, who had no right to expect a "safe place to trespass," the proprietor had no duty at common law other than not to intentionally injure him. While police officers and fire fighters have traditionally been held to be merely licensees, coming onto business premises on a privilege given by their legal authority rather than on the basis of an express or implied invitation by the proprietor, there is some movement away from this recently. *See* PROSSER AND KEETON, *supra* note 4, Sec. 61 and SECOND RESTATEMENT OF TORTS, Sec. 345, Comment e. Finally, it should be clear to all business owners that their own employees are "invitees" who are there for the benefit of their business, and therefore there is a duty to furnish them with a reasonably safe workplace, which may include protecting them against assaults by third parties, according to some courts. *See, e.g.,* Streeter v. Sullivan, 509 So. 2d 268 (Fla. 1987).

chandise. The cases which have imposed liability for inadequate or negligent security have been based on the notion that, for some businesses at least, the occurrence of criminal activity by third parties—ranging from property thefts to assaults, rapes, and murders—is a foreseeable danger and that the business therefore must take reasonable measures to protect customers against such crimes.

PRIOR SIMILAR CRIMES AND FORESEEABILITY

A key condition is normally the existence of past crimes—particularly similar crimes—on the premises or in the general vicinity, since this has an impact on the foreseeability of future crimes. In *Taco Bell v. Lannon,*[5] the Colorado Supreme Court for the first time held that a business has a duty to protect patrons from criminal acts of third parties in some circumstances. In language which the Michigan Supreme Court disagreed with in the aforementioned *Williams* case, it found that it was for the jury to decide whether this duty was breached by the failure to provide armed security guards. In this case, the restaurant which was robbed had suffered ten prior armed robberies during the three years prior to the incident giving rise to the present lawsuit.

The court rejected the argument that the robbery was not foreseeable, since armed robberies occur "randomly and without notice of the specific time and the specific manner in which they will take place." This, the court stated, is too limited a concept of foreseeability. It is not necessary that the business owner know the time and place of the next robbery, merely that it is likely enough to occur so that a "reasonably thoughtful person" would take account of it in guiding their practical conduct. The court also rejected the argument that the customer's injury was not foreseeable since none of the previous armed robberies at the restaurant resulted in injuries to customers. "We have little difficulty in concluding that armed robberies present a significant risk of injury to persons unfortunate enough to be present when one occurs."[6]

Generally, though, courts will not impose such duties merely on the basis of a general allegation that a neighborhood is in a "high crime area." A more direct connection with a particular business will normally be required.[7] In some

---

5. 744 P.2d 43 (Colo. 1987).

6. *See also* Winn Dixie Stores v. Estate of Castano, 544 So. 2d 215 (Fla. App. 1989) (court upholds verdict against store for assault by criminal on patron after evidence of 93 prior violent crimes in vicinity was presented). In contrast, in Meadows v. Friedman R.R. Salvage Warehouse, 655 S.W.2d 718 (Mo. App. 1983), the court found no liability on the part of the warehouse owner or security company guarding the premises for an assault on a patron in a "high crime" area absent allegations of specific prior attacks. *See also* Childers v. Winn-Dixie Stores, Inc., 514 So. 2d 879 (Ala. 1987) (store had no duty to protect customer against theft of purse outside store when no prior thefts in area shown).

7. *See* Petrauskas v. Wexenthaller Realty Management, Inc., 542 N.E.2d 902 (Ill. App. 1989) (landlord did not have duty to protect female tenant against rape based on the "high crime area" concept when all the criminal activity shown had no connection to the building in question).

instances, a pattern of motel robberies in the area imposed a duty on each motel to protect its patrons, since it was foreseeable that further such robberies would occur.[8]

However, evidence of dissimilar crimes in the area or on the premises may be excluded by many courts in determining foreseeability. Thus, several property offenses—such as shoplifting or purse snatching—might not be found to give a merchant sufficient notice to take specific measures to attempt to prevent violent assaults, such as a rape or murder.[9]

Additionally, even courts which impose liability for negligent or inadequate security in some circumstances will not impose liability for "freak" occurrences which no one could possibly foresee, and for which it is difficult to establish preventive measures. For instance, in one recent California case,[10] the court held that a business owner was not liable for injuries to a customer inflicted by a "drive-by" shooting. There was no evidence that would have reasonably forecast a potentially homicidal act, or put the business owner on notice that a daytime drive-by shooting of someone on the premises was a "real possibility, yet alone a likely event." The court commented that given the "random nature" of drive-by shootings, it could not discern what the business owner could have done to prevent the injury.[11]

Another excellent example of the sort of event for which courts will not impose liability is illustrated by *Lopez v. McDonald's,*[12] in which the court upheld a summary judgment in favor of McDonald's and its local franchise in a lawsuit arising out of the tragic 1984 massacre at McDonald's restaurant in San Ysidro, California. In this incident, a man entered the restaurant during the day, dressed in camouflage pants and armed with a 9 mm semi-automatic rifle, a semi-automatic 9 mm pistol, and a 12 gauge shotgun, and immediately began indiscriminately slaughtering patrons and employees within the restaurant.

During the hour before he was killed by a police officer, this madman showed no intent to rob the restaurant; made no demands for money; made no effort to take hostages; loaded his weapon several times; and killed 21 people in the restaurant and wounded 11 others. His single apparent purpose was to kill as many people as possible. The court noted that the theft-related and property crimes recorded in the area before—and even the "general assaultive-type activity" experienced—"bear no relationship to purposeful homicide or assassi-

---

8. Crinkley v. Holiday Inns, Inc., 844 F.2d 156 (4th Cir. 1988).

9. *See* Brown v. National Super Markets, Inc., 731 S.W.2d 291 (Mo. App. 1987) (evidence of past nonviolent purse snatchings properly excluded in lawsuit over violent assault by third party in supermarket parking lot).

10. Thai v. Stang, No. D007473, Cal. App., 89 Daily Journal D.A.R. 12881 (October 24, 1989).

11. *See also* White v. Ha, Inc., 782 P.2d 1125 (Wyo. 1989) (bar had no duty to protect patron against shooting, off the premises, by another patron, in absence of notice of danger) and Grandma's Biscuits, Inc. v. Baisden, 386 S.E.2d 415 (Ga. App. 1989) (restaurant was not liable for shooting of patron by unknown assailant in absence of sufficiently similar prior crimes establishing foreseeability).

12. 193 Cal. App. 3d 495, 238 Cal. Rptr. 436 (1987).

nation." This "deranged and motiveless attack" was not foreseeable. There was no causal connection between the restaurant's failure to provide security and the injuries which occurred, and any reasonable protective measure—such as security cameras, alarms, etc., which might have deterred "ordinary criminal conduct"—could not have deterred or hindered the "maniacal, suicidal" shooter.

MINORITY COURT APPROACH: NO PRIOR SIMILAR CRIMES NEEDED

In *Small v. McKennan Hospital*,[13] the South Dakota Supreme Court adopted the "totality of circumstances" test for inadequate security, rejecting an argument that the plaintiff needed to show that "prior similar" crimes had taken place on the premises in order to demonstrate that the crime was foreseeable. Applying this test in the same case on a later appeal,[14] the court upheld a $535,000 jury verdict on behalf of a hospital employee who was raped and murdered after being kidnapped from a hospital parking ramp. Although there was no history of prior violent criminal activity in the parking ramp, the ramp was used by employees, patients, and visitors 24 hours a day, lighting was poor, and the ramp was widely used for consuming alcohol and smoking marijuana, according to the evidence presented. Further, acts of property theft and vandalism had occurred at the parking ramp and the chief of security had requested more security personnel and the installation of television cameras. Those requests had been denied.[15]

The court noted that a "long history of good fortune" in avoiding violent criminal assault "does not relieve a party from exercising ordinary and reasonable care in the operation of his particular business enterprise." In this case, an expert witness for the plaintiff testified that parking areas are "widely known as being inherently dangerous" and that the frequency of the security patrols on the ramp was "totally inadequate." While the approach taken by this court is still a minority one, it seems likely that more courts will adopt it in the future.[16]

---

13. 403 N.W.2d 410 (S.D. 1987).

14. Small v. McKennan Hospital, 437 N.W.2d 194 (S.D. 1989).

15. Ignoring a request for additional security personnel, or a report from security managers pointing to the need for additional security devices, may return to haunt a business proprietor, since this may be evidence that the assault on a customer, absent such measures, was foreseeable and might have been prevented—perhaps at modest cost—had the recommendations not been ignored. In one such case, the plaintiff's lawyer put into evidence the cost of installation of security cameras in an elevator in which a patron was assaulted. Craigo v. Circus-Circus Enterprises, Inc., No. 18515, Nevada Supreme Court, slip opinion, January 23, 1990. (Upholding award of $45,000 in compensatory damages, but overturning $1 million punitive damages award).

16. *See* Erickson v. Curtis Inv. Co., 447 N.W.2d 165 (Minn. 1989) (hotel and security firm owed duty to reasonably protect woman against rape in adjoining parking ramp despite absence of prior violent crimes there.)

SPECIAL PROBLEM AREAS

There are several special problem situations in which the pattern of lawsuits being filed clearly indicates the need for extra attention by security management and personnel. Inadequate security in parking lots is an increasing area of concern in relationship to allegations of inadequate security and has led in some instances to million dollar jury verdicts.[17] Similarly, there are many cases in which liability was based, in whole or part, upon a claim that the lighting provided by a business owner was inadequate enough to be a causal factor by creating the conditions for criminal assaults—dark places in which criminals could lurk, waiting for victims.[18]

Even if there otherwise would not be a duty to provide security or a certain level of security, the representation to patrons that a certain level of security will be provided may impose either a contractual duty to do so, or impose a duty to do so based on the patron's reasonable reliance on such representations.[19]

In one case, a jury awarded $2 million to a young student who was abducted from a parking lot and raped.[20] She had chosen the lot to park in on a regular basis because of a sign advertising that there was a security guard on duty during the hours when she would be there. The evidence showed that the guard provided was a 67-year-old retired truck driver, with no experience or training as a security guard, who had been told to remain in his guard shack. He had

17. *See* Knor v. Parking Co. of Am., Ohio, Hamilton County Court of Common Pleas, No. A85-09133, July 14, 1989, reported in 32 ATLA L. Rep. 474 (December 1989) (young student abducted from parking lot and raped, awarded $2 million; security guard was instructed not to patrol lot); Becker v. Diamond Parking, Inc., 768 S.W.2d 169 (Mo. App. 1989) (reversing summary judgment for operator of parking ramp in case brought by patron assaulted there by third party); General Syndicators of America v. Green, 522 So. 2d 1081 (Fla. App. 1988) (owner of shopping mall liable for $59,000 for injuries of employee whose purse was snatched in parking lot); Jardel Co. Inc. v. Hughes, 523 A.2d 518 (Del. 1987) (upholding award of $530,000 to woman raped after abduction from shopping mall parking lot); Aisner v. Lafayette Towers, 341 N.W.2d 852 (Mich. App. 1983) (landlord could be liable for visitor's robbery and sexual assault in parking lot); Allen v. Babrab, Inc., 438 So. 2d 356 (Fla. 1983) (tavern owner liable for assault of patron in parking lot); Daily v. K-Mart, Hamilton, Ohio, #CV80-07-0644 (Ohio 1982) (store ordered to pay $1.9 million to female abducted in parking lot and shot); and Butler v. Acme Markets, Inc., 445 A.2d 1141 (N.J. 1982) (store ordered to pay damages for failure to provide adequate security to patron mugged in store's parking lot).

18. *See, e.g.,* Roberts v. Clark Financial Corp., Tex. Tarrant County 17th Judicial District Court, No. 17-100421-86, Oct. 21, 1987, 30 ATLA L. Rep. 465 (Dec. 1987) ($75,000 settlement for tenant beaten in apartment complex parking lot; suit alleged inadequate lighting); Lockhart v. Howard Johnson Co., U.S. District Ct., C.D. Cal., No. CV 850-6873-JSL, Oct. 7, 1986, reported in 30 ATLA L. Rep. 86 (March 1987) (hotel liable for wrongful death based on inadequate lighting and security). But *see* C.S. v. Sophir, 368 N.W.2d 444 (Neb. 1985) (inadequate lighting and overgrown shrubbery not grounds for liability for assault on patron).

19. *See* Kivel v. Clark Fin. Corp., Ariz. Pima County Superior Court, No. 250785, April 12, 1989, reported in 32 ATLA L. Rep. 409 (Nov. 1989) (violent knife attack on two women in their apartment leads to $1.2 million award against building owners; misrepresentation of presence of security guards).

20. Knor v. Parking Co. of Am., Ohio, Hamilton County Court of Common Pleas, No. A85-09133, July 14, 1989, reported in 32 ATLA L. REP. 474 (December 1989).

also been told not to patrol the lot, and was unarmed. In addition, the guard indicated that he had told his employers about problems with a burned-out building next door which was being used by transients and alcoholics, but that nothing was done. This building was where the assailants testified they had spent a night. In addition, there had been two prior crimes in the parking lot. It was a combination of the knowledge or presumption of knowledge on the part of management, combined with the patron's reasonable reliance on the promise of security—a factor that was decisive in achieving the size of the verdict.

Another area in which courts have increasingly imposed liability for negligence in security by businesses is alleged negligence in their own hiring, disciplining, training, and retention of employees.[21] When an employee, who was negligently screened by the employer prior to hiring, assaults, rapes, or kills a patron, the failure of the employer to have discovered the past criminal record may be the basis for liability under certain circumstances. In one such case,[22] for instance, the employee's past crimes consisted of violent acts. Although there is no general duty on all employers to inquire into the possible criminal record of all potential employees, in this case, the employer knew that the employee did have a criminal record but failed to investigate the details of it. Under these circumstances, the employer might be liable for negligent retention of the employee who later assaulted a patron.[23]

BUSINESSES WHICH SERVE LIQUOR

Businesses where liquor is served, whether in restaurants, taverns, or nightclubs, as well as businesses engaged in the package sale of liquor, should have some special concern about their liability for the criminal, or even negligent, acts of others. Court decisions and statutes in many jurisdictions impose "dram shop" liability on such businesses, whereby the victims of car accidents or of assaults by intoxicated individuals who obtained their liquor at a particular business may be able to sue not only the consumer but also the seller. A normal requirement before imposing such liability is that the business had some notice that the individual was intoxicated when served, and therefore should not be served any additional liquor,

---

21. *See generally* Annot., *Liability for Negligent Hiring, Supervision, and Retention of Security Guard,* 44 A.L.R.4th 620. *See also* Besta v. Consolidated Rail Corp., 580 F. Supp. 869 (S.D.N.Y. 1984) (alleged negligent retention of railroad security guard could result in liability); Gonzales v. Southwest Sec. & Protection, 665 P.2d 810 (N.M. App. 1983) ($15,000 awarded against security company which negligently hired and trained guards who beat a spectator; Gregor v. Kleiser, 443 N.E.2d 1162) (Ill. App. 1982) (employer could be liable for hiring bouncer known to be violent).

22. Foster v. Loft, Inc., 526 N.E.2d 1309 (Mass. App. 1988). For a discussion of criminal records checks of employees, see Chapter 8.

23. *See also* Montauban v. Haitian Transfer Express Co., N.Y., Kings County Supreme Court, No. 29/84, April 15, 1988, reported in 31 ATLA L. REP. 319 (Sept. 1988) ($1.4 million settlement in killing of store customer by security guard; suit alleged that guard was negligently hired and entrusted with weapons).

because it may be foreseeable that such a person will become involved in an accident while driving his car. Liability for an assault may also require notice of a patron's violent propensities.[24]

In addition to liability of this sort, businesses that serve liquor may have more than their share of problems with customers fighting each other or engaging in altercations with employees. Also leading to liability for assault and battery is the conduct by "bouncers" who may use an unnecessary level of force in ejecting unruly patrons. Liability may also be incurred for a failure to adequately control intoxicated patrons who then attack others.[25]

HOSPITALS

Hospitals and other businesses that treat or otherwise deal with persons with medical problems as their primary patrons may have some special protective obligations. Many members of the public who are not residential hospital patients come in and out of the hospital for a variety of purposes—including visiting patients, receiving outpatient treatment and follow-up care, having blood tests or other tests taken for marriage license, insurance, or other purposes, volunteering services, or accompanying friends and family members coming to the hospital for any of these purposes. There are many persons, therefore, who are not patients or employees, who have a legitimate right to be on the premises. A variety of accommodations are necessarily provided to meet their needs, including public restrooms, cafeterias, and vending machine areas, phone booth areas, and gift shops.

At the same time, a hospital is understandably concerned that criminals may congregate in the parking lots, lobbies, or restrooms of its facilities, seeking to prey on the ill and infirm. Additionally, the presence of large quantities of controlled substances, albeit for legitimate medical purposes, can also be a magnet attracting individuals with no good in mind. Adequate security measures are therefore essential.

Courts have disagreed about whether the special circumstances presented by hospitals, and the particular problems of their patients, result in hospitals having,

---

24. *See, e.g.*, De Villez v. Schifano, 23 Mich. App. 72, 178 N.W.2d 147 (1970); Espadero v. Feld, 649 F. Supp. 1480 (D. Colo. 1986); Cimino v. Milford Key, 385 Mass. 323, 431 N.E.2d 920 (1982). Some states do not impose such liability, however. *See* Arant v. G.H. Inc., 428 N.W.2d 631 (Neb. 1988) (court would not judicially impose dram shop liability after legislature repealed the statute).

25. *See, e.g.*, S&A Beverage Co. of Beaumont, No. 2 v. DeRouen, 753 S.W.2d 507 (Tex. App. 1988) (customer of tavern, raped by another patron, awarded $75,000 against tavern operators); Aanenson v. Bastien, 438 N.W.2d 151 (N.D. 1989) (injured party's complicity in a drinking companion's intoxication is no defense to dram shop action in North Dakota); Tilton v. Brombacher, 556 A.2d 1337 (N.J. Super. 1989) (court expands dram shop liability to encompass package sale of alcohol to intoxicated persons). An increasing area of concern and liability is the sale of liquor to underage persons. *See, e.g.*, Finney v. Ren-Bar, Inc., 551 A.2d 535 (N.J. Super. A.D. 1988) (fire caused by underage drinker was foreseeable; tavern liable for $225,000 for personal injuries).

in essence, an implied contract to ensure the safety of its patients.[26] In some instances, legislatures have recognized the difficult task that hospitals face in providing adequate security, and the importance of preserving assets of health care facilities for their primary purposes. Statutes have been passed, therefore, which provide immunity from claims except in instances of "gross negligence" or "willful misconduct."[27]

Hospitals almost universally have adopted a system of badges for visitors to residential patient floors. A hospital with good security will attempt to remove loiterers, derelicts, and intoxicated or drug-abusing individuals from its premises. One recent case, however, points out the necessity of adequate special training and procedures, given the hospital's role as a medical care provider.[28] A diabetic man was waiting in the lobby of a hospital for a friend and her daughter when he began suffering from a diabetic crisis. He left the lobby to go to the cafeteria, but felt weak and returned to the lobby. By the time he got there, he had trouble walking. He appeared intoxicated because of his behavior and was experiencing a condition known as ketosis, which produces an odor on the breath that can be mistaken for alcohol. Security guards removed him from the lobby and left him outside. He sued the hospital for assault and battery.

The plaintiff claimed that the guards commenced picking him up without saying a word, that he told them he was diabetic and needed help, and that they held him under his armpits and led him out of the hospital. One of the guards, on the other hand, testified that the plaintiff was leaning against a tree in the lobby, was asked whether he was lost or injured or needed assistance, and he was incoherent and only said "ahhh," later replying that he was looking for his car. The court held that even if the security guards acted to help the man and did not have intent to harm him, the plaintiff's testimony raised at least a factual question for the jury as to whether any apprehension for this contact constituted an assault and whether the contact was offensive and thus a battery.

The hospital argued that even if the action of the guards was an assault and battery, it was privileged by the hospital's "right and duty" to remove potentially dangerous individuals from the building for the safety of patients. While agreeing that there was such a "right and duty,"[29] the court found that the plaintiff's alleged statement that he was a diabetic raised a factual issue as to whether the guards' actions in removing him were reasonable.

26. *Compare* G.L. v. Kaiser Foundation Hospitals, Inc., 306 Or. 54, 757 P.2d 1347 (Or. 1988) (holding that hospital had no implied contract to ensure the safety of its patients from sexual assault by employees) and K.M.H. v. Lutheran General Hospital, 230 Neb. 269, 431 N.W.2d 606 (1988) (hospital patient could sue hospital for breach of implied contract to provide security after male nurse sexually assaulted her). *See also* Associated Health Systems, Inc. v. Jones, 366 S.E.2d 147 (Ga. App. 1988).

27. *See* Farago v. Sacred Heart General Hospital, 562 A.2d 300 (Pa. 1989) (hospital was immune under state law from liability for rape of mental patient by another patient, in the absence of "willful misconduct or gross negligence.")

28. Mason v. D.C. Department of Employment Services, 562 A.2d 644 (D.C. 1989).

29. For a general discussion of the right of businesses to eject persons from their premises, see Chapter 7.

While such occurrences are not unheard of at other business premises, a hospital, for all the reasons previously outlined, can anticipate encountering them much more frequently. Hospitals hold themselves to the community to be places where the ill can receive medical care. A good suggestion for hospital security managers, therefore, is that personnel should receive special training and information on such topics as distinguishing a diabetic in crisis (likely to have rapid respiration) from an alcoholic (likely to have slow breathing, given alcohol's depressive properties); handling mentally disturbed individuals; and similar topics. Hospitals with psychiatric wings, alcohol and drug abuse clinics, and similar facilities, may face more frequent instances of such difficulties. Hospital medical personnel can play a vital role in helping to provide such information and training to security officers. In this manner, adequate security can be provided to safeguard the well being of a hospital's patients and other members of the public legitimately on the premises, while medical attention is given to those requiring it.

PREVENTIVE MEASURES

Adequate security is a good business practice, in addition to being helpful in preventing liability. Customers are more comfortable coming to business premises which are adequately guarded, e.g., parking in lots that are adequately lit and shopping in frequently patrolled shopping malls. In reviewing the many cases when liability has been imposed for inadequate or negligent security, it is clear that the key preventive measures available to businesses should include: (1) careful screening in hiring, and proper training of security personnel; (2) careful record keeping of past incidents and taking corrective measures where a problem has been shown to exist; (3) paying attention to complaints and suggestions by customers and security personnel. The security manager could ask himself, concerning the business premises, including adjacent facilities, such as parking ramps: "Would I feel safe coming here during all the hours our business is open? Would I feel safe and confident allowing my family members to come here?" If the answer is "no" or "uncertain," corrective steps are clearly indicated.

A business is not the insurer of its customers' safety, and in today's world there are no security measures that can prevent criminal assaults with absolute certainty. Businesses are understandably concerned with property theft, including shoplifting, inventory "shrinkage" involving employees, and robbery, and most businesses take measures to deter these acts. Similar attention must be paid to the protection of another one of any business's most vital assets—its customers.[30]

30. It is important to keep up to date on the law concerning liability for inadequate security and other security legal questions because many security problems faced by different businesses share common features. An excellent monthly journal which summarizes new case law in this area, *Security Legal Update*, is published by Americans for Effective Law Enforcement, 5519 N. Cumberland, Suite 1008, Chicago, Illinois 60656-1498.

DUTY OWED TO RESIDENTS OF HOTELS, PUBLIC HOUSING AUTHORITIES, APARTMENT BUILDINGS, AND CONDOMINIUM ASSOCIATIONS

When a landlord rents an apartment or a house to a tenant, it is the tenant who has the right to possession of the premises. The landlord has "no right even to enter without the permission of the lessee."[31] As a result, the traditional common law rule was that the landlord had no obligation to keep the premises in good repair, or, in any way, to protect the tenant from harm occurring there.[32] The modern trend, however, has been to create more and more exceptions to this rule, until the exceptions may be said to have swallowed up the rule.[33] Nevertheless, there is still much authority for the proposition that the landlord has no general duty to protect the tenant from criminal assault by third parties.[34]

Liability has increasingly been imposed, nevertheless, on landlords for providing inadequate or negligent security, on a variety of theories. One of the most widespread is simply that of a duty of reasonable care on the basis of the landlord's retention of control over the "common areas" of the building.[35] The landlord normally has not rented the hallways, lobbies, staircases, and elevators of the premises to any particular tenant (at least in multitenant buildings).

31. PROSSER and KEETON, THE LAW OF TORTS, *supra* note 4, Sec. 63 (5th ed. 1984).
     Many of the points made in the earlier portion of this chapter regarding the duties owed to invitees by business owners and their security personnel also apply to hotel and apartment building circumstances, such as the special problems with parking lots, the detailed discussion of the test for foreseeability, etc. For a discussion of landlord liability for inadequate security in the context of business, as opposed to residential, premises, *see* generally, URI KAUFMAN, *When Crime Pays: Business Landlords' Duty to Protect Customers from Criminal Acts Committed on the Premises*, 31 S. TEX. L. REV. 89-120 (February 1990).

32. Thomas v. Barnes, 634 S.W.2d 554 (Mo. App. 1982); Seago v. Roy, 424 N.E.2d 640 (Ill. App. 1981); Powell v. United Oil Corp., 160 Ga. App. 810, 287 S.E.2d 667 (1982).

33. PROSSER and KEETON, *supra* note 4, at 434-435.

34. *See, e.g.,* Duncavage v. Allen, 497 N.E.2d 433 (Ill. App. 1986), *appeal denied,* 505 N.E.2d 352 (Ill. 1986).

35. *See* Kline v. 1500 Massachusetts Ave. Corp., 439 F.2d 477, 481-82 (D.C. Cir. 1970), in which the court noted that when the landlord "reserves under his own control the halls, stairs, or other parts of the property for use in common by all tenants, he has a duty to all those on the premises of legal right to use ordinary care and diligence to maintain the retained portions in a reasonably safe condition." Further, "[t]he value of the lease to the modern apartment dweller is that it gives him a well known package of goods and services—a package which includes not merely walls and ceilings, but also adequate heat, light and ventilation, serviceable plumbing facilities, secure windows and doors, proper sanitation, and proper maintenance." In this case, the court held that "[w]e place the duty of taking protective measures guarding the entire premises and the areas peculiarly under the landlord's control against the perpetration of criminal acts upon the landlord, the party to the lease contract who has effective capacity to perform these necessary acts." At the same time, a landlord who has actually *not* retained control will often be able to argue that those to whom he has delegated such control are the responsible parties. *See, e.g.,* Ross v. Texas One Partnership, 796 S.W.2d 206 (Tex. App. 1990), in which the court held that the owner of an apartment building could not be held liable for a security guard's alleged wrongful shooting of a man on the premises when the company

As a result, having control over that portion of the premises, the landlord must act as a reasonable person in exercising its control.[36]

In many apartment buildings, the building's owners or managers may have voluntarily undertaken to provide security of one kind or another, and once having undertaken this, must not perform that responsibility negligently.[37] In some instances, tenants may have been specially assured that the building provides security guards or is otherwise a "high security" or "secure" building. Such representations, if false, may well give rise to liability for later criminal assaults by third parties, based on the theory that the tenants relied on these representations to their detriment, and that these representations essentially became an implicit part of the contract between the landlord and the tenant.[38]

For conduct to be negligent, there first must be a duty of care, and then a breach of that duty which "proximately" causes damage. For there to be a duty to prevent the harm, the harm must have been the type of incident which was reasonably foreseeable. Negligence is based on a person with a duty acting "unreasonably" under the circumstances—but it is not "unreasonable" to neglect to act to prevent something which could not be foreseen.[39]

which supplied the security guard was an independent contractor. The facts showed that the apartment owner did not have the authority to control the details of how the supplied security guards did their job, nor did it train the guards. Without the right to control, the owner could not be held liable. The court also rejected the claim that the building owner was negligent in hiring the security company. The security company had provided documentation to the owner showing that it was licensed by the state, together with favorable references. There was no evidence to the contrary establishing that the owner knew or should have known that the security company was incompetent when hired.

See also Craig v. A.A.R. Realty Corp., 576 A.2d 688 (Del. Super. 1989) in which the nonpossessory landlord of a shopping mall, who had no actual control over the premises, was found to have no duty to protect customers and employees of its tenants against criminal attack, and in particular no liability for the kidnap-rape and murder of a female store employee.

36. SECOND RESTATEMENT OF TORTS, Sec. 360-61; SECOND RESTATEMENT OF PROPERTY, Sec. 17.3-.4.

37. Marshall v. David's Food Store, 515 N.E.2d 134 (Ill. App. 1987) (court finds that hiring of security service to guard parking lot showed knowledge of danger); Landry v. St. Charles Inn, Inc., 446 So. 2d 1246 (La. App. 1984) (woman awarded $20,000 after employee assured her of safety); and Olar v. Schroit, 202 Cal. Rptr. 457 (Cal. App. 1984) (female model violently attacked accuses condominium owners of making false promises of security).

38. Thompson v. Cane Garden Apartment, 442 So. 2d 1296 (La. App. 1983) (landlord could be liable for failing to protect elderly residents, as promised in the lease); Kivel v. Clark Fin. Corp., Ariz. Pima County Superior Court, No. 2507685, April 12, 1989, reported in 32 ATLA L. REP. 409 (Nov. 1989) (violent knife attack on two women in their apartment leads to $1.2 million award against building owners; misrepresentation of presence of security guards); Alvarez v. Harold Farb Investments, Inc., Tex. Harris County 270th Judicial District Court, No. 86-018657, Nov. 17, 1988, reported in 32 ATLA L. REP. 156 (May 1989) (building which advertised security was "second to none" settles lawsuit of tenant raped in parking lot for $100,000); and Conway v. H.R. Management Co., Tex., Harris County 125th Judicial District Court, No. 89-01137, Sept. 14, 1990, reported in 34 ATLA L. Rep. 68 (March 1991) (two female tenants sexually assaulted by an intruder to receive $550,000 each from apartment building owner in settlement of inadequate security and misrepresentation claims based on statements that there was a 24-hour security patrol when the patrol service drove through the parking lot only 2 or 3 times a night).

39. See generally, PROSSER AND KEETON, THE LAW OF TORTS, supra note 4, ch. 5 (5th ed. 1984).

In the landlord-tenant context, whether that of a private landlord, hotel, or public housing authority, there are many particular differences from state to state on the exact parameters of when a duty to protect the tenant will be found, but a common thread is the notion that prior similar crimes occurring in the building (or in some instances in the neighborhood of the building) make it foreseeable that more such crimes will take place.[40]

Although a condominium association is composed of owners of units, rather than tenants, the association typically takes on a management role and controls the "common elements" of the building. For purposes of civil liability for inadequate security, therefore, it typically should be viewed as being little different from a landlord.[41]

A hotel or motel (sometimes called an "innkeeper") actively solicits its guests to stay on the premises, usually on a transitory basis while traveling. An innkeeper essentially promises the guest a "home away from home" which is largely under the control of the innkeeper. In a hotel or motel, the management usually has much more control over the premises than in the apartment building context where more permanent tenants may take on much control. Typically a hotel or motel will even customarily enter guest's rooms to provide fresh linen, empty garbage containers, and do general cleanup. As a result, an innkeeper is held by most courts to have some duty to protect guests against criminal assaults.[42] Traveling individuals are a tempting target for criminals. This is so well known that many jurisdictions have passed statutes mandating that innkeepers post notices warning travelers of the need to safeguard valuables and provide front desk or front office safes for the safekeeping of patron's jewelry, funds, or valuable business papers. Strict compliance with such statutes normally results in a statutory limitation on the amount of monetary liability which the innkeeper could potentially incur for theft of property from patrons' rooms, but has little impact on suits for personal injury to patrons stemming from criminal assaults.[43]

40. *See, e.g.,* Crinkley v. Holiday Inns, Inc., 844 F.2d 156 (4th Cir. 1988) (pattern of motel robberies in area imposed duty to protect matrons; motel franchisor & franchisee liable for $500,000 in damages); Lay v. Dworman, 732 P.2d 455 (Okla. 1986) (landlord had duty to protect tenant from foreseeable criminal acts by third parties); Morrison v. MGM Grand Hotel, 570 F. Supp. 1448 (D. Nev. 1983) (gambling hotel could be liable for robbery in elevator since it had notice of other such robberies).

41. Frances T. v. Village Green Owners Assn., 42 Cal. 3d 490, 723 P.2d 573, 229 Cal. Rptr. 456 (1986) (condominium association and individual directors may be liable for failing to protect residents).

42. *See* Hayward v. Holiday Inns, Inc., 459 F. Supp. 634 (E.D.Va. 1978) (hotel guest awarded $2.5 million in damages for rape in motel room); Kveragas v. Scottish Inns, Inc., 733 F.2d 409 (6th Cir. 1984) (unlike shopping center owners, motel owners need not have actual notice of criminal activity before taking protective measures, such as installing adequate locks). *See* SECOND RESTATEMENT OF TORTS, Sec. 314(A)(2). *See also* Sec. 344, which states that "A possessor of land who holds it open to the public for entry for his business purposes is subject to liability to members of the public while they are upon the land for such purpose, for physical harm caused by the accidental, negligent, or intentionally harmful acts of third persons or animals, and by the failure of the possessor to exercise reasonable care to: (a) discover that such acts are being done or are likely to be done, or (b) give a warning adequate to enable the visitors to avoid the harm or otherwise to protect them against it."

43. *See, e.g.,* Gooden v. Day's Inn, 395 S.E.2d 876 (Ga. App. 1990), in which an innkeeper was found immune, under a state statute, from liability for employee's alleged theft of bag of money found in

Courts have imposed liability on the basis of a landlord or hotel's failure to warn tenants of earlier crimes in the building, to take corrective measures (such as posting additional security guards or installing security devices) or to make repairs (such as fixing a broken lock) after earlier crimes took place, and for failing to control access to master keys thus allowing individuals to enter apartments without authority.[44] Circumstances in which tenants have repeatedly complained about broken locks or unlocked stairwells, only to be ignored, have often resulted in large liability judgments.[45]

Under state negligence law, public housing authorities may in some instances be treated no differently than other landlords, on the theory that providing housing is a "proprietary" rather than governmental function. In some instances, however, there may be governmental immunity doctrines or statutes which apply.[46]

---

guest's room, when it provided a safe for guest's valuables, and the guest failed to avail himself of these safekeeping facilities. A Georgia statute provides that an innkeeper who provides a safe for deposit of his guest's valuables and posts a notice concerning its availability, is relieved for responsibility for such articles. The court rejected the argument that the motel was liable for the theft by virtue of *respondeat superior*. The court found that when the motel employee allegedly took the money, he was acting for himself and not on behalf on the motel, "nor was he acting within the scope of his employment."

44. *See* L.K. v. Water's Edge Assn., 532 So. 2d 1097 (Fla. App. 1988) (failure to instruct jury that landlord was obligated to protect tenant from reasonably foreseeable sexual assault or to warn tenant was grounds for reversal); Glick v. Preferred Fin. Corp. of Cal., Tex Harris County 234th Judicial District Court, No. 88-33120, Dec. 28, 1988, reported in 32 ATLA L. Rep. 261 (Aug. 1989) (tenant raped in apartment after building management allegedly failed to warn of four previous rapes on premises received $675,000 settlement);

45. *See, e.g.,* Vernon v. Benchmark Properties, Tex., Ector County 70th Judicial District Court, No. A-78,726, April 10, 1989, reported in 32 ATLA L. REP. 410 (Nov. 1989) (broken lock on apartment door facilitates tenant's rape; $956,000 jury award against management company which repeatedly failed to repair lock); Cain v. Vontz, 703 F.2d 1279 (11th Cir. 1983) (apartment landlord could be liable for death of tenant after failure to warn broken door locks); Orlando Executive Park, Inc. v. Robbins, 433 So. 2d 491 (Fla. 1983) (motel liable for assault on premises where there should have been three security guards instead of one.)

46. *See* Totten v. More Oakland Residential Housing, Inc., 63 Cal. App. 538, 134 Cal. Rptr. 29 (1976); Pippin v. Chicago Housing Authority, 374 N.E.2d 1055 (Ill. App. 1978); Goldberg v. Newark Housing Authority, 38 N.J. 578, 186 A.2d 291 (1962); McGoughy v. Chicago Housing Authority, 543 N.E.2d 236 (Ill. App. 1989). While providing the housing itself may be a proprietary (nongovernmental) function, immunity may be applied to the provision of a housing authority police force, which clearly is a government function. *See* Bass v. City of New York, 38 A.D.2d 407, 330 N.Y.S.2d 569 (1972). Similar considerations are often present in cases involving public university dormitories. *See* Delaney v. University of Houston, 792 S.W.2d 733 (Tex. App. 1990), in which a state university was not liable to female student raped in a dormitory by an intruder who entered through unrepaired door the student had complained about; state university was immune under a state statute from liability for intentional wrongs. The student's attempt to characterize part of her claims as a breach of contract of her housing contract did not alter the result, since the court found that, regardless of characterization, "the claims in this case arise out of an intentional tort." The court also rejected the argument that the state university should still be held liable on a theory that, in running a dormitory, it was engaged in a "proprietary" rather than "governmental" function and should be held to the same duty of care as any other landlord. The court noted that Texas has not, in past cases, applied a proprietary/governmental function distinction to actions of the state or state agencies, while doing so for municipal and other local government entities. Some states do

The fact that public housing authorities are governmental entities may tempt some to attempt to sue on a theory of violation of civil rights rather than state law negligence doctrines. In a recent important case *DeShaney v. Winnebago County Dept. of Social Services,*[47] however, the United States Supreme Court reemphasized the concept that state and local governments have no duty to protect particular members of the public from harm by private persons. While the Court made it clear that states were certainly free—as a matter of state law—to impose liability for failure to act to protect an individual, there is no constitutional duty to protect a private individual not "in custody" from harm by third persons under the Due Process Clause of the Fourteenth Amendment. Federal civil rights suits against public housing authorities on the basis of a supposed constitutional duty to protect, therefore, should now be easily dismissed.

Hotels, motels, condominium associations, public housing authorities, and the owners and managers of apartment buildings all hire maintenance, security, and other personnel, ranging from maids to doormen to electricians. Tenants and guests in these facilities are therefore unavoidably exposed to contact with many persons who have been hired and trained by the management and who are frequently given access to portions of the building, sometimes including individual apartments or rooms, which is not available to members of the general public. Building management may be held liable under state law for assault and battery by such personnel if they are acting within the scope of their employment.[48] In the instances in which such personnel are not acting within the scope of employment—such as when a security guard sexually assaults a tenant (something which has no connection to his job and which is done for his own purposes rather than to serve any interest of his employer), management may still be liable on a theory of negligent hiring or retention.[49] The negligence in question in those

apply the proprietary/governmental distinction to state agencies such as state universities. *See* Miller v. State, 62 N.Y.2d 506, 467 N.E.2d 493, 478 N.Y.S.2d 829 (1984), a case involving a similar rape of a university co-ed in a dormitory, in which the court found that when the state operates housing, it is held to the same duty as private landlords in the maintenance of physical security devices in the building itself.

47. 109 S. Ct. 998 (1989).

48. *See, e.g.,* Hildreth v. Hilgeford, Fla., Lee County Circuit Court, No. 85-3845 CA JRT, April 15, 1987, reported in 30 ATLA L. REP. 324 (Sept. 1987) (jury awards $255,000 for murder committed by motel manager's son, who used pass key to enter guest's room). But *see* McCarty v. Pheasant Run, Inc., 826 F.2d 1554 (7th Cir. 1987) (hotel guest did not present sufficient evidence to establish hotel's liability for assault in her room; she had failed to lock door); Ramada Inns, Inc. v. Sharp., 711 P.2d 1 (Nev. 1985) (hotel liable for security guard's pushing a woman down a flight of stairs; hotel gave security guards wide latitude in dealing with unescorted females who were not registered guests).

49. *See generally* Annot., *Liability for Negligent Hiring, Supervision, and Retention of Security Guard,* 44 A.L.R.4th 620. The flip side of this, which should not be forgotten, is that the building is the workplace for security guards who are hired, and the employer has some responsibility to provide a reasonably safe workplace for its employees, including such guards. Obviously, security guards know that they will necessarily confront some dangerous situations in the line of duty, but even when they are performing their security function, the landlord-employer may have specific duties to warn them of known dangers. In Robertson v. Sixpence Inns of America, Inc., 789 P.2d 1040

instances may be failure to check into an employee's past criminal record or references or may center around not taking action in response to earlier complaints of wrongful conduct.[50]

Although innkeepers by definition hold themselves out as open to members of the public, private landlords do not. Almost all landlords do some screening of potential tenants from the standpoint of creditworthiness and general desirability (within the boundaries of federal, state, and local laws prohibiting various forms of discrimination on the basis of race, national origin, religion, etc.). Additionally, many residential leases have clauses providing that activities which bother other tenants or use of the premises for illegal activities, constitute breach of the lease by the tenant. As a result, lawsuits against landlords have also occasionally been based on failure to take action against a tenant whose actions make it foreseeable that they will assault or otherwise cause harm to come to others on the premises. In particular, landlords who knowingly tolerate illegal activities such as drug dealing in their buildings may increasingly find themselves subject to suit by tenants who are injured by violent crimes such as robberies and shootings, which gravitate to the scene of such activities.[51] (It should also be noted, in passing, that knowing toleration of such activities may also subject buildings to forfeiture under federal and/or state law.)[52]

(Ariz. 1990), the Arizona Supreme Court held that the widow of a security guard killed by a robber could sue a motel for failure to warn her husband of the fact that the robber was armed, when the manager who summoned the guard knew this fact. "The failure to warn" the guard of the armed robbery, the court commented, "arguably left him at a disadvantage when he confronted" the robber.

50. See Kanne v. Burns International Security Services, Inc., Los Angeles County Superior Court, No. SWC 61883 (May 18, 1984), reported in 28 ATLA L. REP. 78 (liability for negligently hiring guard with prior criminal record).

51. See Simmons v. City of New York, 562 N.Y.S.2d 119 (A.D. 1990). In this case, a tenant in an apartment building told her fellow tenants at a tenants' meeting that another tenant was dealing drugs. This led to a confrontation between her and the alleged drug dealer, after which his roommate allegedly shot her in the back. The injured tenant suffered paralysis in her lower extremities and sued the landlord for negligence. The court found that the defendant landlord owed the injured tenant a duty to act reasonably. The plaintiff alleged that the landlord was aware of an ongoing criminal enterprise on its premises and took no action to stop it. It was a question for a jury to decide whether the landlord's alleged failure to evict the purported drug dealer was a proximate cause of the tenant's injuries. The court therefore refused to enter summary judgment for the landlord. Tolerance of activities far less outrageous than drug dealing may lead to similar lawsuits. In Cardenas v. Thottam Properties, Cal., Los Angeles County Superior Ct., No. C 698 457, Mar. 2, 1990, reported in 33 ATLA L. REP. 302 (Sept. 1990) a landlord was found liable for $249,500 for the blinding of tenant's 3-year-old child by another tenant's son shooting a BB gun, based on allegations that the building manager failed to stop the firing of BB guns on the premises despite earlier complaints.

52. See U.S. v. Premises Known as 418 57th St., Brooklyn, 737 F. Supp. 749 (E.D.N.Y. 1990), in which building owners who knew of drug offenses by tenants on the premises were held not entitled to "innocent owner" defense to forfeiture statute. The U.S. government sued for forfeiture of an apartment building under the Comprehensive Drug Abuse Prevention and Control Act of 1970, 21 U.S.C. Sec. 881(a)(7), because of narcotics activities of tenants in the building. Evidence in the case showed that the rent was always paid in cash. Additionally, the building owners had received a letter from a New York City councilman telling them that there were reports of drugs on the premises and that a tenant's brother, who was living in the building, had been arrested for possession of

Landlords, just as business owners, cannot absolutely guarantee that their tenants and their tenants' legitimate visitors are not subject to criminal activities by third parties (or by other tenants). But the time is clearly here where ownership or management of residential premises carries with it responsibility for taking positive steps to limit the possibility. Careful screening of both employees and tenants is required. Additionally, a defective front hallway lock must now be regarded as just as much of an emergency matter as a leaking pipe. Security measures in a residential building should be reviewed for adequacy at least as frequently as leases are reviewed annually for adequacy of rent. The occurrence of crimes on the premises should always trigger an analysis of whether security measures in force are inadequate to help prevent a recurrence. Taking such steps can both help prevent further harm to tenants and help prevent or limit liability if further crimes, for reasons beyond the control of a landlord, still occur.

drugs in the front yard. The landlords went and spoke to the tenant, who informed them that the brother had a few "joints on him that he used for recreational purposes." The court noted that the "innocent owner" defense is only available if the drug offenses in question had been committed without the knowledge or consent of the owner. In this instance, the evidence showed that the building owners "most certainly did have knowledge of the illegal acts." The fact that they may not have consented to them did not alter the result, since either knowledge or consent is sufficient to prevent assert of the "innocent owner" defense to forfeiture. The government was therefore granted summary judgment on its forfeiture petition. This case illustrates the importance of building owners and managers who acquire information about possible illegal activities of tenants, particularly drug-related activities, taking steps to investigate the possibility and to evict those shown to be engaged in such activities.

12

Crimes, Criminal Law, and Criminal Procedure of Special Interest to Security Personnel

CRIMES IN GENERAL

There are two main categories of crimes: felonies and misdemeanors. Generally, a felony is an offense of such seriousness as to warrant a penitentiary sentence of one year or more, or, as with murder, possibly capital punishment. A misdemeanor is an offense for which the punishment is usually incarceration for less than a year in a penal institution other than the penitentiary, or perhaps a monetary fine only, although some legislative enactments provide for both penalties for certain misdemeanors.

In addition to felonies and misdemeanors, there are also county, city, and village ordinances. Violations of these are generally considered in the judicial system as "quasi-crimes," meaning wrongful conduct that is not quite a crime in the traditional sense. They are usually punishable by monetary fine only. Some business regulatory ordinances, however, allow for suspension or revocation of licenses issued by a county board or a city or village council through a licensing agency.

The English common law was originally the basis for judging and punishing crimes in the American colonies. The common law was based on accumulated court decisions that relied heavily on the attitudes and customary habits of the people.

Much of the common law has been replaced, first by separate acts (statutes) of the various legislatures, and in many states by comprehensive criminal codes. Under some of the codes the common law has been specifically abolished, in consequence of which no conduct can be considered a crime unless declared so in the codes, or by subsequent legislative amendments, or entirely new enactments.[1]

---

1. *See, e.g.,* Illinois 720 ILCS, Sec. 5/21–3.

In the federal system, crimes can be only that conduct specifically declared to be so by Congress. There have never been, on the federal level, any common law crimes, although many of the concepts, and even much of the common law language, have been perpetuated by Congressional enactments.

The following is a list of and brief commentary about various crimes that are relevant to, or sometimes associated with, private business security functions. We then present a discussion of certain legal principles of importance in the interpretation and enforcement of the criminal law.

CRIMES

- *Assault and Battery*—This is often treated as one crime, although it actually consists of two separate crimes. An assault occurs when a person, without lawful authority, does something that places another person in reasonable apprehension of being physically hurt. A battery, however, involves actual physical harm or contact, knowingly inflicted, without legal justification, and in an insulting or provoking manner.

  In many states the penalty for each offense is more severe if the offender brandishes or uses a deadly weapon, in which instances the offenses are generally known as *aggravated assault* or *aggravated battery.*
- *Attempt*—The attempt to commit a crime may itself constitute a crime. This is the case when a person harboring an intent to commit a specific offense performs an act that amounts to a "substantial step" toward its commission. Mere preparation does not fulfill this requirement, and the difference between conduct that is a substantial step and that which is mere preparation is one of degree and must be determined by the circumstances of each case. An example of an attempt situation is one where an employee has removed some of the employer's goods or equipment to a secluded place on the premises from which they could secretly be removed during nonwork time.

  Ordinarily, however, the prudent procedure would be to keep watch on the area and wait until the property is in the actual process of being removed.
- *Bribery* (See also *Commercial Bribery*)—A person commits bribery when she promises or actually gives something of value or of some personal advantage to someone who is or is believed to be a public official, with the intention of influencing the performance of an official act. A public official commits bribery by accepting or soliciting such an offer.
- *Burglary*—At common law, this offense consisted of "breaking and entering" into the "dwelling house" of another "in the night time" with the "intent to steal." To remove the uncertainties and inadequacies of the offense as originally defined, present-day statutes generally provide that "a person commits burglary when without authority he knowingly enters or without authority remains within a building, housetrailer, watercraft, aircraft, motor vehicle . . . railroad car, or any part thereof with intent to commit therein a felony or theft."[2]

2. *See, e.g.,* Illinois 720 ILCS, Sec. 5/19–1(a).

- *Burglary Tools Possession*—The possession of any device suitable for breaking into a building coupled with an intent to use it to commit a crime therein constitutes this offense. The "intent" requirement is usually very difficult to establish.
- *Commercial Bribery* (See also *Bribery*)—This is a separate crime from traditional bribery and usually applies only to conduct involving nonpublic, business personnel.

  Commercial bribery is committed when a person confers, or offers or agrees to confer, any benefit upon an employee, without consent of the employer, with intent to influence the employee's conduct in relation to her employer's affairs.

  Commercial bribery is also committed when the employee solicits, agrees to, or accepts such a benefit.
- *Compounding a Crime*—This is the offense of receiving or offering to give monies or other consideration in return for a promise not to prosecute or aid in the prosecution of a criminal offender. It is also know as *misprision of felony*.

  In addition to state statutes, there is a federal one that provides that "[w]hoever, having knowledge of the actual commission of a federal felony conceals it and does not as soon as possible make [it known to a federal judge or other authority] shall be fined not more than $500 or imprisoned for not more than three years or both."[3] The statute has been interpreted by the courts to require not only knowledge of a crime but also an affirmative act of concealment.
- *Confidence Game*—This is an offense created by statute to plug up a loophole in common law larceny. A person who fleeces another out of money or property by gaining the confidence of the owner plays a "confidence game," for which the punishment is usually of felony grade. In contrast, obtaining something of value by deception without first building up a confidence or trust constitutes a false pretense crime, usually punishable as a misdemeanor.

  Modern "theft" statutes usually cover both activities.
- *Conspiracy*—A conspiracy is an agreement between two or more persons to commit a crime. It is an offense separate and distinct from the underlying substantive offense. Merely discussing the possibility or the ease with which a crime may be committed does not amount to a conspiracy; there must be a planning, and, according to most conspiracy laws, someone in the group must perform at least one overt act toward its accomplishment.
- *Counterfeit Currency Transactions*—The forgery of currency or other legal tender, and the possession, passing, or sale of counterfeit currency or other obligations, are punishable offenses. Because mere possession without knowledge or criminal intent is not a crime, extreme caution is required with respect to a customer or other person who has transferred or attempted to transfer counterfeit currency. The prudent practice, therefore, is for a merchant to retain the currency, request the name, address, and telephone number of the passer, and then notify the local police or federal authorities. This procedure will offer protection against false arrest accusations.
- *Credit Card Misuse*—Because credit cards are of recent origin, state laws have been enacted that specifically provide that it is unlawful to possess, use, or sell

3. 18 U.S.C. Sec. 4.

stolen, lost, or counterfeit credit cards. In addition to the state laws, a federal statute prohibits the interstate commerce of any stolen, lost, counterfeit, altered, or fraudulently obtained credit card. It is also a federal offense for a person to use such a credit card to purchase goods valued at more than $1,000 in a transaction affecting interstate commerce or if the goods were transported interstate.

- *Disorderly Conduct*—Knowingly committing acts in such an unreasonable manner as to alarm or disturb another person or persons constitutes this offense. Examples of disorderly conduct are the creation or maintenance of loud or raucous noises of all sorts, threats to damage property or to cause bodily harm, and, of course, fighting.
- *Embezzlement*—An individual who converts to her own use money or other personal property entrusted to her possession commits the offense of embezzlement.

   Modern theft statutes usually cover embezzlement and have eliminated the problem of whether the converter had possession or mere custody.
- *Extortion* (See also *Intimidation*)—This crime is frequently referred to as "blackmail." It is the offense a public official commits when she compels someone to "pay her off" for withholding the performance of her lawful duty or for resorting to wrongful conduct under the guise of official duty.

   A federal law, the Hobbs Act, makes extortion a federal offense when the conduct affects "interstate commerce." Another federal crime occurs when the U.S. mail is used in an extortion situation.
- *False Pretenses* (See *Confidence Game*).
- *Forgery*—A person commits forgery when, with intent to defraud, she makes or alters any document apparently capable of defrauding another, or issues or delivers such a document knowing it to have been thus made or altered, or possesses it with such an intent.
- *Intimidation* (See also *Extortion*)—This is an offense comparable to extortion, the essential difference being its application to all persons, not just those involved in public official transactions.

   A person commits intimidation when, with intent to cause another to perform or omit the performance of any act, she communicates to another a threat to inflict physical harm, or to make a criminal accusation, or to expose a person to hatred, contempt, or ridicule, or to bring about or continue to strike or boycott, etc.
- *Larceny*—This is the taking and carrying away of the personal property of another with intent to deprive the owner of it permanently.

   Some statutes have two grades of larceny, grand and petty, depending on the amount of money or the value of the article taken—e.g., grand: over $150; petty: under $150.

   Larceny from the person of another (e.g., pickpocketing) is also punishable more seriously.

   Under modern penal codes, the offense of "theft" includes what was formerly labeled larceny.
- *Malicious Mischief*—This is criminal damage to property. If fire or an explosive is used, the offense is arson.
- *Misprision of Felony* (See *Compounding a Crime*)

- *Perjury*—This is when a person knowingly makes, under oath, a false statement about an issue before a court, legislature, grand jury, or an executive branch of government.
- *Pickpocketing* (See also *Larceny* and *Theft*)—Stealthily removing something of value from the pocket of another person, with intent to keep it, is larceny (or theft). Because of the risk of bodily harm which it entails, this type of stealing carries a more severe penalty than ordinary stealing.
- *Purse Snatching* (See also *Larceny, Theft,* and *Robbery*)—Grabbing a person's purse with intent to steal it or its contents is larceny or, in some jurisdictions, theft. Because of the personal danger involved, it is usually punished more severely than simple larceny or theft. Moreover, if the taker encounters physical resistance and forcibly overcomes it, the offense escalates to robbery.
- *Retail Theft* (See also *Theft*)—This is a specialized form of the basic crime of theft. Statutes have been enacted for the primary purpose of affording additional protection from shoplifting. (Examples of such statutes appear in the Appendix.)
- *Robbery*—The taking of money or other property from the person or presence of another by the use of force or by threatening the immediate use of force constitutes this offense.
- *Shoplifting* (See also *Larceny, Theft,* and *Retail Theft*)—This is the theft of merchandise displayed for sale.
- *Solicitation*—A person who intends to have an offense committed, and who commands, encourages, or requests another person to commit it, thereby commits the crime of solicitation.
- *Stolen Property (Possessing/Receiving)*—A person commits the offense of possessing or receiving stolen property when she knows or reasonably should know it has been stolen. (See the discussion of Presumption in the next section.)
- *Theft* (See also *Retail Theft*)— Over the years, the word *theft* merely described a general type of criminal conduct ("stealing"), but it is now used in some statutes as a specific crime label. As such, it embraces a number of formerly separate offenses such as larceny, embezzlement, false pretenses, and receiving stolen property. For instance, under the Illinois Criminal Code, a person commits theft when she knowingly obtains or exercises unauthorized control over property of the owner, or does so by deception, or knows that the property she has received has been stolen and has the intent to deprive the owner of it permanently.
- *Trespass*—This offense consists in entering on the property of another without consent, after receiving, immediately prior to entry, notice that entry is prohibited, or remaining on the property after receiving notice to depart.

CRIMINAL LAW PRINCIPLES

Intent

The general criminal law principle most relevant to the security function is the element of intent that is required to prove most offenses. A commonplace illustration is presented by a typical shoplifting case: While in a department store, a woman picks up a silk scarf, looks around, and then carries it past a cashier and proceeds in the direction of one of the store exits. An experienced security officer has observed all this and is convinced the woman is about to make off without paying for the scarf. May she arrest her? There is no question that the scarf was "taken" and "carried away," two of the requirements for larceny (plus the fact that the scarf was in the "personal property" category), but was there the indispensable factor of "intent to steal"? If apprehended, the scarf carrier could say that she was only taking it to get a better view in the sunlight coming through the exit door. In defense of a false arrest suit, the store would have great difficulty in proving criminal intent so as to justify an arrest. Suppose, however, the taker of the scarf has placed it in her purse, closed the purse, and walked away. Here the intent to steal becomes very evident, and an arrest would be justified. Likewise, consider the case of a person who takes a scarf from a windowed, well-lit second floor, where a cashier is readily available, and walks down a stairway with the scarf to an area where only luggage is sold. Again, the intent to steal is clear. Nevertheless, the usual procedure in shoplifting cases is to withhold an arrest until the person has left the store, so as to render more convincing to a judge or jury that there was the intent to steal. It is important to remember, however, that this is a precautionary measure and not a legal requirement; in many cases the intent to steal may be clearly established without having to wait for the person to depart from the premises.

The 1981 decision of the highest court of New York in *People v. Olivo*, 52 N.Y.2d 309, 420 N.E.2d 40, is an excellent demonstration of the general proposition that shoplifting may occur without the taker leaving the premises. It also contains references to similar cases in other jurisdictions.

Presumption

The meaning of a legal presumption may be best explained by the following two examples: (1) The possession of recently stolen property gives rise to the reasonable assumption that the possessor knew it was stolen when she received it; and (2) the concealment of unpaid merchandise is presumed to evidence intent to steal. In both cases, however, other facts or circumstances are required either to prove guilt beyond a reasonable doubt or to explain away the inference of guilt.

A presumption is either valid or invalid depending "upon whether, based on life and life's experiences," there is "a rational connection between the fact proved and the ultimate fact presumed."

Entrapment

Mindful of the frailties of human nature (and the cynical notion that "every man has his price"), the principle has been established that if the police "entice" or "induce" a person to commit an act that is criminally punishable, that person should not be punished for what she did. The belief is that were it not for the persuasion and temptation by the police, the individual might have remained honest. Accordingly, the defense of entrapment requires that an accused person be granted immunity for what she did as a result of police encouragement. On the other hand, that defense will not prevail when police merely afford a person an *opportunity* to commit a crime.

Although the entrapment defense is almost always invoked in cases that involve police investigations, some courts might be inclined to apply the doctrine even when strictly private security officers are participants. For that reason, as well as on moralistic grounds, no investigator should go beyond the mere presentation of an opportunity to perform the act.

PROCEDURES FROM ARREST THROUGH TRIAL

There will be occasions when a business person or security officer will find it helpful to know about the judicial processes that may occur after the arrest of a suspected shoplifter, or embezzler, or someone arrested for another offense committed while on the premises.

Post Arrest Requirement

In most states there is a statutory provision to the effect that an arrested person must be taken without unnecessary delay before the nearest judge or magistrate. What happens after presentation to the judge or magistrate will depend upon whether the arrested person is accused of a felony or a misdemeanor. If the charge is a misdemeanor, the judge or magistrate will sometimes have the power and authority to hear the case herself, and she may proceed with the trial unless the accused demands trial by jury or a continuance is requested or ordered for some reason. If the offense charged is a felony, the judge or magistrate before whom the accused is brought will ordinarily lack the constitutional or legislative authority to conduct trials for crimes of that degree of seriousness, and in such instances she only conducts what is known as a *preliminary hearing*.

The Right to Bail

After arrest, the first decision made by a court is, frequently, whether the accused is entitled to be released on bail. Subject to some exceptions for persons charged with death penalty offenses, persons on parole, and others, an accused is entitled to have the court set bail. Bail is fixed at a specific dollar amount. If the accused places cash or property worth that amount with the clerk of court, she will be at liberty pending her trial. If the accused appears at the required proceedings, bail is refunded, but failure to appear results in forfeiture of bail. In some states, professional bail bondsmen will, in effect, deposit bail in exchange for a nonrefundable fee from the defendant. In other states, a defendant is allowed to deposit a portion of the bail (usually equivalent to the bondsman's fee, i.e., 10%), most of which is refunded if the defendant honors her obligation to appear. Moreover, courts generally have the power to allow release without any deposit—merely accepting the defendant's signature on a bond that makes her liable for the amount of bail if she fails to appear. Such defendants, usually those thought to be highly likely to appear for trial, are said to be released on recognizance, signature, or individual bond. Finally, an accused has no right to have bail set at an amount she can meet. Many defendants will fail to "make" bail and remain in jail pending trial.

The Right to an Attorney

The Sixth Amendment to the Constitution of the United States provides that "in all criminal prosecutions, the accused shall enjoy the right . . . to have the assistance of Counsel for his defense." The Supreme Court of the United States has also held that where incarceration may be a consequence of the prosecution, the defendant is entitled to appointed counsel in the event she cannot afford one. A preliminary hearing, of course, is a part of the "criminal prosecution." Thus, in that proceeding as well, the defendant is entitled to counsel.

Preliminary Hearing

A preliminary hearing is a relatively informal proceeding whereby a determination is made as to whether there are reasonable grounds to believe that the accused person committed the offense—that is, whether it is fair, under the circumstances, to require her to stand a regular trial. If after such a hearing the judge or magistrate decides that the accusation is without probable cause, the accused will be discharged. This discharge, however, will not bar a grand jury indictment if subsequently developed evidence (or the same evidence presented at the preliminary hearing) satisfies the grand jury that the accusation is well founded.

If the preliminary hearing judge or magistrate decides that the accusation is a reasonable one, the accused will be "bound over" to the grand jury—that is, held in jail until the charge against her is presented for grand jury consideration. If the offense is a bailable one, however, the accused may be released after a bond of a certain amount is given to ensure her presence until the grand jury has acted in the matter. (The nature and composition of a grand jury and the difference between it and a petit or trial jury is described later in this chapter.)

In some jurisdictions, once the magistrate has found probable cause, the prosecutor may bypass the grand jury and file a felony "information" upon which the accused will be tried.

The Habeas Corpus Writ

In the event an arrested person is not formally charged with an offense and is not taken before a judge or other magistrate "without unnecessary delay," she, or rather someone on her behalf, may petition a judge for a "writ of habeas corpus" (that is, "you have the body," which is the literal meaning of the term *habeas corpus*) and thereby attempt to secure her release or at least compel the police to file a specific charge against her. In the latter event, she may then seek to be released on bond. If the court issues the writ, the police or other custodians of the arrested person are required, either immediately or at an early designated time, to bring her into court, and explain to the court the reason or justification for holding the accused person in custody.

Upon the police showing adequate cause, a court may continue the hearing in order to give the police a little more time to conduct a further investigation before making the formal charge against the arrestee. Many times, however, the police are required to file their charges immediately or release the prisoner. In some jurisdictions, the prosecutor makes the decision as to whether the initial charge shall be filed.

The Grand Jury

Misdemeanors are usually prosecuted based on *information* filed by the prosecuting attorney after she has received and considered the sworn complaint of the victim or of some other person with knowledge of the facts. For felonies, however, many states require that the matter must first be submitted to a grand jury. Then, after hearing the alleged facts related by the victim or other persons, the grand jury determines whether there are reasonable grounds for proceeding to an actual trial of the person charged.

A grand jury is usually composed of twenty-three citizen-voters, sixteen of whom constitute a quorum. The votes of twelve members are necessary to the return of an "indictment." This indictment is also known as a "true bill."

The Constitution of the United States does not require that state prosecutors use a grand jury to charge felony offenses, and there is an increasing tendency to enact statutes that permit the prosecution to charge felonies by filing an information. Ordinarily, a person charged by information must have a preliminary hearing before she can be tried for the charge. A defendant charged by a grand jury, however, may not have a right to a preliminary hearing, because it is thought that her rights are adequately safeguarded by her fellow citizens who serve on the grand jury.

One highly significant and increasing modern purpose of the grand jury is to investigate complex crimes. The grand jury has the right to subpoena witnesses, to ask them questions, and to require the production of books and records. It may exercise these rights before any charge is filed and before the specific crime or its perpetrator is known. Police agencies usually do not possess this authority to compel the production of evidence, and it is generally conceded that such a right is required for effective investigation of much financial crime, official corruption, and organized crime.

The consideration of a felony charge by a grand jury is in no sense of the word a trial. Only the state's evidence is presented and considered; the suspected offender is usually not even heard, nor is her lawyer present to offer evidence on her behalf. Some state laws, however, now provide that the suspect has a right to appear before the grand jury if she elects to do so, but very few suspects exercise that option. Other laws provide that a "target" of the grand jury investigation has the right to have counsel present if she is summoned to appear before the grand jury.

The Arraignment and Plea

Following an indictment, the next step in felony cases is the appearance of the accused person before a judge who is empowered to try felony cases. The indictment is read to the defendant or the essence of its contents is made known to her; in other words, she is advised of the criminal charges made against her. If she pleads guilty, the judge can sentence her immediately or take the matter under advisement for a decision at an early date. If the accused pleads not guilty, a date is then set for the actual trial.

In some states, and in the federal system, the defendant may enter a plea of "nolo contendere," a plea which has the same effect as a plea of guilty, except that the admission thereby made cannot be used as evidence in any other action.

Pretrial Motions

After the formal charge has been made, the accused may, in advance of trial, seek to terminate the prosecution's case, or a least seek to prepare a better defense, by utilizing a procedure known as making or filing a *motion*. A motion is merely a request for a court ruling or order that will afford the defendant the assistance or remedy she is thereby seeking. Some of the more frequently used motions are the following:

> *Motion to Quash the Indictment.* With this motion the defendant may question the legal sufficiency of the indictment. If the court decides that the indictment adequately charges a criminal offense, and that it was obtained in accordance with the prescribed legal procedures, the motion will be overruled; otherwise the indictment will be considered invalid and "quashed." Even after an indictment has been thus rejected and set aside, the prosecutor may proceed to obtain another proper indictment. Moreover, the prosecution is entitled to appeal a court order to quash an indictment; at this stage of the proceedings the defendant has not been placed in jeopardy, and consequently a subsequent indictment and trial would not constitute a violation of her constitutional privilege against double jeopardy.

Motion to Suppress Evidence. A defendant has the privilege to file with the court, normally in advance of trial, a "motion to suppress" evidence that she contends has been obtained in an unconstitutional manner. The evidence in question may be, on the one hand, tangible items such as guns, narcotics, or stolen property or, on the other hand, intangible items such as confessions or the testimony of eyewitnesses who are expected to identify the accused as the offender. If the court is satisfied that the evidence has been illegally obtained, it will order the evidence suppressed, which means that it cannot be used at the trial. If the court decides that the evidence was lawfully obtained, it is usable against the defendant at the trial.

The Trial

In all states, and in the federal system, the accused is entitled to a "speedy trial." This right to an early trial is guaranteed by the various constitutions, and the constitutional provisions are generally supplemented by legislative enactments that particularize and specifically limit the pretrial detention period. In Illinois, for instance, once a person is jailed on a criminal charge, she must be tried within 120 days, unless the delay has been occasioned by her, or is necessitated by a hearing to determine her mental competency to stand trial or by certain appeals from evidentiary rulings. If the accused is out on bail, she can demand trial within 160 days. In either instance, however, if the court determines that the prosecution has exercised, without success, due diligence to obtain evidence material to the case, and that there are reasonable grounds to believe that such evidence will be forthcoming, the time for trial may be extended for another sixty days.[4] These time limits vary from state to state, but the consistent rule is that unless tried within the specified period of time the accused must be released and is thereafter immune from prosecution for that offense.

The federal courts are governed by the Speedy Trial Act of 1974, which is a statutory scheme that provides time periods within which federal trials must begin. Subject to narrow exceptions, a federal trial must commence within seventy days of indictment. Even under the new federal act, some circumstances permit the accused to waive this right to a trial within the statutory period.[5]

Jury Trial—Trial by Judge Alone

A person accused of a "serious crime," which is considered one for which there may be incarceration beyond six months, is entitled to trial by jury as a matter of constitutional right. She may waive this right, however, and elect to be tried by a

4. 725 ILCS§5/103–5.
5. 18 U.S.C. § 3161–3174.

judge alone. In some jurisdictions the defendant has an absolute right to this waiver (e.g., Illinois);[6] in others (e.g., the federal system) it is conditioned upon the concurrence of the judge and the prosecution.

If the case is tried without a jury, the judge hears the evidence and decides whether the defendant is guilty or not guilty. Where the trial is by a jury, the jury determines the facts and the judge serves more or less as an umpire or referee; it is her function to determine what testimony or evidence is legally "admissible," that is, to decide what should be heard or considered by the jury. But the ultimate decision as to whether the defendant is guilty is one to be made by the jury alone.

Jury Selection

In the selection of the jurors, usually twelve in number, who hear the defendant's case, most states permit the accused's attorney as well as the prosecuting attorney to question a larger number of citizens who have been chosen for jury service from the list of registered voters. In the federal system and in a growing number of states, however, most trial judges will do practically all the questioning, with very little opportunity for questioning accorded the prosecutor and defense counsel. Nevertheless, each lawyer has a certain number of "peremptory challenges," which means that she can arbitrarily refuse to accept as jurors a certain number of those who appear as prospective jurors.[7] In some states, by statutory provision, the defendant in larceny cases has ten such challenges and the state has an equal number; in a murder case the defendant and the state each have twenty peremptory challenges; and in minor criminal cases, such as petit larceny, the challenges are five for each side. In all cases, if any prospective juror's answers to the questions of either attorney reveal a prejudice or bias that prevents her from being a fair and impartial juror, the judge, either on her own initiative or at the suggestion of either counsel, will dismiss that person from jury service. Although the desired result is not always achieved, the avowed purpose of this practice is to obtain twelve jurors who will be fair to both sides of the case.

6. 725 ILCS § 5/103–6.

7. In Batson v. Kentucky, 476 U.S. 79 (1986), an exception to this was established, with the Court holding that a prosecutor could not exercise such peremptory challenges to remove potential jurors on the basis of their race. In instances where it appears that race is the basis for such a challenge, the prosecutor must be able to articulate, to the court's satisfaction, other, nonracial grounds on which she based her peremptory challenge. This principle has been extended by the U.S. Supreme Court to bar peremptory challenges on the basis of gender. J.E.B. v. Alabama Ex Rel. T.B., 114 S. Ct. 1419 (1994). The Court applied to principle in Batson to civil lawsuit jury selection and to peremptory challenges by private parties (such as the criminal defendant) as well as governmental parties (such as the prosecutor). See Powers v. Ohio, 499 U.S. 400 (1991), Edmonson v. Leesville Concrete Co., 500 U.S. 614 (1991), and Georgia v. McCollum, 112 S. Ct. 2348 (1992). Some state courts have also barred peremptory challenges on the basis of religion or various other categories. See Joseph v. Florida, 636 So. 2d 777 (Fla. App. 1994) (exclusion of juror by peremptory challenge based on Jewish religion violates Florida constitution), and Florida v. Alen, 616 So. 2d 452 (Fla. 1993) (peremptory challenge could not be used to discriminate against potential jurors who were Hispanics or other ethnic groups which constitute a "cognizable class").

Opening Statements

After the jury is selected, both the prosecuting attorney and the defense lawyer are entitled to make "opening statements" in which each outlines what she intends to prove. The purpose of this is to acquaint the jurors with each side of the case, so that it will be easier for them to follow the evidence as it is presented.

The Prosecution's Evidence

After the opening statements the prosecuting attorney produces the prosecution's testimony and evidence. She has the burden of proving the state's case "beyond a reasonable doubt." If, at the close of the prosecution's case, the judge is of the opinion that reasonable jurors could not conclude that the charge against the defendant has been proved, she will "direct a verdict" of acquittal. At that point, the matter is ended and the defendant goes free—forever immune from further prosecution for the crime, just as if a jury had heard all the evidence and found her not guilty.

The Defendant's Evidence

If, at the close of the prosecution's case, the court does not direct the jury to find the defendant not guilty, the defendant may, if she wishes, present evidence in refutation. She herself may or may not testify, and if he chooses not to appear as a witness, the prosecuting attorney is not permitted to comment on that fact to the jury. The basis for this principle whereby the defendant is not obligated to speak on her own behalf is the constitutional privilege that protects a person from self-incrimination.

The prosecution is given an opportunity to rebut the defendant's evidence, if any, and the presentation of testimony usually ends at that point. Then, once more, defense counsel will try to persuade the court to direct a verdict in favor of the defendant. If the court decides to let the case go to the jury, the prosecuting attorney and defense counsel make their closing arguments.

The defense and the prosecution have the right to subpoena witnesses and require them to testify at trial or to produce records if such evidence would be of value at trial. It is possible in certain case situations to enforce subpoenas against out-of-state witnesses and, in some instances, against witnesses in foreign countries.

The prosecution has the obligation in most, if not all, cases to notify the defense of any evidence that would be of significance in exculpating the accused or in mitigating her sentence, if the prosecution is aware of this evidence.

Closing Arguments

In their closing arguments the prosecutor and defense counsel review and analyze the evidence and attempt to persuade the jury to render a favorable verdict.

After the closing arguments are completed, the judge in most jurisdictions will read and give to the jury certain written instructions as to the legal principles that should be applied to the facts of the case as determined by the jury. The judge also gives the jury certain written forms of possible verdicts. The jury then retires to the jury room, where they are given an adequate opportunity to deliberate on the matter away from everyone, including the judge herself.

The Verdict of the Jury

When the jurors have reached a decision, they advise the bailiff that they have reached a verdict and then return to the courtroom. The foreman, usually selected by the jurors themselves to serve as their leader and spokesperson, announces the verdict of the jury. Jury participation in the case then ends.

If acquitted, the defendant is free forever from any further prosecution by that particular state or jurisdiction for the crime for which she was tried. If found guilty, then, in most types of cases and in most jurisdictions, it becomes the function of the trial judge to fix the sentence within the legislatively prescribed limitations.

In the event the jurors are unable to agree on a verdict—and it must be unanimous in most states—the jury, commonly referred to as a "hung jury," is discharged, and a new trial date may be set for a retrial of the case before another jury. The retrial does not constitute a violation of the constitutional protection against double jeopardy—trying a person twice for the same offense—because there actually has not been a first trial; in other words, it has been terminated by the failure of the jury to agree on a verdict.

The Motion for a New Trial

After a verdict of guilty, there are still certain opportunities provided the defendant to obtain her freedom. She may file a "motion for a new trial," in which she alleges certain "errors" were committed in the course of the trial; if the trial judge agrees, the conviction is set aside and the defendant may be tried again by a new jury and usually before a different judge. Where this motion for a new trial is "overruled" or "denied," the judge will then proceed to sentence the defendant.

The defendant may also seek a new trial on the grounds of newly discovered evidence favorable to her. Such motions are rarely granted. The defendant must establish that she was not aware of the evidence, that she could not have discovered it by exercising due diligence, and that it would probably change the result of the trial.

The Sentence

In cases tried without a jury, the judge, of course, will determine the sentence to be imposed. In jury cases the practice varies among the states, with most of them following the practice of confining the jury function to a determination of guilt or innocence and permitting the judge to fix the penalty. For capital crimes of murder and rape, however, most states place both responsibilities on the jury.

In some states there are statutory provisions that prescribe that upon conviction of a felony, the defendant must be sentenced for a specified minimum-maximum term in the penitentiary—for example, one year to ten years for burglary. In many states a judge is permitted to set a minimum-maximum period anywhere within the minimum-maximum term prescribed by the legislature. In other words, the sentence given for grand larceny may be one to ten years, the statutory range, or one or two, nine to ten, or any other combination between one and ten. The minimum-maximum term means that the defendant cannot be released before serving the minimum period, less "time off for good behavior," nor can she be kept in the penitentiary longer than the maximum period, less "time off for good behavior." In between this minimum-maximum period the convict is eligible for "parole." The determination of the appropriate time for release within that period is made by a "parole board," whose judgment in that respect is based on the extent of the convict's rehabilitation, the security risk involved, and similar factors.

In instances where imprisonment is fixed at a specified number of years, rather than for an indeterminate period, the law usually provides that the convicted person must serve one-third of the sentence before becoming eligible for parole.

Recently, there has been an increase in two new forms of incarceration. "Work release" allows an inmate to work at a job and return to custody during nonworking hours. "Periodic imprisonment" allows an inmate her freedom except for certain specified periods, e.g., weekends.

In addition, some states have adopted a plan that limits the sentencing discretion of judges and the release powers of parole boards, or that even abolishes parole boards. Under this new system the judge is required to set a specific term according to more or less strict guidelines. The sentence may be reduced by "good time" allowance (for "good behavior") in prison, which is calculated by a set formula. When the inmate serves her sentence less "good time," she is automatically released.

13

The Courts and Their Organization

In accordance with our unique concept of government, there are two distinct court systems for criminal prosecution: the federal system and the state system. Courts are created, organized, and empowered to act either by constitutional or legislative provisions, or both.[1]

The Constitution of the United States vests the federal judicial power in "one Supreme Court and in such inferior courts as the Congress may from time to time ordain and establish."[2] Under the federal–state relationship established by the Constitution, each state is free to decide on the kind and nature of the court system of that state. There are, therefore, not only conceptual and organizational differences between the state and federal courts, but also differences among the court systems of the individual states. Although the names, character, and authority of the state and federal court systems may vary, there is one common thread that runs through the organizations of all courts: each system has both a trial and an appellate branch. We shall begin with a description of the state system, with primary attention, of course, to the criminal courts.

STATE COURTS

State constitutions usually contain provisions that refer to the system of courts to be established, often in the form of a declaration that judicial power is to be vested in certain kinds of courts. Such constitutional provisions vary in that some specify the courts to be established,[3] whereas others list certain types of

---

1. Omitted from consideration in this chapter are the clerks, sheriffs, bailiffs, and reporters within the court systems. These ministerial officials are not an inherent part of the court; they only help the court function on a day-to-day basis.

2. Art. 3, § 1.

3. For example, Ark. Constitution, art. 7, § 1 et seq., and Fla. Constitution, art. 5, § 1 et seq.

courts and provide that additional courts of lesser jurisdictions may be created by legislation.[4]

The states, by their own constitutions or by statutes or local ordinances, usually provide for the following general organization of courts with criminal jurisdiction:

1. minor trial courts with limited jurisdiction—for example, municipal courts, county courts, justices of the peace, and magistrates;
2. major trial courts—for example, circuit courts, district courts, and superior courts, all of which titles are usually synonymous;
3. juvenile courts;
4. intermediate appellate courts;
5. courts of last resort—known by various names, such as supreme courts, courts of appeals, supreme judicial courts, or supreme courts of appeal.

In considering the seemingly complex state court systems described in this chapter, the reader should be mindful of the fact that only a small percentage of criminal cases go through a full-blown trial and appellate process. In many instances the role of the courts is to receive, review, and approve negotiations between the prosecutor and the defense counsel and the defendant that have resulted from the defendant's decision to plead guilty.

TRIAL COURT

Minor Trial Courts—Courts of Limited Jurisdiction.   The jurisdiction of minor trial courts is prescribed by statutes or by local ordinances. Because the statutes and ordinances may vary from state to state in the kind of courts prescribed and the extent of their jurisdiction, the relevant statutes and ordinances must be consulted whenever there is a question as to a particular court's jurisdiction over a given case. The question of whether or not a court possesses the necessary jurisdiction is determined by the allegations of the complaint rather than by the facts that may ultimately be proved at trial.

The jurisdiction of local courts—those created by county or city ordinances—is in some instances exclusive of the jurisdiction of other state courts, but the jurisdiction may be concurrent with them. In other instances special statutes prescribe that the local courts have the same jurisdiction in criminal cases within a city or county limit as that possessed by state-established courts. Generally, the jurisdiction of local courts is limited to petty offenses such as misdemeanors or ordinance violations. The same unlawful conduct, however, may constitute an offense against both a state statute and a local ordinance. In the absence of statutory or constitutional provisions that confer concurrent jurisdiction, inferior state courts have jurisdiction only over offenses that are punishable as violations of state laws, whereas local courts have jurisdiction over offenses punishable as ordinance violations.

---

4. For example, Kans. Constitution, art. 3, § 1 et seq.; Mo. Constitution, art. 5, § 1 et seq.; N.J. Constitution, art. 6 and 7; Utah Constitution, art. 8, § 1 et seq.; Wis. Constitution, art. 7, § 1 et seq.

Inferior courts such as justices of the peace and police justices sit as state courts of limited criminal jurisdiction. Their jurisdiction ordinarily extends to the trial of a limited class or misdemeanors of minor offenses such as disorderly conduct, breach of the peace, vagrancy, and some traffic offenses. They generally do not have jurisdiction over felonies except as committing magistrates for the initial appearance of the accused before a court.

Trial Courts. The major trial courts, usually called circuit courts, district courts, or superior courts, are state courts that have general jurisdiction over criminal prosecutions. They are concerned mainly with the trial of felony offenses before a judge or jury. The general types of crimes heard by such courts range from violent crimes such as murder, rape, and robbery to such nonviolent crimes as check offenses and credit card fraud.

Juvenile Courts. Juvenile courts are generally created by state statutes and are given jurisdiction over certain cases relating to delinquent children, with the goal of directing the juveniles away from criminal activity. The purpose of juvenile courts is to help reform delinquent children rather than to punish them. Emphasis is placed on the future development of the delinquent minor rather than on his past shortcomings.

In the juvenile courts there are fewer technicalities and formalities than are required in adult criminal proceedings. The United States Supreme Court has held, however, that the substantive due process protection accorded adults must also be given children in juvenile court proceedings.[5]

Typically, the statutes that set up juvenile courts narrowly limit their jurisdiction. Some state statutes give juvenile courts exclusive jurisdiction over proceedings arising out of the commission of certain proscribed acts by juveniles. Some of these statutes, however, give the juvenile court authority to determine whether it will retain jurisdiction over the unlawful conduct or transfer the case to a criminal court. Other statutes do not deprive the criminal courts of jurisdiction to try juveniles for serious offenses. The most common examples are statutes that permit the criminal courts to try juveniles for crimes punishable by death or life imprisonment.

APPELLATE COURTS

If a defendant is convicted in the trial court and is unsuccessful in his post-trial motions, he may appeal his conviction to a higher state court. Generally a time limit is placed upon the period during which an appeal may be taken.

In some jurisdictions, a defendant who is convicted of a minor offense in an inferior trial court has the right to a new trial ("trial de novo") in a major trial court. In most cases, and in all cases involving serious offenses, the right to appeal is limited to the right to have an appellate court examine the record of the trial

---

5. *In re* Gault, 387 U.S.1, 87 S. Ct. 1428 (1967).

proceedings for error. If error is found, the appellate court either may take definitive action, such as ruling that the prosecution be dismissed, or may set aside the conviction and remand the case for a new trial. The latter gives the prosecution the opportunity to obtain a valid conviction.

A considerable period of time is often required for a case to be disposed of on appeal. Generally, the appellate process involves the following four states:

1. A notice of appeals must be filed. In some states the notice of appeal may be filed up to six months after the imposition of the sentence; in other states the appeal must be filed within ten days after the imposition of sentence. This notice of appeal will indicate whether the defendant is appealing as a matter of right or is asking the court to hear an appeal as a matter of discretion.

2. Assuming the court must or will hear the appeal, a record is filed by the defendant of the proceedings in the trial court below. The permissible time interval for filing varies from twenty days in one state to two years in another.

3. Both the defendant and the prosecutor file briefs, which are legal arguments in support of their respective positions. The time permitted for the filing of briefs varies from three weeks to 105 days, and extensions of time for filing are common. After filing the briefs, there are oral arguments by the defense and prosecutor, unless the parties or the court have indicated the oral argument is not necessary.

4. The court announces its decision. This may take only a few days after oral arguments, or perhaps many months. Some appellate courts follow the practice of affirming convictions without opinion, or by per curiam memorandum (meaning that all judges are in agreement), if no novel principle of law is involved. If a novel principle of law is involved, the court will issue a written opinion that will be used as a guide by lower court judges, prosecutors, and defense counsel in conducting subsequent trials. The appellate process in most states takes from ten to eighteen months from sentence to final disposition of an appeal.

Many states have only one appellate court, which acts as the state court of last resort. Other states have not only a state court of last resort but also an intermediate appellate court. An intermediate appellate court is an additional level of review between the trial court and the highest appellate court. This intermediate appellate court not only provides an additional mechanism for screening cases but also helps to reduce the workload of the highest appellate court. In most states with intermediate appellate courts, all criminal cases must be first appealed to them rather than directly to the highest appellate court, with the exception of those cases where the defendant has been sentenced to death.

The highest state appellate court generally has authority to review all criminal proceedings. This court consists of an odd number of justices, generally not less than five nor more than nine. A decision is arrived at by a majority vote. One of the majority justices writes the opinion of the court. The judges on the minority of the vote may write what is called a *dissenting opinion*, setting forth the reasons they disagree with the majority. In addition, a judge may write his own special *concurring opinion*, indicating added or other reasons why he agrees or disagrees with the majority ruling. A decision from the state's highest appellate court becomes a permanent part of the state's law and a guide in deciding new cases at all levels of the state judiciary.

Some intermediate appellate courts are organized centrally, but others are organized regionally, with the state being divided into different appellate divisions. Regardless of the geographic organization, an appeal is generally decided by a panel of at least three judges. As with the highest appellate court, the opinion of the majority of the judges prevails as the court's opinion, and one of the majority judges will draft an opinion of the court.

FEDERAL COURTS

As previously noted, the Constitution has vested the judicial power of the United States in one Supreme Court and in such inferior courts as Congress may from time to time ordain and establish.[6] In accordance with this authorization, Congress established a federal judicial system by the Judiciary Act of 1789 and has enacted subsequent legislation on the subject. The various enactments have created and delineated the powers of the United States Supreme Court, the United States Court of Appeals, United States district courts, and United States magistrates to deal with the criminal prosecutions of persons charged with violating the criminal laws established by Congress. The United States district courts, assisted by United States magistrates, constitute the federal criminal trial courts. The United States Supreme Court and the various United States courts of appeal comprise the federal appellate system. All judges of the United States District Court, the Court of Appeals, and the Supreme Court are appointed for life by the President, by and with the consent of the Senate; they may be removed from office only by impeachment.[7]

United States District Courts and Magistrates

The United States is divided into numerous federal judicial districts as set forth in the United States Code. In each district there is a United States District Court.

Just as state courts have exclusive jurisdiction over offenses against state laws, federal courts have exclusive jurisdiction over offenses against federal laws. A federal statute commonly referred to as the "Assimilative Crimes Act,"[8] however, provides for the applicability of state criminal statutes to criminal acts committed

---

6. Art. 3, § 1.

7. Art. 3.

8. 18 U.S.C. § 13.

within federal enclaves but not specifically covered under federal law.[9] This statute provides for the prosecution in the federal courts of offenses committed within federal enclaves to the degree and extent that such conduct would have been punished had the enclave remained subject to the jurisdiction of the state. Prosecutions under this Act are not to enforce the laws of the state, territory, or district, but rather to enforce federal law, the details of which, instead of being delineated by statute, are adopted by reference.

The practice and procedure of the trial of criminal cases in federal district courts are governed largely by the Federal Rules of Criminal Procedure, which are promulgated by the Supreme Court of the United States. The principles of criminal procedure outlined with regard to state courts also generally apply to federal courts. The initial appearance of a person arrested or indicted for a federal offense is before a United States magistrate, who apprises him of his legal rights and sets bail when required. Under certain conditions minor offenses may be tried before the United States magistrate himself. The term *minor offenses* means misdemeanors punishable under the laws of the United States, the penalty for which does not exceed imprisonment for a period of one year or a fine of not more than $1,000 or both.[10] A person charged with a minor offense may elect to be tried before a district court judge, however, and the magistrate must advise the defendant of such a right. The magistrate cannot try the case himself unless the defendant so consents in writing, specifically waiving both a trial before a district court judge and his right to trial by jury. All offenses other than minor offenses must be tried before a judge of the United States District Court.

Each district court consists of the district judge or judges for the district in regular active service. In addition, there are "senior Judges" (those who have reached "retirement" age) who may conduct court on a part-time basis. Moreover, active judges from another district may be subject to assignment to sit on specific cases.

The proper federal district court for the prosecution of a federal offense is the court within the federal district in which the crime was committed. If a federal district consists of two or more divisions, the trial is to be held in the division in which the offense was committed, unless the defendant consents to be tried in another division within the district.

Unlike many state court systems, the federal district courts do not have a juvenile court or division. However, the Federal Youth Correction Act applies to a convicted person under the age of twenty-two at the time of conviction, and it may, in the court's discretion, be applied to defendants as old as twenty-six.[11] Although a youthful offender may be imprisoned, the act also authorizes the grant of probation to the offender.

Upon his successful completion of a sentence imposed under the Youth

9. The term enclaves refers to places falling within the "special maritime and territorial jurisdiction of the United States," as defined in 18 U.S.C. § 7. Examples of enclaves are army or naval bases and post offices.

10. 18 U.S.C. § 3401.

11. 18 U.S.C. § 5005.

Correction Act there remains no record of conviction. In some situations youthful offenders may be "sentenced" to the custody of the Attorney General, "for observation and study at an appropriate classification center or agency." The matter thereafter rests with the United States Parole Commission.[12]

There is also the Federal Juvenile Delinquency Act which applies to youths under eighteen years of age who are alleged to have violated a federal law for which neither a life nor a death sentence may be imposed.[13] In order to proceed under this Act there must be consent of both the accused and the Attorney General; moreover, the juvenile's consent must be in writing, after having been fully apprised of his rights and of the consequences of that consent.[14] Upon a federal district court determination of delinquency, a juvenile may be placed on probation by the court for a period not exceeding this minority, or he may be committed to the custody of the Attorney General for a like period, provided such commitment does not exceed the term that might have been imposed had the individual been tried and convicted for the alleged violation.[15]

United States Courts of Appeals

If a defendant is convicted in the federal district court and is unsuccessful in his post-trial motions, he may appeal his conviction to the appropriate United States Court of Appeals. The federal prosecutor, just like his state counterpart, has no right to an appeal absent direct statutory authorization in certain types of proceedings.[16]

The United States Court of Appeals is a appellate court without power or jurisdiction to retry criminal cases. Its authority is limited to reviewing the trial court record and correcting errors of law that may have been committed. Thus, on an appeal from a judgment of conviction in the district court, the Court of Appeals will not hear cases anew (de novo).

The appellate process for courts of appeals involves the same basic stages as for state appellate courts. After filing written briefs, there are oral arguments by the defense and prosecution, unless the parties or the court have indicated that oral

12. 18 U.S.C. § 5010.

13. 18 U.S.C. § 5031.

14. 18 U.S.C. § 5033.

15. 18 U.S.C. § 5034.

16. The Criminal Appeals Act, 18 U.S.C. § 3731, provides that in all criminal cases an appeal by the United States attorney shall lie to a court of appeals from a decision, judgment, or order of a district court dismissing an indictment or information on one or more counts where the defendant has not been put in double jeopardy. In addition, an appeal by the United States Attorney lies to a court of appeals from a decision or order of a district court suppressing or excluding evidence or requiring the return of seized property in a criminal proceeding, before the verdict or finding on an indictment or information and where the defendant has not be put in double jeopardy, if the United States Attorney certifies to the district court that the appeal is not taken for the purpose of delay and that the evidence is a substantial proof of a fact material in the proceeding.

argument is not necessary. The court of appeals may announce its decision as quickly as a few days or as long as several months after oral argument. Unless there is a novel principle of law involved, the courts follow the practice of affirming convictions by a rather short per curiam memorandum; otherwise there will be a full written opinion in the name of one of the judges. As with state appellate court opinions, a written opinion will serve as a guide for the district court judges and the attorneys practicing in that circuit.

The United States is geographically divided into twelve judicial circuits,[17] in each of which there is a United States Court of Appeals with appellate jurisdiction over the United States district courts within that circuit.[18]

The court of appeals consists of the circuit judges of that circuit who are in regular active service, although justices from other circuits, or other designated or assigned judges, are also competent to serve on that court.[19] A case before the court of appeals is heard and determined by a court or division of not more than three judges unless a hearing or rehearing before the court en banc (all the judges of the circuit) is ordered by a majority of the circuit judges of the circuit who are in regular active service.

A criminal defendant has the right to have his district court conviction reviewed by a court of appeals. He need not petition that court for an exercise of its discretion in order to bring his case before the court; the only condition required is that he meet the time limitations within which various procedural steps must be completed.

Supreme Court of the United States

As previously mentiond, the United States Constitution vests the highest federal judicial power of the United States in "one Supreme Court." It consists of a "Chief Justice of the United States" and eight Associate Justices, any six of whom constitute a quorum.

The Constitution provides for the appointment of Justices of the Supreme Court by the President by and with the advice and consent of the Senate, and it further provides that the Justices of the Supreme Court shall hold office "during good behavior."[20] They may be removed only by impeachment.

The United States Supreme Court exercises not only appellate review but also,

---

17. 28 U.S.C. § 41. The first circuit includes Me., Mass., N.H., P.R., R.I.; the second, Conn., N.Y., Vt.; the third, Del., N.J., Pa., V.I.; the fourth, Md., N.C., S.C., Va., W.Va.; the fifth, La., Miss., Tex., and C.Z.; the sixth, Ky., Mich., Ohio, Tenn.; the seventh, Ill., Ind., Wis.,; the eighth, Ark., Iowa, Minn., Mo., Neb., N.D., S.D.; the ninth, Alas., Ariz., Cal., Idaho, Mont., Nev., Oreg., Wash., Guam, Hawaii; the tenth, Colo., Kan., N.M., Okla., Utah, Wyo.; and the eleventh, Ala., Fla., and Ga. The remaining circuit is not designated by number; it encompasses the D.C. and is known by that name. 28 U.S.C. § 41. In addition, there is a special U.S. Court of Appeals for the federal circuit that handles only certain special cases from around the country, such as patent and trademark appeals.

18. 28 U.S.C. § 43, §§ 1291–1294.

19. The chief justice and associate justices of the Supreme Court are allotted as circuit justices among the circuits by order of the Court, and a justice may be assigned to more than one circuit, or more than one justice may be assigned to the same circuit. See 28 U.S.C. § 42.

20. Art. 2, § 2.

in certain types of civil cases, original jurisdiction—for instance, cases affecting ambassadors or the states themselves.[21] To the degree that certain decisions of the highest court of a state are reviewable and may be set aside by the United States Supreme Court, it occupies a unique and supreme position within the dual system of federal and state jurisdiction. For the convicted defendant in either the federal or state system, the Supreme Court is the court of last resort.

There is one method of appeal to the Supreme Court—a review by "certiorari." It consists of an order (a "writ") from the Court to a lower court to supply the existing records for examination. The writ is not a matter of right but a matter of the Court's discretion.[22] Although the power granted to the Supreme Court to issue the writ of certiorari is comprehensive and unlimited, it is in fact exercised sparingly and only in cases of gravity and importance.

The writ of certiorari is granted only when four justices deem it desirable to review a lower court decision. Denial of such a writ with regard to a lower federal court decision does not imply any view by the Supreme Court as to the merits of the case. Denial by the Supreme Court of a writ of certiorari to review a state court's decision, however, although not an absolute expression of approval of the decision, may be an indication of its correctness.

The scope of review by the Supreme Court generally is restricted to matters raised and decided below. However, on its own motion, the Supreme Court may take notice of errors to which no exception has been noted if the Court feels that the errors would seriously affect the fairness or integrity of the lower judicial proceeding. Generally, the Court will accept the verdict and findings of fact as conclusive and will not question the lower courts' evaluation of the credibility of witness. The scope of Supreme Court review of state court decisions in criminal cases is solely to determine whether the state court permitted violations of the basic safeguards of the Fourteenth Amendment. However, that Amendment is considered to embrace the first eight amendments, known as the Bill of Rights, as obligations on the states as well as the federal government.

The four stages of the appellate process as previously described are the same for appeals to the United States Supreme Court. Oral argument is usually required for the purpose of clarifying the written argument appearing in the briefs filed by the parties in support of their respective positions. In fact, the United States Supreme Court looks with disfavor on the submission of cases on briefs without oral argument and may require oral argument by the parties. In the Supreme Court, as in the highest state appellate courts, a decision is arrived at by a majority vote of justices. Because by the very nature of the Supreme Court's position every decision is a major decision that involves novel principles of law, the decisions of the United States Supreme Court are rendered through written opinions that become legal precedent for both state and federal courts.

21. Art. 3, § 2.
22. Supreme Court Rule 10.

14

Security Officer's
Preparation for Trial
and Testimony in Court

The preparation of a case for criminal prosecution should begin immediately after the discovery of the offense—regardless of whether a suspect has been arrested. Moreover, this practice should be followed even if the employer's business practice is to avoid criminal prosecutions whenever possible. One reason for this suggestion is that the security officer can never be certain that the case she investigates will not develop into a prosecution, despite the prevailing office policy. Second, if the matter is treated as one for potential prosecution, the facts that are developed—and a preserved record of them—may serve a very valuable purpose in the defense of a civil suit that may be filed by the arrested or accused person. Then, too, those facts may be necessary for the presentation of a claim for restitution from an insurance company covering a loss or damage.

Two types of crimes require the attention of private security officers. One type involves offenses typically committed by employees or customers, or by other persons presumably with legitimate reasons for being on the premises. The other type involves participants unassociated with the business operation, such as burglars and robbers. Suggestions for the investigation of offenses of the first type were presented in the first six chapters of this book dealing with arrest, search and seizure, temporary detentions, interrogations, scientific evidence, and surveillance. Our primary concern in this chapter will be the second type of crimes—burglaries, robberies, and the like—although, to be sure, some of what follows will be applicable to the first type as well.

Case preparation is essentially the gathering and cataloging of facts with a view toward prosecution. Although the following discussion should not be considered exhaustive, we believe that its presentation, under a few topical headings, contains the basic information needed by security officers.

PROTECTION OF THE CRIME SCENE

The "crime scene" is nothing more than the location where an offense has occurred. A security officer can effectively and significantly aid in the successful apprehension and prosecution of criminal offenders by protecting the crime scene
so that vital evidence is left undisturbed until police investigators and evidence
technicians arrive. Following is an actual case illustration of the importance of protecting the crime scene:

> A local police department received a report one afternoon that a certain business es-
> tablishment had been burglarized. Upon arrival at the scene the police learned that
> the security officer had been informed of the burglary early that morning, and had
> reported it to the manager, who had instructed him to determine the loss and call the
> police.
>
> By the time the police investigators and evidence technicians arrived, numerous
> items that the burglars had handled had been returned to their original locations.
> Merchandise and file drawers rifled by the burglars had been put in order and placed
> in their proper position. The unsightly evidence of forced entry had been cleared up,
> and the door lock was in the process of being replaced.
>
> Because the security officer failed to protect the crime scene, some crucial evi-
> dence that might have helped significantly to detect, apprehend, and prosecute the
> burglars was lost.

The security officer in the preceding case situation violated the cardinal rule
that nothing in the general area of a crime should be touched or disturbed until
after the proper police personnel have arrived.

There is a popular misconception that preserving the crime scene for police investigators and evidence technicians is only important when the criminal offender
is still at large; the theory being that evidence at the crime scene merely helps to
identify a criminal. To the contrary, preservation of the crime scene aids not only
in the identification of the criminal offender but also in the successful prosecution
of that offender. As experienced prosecutors can attest, mere identification of the
criminal offender is not enough for successful prosecution; there is also a need for
competent evidence linking the accused to the crime. This evidence can best be
obtained from a careful examination of the crime scene.

The reasons for having the security officer protect the crime scene are: (1) to
prevent the removal, destruction, rearrangement, or concealment of physical evidence by employees or others; (2) to preserve the crime scene in its natural state
until the police arrive and perform their investigatory and technical tasks; and
(3) to keep out unauthorized persons who may purposely or unwittingly interfere
with significant evidence.

The security officer who first arrives at the crime scene should be responsible
for its protection. She should explain to the employees and others present that the
apprehension and prosecution of the criminal offender may be seriously jeopar-
dized, if not completely defeated, by any disturbance of the crime scene. She
should also instruct them not to touch, handle, or move anything until the police
investigators and evidence technicians arrive.

In protecting the crime scene, a security officer should not take too restrictive a view of what the actual crime scene is. The approaches to the scene, adjoining areas, and avenues of escape are as important as the exact spot where the offense was committed, because valuable clues may be found in such locations. For example, in burglary cases a particular interior part of a building may bear the most identifiable signs of the commission of the crime. However, the area through which the criminal offenders entered and left the premises is of comparable importance, or perhaps of greater importance in many cases.

A criminal offender may leave tool marks or fingerprints on the door or window by which she entered the building. There may be footprints in dirt around the outside of the building near the point of entry or departure. In fleeing the scene, the criminal offender may have hidden or unintentionally dropped weapons, tools, or personal property that could help in identifying her. In entering or fleeing the area, the criminal offender may have caught and torn her clothing on bushes, fences, or other objects and thus have left behind threads of fabric that could aid in a successful prosecution. Because of these possibilities the entire area should be protected until a search is made by police evidence technicians.

Statistical studies have indicated the importance of properly preserving evidence at the point of entry in the investigation of a burglary; of all the identifiable latent prints found at a burglary scene, most are found at the places of entry and departure. Police evidence technicians will want to dust there for fingerprints of the offender, but they may be thwarted in their efforts if other persons have been permitted to place their own fingerprints on the places of entry and departure, or on objects that may have been handled by the offender.

Upon arriving at the crime scene, the security officer's first action should be to remove all persons present, or, if operation of the business makes this impossible, she should at least keep everyone away from direct contact, perhaps by roping off the area. In any event, no one should be allowed to enter except police officers, investigators, and evidence technicians. Other employees, curiosity seekers, and newspaper reporters should not be allowed entry until after the police have completed their investigation and searched for evidence.

Persons other than the police or security personnel should be restrained from participating in the protection of the crime scene or in the investigation except to answer questions or supply information they may have. All witnesses and the person(s) who discovered the crime should be persuaded to remain. They should either be separated or instructed not to discuss the case among themselves. This will afford the police investigators an opportunity to interview them effectively. (We may note at this point that there are occasions when the apparent discoverer of a crime is the one who actually committed it; she reports it to divert suspicion from herself.)

If apprehended, the offender should be detained in a separate and secure place until the police arrive. Care should be taken to ensure that the criminal offender does not destroy any physical evidence either at the scene or on her person.

Security officers should be careful not to contaminate anything that may be of evidentiary value. Their unnecessary or careless handling of objects that have the potential of carrying the offender's latent fingerprints could result in the obliteration of the prints.

Because a security officer, who is usually the first professional law enforcement agent on the crime scene, may not immediately recognize the evidentiary value or location of all the evidence that may be present, everything at the scene should be treated as having potential value until an expert detailed analysis proves otherwise.

PHOTOGRAPHS OF THE SCENE

Photographs should always be taken of a crime scene. Although this is a police function, photographs ordinarily are taken by them only when the crime on a business premise is of a most serious nature, such as murder. In less serious crime cases, we suggest that whenever feasible photographs be taken by the security officer or some other available person. Photographs may not only be helpful to the public interest of successfully prosecuting criminals but may also work to the benefit of the employer, as, for instance, where a civil suit arises out of the incident, or a dispute develops over an insurance claim.

In lieu of photographs, sketches or diagrams may be made of crime scenes. They, too, may serve a very valuable purpose at trial.

PROPER PRESERVATION OF PHYSICAL EVIDENCE

Police investigators and evidence technicians normally perform the task of gathering, marking, and storing physical evidence. On occasion, however, they may seek the assistance of security officers employed on the premises where the crime occurred, even to the extent of inventorying the evidence and storing it until the time for either a crime laboratory examination or presentation in court.

Among the tangible objects that can link the perpetrator to a crime, the obvious ones are guns, knives, and other large objects that are clearly observable. A security officer should also diligently search for other, less conspicuous objects, such as hair, cloth fibers, and bits of glass. For example, fragments of glass found on the ground immediately beneath a broken window might match fragments of glass embedded in the offender's clothing.

All the observed evidence should be left undisturbed so that it may be examined in its original state by the police. Where circumstances require prior action by the security officer, she should take certain precautions, some of which have been discussed in Chapter 5. If the proper method for preserving a particular object is not specifically known to the security officer, an exercise of plain common sense, based on an awareness of the object's potential for scientific examination, will usually suffice. The mistakes made by the collector of physical evidence will ordinarily result from either ignorance of its investigative value or else plain recklessness. For instance, picking up a gun or knife and handling it in the same way a user would will very likely obliterate or damage fingerprints that may have been left by the perpetrator. Using gloves or cloth on such an object could have a similar effect.

For physical evidence to be admissible in a criminal trial, the prosecution must establish who had possession of the physical evidence, and an account must be made of every step in the handling of the evidence from the time it was found at the crime scene up to the moment it was presented at the trial. Consequently, a careful record should be kept of its transmission history. Moreover, every effort should be made to minimize the number of persons involved in the transmission process. Ordinarily, a single security officer should be responsible for the recovery, storage, and transmission. Then, at the time of trial she will be the only employee needed to trace the exhibit properly and thus satisfy courtroom admissibility requirements. Moreover, the time and cost to the employer will be thereby minimized.

If a security officer fails to adequately segregate, secure, and identify physical evidence, it will be inadmissible at a criminal trial. This ruling, of course, can seriously jeopardize the success of the criminal prosecution. Thus the security officer should set up an evidence storage procedure and a control area. Identifying marks or tags should be placed on all sizable pieces of evidence or on the separate containers into which smaller pieces may have had to be placed. The evidence control area can be as large as a locked room or as small as a locked filing cabinet, depending on the needs that exist; the area also should be thoroughly secured, with access limited to only one person if at all possible.

STATEMENTS OF WITNESSES

In serious crime investigations, the police usually will interview witnesses and arrange for the taking of written statements. If this function has to be assumed by the security officer, however, several factors need to be kept in mind. First of all, as stated in Chapter 4, there is no legal requirement that she issue warnings of constitutional rights to any witness! Second, it is a good practice to have a witness relate, in a conversational manner, just what she observed, and only after she has committed herself to a story should any attempt be made to reduce her statement to writing. The reason for this is the natural reluctance of people to have their statements reduced to writing and signed. If abruptly confronted with paper and pen, they may repress their willingness to be helpful. Most people are more willing to talk than to write; or more willing to talk than to have what they say reduced to writing and then sign it. Consequently, only after they have expressed themselves in an informal way should the interrogator make any overture toward a transcription to writing. Proceeding in a casual fashion, as though it were only a routine procedure, the interrogator should say she would like to jot down what the witness says, and the statement can be recorded as though the witness were writing it out herself. Then the witness should be asked to read it and told that if it is accurate, "Please put your name at the end of it." Even if a witness says, "That's accurate, but I don't want to sign anything," all is not lost, and no issue should be made of the refusal. The security officer will still have a record of what the witness said, which will be extremely helpful to the prosecutor in the preparation and trial of the case.

SECURITY OFFICER'S NOTES

A written record should be made by the security officer of all relevant information about the case. What has been ascertained should not be left to memory alone. Many details may be forgotten weeks or months later, whereas notes may refresh recollection and, in some circumstances, the record itself may be used as evidence. The record, therefore, should be as complete as possible. Among other reasons, completeness will avoid impeachment by a cross-examiner who otherwise might effectively disclose that certain essential facts were left out of the report.

Before testifying, the security officer should review her notes. These notes may also be used to refresh the recollection of other witnesses to the event.

LEGALISTIC INFORMATION FOR TESTIMONY AT TRIAL

Proof of Corporate Existence

In cases that involve the theft of store merchandise or money from an incorporated business, the indictment or complaint will state that the stolen goods or money belonged to the store, "a corporation." It will be necessary for the prosecutor to identify the owner very specifically, and this means proving that the owner is in fact a corporation in the strict legal sense of that term.

Although many states have statutory provisions that seem to simplify the proof of corporate existence, the courts have been very particular in their requirements. The mere statement of an officer or employee of the company that it does business as a corporation may be insufficient. As a general practice, corporate existence must be proved either by the charter or articles of incorporation or by proof of the exercise of corporate powers and functions. The best way to prove that the business is a corporation is to present to the court a certified copy of the articles of incorporation and have the prosecuting attorney offer it into evidence.

It is advisable for the security department of a corporation to have several certified copies of the store's articles of incorporation on hand at all times. They can be obtained at very small cost from the appropriate state official.

After a certified copy of the articles of incorporation has been used in a case, and the case is finally disposed of, the prosecutor's office will, upon request, return the copy. It can then be used over and over again in subsequent cases in which proof of corporate existence is required.

Proof of Value of Merchandise

In cases that involve the theft of merchandise, it is necessary to establish its value. This is particularly important in proving that a theft is a felony rather than a misdemeanor.

Neither the prosecutor nor the judge will make an assumption about the value of a stolen article. If, for instance, the statutory dividing line between a felony and a misdemeanor is $300, the value of an article of that or greater value must be proved, even though that fact may be quite obvious for ordinary purposes. In court, however, the "fair, cash market value" at the time and place of the theft must be established. For instance, if a theft of a jacket occurred in Chicago on January 15, 1996, its value in a suburb or in another town on that date will not suffice, nor will its value in Chicago on June 15, 1995, or on January 15, 1997.

The safest way to establish the "fair, cash market value" of stolen merchandise is to have a store buyer testify to that fact. She is the one best qualified for that purpose. Because there are occasions when the buyer is unavailable, however, or instances where the nature of the case or circumstances may not warrant her participation, the security officer will at times have to assume this obligation. In anticipation of the experience of testifying, the security officer should make some special preparations in every case by consulting the store buyers and some salespersons regarding the purchase price of merchandise involved in the case. It is also advisable, if time and circumstances permit, for the agent to observe sales of that kind of merchandise soon after the arrest of an offender has occurred; in this way she can obtain first-hand knowledge of the existing purchase price. The purchase price is competent evidence of the "fair, cash market value."

COOPERATION WITH PROSECUTING ATTORNEY

Because the prosecutor assigned to a case will usually be engaged in several other legal matters, the security officer should display interest in her own case by first finding out from the prosecutor's office which assistant is to try it, and then contacting her to inquire whether anything can be done to assist in its preparation. She should find out which judge is to hear the case and then ascertain the date set for trial. A few days before the scheduled trial, the security officer should go to the prosecutor's office to discuss the details of the case with her. In all this, of course, the officer must be very discreet and avoid giving the impression that she lacks confidence in the prosecutor. Nevertheless, no harm, but a lot of good, can come from an expressed interest and an offer of cooperation. Furthermore, within a very busy prosecutor's office, the cases in which the prosecution witnesses exhibit an active interest are the ones likely to receive the best attention from the prosecutor's staff.

Before appearing in court as a witness, the security officer should review her initial crime report and all the facts, statements, and other evidence that have come to her attention during the investigation of the crime. She should also review all crime reports, supplemental reports, and notes, in chronological order. She should also check to see if physical evidence held by the business is still properly stored in its original condition, and the necessary arrangements should be made for obtaining it for court presentation.

It is of the utmost importance that the security officer appear in court each time the police or prosecuting attorney requests her presence. The security officer should arrive in court and report to the prosecutor at the time indicated on the subpoena or requested by the prosecutor.

The security officer can be a great help to a prosecutor by arranging to accompany employee witnesses to court, and by soothing their nervousness about the experience of testifying. Toward that end it will be helpful to review with them the facts about which they are to testify and to let them read the statements they made during the investigation. In doing so, let them know that this pretrial discussion is a perfectly proper one, and, if asked by defense counsel, they should have no hesitation in admitting that the conversation occurred. In the event a subpoenaed witness displays a reluctance to appear in court, she should be reminded that a refusal to honor the subpoena could subject her to a fine or jail sentence.

SECURITY OFFICER AS WITNESS

Demeanor in Court

The following suggestions are for the security officer who is asked to testify in a court proceeding.

Your demeanor as a witness—the manner in which you testify and the appearance you make on the witness stand—may be crucial to the prosecution's success at trial. This is particularly true in a jury case, where the impressions a witness makes are often as important as the substance of her testimony.

It is generally advisable to refrain from discussing your testimony with any persons other than fellow officers or the prosecutor. If you are approached by defense counsel to give a statement prior to the trial, consult first with the prosecutor.

An important piece of advice to a prospective security officer witness is this: You are a professional; look and act like one! A security officer's professional-looking appearance and conduct will render her courtroom testimony more effective, and will also reflect credit on her agency and on her profession generally. It is best to appear in court in civilian dress rather than a uniform. Of course, no security officer should ever take the witness stand with gum, tobacco, or any other such substance in her mouth. If the security officer witness must come to court in uniform, the uniform should be clean and the entire appearance neat; never wear a gun or other weapon in the courtroom.

When the oath is administered, affirm clearly and distinctly. While on the stand, sit erect and speak slowly, distinctly, and loud enough for the juror farthest away to hear you. When speaking, you should look in the general direction of the jury box, unless you are responding to a question from the judge. Concentrate on your testimony; for when you do, the personal nervousness or discomfort that most witnesses experience will be more controllable. Avoid the use of profanity, except when repeating words spoken by another.

There are rules of evidence that preclude certain questions and certain answers. When you are not permitted to answer because the rules exclude it, do not show annoyance or frustration. If you do, the jury will be offended by your lack of professionalism.

When the prosecutor questions you, do not volunteer a statement that is not asked for. By volunteering an answer not requested by the prosecutor, you may open the door to material that defense counsel can then inject during cross-examination that could severely damage the prosecution. Remember—the prosecutor is in charge of the case. During the preparation for your testimony, she has determined what material is important. Let her decide what matters will be brought out from you on the witness stand. Particular care should be taken to avoid any unsolicited information about a defendant's prior criminal record, whether it be a conviction or a mere arrest. Anything of that sort may result in a mistrial or reversal on appeal.

During direct examination, the prosecutor may ask you to testify in narrative terms, or you may be asked specific questions. For the narration, the question may be: "Officer, will you please tell us what you observed when you came upon the scene?" Specific questions may be: "Whom did you see when you arrived?" "What time was it when you got there?" "Who was with you when you received the call to go to the scene?" The form used will be determined by the prosecutor in the exercise of her discretion as to the effective course to follow in the particular case.

When testifying, avoid using words and expressions that are not commonly used by ordinary citizens; in other words, you should not use law enforcement jargon.

When referring to the victim of the crime, her last name should be used instead of "the victim." Rather than speaking of "apprehending" the defendant, you should use the expression "caught" or "arrested"—expressions that mean more to the layperson than "apprehended." Also, the defendant should be referred to as such, rather than as "the offender," which implies, of course, that she is guilty, a determination yet to be made by the judge or jury. When giving the time of an incident or occurrence, you should not use military-police terminology, such as 15:06, but rather civilian terminology, such as 3:06 p.m.

When answering a question asked by either the prosecutor or defense counsel, you should avoid any such prefatory statements as "To tell you the truth" or "To be honest with you . . ." Such statements detract from the persuasiveness of the answer. Obviously, however, if you are not sure or do not know which the answer is, you should say so. You are not expected to know everything about which you are to be questioned. You should have no reluctance, therefore, to respond at times with the blunt answer of "I don't know." This answer is far more honest and far less damaging to the prosecutor's case than a halting, equivocal answer that will afford defense counsel an opportunity to discredit all your testimony by exposing your apparent lack of frankness and honesty. Likewise, if you are asked a question that pertains to a fact or incident about which you now have no present recollection, you should simply reply "I do not remember." This response is far better than bluffing or guessing at an answer that is later exposed as incorrect.

The real test of a security officer witness's credibility will come when she is under cross-examination by defense counsel.

All security officer witnesses should recognize that in contrast to their function—the impartial presentation of the facts as they know them to be—defense counsel is expected to perform in a partisan manner. Her primary obligation is to her client, and she is duty bound to do the best she can to test out the credibility and the accuracy of the prosecutor's witnesses. Once this function is recognized, security officer witnesses will realize that except for the rarest of cases, the issue is not a personalized one; the aim is not to embarrass or ridicule you as a person, but to disclose the possible weaknesses in your testimony as a security officer. The best impression is made when you treat defense counsel with the same respect that you do the prosecutor.

Some defense counsel will delight in employing ridicule and insult in an effort to rattle a prosecution witness. They know that a rattled witness is apt to be an ineffective witness, and if you try to do battle with them, you will almost certainly lose. They know all the rules and will usually have an advantage in any verbal sparring with you as a witness. Thus, the only way to counter an abusive cross-examination is to maintain your composure and rely on the prosecutor and the judge for corrective action.

No sarcasm should be employed toward defense counsel, even when a justifiable impulse exists. For instance, when counsel asks repetitious questions, the natural impulse is to say, "I've already answered that," but it is far better to respond without making any such remark. Then, too, it is better to address the cross-examiner by her name rather than refer to her as "counsel," because it is difficult for a harassed witness to conceal her annoyance or anger when she says "counsel." The concealment is easier with the appellation "Ms. Smith." In addressing the judge, the preferred designation is "Your Honor," rather than "Judge."

When questioned by defense counsel, avoid looking at the prosecutor. You should not give the jury the impression that you are seeking the prosecutor's approval in answering, or help in avoiding an answer to, a question. If the question is legally improper, the prosecutor will make an objection. She will do this on her own and does not need a signal from you to do so. She does, however, need ample time to invoke her objection. Therefore, after defense counsel's question is completed, it is important to hesitate briefly before answering. This will allow the prosecutor to interpose an objection should the question be improper.

As stated earlier, it is important to give the appearance of perfect candor when undergoing cross-examination. Competent prosecutors will attempt to confer in advance of trial, or certainly prior to a call to the witness stand, with the persons she expects to use as witnesses, including the security officers themselves. This procedure is ethical and legally permissible. It is also proper for a prospective security officer witness to discuss the case and any aspect of it with fellow security officers. Some witnesses have sustained a terrible embarrassment, or even seriously damaged the prosecutor's case, by being unwilling, or even merely hesitant, to admit to a pretrial conference or discussion about the case. Sensing a dishonest answer, the judge or jury might discount all of the witness's testimony, despite its absolute truthfulness. Thus, if, while under cross-examination by defense counsel, you are asked whether you discussed the case with the prosecutor or another security officer prior to taking the witness stand, the answer should be an unhesitating yes. Sometimes defense counsel, discontent with such a truthful answer, will then inquire: "Didn't the prosecutor [or your commanding officer, or someone else] tell you what to say?" You should not hesitate to respond truthfully with "No," or, where it can be truthfully said, the answer may be: "She told me to relate the facts as I know them to be; in other words, tell the truth."

If defense counsel requests you to tender your notes to her or if the judge orders you to do so, be prepared to comply promptly. If defense counsel is not entitled to them, the prosecutor will take care of the matter with an objection. In any event, have your notes with you when you go to court in order to avoid causing a trial delay while obtaining them.

Be sure you have been excused by both attorneys and the judge before leaving the witness stand. When excused, *leave the courtroom* without conversing with or contacting anyone in the courtroom. Whatever temptation you may have to remain in court, control it. By leaving you demonstrate to the jury that you are a disinterested, unbiased witness. Moreover, if you stay during defense counsel's closing argument, do not be surprised if she works your presence into her closing argument. She may point to you dramatically and state, "Look at this witness, ladies and gentlemen. She is so vindictive toward this defendant that she is not satisfied with merely testifying, but remains here throughout the case."

During the balance of the trial, after your testimony, do not discuss the testimony you have given with anyone other than the prosecutor. If you realize after testifying that you have made a mistake, immediately notify the prosecutor. She will best determine how to handle the problem and may even decide to recall you to the stand to correct the error.

The best advice we can offer to the security officer as a witness is that she should tell the truth. If some testimony you give is favorable to the defense, give it as freely and truthfully as your other testimony; to do otherwise than testify honestly could endanger the life or liberty of an innocent person. It could also destroy your credibility as a professional and as a believable witness. Moreover, the prosecution's case could be severely undermined if you are subsequently exposed as not having testified with complete candor.

Appendix

This Appendix contains a collection of state statutes of particular concern to merchants and security officers. Three general types of statutes are included: (1) statutes dealing with the right of private persons to make "citizen arrests"; (2) statutes that pertain to the rights of retail merchants to temporarily detain and question suspected shoplifters, or to examine the contents of shopping bags and other such containers; and (3) criminal law statutes which are specifically directed toward "retail theft," or, where such a statute has not been enacted, we have reproduced the state's general theft statute which, of course, includes the criminal conduct of theft of merchandise. The statutes vary considerably from state to state, and some have only one or two of the three types. Also keep in mind the fact that where we have noted that certain states have no statute on arrest by private persons, or the detention of suspected shoplifters, this does not necessarily signify that the right is nonexistent, because court case law may have already established those rights and the limitations upon them.

A word of caution! Since legislatures may change state laws whenever they wish, either by repeal or modification, readers of the present publication should make inquiries, of either their own lawyers or the prosecuting attorney of the county or city, to ascertain whether the law has remained as it was at the time of this book's publication.

Apart from the obvious value of the information about the statutes of a particular state to the security officer, merchant, or lawyer in a particular state, the compilation of the statutory provisions of the various other states may afford valuable assistance to merchants or their lawyers who seek to have their own state laws enacted or modified to conform to more suitable ones that have evolved in the other states.

ALABAMA

1. Arrest by Private Persons
(15-10-7, Ala. Code)

(a) A private person may arrest another for any public offense:
  (1) Committed in his presence;
  (2) Where a felony has been committed, though not in his presence, by the person arrested; or
  (3) Where a felony has been committed and he has reasonable cause to believe that the person arrested committed it.
(b) An arrest for felony may be made by a private person on any day and at any time.
(c) A private person must, at the time of the arrest, inform the person to be arrested of the cause thereof, except where such person is in the actual commission of an offense, or arrested on pursuit.
(d) If he is refused admittance, after notice of his intention, and the person to be arrested has committed a felony, he may break open an outer or inner door or window of a dwelling house.
(e) It is the duty of any private person, having arrested another for the commission of any public offense, to take him without unnecessary delay before a judge or magistrate, or to deliver him to some one of the officers specified in section 15-10-1, who must forwith take him before a judge or magistrate.

2. Detention
(15-10-14, Ala. Code)

(a) A peace officer, a merchant or a merchant's employee who has probable cause for believing that goods held for sale by the merchant have been unlawfully taken by a person and that he can recover them by taking the person into custody may, for the purpose of attempting to effect such recovery, take the person into custody and detain him in a reasonable manner for a reasonable length of time. Such taking into custody and detention by a peace officer, merchant or merchant's employee shall not render such police officer, merchant or merchant's employee criminally or civilly liable for false arrest, false imprisonment or unlawful detention.
(b) Any peace officer may arrest without warrant any person he has probable cause for believing has committed larceny in retail or wholesale establishments.
(c) A merchant or a merchant's employee who causes such arrest as provided for in subsection (a) of this section of a person for larceny of goods held for sale shall not be criminally or civilly liable for false arrest or false imprisonment where the merchant or merchant's employee has probable cause for believing that the person arrested committed larceny of goods held for sale.

3. Theft
(13A-8-2, Ala. Code)

A person commits the crime of theft of property if he:

(1) Knowingly obtains or exerts unauthorized control over the property of another, with intent to deprive the owner of his property; or

(2) Knowingly obtains by deception control over the property of another, with intent to deprive the owner of his property.

[In addition to the foregoing general theft provision, Alabama has a special statute regarding the removal of shopping carts. It follows:]

(13A-8-60, 61, 62, 63, Ala. Code)

The term "shopping cart," when used in this article, shall mean those pushcarts of the type or types which are commonly provided by grocery stores, drugstores or other merchant stores or markets for the use of the public in transporting commodities in stores and markets and incidentally from the store to a place outside the store.

It shall be unlawful for any person to remove a shopping cart from the premises, posted as provided in Section 13A-8-63, [which follows] of the owner of such shopping cart without the consent, given at the time of such removal, of the owner or of his agent, servant or employee. For the purpose of this section, the "premises" shall include all the parking area set aside by the owner, or on behalf of the owner, for the parking of cars for the convenience of the patrons of the owner.

It shall be unlawful for any person to abandon a shopping cart upon any public street, sidewalk, way or parking lot, other than a parking lot on the premises of the owner. The owner of the store in which the shopping cart is used shall post in at least three prominent places in his store, and at each exit therefrom, a printed copy of this article, which copy shall be printed in type no smaller than 12 points.

ALASKA

1. Arrest by Private Persons
(12.25.030, Alaska Stats.)

(a) A private person or a peace officer without a warrant may arrest a person
   (1) for a crime committed or attempted in the presence of the person making the arrest;
   (2) when the person has committed a felony, although not in the presence of the person making the arrest;
   (3) when a felony has in fact been committed, and the person making the arrest has reasonable cause for believing the person to have committed it.

2. Detention
(11.46.230, Alaska Stats.)

Reasonable detention as a Defense. (a) In a civil or criminal action upon the complaint of a person who has been detained in or in the immediate vicinity of a commercial establishment for the purpose of investigation or questioning as to the ownership of merchandise, it is a defense that

   (1) the person was detained in a reasonable manner and for not more than a reasonable time to permit investigation or questioning by a peace officer or by the owner of the commercial establishment or the owner's agent; and
   (2) the peace officer, owner, or owner's agent had probable cause to believe that the person detained was committing or attempting to commit concealment of merchandise.

(b)   As used in this section, "reasonable time" means the time necessary to permit the person detained to make a statement or refuse to make a statement, and any additional time necessary to examine employees and records of the commercial establishment relative to the ownership of the merchandise.

3.   Concealment of Merchandise
(11.46.220, 45.45.100, Alaska Stats.)

(a)   A person commits the crime of concealment of merchandise if without authority the person knowingly conceals on or about the person the merchandise of a commercial establishment, not purchased by the person, while still upon the premises of the commercial establishment, with intent to deprive the owner of the merchandise or with intent to appropriate the merchandise.

(b)   Merchandise found concealed upon or about the person which has not been purchased by the person is prima facie evidence of a knowing concealment. [Penalties are prescribed on the basis of the value of the merchandise concealed.]

A merchant may request an individual on the merchant's premises to place or keep in full view merchandise that the individual removes, or that the merchant believes the individual may have removed, from its place of display or elsewhere, whether for examination, purchase, or another purpose. A merchant is not criminally or civilly liable for making this request.

4.   Removal of Identification Marks
(11.46.260, Alaska Stats.)

A person commits the crime of removal of identification marks if, with intent to cause interruption to the ownership of another, the person defaces, erases, or otherwise alters or attempts to deface, erase, or otherwise alter any serial number or identification mark placed or inscribed on a propelled vehicle, bicycle, firearm, movable or immovable construction tool or equipment, appliance, merchandise, or other article or its component parts. [Penalties are prescribed on the basis of the value of merchandise from which the identification is removed.]

ARIZONA

1.   Arrest by Private Persons
(13.3884, 13.3889, 13.3900, Ariz. Rev. Stats. Ann.)

A private person may make an arrest:

1.   When the person to be arrested has in his presence committed a misdemeanor amounting to a breach of the peace, or a felony.
2.   When a felony has been in fact committed and he has reasonable ground to believe that the person to be arrested has committed it.

A private person when making an arrest shall inform the person to be arrested of the intention to arrest him and the cause of the arrest, unless he is then engaged in the commission of an offense, or is pursued immediately after its commission or after an escape, or flees or forcibly resists before the person making the arrest has opportunity so to inform him, or when the giving of such information will imperil the arrest.

A private person who has made an arrest shall without unnecessary delay take the person arrested before the nearest or most accessible magistrate in the county in which the arrest was made, or deliver him to a peace officer, who shall without unnecessary delay take him before such magistrate. The private person or officer so taking the person arrested before the magistrate shall make before the magistrate a complaint, which shall set forth the facts showing the offense for which the person was arrested. If, however, the officer cannot make the complaint, the private person who delivered the person arrested to the officer shall accompany the officer before the magistrate and shall make to the magistrate the complaint against the person arrested.

2. Detention

[Covered in next section (C and D) on Shoplifting.]

3. Shoplifting
(13.1805, Ariz. Rev. Stats. Ann.)

(a). A person commits shoplifting if, while in an establishment in which merchandise is displayed for sale, such person knowingly obtains such goods of another with the intent to deprive him of such goods by:
  1. Removing any of the goods from the immediate display or from any other place within the establishment without paying the purchase price; or
  2. Charging the purchase price of the goods to a fictitious person or any person without his authority; or
  3. Paying less than the purchase price of the goods by some trick or artifice such as altering, removing, substituting or otherwise disfiguring any label, price tag or marking; or
  4. Transferring the goods from one container to another; or
  5. Concealment.

(b). Any person who knowingly conceals upon himself or another person unpurchased merchandise of any mercantile establishment while within the mercantile establishment shall be presumed to have the necessary culpable mental state pursuant to subsection A of this section.

(c). A merchant, or his agent or employee, with reasonable cause, may detain on the premises in a reasonable manner and for a reasonable time any person suspected of shoplifting as defined in subsection (a) of this section for questioning or summoning a law enforcement officer.

(d). Reasonable cause is a defense to a civil or criminal action against a peace officer, a merchant or an agent or employee of such merchant for false arrest, false or unlawful imprisonment or wrongful detention.

(e). If a minor engages in conduct which violates subsection (a) of this section notwithstanding the fact that such minor may not be held responsible because of his minority, any merchant injured by the shoplifting of such minor may bring a civil action against the parent or legal guardian of such minor [. . .] [and may recover the retail value of the obtained goods, as well as a penalty of not less than 100 dollars nor more than 100 dollars plus actual damages to the merchant].

(f).   Any merchant injured by the shoplifting of an adult or emancipated minor in violation of subsection (a) of this section may bring a civil action against the adult or emancipated minor [. . .] [and may recover the retail value of the obtained goods, as well as a penalty of not less than 100 dollars nor more than 100 dollars plus actual damages to the merchant].

(g).   [Penalties are prescribed based on the value of the property shoplifted.]

(h).   The court may, in imposing sentence upon a person convicted of violating this section, require any person to perform public services designated by the court in addition to or in lieu of any fine which the court might impose.

ARKANSAS

1. Arrest by Private Persons
(16-81-106(d), Ark. Code Ann.)

A private person may make an arrest where he has reasonable grounds for believing that the person arrested has committed a felony.

2. Detention & Shoplifting
(5-36-116, 5-36-102(b) Ark. Code Ann.)

(a)   A person engaging in conduct giving rise to a presumption under Sec. 5-36-102(b) [which appears below in Section 3] may be detained in a reasonable manner and for a reasonable length of time by a peace officer or a merchant or a merchant's employee in order that recovery of such goods may be effected. The detention by a peace officer, merchant, or merchant's employee shall not render the peace officer, merchant, or merchant's employee criminally or civilly liable for false arrest, false imprisonment, or unlawful detention.

(b)   (1)   The activation of an antishoplifting or inventory control device as a result of a person exiting the establishment or a protected area within the establishment shall constitute reasonable cause for the detention of the person so exiting by the owner or operator of the establishment or by an agent or employee of the owner or operator, provided sufficient notice has been posted to advise the patrons that such a device is being utilized. Each such detention shall be made only in a reasonable manner and only for a reasonable period of time sufficient for any inquiry into the circumstances surrounding the activation of the device or for the recovery of goods. Such detention by a peace officer, merchant, or merchant's employee shall not render such peace officer, merchant, or merchant's employee criminally or civilly liable for false arrest, false imprisonment, or unlawful detention.

(2)   For purposes of this section, "antishoplifting" or "inventory control device" means a mechanism or other device designed and operated for the purpose of detecting the removal from a mercantile establishment or similar enclosure or from a protected area within such an enclosure of specially marked or tagged merchandise.

(c)   A peace officer may arrest without a warrant upon probable cause for believing the suspect has committed the offense of shoplifting. The peace officer, merchant, or merchant's employee who has observed the person accused of committing the offense of shoplifting shall provide a written statement which shall serve as probable cause to justify the arrest. The accused shall be brought before a magistrate forthwith and afforded the opportunity to make a bond or recognizance as in other criminal cases.

3. Theft
(5-36-102, Ark. Code Ann.)

(a) (1) Conduct denominated theft in this chapter constitutes a single offense embracing the separate offenses heretofore known as larceny, embezzlement, false pretense, extortion, blackmail, fraudulent conversion, receiving stolen property, and other similar offenses.

(2) A criminal charge of theft may be supported by evidence that it was committed in any manner that would be theft under this chapter, notwithstanding the specification of a different manner in the indictment or information, subject only to the power of the court to ensure fair trial by granting a continuance or other appropriate relief where the conduct of the defense would be prejudiced by lack of fair notice or by surprise.

(b) The knowing concealment, upon his person or the person of another, of unpurchased goods or merchandise offered for sale by any store or other business establishment shall give rise to a presumption that the actor took goods with the purpose of depriving the owner, or another person having an interest therein.

(c) (1) The amount involved in a theft shall be deemed to be the highest value, by any reasonable standard, of the property or services which the actor obtained or attempted to obtain.

(2) Amounts involved in theft committed pursuant to one (1) scheme or course of conduct, whether from one (1) or more persons, may be aggregated in determining the grade of the offense.

CALIFORNIA

1. Arrest by Private Persons
(837, 847, Cal. Penal Code)

A private person may arrest another:

1. For a public offense committed or attempted in his presence.
2. When the person arrested has committed a felony, although not in his presence.
3. When a felony has been in fact committed, and he has reasonable cause for believing the person arrested to have committed it.

A private person who has arrested another for the commission of a public offense must, without unnecessary delay, take the person arrested before a magistrate, or deliver him to a peace officer.

2. Detention
(490.5(f), Cal. Penal Code)

(1) A merchant may detain a person for a reasonable time for the purpose of conducting an investigation in a reasonable manner whenever the merchant has probable cause to believe the person to be detained is attempting to unlawfully take or has unlawfully taken merchandise from the merchant's premises.

A person employed by a library facility may detain a person for a reasonable time for the purpose of conducting an investigation in a reasonable manner whenever the person employed by a library facility has probable cause to believe the person to be detained is attempting to unlawfully remove or has unlawfully removed books or library materials from the premises of the library facility.

(2) In making the detention a merchant or a person employed by a library facility may use a reasonable amount of nondeadly force necessary to protect himself or herself and to prevent escape of the person detained or the loss of property.

(3) During the period of detention any items which a merchant or any items which a person employed by a library facility has probable cause to believe are unlawfully taken from the premises of the merchant or library facility and which are in plain view may be examined by the merchant or person employed by a library facility for the purposes of ascertaining the ownership thereof.

(4) A merchant, a person employed by a library facility, or an agent thereof, having probable cause to believe the person detained was attempting to unlawfully take or has taken any item from the premises, may request the person detained to voluntarily surrender the item. Should the person detained refuse to surrender the item of which there is probable cause to believe has been unlawfully taken from the premises, or attempted to be unlawfully taken from the premises, a limited and reasonable search may be conducted by those authorized to make the detention in order to recover the item. Only packages, shopping bags, handbags or other property in the immediate possession of the person detained, but not including any clothing worn by the person, may be searched pursuant to this subdivision. Upon surrender or discovery of the item, the person detained may also be requested, but may not be required, to provide adequate proof of his or her true identity.

(5) A peace officer who accepts custody of a person arrested for an offense contained in this section may, subsequent to the arrest, search the person arrested and his or her immediate possessions for any item or items alleged to have been taken.

(6) In any civil action brought by any person resulting from a detention or arrest by a merchant, it shall be a defense to such action that the merchant detaining or arresting such person had probable cause to believe that the person had stolen or attempted to steal merchandise and that the merchant acted reasonably under all the circumstances.

3. Theft of Merchandise
(490.5, Cal. Penal Code)

(a) Upon a first conviction for petty theft involving merchandise taken from a merchant's premises or a book or other library materials taken from a library facility, a person shall be punished by a mandatory fine of not less than fifty dollars

($50) and not more than one thousand dollars ($1,000) for each such violation; and may also be punished by imprisonment in the county jail, not exceeding six months, or both such fine and imprisonment.

(b)   When an unemancipated minor's willful conduct would constitute petty theft involving merchandise taken from a merchant's premises or a book or other library materials taken from a library facility, any merchant or library facility who has been injured by that conduct may bring a civil action against the parent or legal guardian having control and custody of the minor. For the purposes of those actions the misconduct of the unemancipated minor shall be imputed to the parent or legal guardian having control and custody of the minor. The parent or legal guardian having control or custody of an unemancipated minor whose conduct violates this subdivision shall be jointly and severally liable with the minor to a merchant or to a library facility for damages of not less than fifty dollars ($50) nor more than five hundred dollars ($500), plus costs. In addition to the foregoing damages, the parent or legal guardian shall be jointly and severally liable with the minor to the merchant for the retail value of the merchandise if it is not recovered in a merchantable condition, or to a library facility for the fair market value of its book or other library materials. Recovery of these damages may be had in addition to, and is not limited by, any other provision of law which limits the liability of a parent or legal guardian for the tortious conduct of a minor. An action for recovery of damages, pursuant to this subdivision, may be brought in small claims court if the total damages do not exceed the jurisdictional limit of that court, or in any other appropriate court; however, total damages, including the value of the merchandise or book or other library materials, shall not exceed five hundred dollars ($500) for each action brought under this section.

The provisions of this subdivision are in addition to other civil remedies and do not limit merchants or other persons to elect to pursue other civil remedies, except that the provisions of Section 1714.1 of the Civil Code shall not apply herein.

(c)   When an adult or emancipated minor has unlawfully taken merchandise from a merchant's premises, or a book or other library materials from a library facility, the adult or emancipated minor shall be liable to the merchant or library facility for damages of not less than fifty dollars ($50) nor more than five hundred dollars ($500), plus costs. In addition to the foregoing damages, the adult or emancipated minor shall be liable to the merchant for the retail value of the merchandise if it is not recovered in merchantable condition, or to a library facility for the fair market value of its book or other library materials. An action for recovery of damages, pursuant to this subdivision, may be brought in small claims court if the total damages do not exceed the jurisdictional limit of such court, or in any other appropriate court. The provisions of this subdivision are in addition to other civil remedies and do not limit merchants or other persons to elect to pursue other civil remedies.

(d)   In lieu of the fines prescribed by subdivision (a), any person may be required to perform public services designated by the court, provided that in no event shall any such person be required to perform less than the number of hours of such public service necessary to satisfy the fine assessed by the court as provided by subdivision (a) at the minimum wage prevailing in the state at the time of sentencing.

COLORADO

1. Arrest by Private Persons
(16-3-201, Colo. Rev. Stats.)

A person who is not a peace officer may arrest another person when any crime has been or is being committed by the arrested person in the presence of the person making the arrest.

2. Detention
(18-4-407, Colo. Rev. Stats.)

If any person conceals upon his person or otherwise carries away any unpurchased goods, wares, or merchandise held or owned by any store or mercantile establishment, the merchant or any employee thereof or any peace officer, acting in good faith and upon probable cause based upon reasonable grounds therefor, may detain and question such person, in a reasonable manner for the purpose of ascertaining whether the person is guilty of theft. Such questioning of a person by a merchant, merchant's employee, or peace or police officer does not render the merchant, merchant's employee or peace officer civilly or criminally liable for slander, false, arrest, false imprisonment, malicious prosecution, or unlawful detention.

3. Concealment of Merchandise/Theft
(18-4-406, Colo. Rev. Stats.)

If any person willfully conceals unpurchased goods, wares, or merchandise owned or held by and offered or displayed for sale by any store or other mercantile establishment, whether the concealment be on his own person or otherwise and whether on or off the premises of said store or mercantile establishment, such concealment constitutes prima facie evidence that the person intended to commit the crime of theft.

CONNECTICUT

1. Arrest by Private Persons
(53a-22(f), Vol. 27A, Conn. Gen. Stats.)

A private person acting on his own account is justified in using reasonably physical force upon another person when and to the extent that he reasonably believes such to be necessary to effect an arrest or to prevent the escape from custody of an arrested person whom he reasonably believes to have committed an offense and who in fact has committed such offense; but he is not justified in using deadly physical force in such circumstances, except in defense of person as prescribed (elsewhere in the penal code).

2. Detention
(53a-119a, Vol. 27A, Conn. Gen. Stats.)

(a) Any owner, authorized agent or authorized employee of a retail mercantile establishment, who observes any person concealing or attempting to conceal goods displayed for sale therein, or the ownership of such goods, or transporting such goods from such premises without payment therefor, may question such person as to his name and address and, if such owner, agent or employee has reasonable grounds to believe that the person so questioned was then attempting to commit or was committing larceny of such goods on the premises of such establishment, may detain such person for a time sufficient to summon a police officer to the premises. Any person so questioned by such owner, authorized agent or authorized employee pursuant to the provisions of this section shall promptly identify himself by name and address. No other information shall be required of such person until a police officer has taken him into custody. For the purposes of this subsection, "reasonable grounds" shall include knowledge that a person has concealed unpurchased merchandise of such establishment while on the premises or has altered or removed identifying labels on such merchandise while on the premises or is leaving such premises with such unpurchased or concealed or altered merchandise in his possession. . . .

(c)   In any civil action by a person detained under the provisions of subsection (a) [. . .] of this section against the person so detaining him or the principal or employer of such person arising out of such questioning or detention by any such owner, agent or employee, evidence that the defendant had reasonable grounds to believe that the plaintiff was, at the time in question, committing or attempting to commit larceny or mutilating, defacing or destroying a book or other archival library materials shall create a rebuttable presumption that the plaintiff was so committing or attempting to commit larceny or mutilating, defacing or destroying a book or other archival library materials.

3.   Shoplifting & Liability for Shoplifting
(53 a-119(9), 52-564a, Vol. 27A, Conn. Gen. Stats. Ann.)

Shoplifting. A person is guilty of shoplifting who intentionally takes possession of any goods, wares or merchandise offered or exposed for sale by any store or other mercantile establishment with the intention of converting the same to his own use, without paying the purchase price thereof. A person intentionally concealing unpurchased goods or merchandise of any store or other mercantile establishment, either on the premises or outside the premises of such store, shall be prima facie presumed to have so concealed such article with the intention of converting the same to his own use without paying the purchase price thereof.

Liability for Shoplifting (a) Any person eighteen years of age or older or an emancipated minor who takes possession of goods or merchandise displayed or offered for sale by any mercantile establishment, or who takes from any real property any agricultural produce kept, grown or raised on the property for purposes of sale, without the consent of the owner and with the intention of converting such goods, merchandise or produce to his own use without having paid the purchase price thereof, or who alters the price indicia of such goods or merchandise, shall be liable in a civil action to the owner of the goods, merchandise or produce for (1) the actual and reasonable costs of maintaining the action, including court costs and a reasonable attorney's fee, (2) the retail value of the goods, merchandise or produce taken, if not recovered by the time of the commencement of the action or if recovered in an unmerchantable condition, and (3) punitive damages in an amount not to exceed three hundred dollars.

(b) A conviction of larceny by shoplifting, [. . .] shall not be a condition precedent to the maintenance of a civil action under this section.

(c) In any action brought pursuant to subsection (a) of this section, if the plaintiff does not prevail, the court may award to the defendant his costs, including a reasonable attorney's fee, and damages not to exceed three hundred dollars.

(d) No action shall be brought pursuant to subsection (a) of this section but within two years from the date of the act complained of.

DELAWARE

1. Arrest by Private Persons

[No general statutory right, but limited one, reproduced in next section 2.]

2. Detention
(Tit. 11, 840, Del. Code Ann.)

A merchant, a store supervisor, agent or employee of the merchant 18 years of age or older, who has probable cause for believing that a person has intentionally concealed unpurchased merchandise or has committed shoplifting as defined in subsection (a) of this section, may, for the purpose of summoning a law-enforcement officer, take the person into custody and detain him in a reasonable manner on the premises for a reasonable time.

A merchant, a store supervisor, agent or employee of the merchant 18 years of age or older, who detains, or a merchant, a store supervisor, agent or employee of the merchant who causes or provides information leading to the arrest of any person under subsection (a), (b) or (c) of this section, shall not be held civilly or criminally liable for such detention or arrest provided he had, at the time of such detention or arrest, probable cause to believe that the person committed the crime of shoplifting as defined in subsection (a) of this section.

3. Shoplifting
(Tit. 11, 840, Del. Code Ann.)

(a) A person is guilty of shoplifting if, while in a mercantile establishment in which goods, wares or merchandise are displayed for sale, he:

(1) removes any such goods, wares or merchandise from the immediate use of display or from any other place within the establishment, with intent to appropriate the same to the use of the person so taking, or to deprive the owner of the use, the value or possession thereof without paying to the owner the value thereof; or

(2) obtains possession of any goods, wares or merchandise by charging the same to any person without the authority of such person or to a fictitious person with a like intent; or

(3) conceals any such goods, wares or merchandise with like intent; or

(4) alters, removes or otherwise disfigures any label, price tag or marking upon any such goods, wares or merchandise with a like intent; or

(5) transfers any goods, wares or merchandise from a container in which same shall be displayed or packaged to any other container with like intent; or

(6) Uses any instrument whatsoever, credit slips or choose in action to obtain any goods, wares or merchandise with intent to appropriate the same to the use of the person so taking or to deprive the owner of the use, the value or the possession thereof without paying to the owner the value thereof.

(b) Any person wilfully concealing unpurchased merchandise of any store or other mercantile establishment, inside or outside the premises of such store or other mercantile establishment, shall be presumed to have so concealed such merchandise with the intention of converting the same to his own use without paying the purchase price thereof within the meaning of subsection (a) of this section, and the finding of such merchandise concealed upon the person or among the belongings of such person, outside of such store or other mercantile establishment, shall be presumptive evidence of intentional concealment; and if such person conceals or causes to be concealed such merchandise upon the person or among the belongings of another, the finding of the same shall also be presumptive evidence of intentional concealment on the part of the person so concealing such merchandise.

DISTRICT OF COLUMBIA

1. Arrest by Private Persons
(23-582, D.C. Code, 1994 ed.)

A private person may arrest another—

(1) who he has probable cause to believe is committing in his presence—
(A) a felony, or
(B) [Certain other offenses enumerated in section 23-581 (a) (2)]; or
(2) in aid of a law enforcement officer or special policeman, or other person authorized by law to make an arrest.

Any person making an arrest pursuant to this section shall deliver the person arrested to a law enforcement officer without unreasonable delay.

2. Detention
[No statute]

3. Theft
(22-3811, D.C. Code)

For the purpose of this section, the term "wrongfully obtains or uses" means: (1) Taking or exercising control over property; (2) making an unauthorized use, disposition, or transfer of an interest in or possession of property; or (3) obtaining property by trick, false pretense, false token, tampering, or deception. The term "wrongfully obtains or uses" includes conduct previously known as larceny, larceny by trick, larceny by trust, embezzlement, and false pretenses.

A person commits the offense of theft if that person wrongfully obtains or uses the property of another with intent:

(1) To deprive the other of a right to the property or a benefit of the property; or
(2) To appropriate the property to his or her own use or to the use of a third person.

FLORIDA

1. Arrest by Private Persons
[No statute]

2. Detention
[Covered in the following provisions on retail theft—in sections 3, 4, 5 & 6.]

3. Theft and Retail Theft
(812.014 and 812.015, Fla. Stat. Ann.)

Theft (1) A person commits theft if he knowingly obtains or uses, or endeavors to obtain or to use, the property of another with intent to, either temporarily or permanently:

(a) Deprive the other person of a right to the property or a benefit therefrom.
(b) Appropriate the property to his own use or to the use of any person not entitled thereto.

Retail Theft. (1) As used in this section:

(a) "Merchandise" means any personal property, capable of manual delivery, displayed, held, or offered for retail sale by a merchant.
(b) "Merchant" means an owner or operator, or the agent, consignee, employee, lessee, or officer of an owner or operator, of any premises or apparatus used for retail purchase or sale of any merchandise.
(c) "Value of merchandise" means the sale price of the merchandise at the time it was stolen or otherwise removed, depriving the owner of his lawful right to ownership and sale of said item.
(d) "Retail theft" means the taking possession of or carrying away of merchandise, money, or negotiable documents; altering or removing a label or price tag; transferring merchandise from one container to another; or removing a shopping cart, with intent to deprive the merchant of possession, use, benefit, or full retail value.
(h) "Antishoplifting or inventory control device" means a mechanism or other device designed and operated for the purpose of detecting the removal from a mercantile establishment or similar enclosure, or from a protected area within such an enclosure, of specially marked or tagged merchandise.
(2) Upon a second or subsequent conviction for petit theft from a merchant or farmer, the offender shall be punished as provided in s. 812.014 (2) (d), except that the court shall impose a fine of not less than $50 or more than $1,000. However, in lieu of such fine, the court may require the offender to perform public services designated by the court. In no event shall any such offender be required to

perform fewer than the number of hours of public service necessary to satisfy the fine assessed by the court, as provided by this subsection, at the minimum wage prevailing in the state at the time of sentencing.

(3) (a) A law enforcement officer, a merchant, a merchant's employee, or a farmer who has probable cause to believe that retail or farm theft has been committed by a person and that he can recover the property by taking the person into custody may, for the purpose of attempting to effect such recovery or for prosecution, take the person into custody and detain him in a reasonable manner for a reasonable length of time. In the case of a farmer, taking into custody shall be effectuated only on property owned or leased by the farmer. In the event the merchant, merchant's employee, or farmer takes the person into custody, a law enforcement officer shall be called to the scene immediately after the person has been taken into custody.

(b) The activation of an antishoplifting or inventory control device as a result of a person exiting an establishment or a protected area within an establishment shall constitute reasonable cause for the detention of the person so exiting by the owner or operator of the establishment or by an agent or employee of the owner or operator, provided sufficient notice has been posted to advise the patrons that such a device is being utilized. Each such detention shall be made only in a reasonable manner and only for a reasonable period of time sufficient for any inquiry into the circumstances surrounding the activation of the device.

(c) The taking into custody and detention by a law enforcement officer, merchant, merchant's employee, or farmer, if done in compliance with all the requirements of this subsection, shall not render such law enforcement officer, merchant, merchant's employee, or farmer criminally or civilly liable for false arrest, false imprisonment, or unlawful detention.

(4) Any law enforcement officer may arrest, either on or off the premises and without warrant, any person he has probable cause to believe has committed theft in a retail or wholesale establishment or on commercial or private farm lands of a farmer.

(5) A merchant, merchant's employee, or farmer who takes a person into custody, as provided in subsection (3), or who causes an arrest, as provided in subsection (4), of a person for retail theft or farm theft shall not be criminally or civilly liable for false arrest or false imprisonment when the merchant, merchant's employee, or farmer has probable cause to believe that the person committed retail theft or farm theft.

(6) An individual who, while committing or after committing theft of property, resists the reasonable effort of a law enforcement officer, merchant, merchant's employee, or farmer to recover the property which the law enforcement officer, merchant, merchant's employee, or farmer had probable cause to believe the individual had concealed or removed from its place of display or elsewhere commits a misdemeanor of the first degree, punishable as provided in section. 775.082 or section 775.083, unless the individual did not know, or did not have reason to know, that the person seeking to recover the property was a law enforcement officer, merchant, merchant's employee, or farmer. For purposes of this section the charge of theft and the charge of resisting may be tried concurrently.

GEORGIA

1. Arrest by Private Persons
(17-4-60, Ga. Code Ann.)

A private person may arrest an offender if the offense is committed in his presence or within his immediate knowledge. If the offense is a felony and the offender is escaping or attempting to escape, a private person may arrest him upon reasonable and probable grounds of suspicion.

2. Detention
(51-7-61, Ga. Code Ann.)

Whenever the owner or operator of a mercantile establishment or any agent or employee of the owner or operator detains, arrests, or causes to be detained or arrested any person reasonably thought to be engaged in shoplifting and, as a result of the detention or arrest, the person so detained or arrested brings an action for false arrest or false imprisonment against the owner, operator, agent, or employee, no recovery shall be had by the plaintiff in such action where it is established by competent evidence:

(1)   That the plaintiff had so conducted himself or behaved in such manner as to cause a man of reasonable prudence to believe that the plaintiff, at or immediately prior to the time of the detention or arrest, was committing the offense of shoplifting, as defined by Code Section 16-8-14; or

(2)   That the manner of the detention or arrest and the length of time during which such plaintiff was detained was under all the circumstances reasonable.

[The following provision, Sec. 51-7-6, deals specifically with detention rights by businesses equipped with anti-shoplifting or inventory control devices.]

(a)   As used in this Code section, the term: "antishoplifting or inventory control device" means a mechanism or other device designed and operated for the purpose of detecting the removal of specially marked or tagged merchandise from a mercantile establishment or similar enclosure or from a protected area within such an enclosure.

(b)   In the case of a mercantile establishment utilizing an antishoplifting or inventory control device, the automatic activation of the device as a result of a person exiting the establishment or a protected area within the establishment shall constitute reasonable cause for the detention of the person so exiting by the owner or operator of the establishment or by an agent or employee of the owner or operator. Each detention shall be made only in a reasonable manner and only for a reasonable period of time sufficient for any inquiry into the circumstances surrounding the activation of the device.

(c)   This Code section shall apply only with respect to mercantile establishments in which a notice has been posted in a clear and visible manner advising patrons of the establishment that an antishoplifting or inventory control device is being utilized in the establishment.

3. Shoplifting
(16-8-14, Ga. Code Ann.)

(a) A person commits the offense of theft by shoplifting when he alone or in concert with another person, with the intent of appropriating merchandise to his own use without paying for the same or to deprive the owner of possession thereof or of the value thereof, in whole or in part, does any of the following:

   (1) Conceals or takes possession of the goods or merchandise of any store or retail establishment;

   (2) Alters the price tag or other price marking on goods or merchandise of any store or retail establishment;

   (3) Transfers the goods or merchandise of any store or retail establishment from one container to another;

   (4) Interchanges the label or price tag from one item of merchandise with a label or price tag for another item of merchandise; or

   (5) Wrongfully causes the amount paid to be less than the merchant's stated price for the merchandise.

(b) (1) A person convicted of the offense of theft by shoplifting, as provided in subsection (a) of this Code section when the property which was the subject of the theft is $100.00 or less in value, shall be punished as for a misdemeanor; provided, however, that:

      (A) Upon conviction of a second such offense, in addition to or in lieu of any imprisonment which might be imposed, the defendant shall be fined not less than $250.00 and the fine shall not be suspended or probated;

      (B) Upon conviction of a third such offense, in addition to or in lieu of any fine which might be imposed, the defendant shall be punished by imprisonment for not less than 30 days; and such sentence of imprisonment shall not be suspended, probated, deferred, or withheld; and

      (C) Upon conviction of a fourth or subsequent such offense, the defendant commits a felony and shall be punished by imprisonment for not less than one nor more than ten years; and the first year of such sentence shall not be suspended, probated, deferred, or withheld.

   (2) A person convicted of the offense of theft by shoplifting, as provided in subsection (a) of this Code section, when the property which was the subject of the theft exceeds $100.00 in value commits a felony and shall be punished by imprisonment for not less than one nor more than ten years.

(c) In all cases involving theft by shoplifting, the term "value" means the actual retail price of the property at the time and place of the offense. The unaltered price tag or other marking on property, or duly identified photographs thereof, shall be prima-facie evidence of value and ownership of the property.

HAWAII

1. Arrest by Private Persons
(803-3 and 4, Hawaii Rev. Stats.)

Anyone in the act of committing a crime, may be arrested by any person present, without a warrant.

Whenever a crime is committed, and the offenders are unknown, and any person is found near the place where the crime was committed, either endeavoring to conceal oneself, or endeavoring to escape, or under such other circumstances as to justify a reasonable suspicion of the person being the offender, the person may be arrested without warrant.

["Crime" is defined in 701-107 as an offense "for which a sentence of imprisonment is authorized." It includes misdemeanors as well as felonies.]

2. Detention
(663-2, Hawaii Rev. Stats.)

In any action for false arrest, false imprisonment, unlawful detention, defamation of character, assault, trespass, or invasion of civil rights, brought by any person by reason of having been detained on or in the immediate vicinity of the premises of a retail mercantile establishment for the purpose of investigation or questioning as to the ownership of any merchandise, it shall be a defense to the action that the person was detained in a reasonable manner and for not more than a reasonable time to permit such investigation or questioning by a police officer or by the owner of the retail mercantile establishment, the owner's authorized employee, or agent, and that such police officer, owner, employee, or agent had reasonable grounds to believe that the person so detained was committing or attempting to commit larceny of merchandise on the premises.

As used in this section, "reasonable grounds" includes, but is not limited to, knowledge that a person has concealed possession of unpurchased merchandise of the retail mercantile establishment, and a "reasonable time" means the time necessary to permit the person detained to make a statement or to refuse to make a statement, and the time necessary to examine employees and records of the mercantile establishment relative to the ownership of the merchandise.

For the purpose of this section, the term "retail mercantile establishment" means a place where goods, wares, or merchandise are offered to the public for sale.

(707-722, Hawaii Rev. Stats.)

(1) A person commits the offense of unlawful imprisonment in the second degree if he knowingly restrains another person. ***

(3) In any prosecution under this section it is an affirmative defense, that the person restrained (a) was on or in the immediate vicinity of the premises of a retail mercantile establishment for the purpose of investigation or questioning as to the ownership of any merchandise; (b) was restrained in a reasonable manner and for not more than a reasonable time; (c) was restrained to permit such investigation or questioning by a police officer or by the owner of the retail mercantile establishment, his authorized employee or agent; and (d) that such police officer, owner, employee or agent had reasonable grounds to believe that the person so detained was committing or attempting to commit theft of merchandise on the premisees [premises].

3. Theft/Shoplifting/Liability for Shoplifting/ Removal of Shopping Carts
(708-830, Hawaii Rev. Stats.)

A person commits theft if he does any of the following:

(1) Obtains or exerts unauthorized control over property. He obtains, or exerts control over, the property of another with intent to deprive him of the property.

(2)   Property obtained or control exerted through deception. He obtains, or exerts control over, the property of another by deception with intent to deprive him of the property.

(8)   Shoplifting.

    (a)   He conceals or takes possession of the goods or merchandise of any store or retail establishment, with intent to defraud.

    (b)   He alters the price tag or other price marking on goods or merchandise of any store or retail establishment, with intent to defraud.

    (c)   He transfers the goods or merchandise of any store or retail establishment from one container to another, with intent to defraud.

The unaltered price or name tag or other marking on goods or merchandise, or duly identified photographs thereof, shall be prima facie evidence of value and ownership of such goods or merchandise. Photographs of the goods or merchandise involved, duly identified in writing by the arresting police officer as accurately representing such goods or merchandise, shall be deemed competent evidence of the goods or merchandise involved and shall be admissible in any proceedings, hearings, and trials for shoplifting, to the same extent as the goods or merchandise themselves.

(708-833.5, Hawaii Rev. Stats.)

A person convicted of committing the offense of shoplifting as defined in section 708-830 shall be sentenced as follows:

(1)   In cases involving property the value or aggregate value of which exceeds $300: as a class C felony, provided that the minimum fine shall be four times the value or aggregate value involved;

(2)   In cases involving property the value or aggregate value of which exceeds $100: as a misdemeanor, provided that the minimum fine shall be three times the value or aggregate value involved;

(3)   In cases involving property the value or aggregate value of which is $100 or less: as a petty misdemeanor, provided that the minimum fine shall be twice the value or aggregate value involved;

(4)   If a person has previously been convicted of committing the offense of shoplifting as defined in section 708-830, the minimum fine shall be doubled that specified in paragraphs (1), (2), and (3), respectively, as set forth above; provided in the event the convicted person defaults in payment of any fine, and the default was not contumacious, the court may sentence the person to community services as authorized by section 706-605(1)(e).

(663A-2, Hawaii Rev. Stats.)

(a)   Any person who takes possession of any merchandise displayed or offered for sale by any mercantile establishment without the consent of the owner and with the intention of converting such merchandise to the individual's own use without having paid the purchase price thereof, who alters the price indicia of such merchandise, or who takes any other action that constitutes the offense of shoplifting, shall be civilly liable to the owner of the mercantile establishment for either:

    (1)   Actual damages and a civil penalty of $75, if a written demand is made pursuant to subsection (e), for the actual damages and this civil penalty; or

    (2)   Actual damages, a civil penalty of $75, and an additional civil penalty of not less than $50 nor more than $500, to recover the costs and expenses of bringing a civil suit, as determined by the court.

(b)   A conviction for theft under section 708-830 to 708-833 is not a condition precedent to the maintenance of a civil action under this section.

(c)   A civil liability under this section is not limited by another law that limits liability of parents or minor children.

(d)   An action for recovery of damages and the assessment of the civil penalties under this section may be brought in any court of competent jurisdiction, including the small claims division of a district court.

(e)   The fact that an owner of a mercantile establishment may bring an action against an individual for damages as provided in this section shall not limit the right of the owner of a mercantile establishment to demand, in writing, prior to the commencement of any legal action, that a person who is liable for damages under this section remit said damages and the amount of civil penalty allowed in section 663A-2.

(633-16, Hawaii Rev. Stats.)

(a)   A person shall not remove, without proper authorization, a shopping cart, shopping basket, or similar device from the premises of any business establishment, including any parking area maintained for the customer of the business establishment, or any sidewalk or passageway adjacent to the business establishment, for any purpose whatsoever.

(b)   This section shall not apply unless:

    (1)   The shopping cart, shopping basket, or other similar device has securely affixed to it a conspicuous sign identifying it as belonging to the business establishment; and

    (2)   There is posted at the place or places where the shopping carts, shopping baskets, or other similar devices are stored for customer use, a sign or signs conspicuously positioned in order to be seen by an ordinarily observant person, to notify customers and the general public that the carts, baskets, or devices shall not be removed from the premises, parking areas, sidewalks, or passageways adjacent thereto.

(c)   The following shall not be subject to this section:

    (1)   The owner of the shopping cart, shopping basket, or similar device;

    (2)   Any agent of the owner;

    (3)   Any employee of the business establishment;

    (4)   Any person possessing the written consent of the owner or manager of the business establishment.

(d)   Any business establishment which is damaged in its business or property by reason of a violation of subsection (a):

    (1)   May sue in the small claims division of the district court in the circuit where the business establishment is situated for damages sustained, and if the judgment is for the business establishment, it may be awarded a sum equal to the replacement value of the shopping cart, shopping basket, or similar device together with the costs of the suit; and

(2)   May bring proceedings to enjoin further unauthorized removal of shopping carts, shopping baskets, or similar devices.

(e)   In the case of repossession proceedings, the business establishment entitled to the possession of the shopping cart, shopping basket, or other similar device, shall bring and prosecute its action in the small claims division of the district court in the circuit where the business establishment is situated.

(f)   The court in the small claims division shall grant judgment in favor of the business establishment if:

(1)   The plaintiff is the lawful owner of the shopping cart, shopping basket, or similar device which has been adequately identified;

(2)   The plaintiff has given notice as provided in subsection (b)(2) that the unauthorized removal of shopping carts, shopping baskets, or similar devices is prohibited;

(3)   The shopping device has been removed from the premises of the business establishment without proper authorization; and

(4)   The defendant is in possession or has control of the shopping devices.

(g)   A person who has been found by court to have removed, without proper authorization, a shopping cart, shopping basket, or similar device may be liable for payment of an award under this section or a criminal fine under section 706-640, but not both.

IDAHO

1.   Arrest by Private Persons
(19-604 and 614 Idaho Code)

A private person may arrest another:

1.   For a public offense committed or attempted in his presence.
2.   When the person arrested has committed a felony, although not in his presence.
3.   When a felony has been in fact committed, and he has reasonable cause for believing the person arrested to have committed it.

A private person who has arrested another for the commission of a public offense must, without unnecessary delay, take the person arrested before a magistrate, or deliver him to a peace officer.

2.   Detention
(48-704 and 705, Idaho Code)

(a)   Any merchant may request a person on his premises to place or keep in full view any merchandise such person may have removed, or which the merchant has reason to believe he may have removed, from its place of display or elsewhere, whether for examination, purchase or for any other purpose. No merchant shall be criminally or civilly liable on account of having made such a request.

(b)   Any merchant who has reason to believe that merchandise has been taken by a person in violation of this act and that he can recover such merchandise by taking such a person into custody and detaining him may, for the purpose of attempting to effect such recovery or for the purpose of informing a peace officer of the circumstances of such detention, take the person into custody and detain him, in a reasonable manner and for a reasonable length of time.

No merchant shall be entitled to immunity from liability provided for in this act unless there is displayed in a conspicuous place on his premises a notice not less than thirteen (13) inches wide and twenty-one (21) inches long, clearly legible and in substantially the following form:

Any merchant or his agent who has reason to believe that merchandise has been removed or concealed by a person in violation of this act may detain such person for the purpose of recovering the property or notifying a peace officer. A person or the parents or legal guardian of a minor who knowingly removes merchandise without paying therefore, or conceals merchandise to avoid paying therefore, is civilly liable for its value, and additional damages.

3.   Retail Theft/Concealment of Merchandise
(18-4624, 4625, 4626, Idaho Code)

A person steals property and commits theft by the alteration, transfer or removal of any label, price tag, marking, indicia of value or any other markings which aid in the determination of value of any merchandise displayed, held, stored, or offered for sale, in a retail mercantile establishment, for the purpose of attempting to purchase such merchandise either personally or in consort with another, at less than the retail price with the intention of depriving the merchant of the value of such merchandise.

In any prosecution for a violation of this chapter, photographs of the goods or merchandise alleged to have been taken or converted shall be deemed competent evidence of such goods or merchandise and shall be admissible in any proceeding, hearing or trial to the same extent as if such goods and merchandise had been introduced as evidence. Such photographs shall bear a written description of the goods or merchandise alleged to have been taken or converted, the name of the owner of such goods or merchandise, or the store or establishment wherein the alleged offense occurred, the name of the accused, the name of the arresting peace officer, the date of the photograph and the name of the photographer. Such writing shall be made under oath by the arresting peace officer, and the photographs identified by the signature of the photographer. Upon the filing of such photograph and writing with the authority or court holding such goods and merchandise as evidence, such goods or merchandise shall be returned to their owner, or the proprietor or manager of the store or establishment wherein the alleged offense occurred.

(a)   Whoever, without authority, wilfully conceals the goods, wares or merchandise of any store or merchant, while still upon the premises of such store or merchant, shall be guilty of a misdemeanor and, upon conviction thereof, shall be punished by a fine of not more than three hundred dollars ($300) or by imprisonment in the county jail for not more than six (6) months, or by both such fine and imprisonment. Goods, wares or merchandise found concealed upon the person shall be prima facie evidence of a wilful concealment.

(b)   Any owner, his authorized employee or agent of any store or merchant, apprehending or detaining a person on or in the immediate vicinity of the premises of any store or merchant, for the purpose of investigation or questioning as to the ownership of any goods, wares or merchandise, shall have as a defense in any action, civil or criminal, that such detention of the person or persons was in a reasonable manner and for not more than a reasonable time to permit such investigation or questioning by a peace officer or by the owner of the store or merchant, his authorized employee or agent, and that such peace officer, owner, employee or agent had probable cause to believe that the person so detained was committing or attempting to commit an offense as set forth in subsection (a) of this section. "Reasonable time" shall mean the time necessary to permit the person detained to make a statement or to refuse to make a statement, and the time necessary to examine employees and records of the store or merchant relative to ownership of the merchandise.

(48-701, 48-702, Idaho Code—Civil Liability for Acts of Shoplifting)

Any person who knowingly removes merchandise from a merchant's premises without paying therefor, or knowingly conceals merchandise to avoid paying therefor, or knowingly commits retail theft, shall be civilly liable to the merchant for the retail value of the merchandise, plus damages of not less than one hundred dollars ($100) nor more than two hundred fifty dollars ($250), costs of suit and reasonable attorneys' fees.

The parent or legal guardian, having legal custody, of a minor who knowingly removes merchandise from a merchant's premises without paying therefor, or knowingly conceals merchandise to avoid paying therefor, or knowingly commits retail theft, shall be civilly liable to the merchant for the retail value of the merchandise, plus damages of not less than one hundred dollars ($100) nor more than two hundred fifty dollars ($250), costs of suit and reasonable attorneys' fees. Recovery under this section is not limited by any other provision of law which limits the liability of a parent or legal guardian for the tortious conduct of a minor. The liability of parents or legal guardian and of the minor under this chapter is joint and several.

A parent or guardian not having legal custody of a minor shall not be liable for the conduct of the minor proscribed by this act.

ILLINOIS

1. Arrest by Private Persons
(725 Ill. Compiled Stats. 5/107-3)

Any person may arrest another when he has reasonable grounds to believe that an offense other than an ordinance violation is being committed.

["Offense" is defined in another statute as "a violation of any penal statute of this State."]

2. Detention
(720 Ill. Compiled Stats. Secs. 5/16A-5, 5/16A-6)

Any merchant who has reasonable grounds to believe that a person has committed retail theft may detain such person, on or off the premises of a retail mercantile establishment, in a reasonable manner and for a reasonable length of time for all or any of the following purposes:

(a) To request identification;
(b) To verify such identification;
(c) To make reasonable inquiry as to whether such person has in his possession unpurchased merchandise and, to make reasonable investigation of the ownership of such merchandise;
(d) To inform a peace officer of the detention of the person and surrender that person to the custody of a peace officer;
(e) In the case of a minor, to inform a peace officer, the parents, guardian or other private person interested in the welfare of that minor of this detention and to surrender custody of such minor to such person.

A merchant may make a detention as permitted herein off the premises of a retail mercantile establishment only if such detention is pursuant to an immediate pursuit of such person.

A merchant shall be deemed to have reasonable grounds to make a detention for the purposes of this Section if the merchant detains a person because such person has in his possession either a theft detection shielding device or a theft detection device remover.

Affirmative Defense. A detention as permitted in this Article does not constitute an arrest or an unlawful restraint, [. . .], nor shall it render the merchant liable to the person so detained.

3. Retail Theft
(720 Ill. Compiled Stats. 5/16A-1)

Legislative declaration. It is the public policy of this State that the substantial burden placed upon the economy of this State resulting from the rising incidence of retail theft is a matter of grave concern to the people of this State who have a right to be protected in their health, safety and welfare from the effects of this crime.

(720 Ill. Compiled Stats. 5/16A-2)

Definitions. For the purposes of this Article, the words and phrases defined in [this statute] have the meanings ascribed to them in those Sections unless a contrary meaning is clear from the context.

Conceal (2.1). To "conceal" merchandise means that, although there may be some notice of its presence, that merchandise is not visible through ordinary observation.

Full Retail Value (2.2). "Full Retail Value" means the merchant's stated or advertised price of the merchandise.

Merchandise (2.3). "Merchandise" means any item of tangible personal property.

Merchant (2.4). "Merchant" means an owner or operator of any retail mercantile establishment or any agent, employee, lessee, consignee, officer, director, franchisee or independent contractor of such owner or operator.

Minor (2.5). "Minor" means a person who is less than 19 years of age, is unemancipated and resides with his parents or legal guardian.

Person (2.6). "Person" means any natural person or individual.

Peace Officer (2.7). "Peace officer" ["is any person who by virtue of his office or public employment is vested by law with a duty to maintain public order or to make arrests for offenses . . . "].

Premises of a Retail Mercantile Establishment (2.8). "Premises of a Retail Mercantile Establishment" includes, but is not limited to, the retail mercantile establishment; any common use areas in shopping centers and all parking areas set aside by a merchant or on behalf of a merchant for the parking of vehicles for the convenience of the patrons of such retail mercantile establishment.

Retail Mercantile Establishment (2.9). "Retail Mercantile Establishment" means any place where merchandise is displayed, held, stored or offered for sale to the public.

Shopping Cart (2.10). "Shopping Cart" means those push carts of the type or types which are commonly provided by grocery stores, drug stores or other retail mercantile establishments for the use of the public in transporting commodities in stores and markets and, incidentally, from the stores to a place outside the store.

Shopping Cart (2.11). "Under-ring" means to cause the cash register or other sales recording device to reflect less than the full retail value of the merchandise.

Theft Detection Shielding Device (2.12). "Theft detection shielding device" means any laminated or coated bag or device designed and intended to shield merchandise from detection by an electronic or magnetic theft alarm sensor.

Theft Detection Device Remover (2.13). "Theft detection device remover" means any tool or device specifically designed and intended to be used to remove any theft detection device from any merchandise.

(720 Ill. Compiled Stats. 5/16A-3)

Offense of Retail Theft. A person commits the offense of retail theft when he or she knowingly:

(a) Takes possession of, carries away, transfers or causes to be carried away or transferred, any merchandise displayed, held, stored or offered for sale in a retail mercantile establishment with the intention of retaining such merchandise or with the intention of depriving the merchant permanently of the possession, use or benefit of such merchandise without paying the full retail value of such merchandise; or

(b) Alters, transfers, or removes any label, price tag, marking, indicia of value or any other markings which aid in determining value affixed to any merchandise displayed, held, stored or offered for sale, in a retail mercantile establishment and attempts to purchase such merchandise personally or in consort with another at less than the full retail value with the intention of depriving the merchant of the full retail value of such merchandise; or

(c) Transfers any merchandise displayed, held, stored or offered for sale, in a retail mercantile establishment from the container in or on which such merchandise is displayed to any other container with the intention of depriving the merchant of the full retail value of such merchandise; or

(d) Under-rings with the intention of depriving the merchant of the full retail value of the merchandise; or

(e) Removes a shopping cart from the premises of a retail mercantile establishment without the consent of the merchant given at the time of such removal with the intention of depriving the merchant permanently of the possession, use or benefit of such cart; or

(f) Represents to a merchant that he or another is the lawful owner of property, knowing that such representation is false, and conveys or attempts to convey that property to a merchant who is the owner of the property in exchange for money, merchandise credit or other property of the merchant; or

(g) Uses or possesses any theft detection shielding device or theft detection device remover with the intention of using such device to deprive the merchant permanently of the possession, use or benefit of any merchandise displayed, held, stored or offered for sale in a retail mercantile establishment without paying the full retail value of such merchandise. A violation of this subsection shall be a Class A misdemeanor for a first offense and a Class 4 felony for a second or subsequent offense; or

(h) Obtains or exerts unauthorized control over property of the owner and thereby intends to deprive the owner permanently of the use or benefit of the property when a lessee of the personal property of another fails to return it to the owner, or if the lessee fails to pay the full retail value of such property to the lessor in satisfaction of any contractual provision requiring such, within 30 days after written demand from the owner for its return. A notice in writing, given after the expiration of the leasing agreement, by registered mail, to the lessee at the address given by the lessee and shown on the leasing agreement shall constitute proper demand.

(720 Ill. Compiled Stats. 5/16A-4)

Presumptions. If any person:

(a) conceals upon his or her person or among his or her belongings, unpurchased merchandise displayed, held, stored or offered for sale in a retail mercantile establishment; and

(b) removes that merchandise beyond the last known station for receiving payments for that merchandise in that retail mercantile establishment such person shall be presumed to have possessed, carried away or transferred such merchandise with the intention of retaining it or with the intention of depriving the merchant permanently of the possession, use or benefit of such merchandise without paying the full retail value of such merchandise.

(720 Ill. Compiled Stats. 5/16A-5)

Detention. [This provision and the "affirmative defense" one in Sec. 5/16A-6, have been reproduced in the foregoing main section 2.]

(720 Ill. Compiled Stats, 5/16A-7)

Civil Liability. (a) A person who commits the offense of retail theft as defined in Section 16A-3 paragraphs (a), (b) or (c) of this Code [720 ILCS 5/16A-3], shall be civilly liable to the merchant of the merchandise in an amount consisting of:

(i) actual damages equal to the full retail value of the merchandise as defined herein; plus

(ii) an amount not less than $100 nor more than $1,000; plus

(iii) attorney's fees and court costs.

(b) If a minor commits the offense of retail theft, the parents or guardian of said minor shall be civilly liable as provided in this Section; provided, however that a guardian appointed pursuant to the Juvenile Court Act or the Juvenile Court Act of 1987 [705 ILCS 405/1-1 et seq.] shall not be liable under this Section. Total recovery under this Section shall not exceed the maximum recovery permitted under

Section 5 of the "Parental Responsibility Law", approved October 6, 1969, as now or hereafter amended [740 ILCS 115/5].

(c)   A conviction or a plea of guilty to the offense of retail theft is not a prerequisite to the bringing of a civil suit hereunder.

(720 Ill. Compiled Stats., 5/16A-9)

Continuation of prior law. The provisions of [the Retail Theft Act] insofar as they are the same or substantially the same as those of [the general theft provisions] shall be construed as a continuation of such [provisions] and not as a new enactment.

INDIANA

1.   Arrest by Private Persons
(Burns Ind. Code Ann. 35-33-1-4)

(a)   Any person may arrest any other person if:
    (1)   The other person committed a felony in his presence;
    (2)   A felony has been committed and he has probable cause to believe that the other person has committed that felony; or
    (3)   A misdemeanor involving a breach of peace is being committed in his presence and the arrest is necessary to prevent the continuance of the breach of peace.

(b)   A person making an arrest under this section shall, as soon as practical, notify a law enforcement officer and deliver custody of the person arrested to a law enforcement officer.

(c)   The law enforcement officer may process the arrested person as if the officer had arrested him. The officer who receives or processes a person arrested by another under this section is not liable for false arrest or false imprisonment.

2.   Detention
(Burns Ind. Code Ann. 35-33-6-2, 3, 4, 5 and 6).

(a)   An owner or agent of a store who has probable cause to believe that a theft has occurred or is occurring on or about the store and who has probable cause to believe that a specific person has committed or is committing the theft may:
    (1)   Detain the person and request the person to identify himself;
    (2)   Verify the identification;
    (3)   Determine whether the person has in his possession unpurchased merchandise taken from the store;
    (4)   Inform the appropriate law enforcement officers; and
    (5)   Inform the parents or others interested in the person's welfare, that the person has been detained.

(b)   The detention must:
    (1)   Be reasonable and last only for a reasonable time; and
    (2)   Not extend beyond the arrival of a law enforcement officer or two (2) hours, whichever first occurs.

An owner or agent of a store who informs a law enforcement officer of the circumstantial basis for detention and any additional relevant facts shall be presumed to be placing information before the law enforcement officer. The placing of this information does not constitute a charge of crime.

A civil or criminal action against an owner or agent of a store or a law enforcement officer may not be based on a detention which was lawful under [this] section []. However, the defendant has the burden of proof that he acted with probable cause under section 2 of this chapter.

An owner or agent of a store may act in the manner permitted by [this] section 2 of this chapter on information received from any employee of the store, if that employee has probable cause to believe that a:

(1)   Theft has occurred or is occurring in or about the store; and

(2)   specific person has committed or is committing the theft.

3.   Theft/Shoplifting
(Burns Ind. Code Ann. 35-43-4-2 and 4)

A person who knowingly or intentionally exerts unauthorized control over property of another person, with intent to deprive the other person of any part of its value or use, commits theft, a Class D felony. However, the offense is a Class C felony if the fair market value of the property is at least one hundred thousand dollars ($100,000).

Evidence from which elements of theft or conversion may be presumed . . .

(a)   The price tag or price marking on property displayed or offered for sale constitutes prima facie evidence of the value and ownership of the property.

(b)   Evidence that a person:

(1)   Altered, substituted, or transferred a label, price tag, or price marking on property displayed or offered for sale or hire; or

(2)   Transferred property displayed or offered for sale or hire from the package, bag, or container in or on which the property was displayed or offered to another package, bag, or container; constitutes prima facie evidence of intent to deprive the owner of the property of a part of its value and that the person exerted unauthorized control over the property.

(c)   Evidence that a person:

(1)   Concealed property displayed or offered for sale or hire; and

(2)   Removed the property from any place within the business premises at which it was displayed or offered to a point beyond that at which payment should be made; constitutes prima facie evidence of intent to deprive the owner of the property of a part of its value and that the person exerted unauthorized control over the property.

IOWA

1.   Arrest by Private Persons
(804.9, 804.10, 804.13, 804.14, 804.24, Iowa Code Ann.)

A private person may make an arrest:

1.   For a public offense committed or attempted in the person's presence.

2.   When a felony has been committed, and the person has reasonable ground for believing that the person to be arrested has committed it.

A private person who makes or assists another private person in making a lawful arrest is justified in using any force which the person reasonably believes to be necessary to make the arrest or which the person reasonably believes to be necessary to prevent serious injury to any person.

A private person who is summoned or directed by a peace officer to assist in making an arrest may use whatever force the peace officer could use under the circumstances, provided that, if the arrest is unlawful, the private person assisting the officer shall be justified as if the arrest were a lawful arrest, unless the person knows that the arrest is unlawful.

A peace officer or other person who has an arrested person in custody is justified in the use of such force to prevent the escape of the arrested person from custody as the officer or other person would be justified in using if the officer or other person were arresting such person.

The person making the arrest must inform the person to be arrested of the intention to arrest the person, the reason for arrest, and that the person making the arrest is a peace officer, if such be the case, and require the person being arrested to submit to the person's custody, except when the person to be arrested is actually engaged in the commission of or attempt to commit an offense, or escapes, so that there is no time or opportunity to do so; if acting under the authority of a warrant, the law enforcement officer need not have the warrant in the officer's possession at the time of the arrest, but upon request the officer shall show the warrant to the person being arrested as soon as possible. If the officer does not have the warrant in the officer's possession at the time of arrest, the officer shall inform the person being arrested of the fact that a warrant has been issued.

A private citizen who has arrested another for the commission of an offense must, without unnecessary delay, take the arrested person before a magistrate, or deliver the arrested person to a peace officer, who may take the arrested person before a magistrate, but the person making the arrest must also accompany the officer before the magistrate.

2.   Detention
(808.12, Iowa Code Ann.)

1. Persons concealing property as set forth in section 714.5 [reproduced below in 3] may be detained and searched by a peace officer, person employed in a facility containing library materials, merchant, or merchant's employee, provided that the detention is for a reasonable length of time and that the search is conducted in a reasonable manner by a person of the same sex and according to subsection 2 of this section.
2. No search of the person under this section shall be conducted by any person other than someone acting under the direction of a peace officer except where permission of the one to be searched has first been obtained.
3. The detention or search under this section by a peace officer, person employed in a facility containing library materials, merchant, or merchant's employee does not render the person liable, in a criminal or civil action, for false arrest or false imprisonment provided the person conducting the search or detention had reasonable grounds to believe the person detained or searched had concealed or was attempting to conceal property as set forth in section 714.5.

3. Theft
(Secs. 714.1 and 714.5, Iowa Code Ann.)

A person commits theft when the person does any of the following:

Takes possession or control of the property of another, or property in the possession of another, with the intent to deprive the other thereof.

The fact that a person has concealed library materials or equipment as defined in section 702.22 or unpurchased property of a store or other mercantile establishment, either on the premises or outside the premises, is material evidence of intent to deprive the owner, and the finding of library materials or equipment or unpurchased property concealed upon the person or among the belongings of the person, is material evidence of intent to deprive and, if the person conceals or causes to be concealed library materials or equipment or unpurchased property, upon the person or among the belongings of another, the finding of the concealed materials, equipment or property is also material evidence of intent to deprive on the part of the person concealing the library materials, equipment or goods.

KANSAS

1. Arrest by Private Persons
(21-3216, Kans. Gen. Stats.)

A private person who makes, or assists another private person in making a lawful arrest is justified in the use of any force which he would be justified in using if he were summoned or directed by a law enforcement officer to make such arrest, except that he is justified in the use of force likely to cause death or great bodily harm only when he reasonably believes that such force is necessary to prevent death or great bodily harm to himself or another.

2. Detention
(21-3424(3), Kans. Gen. Stats.)

Any merchant, or a merchant's agent or employee, who has probable cause to believe that a person has actual possession of and has wrongfully taken, or is about to wrongfully take merchandise from a mercantile establishment, may detain such person on the premises or in the immediate vicinity thereof, in a reasonable manner and for a reasonable period of time for the purpose of investigating the circumstances of such possession. Such reasonable detention shall not constitute an arrest nor criminal restraint.

3. Theft
(21-3701, Kans. Stats. Ann.)

Theft is any of the following acts done with intent to deprive the owner permanently of the possession, use or benefit of the owner's property:

(a) Obtaining or exerting unauthorized control over property; or
(b) obtaining by deception control over property; or

(c) obtaining by threat control over property; or

(d) obtaining control over stolen property knowing the property to have been stolen by another.

[Penalties for theft are imposed based on the value of the property taken.]

KENTUCKY

1. Arrest by Private Citizens
(431.005(4) and 431-025(1) Ky. Rev. Stats.)

A private person may make an arrest when a felony has been committed in fact and he has probable cause to believe that the person being arrested has committed it.

The person making an arrest shall inform the person about to be arrested of the intention to arrest him, and of the offense for which he is being arrested.

2. Detention
(433.236 Ky. Rev. Stats.)

(1) A peace officer, security agent of a mercantile establishment, merchant or merchant's employee who has probable cause for believing that goods held for sale by the merchant have been unlawfully taken by a person may take the person into custody and detain him in a reasonable manner for a reasonable length of time, on the premises of the mercantile establishment or off the premises of the mercantile establishment, if the persons enumerated in this section are in fresh pursuit, for any or all of the following purposes:

(a) To request identification;

(b) To verify such identification;

(c) To make reasonable inquiry as to whether such person has in his possession unpurchased merchandise, and to make reasonable investigation of the ownership of such merchandise;

(d) To recover or attempt to recover goods taken from the mercantile establishment by such person, or by others accompanying him;

(e) To inform a peace officer or law enforcement agency of the detention of the person and to surrender the person to the custody of a peace officer, and in the case of a minor, to inform the parents, guardian, or other person having custody of that minor of his detention, in addition to surrendering the minor to the custody of a peace officer.

(2) The recovery of goods taken from the mercantile establishment by the person detained or by others shall not limit the right of the persons named in subsection (1) of this section to detain such person for peace officers or otherwise accomplish the purposes of subsection (1).

(3) Any peace officer may arrest without warrant any person he has probable cause for believing has committed larceny in retail or wholesale establishments.

3.   Shoplifting/Theft
(433.234 Ky. Rev. Stats.)

(1)   Wilful concealment of unpurchased merchandise of any store or other mercantile establishment on the premises of such store shall be prima facie evidence of an intent to deprive the owner of his property without paying the purchase price therefor.

(2)   All city and county law enforcement agencies shall cause to be made a photograph, a set of fingerprints and a general descriptive report of all persons except juveniles arrested for theft through an act of shoplifting. If convicted, two (2) copies of each item shall be forwarded within thirty (30) days to the Department of State Police of the Justice Cabinet.

(514.030 Ky. Rev. Stats.)

(1)   A person is guilty of theft by unlawful taking or disposition when he unlawfully:
   (a)   Takes or exercises control over movable property of another with intent to deprive him thereof; or
   (b)   Obtains immovable property of another or any interest therein with intent to benefit himself or another not entitled thereto.

(2)   Theft by unlawful taking or disposition is a Class A misdemeanor unless the value of the property is three hundred dollars ($300) or more, or unless the property is a firearm (regardless of the value of the firearm), in which case it is a Class D felony.

LOUISIANA
1.   Arrest by Private Persons
(Arts. 214, 218, 226, and 227, La. Code Crim. Proc. Ann.)

A private person may make an arrest when the person arrested has committed a felony, whether in or out of his presence.

[. . .] A private person, when making an arrest, shall inform the person to be arrested of his intention to arrest him and of the cause of the arrest.

The [. . .] private person making the arrest need not so inform the person to be arrested if the person is then engaged in the commission of an offense, or is pursued immediately after its commission or after an escape, or flees or forcibly resists before the [. . .] person making the arrest has an opportunity to so inform him, or when the giving of the information would imperil the arrest.

A private person who has made an arrest shall immediately turn the prisoner and all effects removed from him over to a peace officer.

If a person lawfully arrested escapes or is rescued, the person from whose custody he escaped or was rescued may pursue and retake him immediately without a warrant at any time and in any place within the state. He may use the same means to retake as are authorized for an arrest.

2.   Detention
(Arts. 215, La. Code Crim. Proc. Ann.)

A.   (1)   A peace officer, merchant, or a specifically authorized employee or agent of a merchant, may use reasonable force to detain a person for questioning on the merchant's premises, for a length of time, not to exceed sixty minutes, unless it is reasonable under the circumstances that the person be detained longer, when he has reasonable cause to believe that the person has committed a theft of goods held for sale by the merchant, regardless of the actual value of the goods. The merchant or his employee or agent may also detain such a person for arrest by a peace officer. The detention shall not constitute an arrest.

(2)   A peace officer may, without a warrant, arrest a person when he has reasonable grounds to believe the person has committed a theft of goods held for sale by a merchant, regardless of the actual value of the goods. A complaint made to a peace officer by a merchant or a merchant's employee or agent shall constitute reasonable cause for the officer making the arrest.

B.   If a merchant utilizes electronic devices which are designed to detect the unauthorized removal of marked merchandise from the store, and if sufficient notice has been posted to advise the patrons that such a device is being utilized, a signal from the device to the merchant or his employee or agent indicating the removal of specially marked merchandise shall constitute a sufficient basis for reasonable cause to detain the person.

C.   As used in this Article, "reasonable under the circumstances" shall be construed in such a manner so as to include the value of the merchandise in question, the location of the store, the length of time taken for law enforcement personnel to respond, the cooperation of the person detained, and any other relevant circumstances to be considered with respect to the length of time a person is detained.

[Louisiana has a unique provision in its Constitution (Art. 1, Sec. 13) and in its Code of Criminal Procedure (Art. 218.1) which reads as follows: "When any person has been arrested or detained in connection with the investigation or commission of any offense, he shall be advised fully of the reason for his arrest or detention, his right to remain silent, his right against self incrimination, his right to the assistance of counsel and, if indigent, his right to court appointed counsel." The implication of the phraseology and the history of the constitutional provision and the statute is that they apply only to police arrests and detentions. This is substantiated by the fact that the constitutional provision was incorporated in the 1974 Constitution and the statutory implementation was enacted in 1975. The foregoing Art. 215 on arrest and detention of shoplifters was enacted in 1976.]

3. Theft
(14.67, La. Rev. Stats.)

A.   Theft is the misappropriation or taking of anything of value which belongs to another, either without the consent of the other to the misappropriation or taking, or by means of fraudulent conduct, practices, or representations. An intent to deprive the other permanently of whatever may be the subject of the misappropriation or taking is essential.

B.   (1)   Whoever commits the crime of theft when the misappropriation or taking amounts to a value of five hundred dollars or more shall be imprisoned, with or without hard labor, for not more than ten years, or may be fined not more than three thousand dollars, or both.

(2)   When the misappropriation or taking amounts to a value of one hundred dollars or more, but less than a value of five hundred dollars, the offender

shall be imprisoned, with or without hard labor, for not more than two years, or may be fined not more than two thousand dollars, or both.

(3) When the misappropriation or taking amounts to less than a value of one hundred dollars, the offender shall be imprisoned for not more than six months, or may be fined not more than five hundred dollars, or both. If the offender in such cases has been convicted of theft two or more times previously, upon any subsequent conviction he shall be imprisoned, with or without hard labor, for not more than two years, or may be fined not more than one thousand dollars, or both.

C. When there has been a misappropriation or taking by a number of distinct acts of the offender, the aggregate of the amount of the misappropriations or taking shall determine the grade of the offense.

MAINE

1. Arrest by Private Persons
(Tit. 17-A, 16, Me. Rev. Stats.)

Except as otherwise specifically provided, a private person shall have the authority to arrest without a warrant:

1. Any person who he has probable cause to believe has committed or is committing:
   A. Murder; or
   B. [Felonies]
2. Any person who, in fact, is committing in his presence and in a public place:
   A. [Misdemeanors.]

2. Detention
(17-3521, Me. Rev. Stats.)

A store owner, manager or supervisor, or that person's designee, may detain on the premises in a reasonable manner and for a period of time not to exceed 1/2 hour any person as to whom there is probable cause to believe is unlawfully concealing merchandise. The purposes of detention shall be: To require the person being detained to provide identification; to verify the identification; to inform a law enforcement officer of the detention and to surrender that person to the officer; and when the detained person is a minor, to inform a law enforcement officer or the parents or guardian of the minor of the detention and to surrender the minor to the person so informed.

[According to Tit. 17-A, Sec. 107, a private person is justified in using "a reasonable degree of nondeadly force upon another when and to the extent that he reasonably believes it necessary to effect an arrest or detention which is lawful for him to make or prevent the escape from such an arrest or detention; or B. Deadly force only when the person reasonably believes such force is necessary: (1) To defend the person or a 3rd person from what the private citizen reasonably believes to be the imminent use of deadly force; or (2) To effect a lawful arrest or prevent the escape from such arrest of a person who in fact: (a) Has committed a crime involving the use or threatened use of deadly force, or is using a dangerous weapon in attempting to escape; and (b) The private citizen has made reasonable efforts to advise the person that the citizen is a private citizen attempting to effect an arrest or prevent the escape from arrest and has reasonable grounds to believe the person is aware of this advice or the citizen reasonably believes that the person to be arrested otherwise knows that the citizen is a private citizen attempting to effect an arrest or prevent the escape from arrest."]

3. Theft/Shoplifting
(353, 351, Me. Rev. Stats.)

A person is guilty of theft if he obtains or exercises unauthorized control over the property of another with intent to deprive him thereof.

["Theft" specifically includes, according to Sec. 351, shoplifting; and in Sec. 352(5)(A), the value of stolen property "means the market value of the property [. . .] at the time and place of the crime, or if such cannot be satisfactorily ascertained, the cost of replacement of [. . .] within a reasonable time after the crime."]

MARYLAND

1. Arrest by Private Persons

[The only Maryland statute pertaining to arrest by private persons is Art. 27, Sec. 294C, Md. Ann. Code, which accords a limited right during times of public emergency. However, according to Art. 41, Sec. 4-905, a security officer appointed as a "special policeman," pursuant to an application of his employer, possesses broad police powers similar to those of a public police officer.]

2. Detention
(5-307, Courts and Judicial Proceedings, Md. Ann. Code.)

A merchant or an agent or employee of the merchant who detains or causes the arrest of any person shall not be held civilly liable for detention, slander, malicious prosecution, false imprisonment, or false arrest of the person detained or arrested, whether the detention or arrest takes place by the merchant or by his agent or employee, if in detaining or in causing the arrest of the person, the merchant or the agent or employee of the merchant had, at the time of the detention or arrest, probable cause to believe that the person committed the crime of "theft," [. . .] of property of the merchant from the premises of the merchant.

3. Theft/Shoplifting
(Art. 27, 341, Md. Ann. Code)

Conduct designated as theft in this subheading constitutes a single crime embracing, among others, the separate crimes heretofore known as larceny, larceny by trick, larceny after trust, embezzlement, false pretenses, shoplifting, and receiving stolen property. An accusation of theft may be proved by evidence that it was committed in any manner that would be theft under this subheading, notwithstanding the specification of a different manner in the information, indictment, warrant, or other charging document, subject only to the power of the court to ensure a fair trial by granting a continuance or other appropriate relief if the conduct of the defense would be prejudiced by lack of fair notice or by surprise.

MASSACHUSETTS

1. Arrest by Private Persons

[No statutory provision, but consider the following from Ch. 266, 30A: "The statement of a merchant or his employee or agent that a person has [committed shoplifting] shall constitute probable cause for arrest by any law enforcement officer . . . "]

2. Detention
(Ch. 231, 94B, Mass. Ann. Laws)

In an action for false arrest or false imprisonment brought by any person by reason of having been detained for questioning on or in the immediate vicinity of the premises of a merchant or an innkeeper, if such person was detained in a reasonable manner and for not more than a reasonable length of time by a person authorized to make arrests or by the merchant or innkeeper or his agent or servant authorized for such purpose and if there were reasonable grounds to believe that the person so detained was committing or attempting to commit a violation of section thirty A of chapter two hundred and sixty-six, or section twelve of chapter one hundred and forty, or was committing or attempting to commit larceny of goods for sale on such premises or larceny of the personal property of employees or customers or others present on such premises, it shall be a defense to such action.

3. Shoplifting/Alteration of Price Tag/Theft of Shopping Cart
(Ch. 266, 30A, Mass. Ann. Laws)

Any person who intentionally takes possession of, carries away, transfers or causes to be carried away or transferred, any merchandise displayed, held, stored or offered for sale by any store or other retail mercantile establishment with the intention of depriving the merchant of the possession, use of benefit of such merchandise or converting the same to the use of such person without paying to the merchant the value thereof; or

Any person who intentionally conceals upon his person or otherwise any merchandise offered for sale by any store or other retail mercantile establishment with the intention of depriving the merchant of proceeds, use or benefit of such merchandise or converting the same to the use of such person without paying to the merchant the value thereof; or

Any person who intentionally alters, transfers or removes any label, price tag or marking indicia of value or any other markings which aid in determining value affixed to any merchandise displayed, held, stored or offered for sale by any store or other retail mercantile establishment and to attempt to purchase such merchandise personally or in consort with another at less than the full retail value with the intention of depriving the merchant of all or some part of the retail value thereof; or

Any person who intentionally transfers any merchandise displayed, held, stored or offered for sale by any store or other retail mercantile establishment from the container in or on which the same shall be displayed to any other container with intent to deprive the merchant of all or some part of the retail value thereof; or

Any person who intentionally records a value for the merchandise which is less than the actual retail value with the intention of depriving the merchant of the full retail value thereof; or

Any person who intentionally removes a shopping cart from the premises of a store or other retail mercantile establishment without the consent of the merchant given at the time of such removal with the intention of permanently depriving the merchant of the possession, use or benefit of such cart, shall be punished for a first offense by a fine not to exceed two hundred and fifty dollars, for a second offense by a fine of not less than one hundred dollars nor more than five hundred dollars and for a third or subsequent offense by a fine of not more than five hundred dollars or imprisonment in jail for not more than two years, or both such fine and imprisonment.

Law enforcement officers may arrest without warrant any person he has probable cause for believing has committed the offense of shoplifting as defined in this section. The statement of a merchant or his employee or agent that a person has violated a provision of this section shall constitute probable cause for arrest by any law enforcement officer authorized to make an arrest in such jurisdiction.

[Massachusetts has a general larceny statute, Ch. 266, 30, which embraces the stealing of any property, regardless of whether it is or is not in the taker's possession at the time of its conversion.]

MICHIGAN

1. Arrest by Private Persons
(28.875, 879, 873, Mich. Stats. Ann.)

A private person may make an arrest in the following situations:

(a) For a felony committed in the private person's presence.

(b) If the person to be arrested has committed a felony although not in the private person's presence.

(c) If the private person is summoned by a peace officer to assist the officer in making an arrest.

(d) If the private person is a merchant, an agent of a merchant, an employee of a merchant, or an independent contractor providing security for a merchant of a store and has reasonable cause to believe that the person to be arrested has violated section 356c or 356d of the Michigan penal code, Act No. 328 of the Public Acts of 1931, being sections 750.356c and 750.356d of the Michigan Compiled Laws, in that store, regardless of whether the violation was committed in the presence of the private person.

A private person, before making an arrest, shall inform the person to be arrested of the intention to arrest him and the cause of the arrest, except when he is then engaged in the commission of a criminal offense, or if he flees or forcibly resists arrest before the person making the arrest has opportunity so to inform him.

A private person who has made an arrest shall without unnecessary delay deliver the person arrested to a peace officer, who shall without unnecessary delay take that person before a magistrate of the judicial district in which the offense is charged to have been committed. The peace officer or private person shall present to the magistrate a complaint stating the charge against the person arrested.

2. Detention
(27A.2917, Mich. Stats. Ann.)

(1)   In a civil action against a library or merchant, an agent of the library or merchant, or an independent contractor providing security for the library or merchant for false imprisonment, unlawful arrest, assault, battery, libel, or slander, if the claim arises out of conduct involving a person suspected of removing or of attempting to remove, without right or permission, goods held for sale in a store from the store or library materials from a library, [. . .] and if the merchant, library, agent, or independent contractor had probable cause for believing and did believe that the plaintiff had committed or aided or abetted in the larceny of goods held for sale in the store, or of library materials, [. . .] damages for or resulting from mental anguish or punitive, exemplary, or aggravated damages shall not be allowed a plaintiff, unless it is proved that the merchant, library, agent, or independent contractor used unreasonable force, detained the plaintiff an unreasonable length of time, acted with unreasonable disregard of the plaintiff's rights or sensibilities, or acted with intent to injure the plaintiff.

3. Larceny
(28.588, Mich. Stats. Ann.)

Any person who shall commit the offense of larceny, by stealing, of the property of another, any money, goods or chattels, or any bank note, bank bill, bond, promissory note, due bill, bill of exchange or other bill, draft, order or certificate, or any book of accounts for or concerning money or goods due or to become due, or to be delivered, or any deed or writing containing a conveyance of land, or any other valuable contract in force, or any receipt, release or defeasance, or any writ, process or public record, if the property stolen exceed the value of $100.00, shall be guilty of a felony, punishable by imprisonment in the state prison not more than 5 years or by fine of not more than $ 2,500.00. If the property stolen shall be of the value of $100.00 or less, such person shall be guilty of a misdemeanor.

MINNESOTA

1.   Arrest by Private Persons
(629.37, 38, and 39, Minn. Stats. Ann.)

A private person may arrest another:

(1)   for a public offense committed or attempted in the arresting person's presence;
(2)   when the person arrested has committed a felony, although not in the arresting person's presence; or
(3)   when a felony has in fact been committed, and the arresting person has reasonable cause for believing the person arrested to have committed it.

Before making an arrest a private person shall inform the person to be arrested of the cause of the arrest and require the person to submit. The warning required by this section need not be given if the person is arrested while committing the offense or when the person is arrested on pursuit immediately after committing the offense. If a person has committed a felony, a private person may break open an outer or inner door or window of a dwelling house to make the arrest if, before entering, the private person informs the person to be arrested of the intent to make the arrest and the private person is then refused admittance.

A private person who arrests another for a public offense shall take the arrested person before a judge or to a peace officer without unnecessary delay. If a person arrested escapes, the person from whose custody the person has escaped may immediately pursue and retake the escapee, at any time and in any place in the state. For that purpose, the pursuer may break open any door or window of a dwelling house if the pursuer informs the escapee of the intent to arrest the escapee and the pursuer is refused admittance.

2.   Detention
(629.366, Minn. Stats. Ann.)

Subdivision 1. Circumstances justifying detention.

(a)   A merchant or merchant's employee may detain a person if the merchant or employee has reasonable cause to believe:
   (1)   that the person has taken, or is taking, an article of value without paying for it, from the possession of the merchant in the merchant's place of business or from a vehicle or premises under the merchant's control;
   (2)   that the taking is done with the intent to wrongfully deprive the merchant of the property or the use or benefit of it; or
   (3)   that the taking is done with the intent to appropriate the use of the property to the taker or any other person.

(b)   Subject to the limitations in paragraph (a), a merchant or merchant's employee may detain a person for any of the following purposes:
   (1)   to require the person to provide identification or verify identification;
   (2)   to inquire as to whether the person possesses unpurchased merchandise taken from the merchant and, if so, to receive the merchandise;
   (3)   to inform a peace officer; or
   (4)   to institute criminal proceedings against the person.

(c)   The person detained shall be informed promptly of the purpose of the detention and may not be subjected to unnecessary or unreasonable force, nor to interrogation against the person's will. A merchant or merchant's employee may not detain a person for more than one hour unless:
   (1)   the merchant or employee is waiting to surrender the person to a peace officer, in which case the person may be detained until a peace officer has accepted custody of or released the person; or
   (2)   the person is a minor, or claims to be, and the merchant or employee is waiting to surrender the minor to a peace officer or the minor's parent, guardian, or custodian, in which case the minor may be detained until the peace officer, parent, guardian, or custodian has accepted custody of the minor.

(d)   If at any time the person detained requests that a peace officer be summoned, the merchant or merchant's employee must notify a peace officer immediately.

Subd. 2. Arrest. Upon a charge being made by a merchant or merchant's employee, a peace officer may arrest a person without a warrant, if the officer has reasonable cause for believing that the person has committed or attempted to commit the offense described in subdivision 1.

Subd. 3. Immunity. No merchant, merchant's employee, or peace officer is criminally or civilly liable for any action authorized under subdivision 1 or 2 if the arresting person's action is based upon reasonable cause.

3. Theft
(609.52, Minn. Stats. Ann.)

Acts constituting theft. Whoever does any of the following commits theft [. . .]:

Intentionally and without claim of right takes, uses, transfers, conceals or retains possession of movable property of another without the other's consent and with intent to deprive the owner permanently of possession of the property; or

Having a legal interest in movable property, intentionally and without consent, takes the property out of the possession of a pledgee or other person having a superior right of possession, with intent thereby to deprive the pledgee or other person permanently of the possession of the property; or

Alters, removes, or obliterates numbers or symbols placed on movable property for purpose of identification by the owner or person who has legal custody or right to possession thereof with the intent to prevent identification, if the person who alters, removes, or obliterates the numbers or symbols is not the owner and does not have the permission of the owner to make the alteration, removal, or obliteration; or

With the intent to prevent the identification of property involved, so as to deprive the rightful owner of possession thereof, alters or removes any permanent serial number, permanent distinguishing number or manufacturer's identification number on personal property or possesses, sells or buys any personal property with knowledge that the permanent serial number, permanent distinguishing number or manufacturer's identification number has been removed or altered.

4. Possession of Shoplifting Gear
(609.521, Minn. Stats. Ann.)

Whoever has in possession any device, gear, or instrument specially designed to assist in shoplifting with intent to use the same to shoplift and thereby commit theft may be sentenced to imprisonment for not more than three years or to payment of a fine of not more than $5,000, or both.

MISSISSIPPI

1. Arrest by Private Persons
(99-3-1, 99-3-7, Miss. Code Ann.)

Arrests for crimes and offenses may be made by the sheriff or his deputy or by any constable or conservator of the peace within his county, or by any marshal or policeman of a city, town or village within the same, or, when in cooperation with local law enforcement officers, by any federal law enforcement officer who is employed by the

United States government, authorized to effect an arrest for a violation of the United States Code, and authorized to carry a firearm in the performance of his duties. Private persons may also make arrests.

An officer or private person may arrest any person without warrant, for an indictable offense committed, or a breach of the peace threatened or attempted in his presence; or when a person has committed a felony, though not in his presence; or when a felony has been committed, and he has reasonable ground to suspect and believe the person proposed to be arrested to have committed it; or on a charge, made upon reasonable cause, of the commission of a felony by the party proposed to be arrested. And in all cases of arrests without warrant, the person making such arrest must inform the accused of the object and cause of the arrest, except when he is in the actual commission of the offense, or is arrested on pursuit.

2. Detention
(97-23-95, Miss. Code Ann.)

If any person shall commit or attempt to commit the offense of shoplifting, or if any person shall wilfully conceal upon his person or otherwise any unpurchased goods, wares or merchandise held or owned by any store or mercantile establishment, the merchant or any employee thereof or any peace or police officer, acting in good faith and upon probable cause based upon reasonable grounds therefor, may question such person in a reasonable manner for the purpose of ascertaining whether or not such person is guilty of shoplifting as defined herein. Such questioning of a person by a merchant, merchant's employee or peace or police officer shall not render such merchant, merchant's employee or peace or police officer civilly liable for slander, false arrest, false imprisonment, malicious prosecution, unlawful detention or otherwise in any case where such merchant, merchant's employee or peace or police officer acts in good faith and upon reasonable grounds to believe that the person questioned is committing or attempting to commit the crime of shoplifting.

3. Shoplifting/Civil Liability for Shoplifting
(97-23-93, Miss. Code Ann.)

(1) Any person who shall wilfully and unlawfully take possession of any merchandise owned or held by and offered or displayed for sale by any merchant, store or other mercantile establishment with the intention and purpose of converting such merchandise to his own use without paying the merchant's stated price therefor shall be guilty of the crime of shoplifting and, upon conviction, shall be punished as is provided in this section.

(2) The requisite intention to convert merchandise without paying the merchant's stated price for the merchandise is presumed, and shall be prima facie evidence thereof, when such person, alone or in concert with another person, wilfully:
   (a) Conceals the unpurchased merchandise;
   (b) Removes or causes the removal of unpurchased merchandise from a store or other mercantile establishment;
   (c) Alters, transfers or removes any price-marking, any other marking which aids in determining value affixed to the unpurchased merchandise, or any tag or device used in electronic surveillance of unpurchased merchandise;

    (d)   Transfers the unpurchased merchandise from one container to another; or

    (e)   Causes the cash register or other sales recording device to reflect less than the merchant's stated price for the unpurchased merchandise.

(3) Evidence of stated price or ownership of merchandise may include, but is not limited to:

    (a)   The actual merchandise or the container which held the merchandise alleged to have been shoplifted; or

    (b)   The content of the price tag or marking from such merchandise; or

    (c)   Properly identified photographs of such merchandise.

(4) Any merchant or his agent or employee may testify at a trial as to the stated price or ownership of merchandise.

(5) A person convicted of shoplifting merchandise for which the merchant's stated price is less than or equal to Two Hundred Fifty Dollars ($250.00) shall be punished as follows:

    (a)   Upon a first shoplifting conviction the defendant shall be guilty of a misdemeanor and fined not more than Seven Hundred Fifty Dollars ($750.00), or punished by imprisonment not to exceed thirty (30) days, or by both such fine and imprisonment.

    (b)   Upon a second shoplifting conviction the defendant shall be guilty of a misdemeanor and fined not more than One Thousand Dollars ($1,000.00) or punished by imprisonment not to exceed ninety (90) days, or by both such fine and imprisonment.

(6) Upon a third or subsequent shoplifting conviction the defendant shall be guilty of a felony and fined not more than One Thousand Dollars ($1,000.00), or imprisoned for a term not exceeding five (5) years, or by both such fine and imprisonment.

(7) A person convicted of shoplifting merchandise for which the merchant's stated price exceeds Two Hundred Fifty Dollars ($250.00) shall be guilty of a felony and, upon conviction, punished as provided in Section 97-17-41 for the offense of grand larceny.

(8) In determining the number of prior shoplifting convictions for purposes of imposing punishment under this section, the court shall disregard all such convictions occurring more than seven (7) years prior to the shoplifting offense in question.

(97-23-96, Miss. Code Ann.)

(1) Any person who proves by clear and convincing evidence that he has been injured in any fashion by reason of any violation of the provisions of Section 97-23-93, Mississippi Code of 1972, has a cause of action for threefold the actual damages sustained or damages in the amount of Two Hundred Dollars ($200.00), whichever is greater, reasonable attorney's fees and court costs in the trial and in any proceedings in appellate courts. The recovery of stolen goods regardless of condition shall not affect the right to the minimum recovery provided herein.

(2) Before filing an action for damages under this section, the person claiming injury must make a written demand for Two Hundred Dollars ($200.00) or threefold the actual damages sustained, whichever is greater, of the person or accused liable for damages under this section. If the accused to whom a written demand is made complies with such demand within thirty (30) days after receipt of the demand, he shall be given a written release from further civil liability for the specific act of shoplifting by the victim making the written demand.

(3) Any victim who has a cause of action under this section may recover the damages allowed under this section from the parents or legal guardian of any unemancipated minor who lives with his parents or legal guardian and who is liable for damages under this section if it is proven that the parents or legal guardian had knowledge of the minor's intent to violate the provisions of Section 97-23-93 or aided and abetted the minor in such violations. Foster parents shall not be liable for the acts of children placed with them.

Nothing in this section shall in any way be construed as to abrogate, compromise or violate any minor's right to confidentiality under any other provision of the Mississippi Code of 1972 or otherwise.

(4) In no event shall punitive damages be awarded under this section.

(5) In awarding damages, attorney's fees, expenses or costs under this section, the court shall not consider the ability of the opposing party to pay such fees and costs. Nothing under this section shall be interpreted as limiting any right to recover damages, attorney's fees, expenses or costs provided under other provisions of law.

MISSOURI

1. Arrest by Private Persons

[No statute except one, 563.051, which prescribes the limitations upon use of force in making an arrest.]

2. Detention
(537.125, Mo. Stats. Ann.)

Any merchant, his agent or employee, who has reasonable grounds or probable cause to believe that a person has committed or is committing a wrongful taking of merchandise or money from a mercantile establishment, may detain such person in a reasonable manner and for a reasonable length of time for the purpose of investigating whether there has been a wrongful taking of such merchandise or money. Any such reasonable detention shall not constitute an unlawful arrest or detention, nor shall it render the merchant, his agent or employee, criminally or civilly liable to the person so detained.

Any person willfully concealing unpurchased merchandise of any mercantile establishment, either on the premises or outside the premises of such establishment, shall be presumed to have so concealed such merchandise with the intention of committing a wrongful taking of such merchandise within the meaning of subsection 1, and the finding of such unpurchased merchandise concealed upon the person or among the belongings of such person shall be evidence of reasonable grounds and probable cause for the detention in a reasonable manner and for a reasonable length of time, of such person by a merchant, his agent or employee, in order that recovery of such merchandise may be effected, and any such reasonable detention shall not be deemed to be unlawful, nor render such merchant, his agent or employee criminally or civilly liable.

Any merchant, his agent or employee, who has reasonable grounds or probable cause to believe that a person has committed a wrongful taking of property, as defined in this section, and who has detained such person and investigated such wrongful taking, may contact law enforcement officers and instigate criminal proceedings against such person. Any such contact of law enforcement authorities or instigation of a judicial proceeding shall not constitute malicious prosecution, nor shall it render the merchant, his agent or employee criminally or civilly liable to the person so detained or against whom proceedings are instigated.

3. Stealing
(570.030, Mo. Stats. Ann.)

A person commits the crime of stealing if he appropriates property or services of another with the purpose to deprive him thereof, either without his consent or by means of deceit or coercion.

MONTANA

1. Arrest by Private Persons
(46-6-502, Mont. Code Ann.)

A private person may arrest another when there is probable cause to believe that the person is committing or has committed an offense and the existing circumstances require the person's immediate arrest.

A private person making an arrest shall immediately notify the nearest available law enforcement agency or peace officer and give custody of the person arrested to the officer or agency.

2. Detention
(46-6-506, 30-11-302, Mont. Code Ann.)

(1) A merchant, [. . .] who has reason to believe that a person has committed or is in the process of committing the offense of theft may stop and temporarily detain that person. The merchant:
   (a) shall promptly inform the person that the stop is for investigation of shoplifting and that upon completion of the investigation, the person will be released or turned over to the custody of a peace officer;
   (b) may demand the person's name and present or last address and question the person in a reasonable manner for the purpose of ascertaining whether or not the person is guilty of shoplifting;
   (c) may take into possession any merchandise for which the purchase price has not been paid and that is in the possession of the person or has been concealed from full view; and
   (d) may detain the person or request the person to remain on the premises until a peace officer arrives.
(2) A stop, detention, questioning, or recovery of merchandise under this section must be done in a reasonable manner and time. Unless evidence of concealment is obvious and apparent to the merchant, this section does not authorize a search of the detained person other than a search of the person's coat or other outer garments and any package, bag, or other container. After the purpose of a stop

has been accomplished or 30 minutes have elapsed, whichever occurs first, the merchant shall allow the person to go unless the person is arrested and turned over to the custody of a peace officer.

(3)   A merchant stopping, detaining, or arresting a person on the belief that the person is shoplifting is not liable for damages to the person unless the merchant acts in a manner contrary to this section.

(4)   As used in this section, the following definitions apply:

   (a)   "Concealment" means any act or deception done purposely or knowingly upon or outside the premises of a wholesale or retail store or other mercantile establishment, with the intent to deprive the merchant of all or part of the value of the merchandise. The following acts or deceptive conduct is prima facie evidence of concealment:

      (i)   concealing merchandise upon the person or in a container or otherwise removing merchandise from full view while upon the premises;

      (ii)   removing, changing, or altering a price tag;

      (iii) transferring or moving any merchandise upon the premises to obtain a lower price than the merchandise was offered for sale for by the merchant; or

      (iv)   abandoning or disposing of any merchandise in such a manner that the merchant will be deprived of all or part of the value of the merchandise.

   (b)   "Shoplifting" means the theft of any goods offered for sale by a wholesale or retail store or other mercantile establishment.

[Note of caution: The Supreme Court of Montana has declared unconstitutional that part of the detention statute regarding the thiry minute detention period. The court specifically stated, however, that it left "in force and effect" the provision "that any ston detention, questioning or recovery of merchandise under the statute shall be done in a reasonable manner and time." Duran v. Buttrey Food, Inc., 616 P.2d 327 (Mont. 1980). The court also ruled that its decision did not affect the merchant's right to make an arrest, as provided in the foregoing Sec. 46-6-502.]

Any merchant shall have the right to request any individual on his premises to place or keep in full view any merchandise such individual may have removed, or which the merchant has reason to believe he may have removed, from its place of display or elsewhere, whether for examination, purchase, or for any other purpose. No merchant shall be criminally or civilly liable for slander, false arrest, or otherwise on account of having made such a request.

3.   Theft
(45-6-301, Mont. Code Ann.)

(1)   A person commits the offense of theft when the person purposely or knowingly obtains or exerts unauthorized control over property of the owner and:

   (a)   has the purpose of depriving the owner of the property;

   (b)   purposely or knowingly uses, conceals, or abandons the property in a manner that deprives the owner of the property; or

   (c)   uses, conceals, or abandons the property knowing that the use, concealment, or abandonment probably will deprive the owner of the property.

(2)   A person commits the offense of theft when the person purposely or knowingly obtains by threat or deception control over property of the owner and:

(a)   has the purpose of depriving the owner of the property;
(b)   purposely or knowingly uses, conceals, or abandons the property in a manner that deprives the owner of the property; or
(c)   uses, conceals, or abandons the property knowing that the use, concealment, or abandonment probably will deprive the owner of the property.

NEBRASKA

1.   Arrest by Private Persons
(29-402 and 29-402.03, Nebr. Rev. Stats.)

Any person not an officer may, without warrant, arrest any person, if a petitlarceny or a felony has been committed, and there is reasonable ground to believe the person arrested guilty of such offense, and may detain him until a legal warrant can be obtained.

A merchant or a merchant's employee who causes the arrest of a person, [. . .] for larceny of goods held for sale shall not be criminally or civilly liable for slander, libel, false arrest, or false imprisonment where the merchant or merchant's employee has probable cause for believing that the person arrested committed larceny of goods held for sale.

2.   Detention
(29-402.01 and 28-315, Nebr. Rev. Stats.)

A peace officer, a merchant, or a merchant's employee who has probable cause for believing that goods held for sale by the merchant have been unlawfully taken by a person and that he can recover them by taking the person into custody may, for the purpose of attempting to effect such recovery, take the person into custody and detain him in a reasonable manner for a reasonable length of time. Such taking into custody and detention by a peace officer, merchant, or merchant's employee shall not render such peace officer, merchant, or merchant's employee criminally or civilly liable for slander, libel, false arrest, false imprisonment, or unlawful detention.

In any prosecution [for false imprisonment, the unlawful restraining of a person], it shall be an affirmative defense that the person restrained (a) was on or in the immediate vicinity of the premises of a retail mercantile establishment and he was restrained for the purpose of investigation or questioning as to the ownership of any merchandise; and (b) was restrained in a reasonable manner and for not more than a reasonable time; and (c) was restrained to permit such investigation or questioning by a police officer, or by the owner of the mercantile establishment, his authorized employee or agent; and (d) that such police officer, owner, employee or agent had reasonable grounds to believe that the person so detained was committing or attempting to commit theft of merchandise on the premises; Provided, nothing in this section shall prohibit or restrict any person restrained pursuant to this section from maintaining any applicable civil remedy if no theft has occurred.

3.   Theft
(Sec. 28-511, Nebr. Rev. Stats.)

A person is guilty of theft if he or she takes, or exercises control over, movable property of another with the intent to deprive him or her thereof.

NEVADA

1. Arrest by Private Persons

(Secs. 171.126, 171.134, 171.1772, and 171.178, Nev. Rev. Stat.)

A private person may arrest another:

1. For a public offense committed or attempted in his presence.
2. When the person arrested has committed a felony, although not in his presence.
3. When a felony has been in fact committed, and he has reasonable cause for believing the person arrested to have committed it.

If a person arrested escapes or is rescued, the person from whose custody he escaped or was rescued may immediately pursue and retake him at any time and in any place within the state.

A private person making an arrest without a warrant shall take the arrested person without unnecessary delay before the nearest available magistrate empowered to commit persons charged with offenses against the laws of the State of Nevada or deliver the arrested person to a peace officer.

Whenever any person is arrested by a private person, [...] for any violation of a county, city or town ordinance or state law which is punishable as a misdemeanor, such person arrested may be issued a misdemeanor citation by a peace officer in lieu of being immediately taken before a magistrate if:

1. The person arrested furnishes satisfactory evidence of identity; and
2. A peace officer has reasonable grounds to believe that the person arrested will keep a written promise to appear in court.

2. Detention

(597.850, Nev. Rev. Stats.)

Any merchant may request any person on his premises to place or keep in full view any merchandise the person may have removed, or which the merchant has reason to believe he may have removed, from its place of display or elsewhere, whether for examination, purchase or for any other purpose. No merchant is criminally or civilly liable on account of having made such a request.

Any merchant who has reason to believe that merchandise has been wrongfully taken by a person and that he can recover the merchandise by taking the person into custody and detaining him may, for the purpose of attempting to effect such recovery or for the purpose of informing a peace officer of the circumstances of such detention, take the person into custody and detain him, on the premises, in a reasonable manner and for a reasonable length of time. Such taking into custody and detention by a merchant does not render the merchant criminally or civilly liable for false arrest, false imprisonment, slander or unlawful detention unless the taking into custody and detention are unreasonable under all the circumstances.

No merchant is entitled to the immunity from liability provided for in this section unless there is displayed in a conspicuous place on his premises a notice in boldface type clearly legible and in substantially the following form:

> Any merchant or his agent who has reason to believe that merchandise has been wrongfully taken by a person may detain such person on the premises of the merchant for the purpose of recovering the property or notifying a peace officer. An

adult or the parents or legal guardian of a minor, who steals merchandise is civilly liable for its value and additional damages. NRS 597.850, 597.860 and 597.870.

The notice must be prepared and copies thereof supplied on demand by the superintendent of the state printing and micrographics division of the department of administration. The superintendent may charge a fee based on the cost for each copy of the notice supplied to any person.

3. Theft
(205.220, 205.240, 597.860, and 597.870, Nev. Rev. Stats.)

[. . .] Every person who feloniously steals, takes and carries away, leads or drives away the personal goods or property of another of the value of $250 or more, or the motor vehicle of another regardless of its value, is guilty of grand larceny, and shall be punished by imprisonment in the state prison for not less than 1 year nor more than 10 years and by a fine of not more than $10,000.

[Every person who:] Steals, takes and carries, leads or drives away the personal goods or property of another, under the value of $250 [. . .] commits petit larceny and is guilty of a misdemeanor.

An adult who steals merchandise from, or damages property on, a merchant's premises is civilly liable for the retail value of the merchandise or the fair market value of the other property, plus damages of not less than $100 nor more than $250, costs of suit and reasonable attorney's fees. An action may be brought even if there has been no criminal conviction for the theft or damage.

The parent or legal guardian, as the case may be, of a minor who steals merchandise from, or damages property on, a merchant's premises is civilly liable for (a) The retail value of the merchandise; and (b) The fair market value of the damaged property, plus damages of not less than $100 nor more than $250, costs of suit and reasonable attorney's fees. An action may be brought even if there has been no criminal conviction for the theft or damage. Recovery under this section may be had in addition to, and is not limited by, any other provision of law which limits the liability of a parent or legal guardian for the tortious conduct of a minor.

NEW HAMPSHIRE

1. Arrest by Private Persons
(627:5(IV), N.H. Rev. Stats. Ann.)

A private person acting on his own is justified in using non-deadly force upon another when and to the extent that he reasonably believes it necessary to arrest or prevent the escape from custody of such other whom he reasonably believes to have committed a felony and who in fact has committed that felony: but he is justified in using deadly force for such purpose only when he reasonably believes it necessary to defend himself or a third person from what he reasonably believes to be the imminent use of deadly force.

2. Detention
(627:8-a, N.H. Rev. Stats. Ann.)

A merchant, or his agent, is justified in detaining any person who he has reasonable grounds to believe has committed the offense of willful concealment or shoplifting, as defined by RSA 644:17, on his premises as long as necessary to surrender the person to a peace officer, provided such detention is conducted in a reasonable manner.

3. Theft/Concealment/Shoplifting
(637:3 and 644:17, N.H. Rev. Stats. Ann.)

A person commits theft if he obtains or exercises unauthorized control over the property of another with a purpose to deprive him thereof.

A person is guilty of willful concealment if, without authority, he willfully conceals the goods or merchandise of any store while still upon the premises of such store. Goods or merchandise found concealed upon the person shall be prima facie evidence of willful concealment.

A person is guilty of shoplifting if, with the purpose of depriving a merchant of goods or merchandise, he knowingly:

(a) Removes goods or merchandise from the premises of a merchant; or

(b) Alters, transfers, or removes any price marking affixed to goods or merchandise; or

(c) Causes the cash register or other sales recording device to reflect less than the merchant's stated or advertised price for the goods or merchandise; or

(d) Transfers goods or merchandise from the container in which such goods or merchandise were intended to be sold to another container.

III. As used in this section:

(a) "Merchant" means the owner or operator of any place of business where merchandise is displayed, held, or stored, for sale to the public, or any agent or employee of such owner or operator.

(b) "Purpose to deprive" means to have the conscious object to appropriate the goods or merchandise of a merchant without paying the merchant's stated or advertised price.

NEW JERSEY

1. Arrest by Private Persons

[No statute. However, the following provision in Sec. 2C:20-11(E) of the N.J. Code of Crim. Justice is of some relevance.]

A merchant who causes the arrest of a person for shoplifting, as provided for in this section, shall not be criminally or civilly liable in any manner or to any extent whatsoever where the merchant has probable cause for believing that the person arrested committed the offense of shoplifting.

2. Detention
(2C:20-11(E), N.J. Code Crim. Justice)

A law enforcement officer, or a special officer, or a merchant, who has probable cause for believing that a person has willfully concealed unpurchased merchandise and that he can recover the merchandise by taking the person into custody, may, for the purpose of attempting to effect recovery thereof, take the person into custody and detain him in a reasonable manner for not more than a reasonable time, and the taking into custody by a law enforcement officer or special officer or merchant shall not render such person criminally or civilly liable in any manner or to any extent whatsoever.

3. Shoplifting/Cart Removal/Civil Liability for Shoplifting
(2C:20-11(B) and (D), 2A:61C-1, N.J. Code Crim. Justice)

Shoplifting shall consist of any one or more of the following acts:

(1) For any person purposely to take possession of, carry away, transfer or cause to be carried away or transferred, any merchandise displayed, held, stored or offered for sale by any store or other retail mercantile establishment with the intention of depriving the merchant of the possession, use or benefit of such merchandise or converting the same to the use of such person without paying to the merchant the full retail value thereof.

(2) For any person purposely to conceal upon his person or otherwise any merchandise offered for sale by any store or other retail mercantile establishment with the intention of depriving the merchant of the processes, use or benefit of such merchandise or converting the same to the use of such person without paying to the merchant the value thereof.

(3) For any person purposely to alter, transfer or remove any label, price tag or marking indicia of value or any other markings which aid in determining value affixed to any merchandise displayed, held, stored or offered for sale by any store or other retail mercantile establishment and to attempt to purchase such merchandise personally or in consort with another at less than the full retail value with the intention of depriving the merchant of all or some part of the value thereof.

(4) For any person purposely to transfer any merchandise displayed, held, stored or offered for sale by any store or other retail merchandise establishment from the container in or on which the same shall be displayed to any other container with intent to deprive the merchant of all or some part of the retail value thereof.

(5) For any person purposely to under-ring with the intention of depriving the merchant of the full retail value thereof.

(6) For any person purposely to remove a shopping cart from the premises of a store or other retail mercantile establishment without the consent of the merchant given at the time of such removal with the intention of permanently depriving the merchant of the possession, use or benefit of such cart.

Any person purposely concealing unpurchased merchandise of any store or other retail mercantile establishment, either on the premises or outside the premises of such store or other retail mercantile establishment, shall be prima facie presumed to have so concealed such merchandise with the intention of depriving the merchant of the possession, use or benefit of such merchandise without paying the full retail value thereof, and the finding of such merchandise concealed upon the person or among the belongings of such person shall be prima facie evidence of purposeful concealment; and if such person conceals, or causes to be concealed, such merchandise upon the person or among the belongings of another, the finding of the same shall also be prima facie evidence of willful concealment on the part of the person so concealing such merchandise.

   a. A person who commits the offense of shoplifting as defined in N.J.S. 2C:20-11 [. . .] shall be liable for any criminal penalties imposed by law and shall be liable to the merchant in a civil action in an amount equal to the following:

     (1) The value of the merchandise as damages, not to exceed $500.00, if the merchandise cannot be restored to the merchant in its original condition;

     (2) Additional damages, if any, arising from the incident, not to include any loss of time or wages incurred by the merchant in connection with the apprehension of the defendant; and

     (3) A civil penalty payable to the merchant in an amount of up to $150.

   b. A parent, guardian or other person having legal custody of a minor who commits the offense of shoplifting or the offense of theft of food or drink from an eating establishment shall be liable to the merchant for the damages specified in subsection a. of this section. This subsection shall not apply to a parent whose parental custody and control of such minor has been removed by court order, decree, judgment, military service, or marriage of such infant, or to a foster parent of such minor.

   c. If a merchant institutes a civil action pursuant to the provisions of this section, the prevailing party in that action shall be entitled to an award of reasonable attorney's fees and reasonable court costs.

   d. Limitations on civil action:

     (1) Before a civil action may be commenced, the merchant shall send a notice to the defendant's last known address giving the defendant 20 days to respond. It is not a condition precedent to maintaining an action under this act that the defendant has been convicted of shoplifting or theft.

     (2) No civil action under this act may be maintained if the defendant has paid the merchant a penalty equal to the retail value of the merchandise where the merchandise was not recovered in its original condition, plus a sum of up to $150.00.

     (3) The provisions of this act do not apply in any case where the value of the merchandise exceeds $500.00.

   e. If the person to whom a written demand is made complies with such demand within 20 days following the receipt of the demand, that person shall be given a written release from further civil liability with respect to the specific act of shoplifting or theft.

NEW MEXICO

1. Arrest by Private Persons
[No statute]

2. Detention
(30-16-23, N.M. Stats. Ann.)

If any law enforcement officer, special officer or merchant has probable cause for believing that a person has willfully taken possession of any merchandise with the intention of converting it without paying for it, or has willfully concealed merchandise, and that he can recover the merchandise by detaining the person or taking him into custody, the law enforcement officer, special officer or merchant may, for the purpose of attempting to affect [effect] a recovery of the merchandise, take the person into custody and detain him in a reasonable manner for a reasonable time. Such taking into custody or detention shall not subject the officer or merchant to any criminal or civil liability.

Any law enforcement officer may arrest without warrant any person he has probable cause for believing has committed the crime of shoplifting. Any merchant who causes such an arrest shall not be criminally or civilly liable if he has probable cause for believing the person so arrested has committed the crime of shoplifting.

3. Shoplifting
(30-16-20, 30-16-22, and 30-16-21, N.M. Stats. Ann.)

A. Shoplifting consists of any one or more of the following acts:
   (1) willfully taking possession of any merchandise with the intention of converting it without paying for it;
   (2) willfully concealing any merchandise with the intention of converting it without paying for it;
   (3) willfully altering any label, price tag or marking upon any merchandise with the intention of depriving the merchant of all or some part of the value of it; or
   (4) willfully transferring any merchandise from the container in or on which it is displayed to any other container with the intention of depriving the merchant of all or some part of the value of it.
B. Whoever commits shoplifting when the value of the merchandise shoplifted:
   (1) is one hundred dollars ($100) or less is guilty of a petty misdemeanor;
   (2) is more than one hundred dollars ($100) but not more than two hundred fifty dollars ($250) is guilty of a misdemeanor;
   (3) is more than two hundred fifty dollars ($250) but not more than two thousand five hundred dollars ($2,500) is guilty of a fourth degree felony;
   (4) is more than two thousand five hundred dollars ($2,500) but not more than twenty thousand dollars ($20,000) is guilty of a third degree felony; or
   (5) is more than twenty thousand dollars ($20,000) is guilty of a second degree felony.
C. Any individual charged with a violation of this section shall not be charged with a separate or additional offense arising out of the same transaction.

Any person who willfully conceals merchandise on his person or on the person of another or among his belongings or the belongings of another or on or outside the premises of the store shall be prima facie presumed to have concealed the merchandise with the intention of converting it without paying for it. If any merchandise is found concealed upon any person or among his belongings it shall be prima facie evidence of willful concealment.

Any person who has reached the age of majority and who has been convicted of shoplifting [. . .] may be civilly liable for the retail value of the merchandise, punitive damages of not less than one hundred dollars ($100) nor more than two hundred fifty dollars ($250), costs of the suit and reasonable attorney's fees. However, the merchant shall not be entitled to recover damages for the retail value of any recovered undamaged merchandise.

NEW YORK

1. Arrest by Private Persons

(Secs. 140.30, 140.35, 140.40 [Crim. Proc.]., N.Y. Stats. Ann., Sec. 35.30 [Penal Law], N.Y. Stats. Ann.)

1. Subject to the provisions of subdivision two, any person may arrest another person (a) for a felony when the latter has in fact committed such felony, and (b) for any offense when the latter has in fact committed such offense in his presence.
2. Such an arrest, if for a felony, may be made anywhere in the state. If the arrest is for an offense other than a felony, it may be made only in the county in which such offense was committed.

A person may arrest another person for an offense pursuant to [the above provision] at any hour of any day or night.

Such person must inform the person whom he is arresting of the reason for such arrest unless he encounters physical resistance, flight or other factors rendering such procedure impractical.

In order to effect such an arrest, such person may use such physical force as is justifiable pursuant to subdivision four of section 35.30 of the penal law.

A person making an arrest pursuant to section 140.30 [the first section above] must without unnecessary delay deliver or attempt to deliver the person arrested to the custody of an appropriate police officer, as defined in subdivision five. For such purpose, he may solicit the aid of any police officer and the latter, if he is not himself an appropriate police officer, must assist in delivering the arrested person to an appropriate officer.

A private person acting on his own account may use physical force, other than deadly physical force, upon another person when and to the extent that he reasonably believes such to be necessary to effect an arrest or to prevent the escape from custody of a person whom he reasonably believes to have committed an offense and who in fact has committed such offense; and he may use deadly physical force for such purpose when he reasonably believes such to be necessary to:

(a) Defend himself or a third person from what he reasonably believes to be the use or imminent use of deadly physical force; or
(b) Effect the arrest of a person who has committed murder, manslaughter in the first degree, robbery, forcible rape or forcible sodomy and who is in immediate flight therefrom.

2. Detention

(Sec. 218 [Art. 12-B, Gen. Bus. Law], N.Y. Stats. Ann.)

In any action for false arrest, false imprisonment, unlawful detention, defamation of character, assault, trespass, or invasion of civil rights, brought by any person by reason of having been detained on or in the immediate vicinity of the premises of (a) a retail mercantile establishment for the purpose of investigation or questioning as to criminal possession of an anti-security item as defined in section 170.47 of the penal law or as to the ownership of any merchandise, [. . .] it shall be a defense to such action that the person was detained in a reasonable manner and for not more than a reasonable time to permit such investigation or questioning by a peace officer acting pursuant to his special duties, police officer or by the owner of the retail mercantile establishment [. . .] his authorized employee or agent, and that such officer, owner, employee or agent had reasonable grounds to believe that the person so detained was guilty of criminal possession of an anti-security item as defined in section 170.47 of the penal law or was committing or attempting to commit larceny on such premises of such merchandise [. . .].

As used in this section, "reasonable grounds" shall include, but not be limited to, knowledge that a person (i) has concealed possession of unpurchased merchandise of a retail mercantile establishment, or (ii) has possession of an item designed for the purpose of overcoming detection of security markings attachments placed on merchandise offered for sale at such an establishment, [. . .] and a "reasonable time" shall mean the time necessary to permit the person detained to make a statement or to refuse to make a statement, and the time necessary to examine employees and records of the mercantile establishment relative to the ownership of the merchandise, or possession of such an item or device.

3. Larceny
(155.05 and 155.20(4) [Penal Law], N.Y. Stats. Ann.)

A person steals property and commits larceny when, with intent to deprive another of property or to appropriate the same to himself or to a third person, he wrongfully takes, obtains or withholds such property from an owner thereof.

Larceny includes a wrongful taking, obtaining or withholding of another's property, with the intent prescribed in subdivision one of this section, committed in any of the following ways:

(a) By conduct heretofore defined or known as common law larceny by trespassory taking, common law larceny by trick, embezzlement, or obtaining property by false pretenses;

Except as otherwise specified in this section, value means the market value of the property at the time and place of the crime, or if such cannot be satisfactorily ascertained, the cost of replacement of the property within a reasonable time after the crime.

When the value of property cannot be satisfactorily ascertained [. . .], its value shall be deemed to be an amount less than two hundred fifty dollars.

NORTH CAROLINA

1. Arrest by Private Persons
[No statute other than the one (15A-405, N.C. Gen. Stats.) regarding such action at the request of a law enforcement officer. For powers of "Company Police," see Sec. 74E-6, N.C. Gen. Stats.]

2.   Detention
(15A-404, N.C. Gen. Stats.)

(a) No Arrest; Detention Permitted—No private person may arrest another person except as provided in G.S. 15A-405. A private person may detain another person as provided in this section.

(b) When Detention Permitted—A private person may detain another person when he has probable cause to believe that the person detained has committed in his presence:

(1) A felony,

(2) A breach of the peace,

(3) A crime involving physical injury to another person, or

(4) A crime involving theft or destruction of property.

(c) Manner of Detention.—The detention must be in a reasonable manner considering the offense involved and the circumstances of the detention.

(d) Period of Detention.—The detention may be no longer than the time required for the earliest of the following:

(1) The determination that no offense has been committed.

(2) Surrender of the person detained to a law-enforcement officer as provided in subsection (e).

(e) Surrender to Officer.—A private person who detains another must immediately notify a law-enforcement officer and must, unless he releases the person earlier as required by subsection (d), surrender the person detained to the law-enforcement officer.

3.   Shoplifting/Civil Liability for Shoplifting
(14-72.1, N.C. Gen. Stats., 1-538.2, N.C. Gen. Stats.)

(a) Any person, other than an unemancipated minor, who commits an act [of shoplifting] is liable for civil damages to the owner of the property. In any action brought by the owner of the property he is entitled to recover the value of the goods or merchandise, if the goods or merchandise have been destroyed, or any loss of value to the goods or merchandise, if the goods or merchandise were recovered, or the amount of any money lost by reason of the embezzlement or fraud of an employee. In addition to the above, the owner of the property is entitled to recover any consequential damages, and punitive damages, together with reasonable attorneys fees. If damages are assessed against the defendant, in favor of the plaintiff, the amount established for actual or consequential damages shall be trebled. The total of all damages awarded to a plaintiff against a defendant in an action under this section shall not exceed one thousand dollars ($1,000).

(b) The parent or legal guardian, having the care, custody and control of an unemancipated minor who commits an act [of shoplifting] is civilly liable to the owner of the property obtained by the act if such parent or legal guardian knew or should have known of the propensity of the child to commit such an act; and had the opportunity and ability to control the child, and made no reasonable effort to correct or restrain the child. In an action brought against the parent or legal guardian by the owner, the owner is entitled to recover the amounts specified in subsection (a) except punitive damages.

(c) A person may not be found liable under this section unless a sign was conspicuously displayed in the place of business at the time the act alleged in the action occurred stating that civil liability for shoplifting and for theft by an employee is authorized under this section. An action may be brought under this section regardless of whether a criminal action is brought or a criminal conviction is obtained for the act alleged in the civil action.

(d) Nothing contained in this act shall prohibit recovery upon any other theory in the law.

Whoever, without authority, willfully conceals the goods or merchandise of any store, not theretofore purchased by such person, while still upon the premises of such store, shall be guilty of a misdemeanor and, upon conviction, shall be punished as provided in subsection (e). Such goods or merchandise found concealed upon or about the person and which have not theretofore been purchased by such person shall be prima facie evidence of a willful concealment.

(c)　A merchant, or the merchant's agent or employee, or a peace officer who detains or causes the arrest of any person shall not be held civilly liable for detention, malicious prosecution, false imprisonment, or false arrest of the person detained or arrested, where such detention is in a reasonable manner for a reasonable length of time, if in detaining or in causing the arrest of such person, the merchant, or the merchant's agent or employee, or the peace officer had at the time of the detention or arrest probable cause to believe that the person committed the offense created by this section. If the person being detained by the merchant, or the merchant's agent or employee, is a minor under the age of 18 years, the merchant or the merchant's agent or employee, shall call or notify, or make a reasonable effort to call or notify the parent or guardian of the minor, during the period of detention. A merchant, or the merchant's agent or employee, who makes a reasonable effort to call or notify the parent or guardian of the minor shall not be held civilly liable for failing to notify the parent or guardian of the minor.

(d)　Whoever, without authority, willfully transfers any price tag from goods or merchandise to other goods or merchandise having a higher selling price or marks said goods at a lower price or substitutes or superimposes thereon a false price tag and then presents said goods or merchandise for purchase shall be guilty of a misdemeanor [. . . .]

Nothing herein shall be construed to provide that the mere possession of goods or the production by shoppers of improperly priced merchandise for checkout shall constitute prima facie evidence of guilt.

NORTH DAKOTA

1.　Arrest by Private Persons
(29-06-20, 29-06-21, 29-06-23, 29-06-24, N.D. Century Code)

A private person may arrest another:

1. For a public offense committed or attempted in his presence.
2. When the person arrested has committed a felony, although not in his presence.
3. When a felony has been in fact committed, and he has reasonable ground to believe the person arrested to have committed it.

A private person making an arrest must inform the person to be arrested of the intention to arrest him, and of the cause of the arrest, unless:

1. The person to be arrested then is engaged in the commission of an offense;
2. Such person is pursued immediately after its commission or after an escape;
3. Such person flees or forcibly resists before the person making the arrest has opportunity to inform him; or
4. The giving of such information will imperil the arrest.

A private person who has arrested another for the commission of a public offense, without unnecessary delay, shall take him before a magistrate or deliver him to a peace officer.

Any person making a lawful arrest shall take from the person arrested all offensive weapons which he may have about his person and shall deliver them to the magistrate before whom he is taken.

2. Detention
(51-21-03 and 51-21-04, N.D. Century Code)

Any peace officer or merchant who reasonably believes that a person has committed, or is in the process of committing, theft may detain such person, on or off the premises of a retail mercantile establishment, in a reasonable manner and for a reasonable length of time for all or any of the following purposes:

1. To require the person to identify himself.
2. To verify such identification.
3. To determine whether such person has in his possession unpurchased merchandise and, if so, to recover such merchandise.
4. To inform a peace officer of the detention of the person and surrender custody of that person to a peace officer.
5. In the case of a minor, to inform a peace officer, the parents, guardian, or other private person interested in the welfare of that minor of this detention and to surrender custody of said minor to the person informed.

Any peace officer or merchant who detains any person as permitted under [the above section] may not be held civilly or criminally liable for any claim for relief allegedly arising from such detention.

3. Retail Theft
(51-21-02 and 51-21-05, N.D. Century Code)

Any person concealing upon his person or among his belongings, or causing to be concealed upon the person or among the belongings of another, unpurchased merchandise displayed, held, offered, or stored for sale in a retail mercantile establishment and removing it to a point beyond the last station for receiving payments in that retail mercantile establishment shall be prima facie presumed to have so concealed such merchandise with the intention of permanently depriving the merchant of possession or of the full retail value of such merchandise.

An adult who commits the offense of theft from a merchant is civilly liable to the merchant for the retail value of the merchandise, plus exemplary damages of not more than two hundred fifty dollars, costs of suit, and reasonable attorney's fees. The parent or legal guardian of an unemancipated minor who while living with the parent or legal guardian commits the offense of theft from a merchant is civilly liable to the merchant for the retail value of the merchandise, plus exemplary damages of not more than two hundred fifty dollars, costs of suit, and reasonable attorney's fees. A conviction or plea of guilty for the theft is not a prerequisite to the bringing of a suit hereunder. A parent or legal guardian of an unemancipated minor is not civilly liable under this section if it is determined by the court that one of the principal rationales for the shoplifting was a desire on the part of the minor to cause his parent or legal guardian to be liable under this section.

OHIO

1. Arrest by Private Persons
(2935.04, 2935.06, and 2935.07, Ohio Rev. Code)

When a felony has been committed, or there is reasonable ground to believe that a felony has been committed, any person without a warrant may arrest another whom he has reasonable cause to believe is guilty of the offense, and detain him until a warrant can be obtained.

A private person who has made an arrest [pursuant to the above section, or a detention pursuant to the detention statute which follows] shall forthwith take the person arrested before the most convenient judge or clerk of a court of record or before a magistrate, or deliver such person to an officer authorized to execute criminal warrants who shall, without unnecessary delay, take such person before the court or magistrate having jurisdiction of the offense. The officer may, but if he does not, the private person shall file or cause to be filed in such court or before such magistrate an affidavit stating the offense for which the person was arrested.

When an arrest is made by a private person, he shall, before making the arrest, inform the person to be arrested of the intention to arrest him and the cause of the arrest.

When a person is engaged in the commission of a criminal offense, it is not necessary to inform him of the cause of his arrest.

2. Detention
(2935.041, Ohio Rev. Code)

(A) A merchant, or his employee or agent, who has probable cause to believe that items offered for sale by a mercantile establishment have been unlawfully taken by a person, may, for the purposes set forth in division (C) of this section, detain the person in a reasonable manner for a reasonable length of time within the mercantile establishment or its immediate vicinity.

(C) [. . .] a merchant or his employee or agent [. . .] may detain another person for any of the following purposes:
(1) To recover the property that is the subject of the unlawful taking, criminal mischief, or theft;
(2) To cause an arrest to be made by a peace officer;
(3) To obtain a warrant of arrest.

(D) The officer, agent, or employee [. . .] or the merchant or his employee or agent [. . .] shall not search the person, search or seize any property belonging to the person detained without the person's consent, or use undue restraint upon the person detained.

3. Theft
(2913.02, Ohio Rev. Code)

(A) No person, with purpose to deprive the owner of property or services, shall knowingly obtain or exert control over either the property or services in any of the following ways:
(1) Without the consent of the owner or person authorized to give consent;

(2) Beyond the scope of the express or implied consent of the owner or person authorized to give consent;
(3) By deception;
(4) By threat.
(B) Whoever violates this section is guilty of theft. [Penalties are exacted based on the value of the property stolen].

OKLAHOMA

1. Arrest by Private Persons
(Tit. 22, 202, 203, 205, 206, Okla. Stats. Ann.)

A private person may arrest another:

1. For a public offense committed or attempted in his presence.
2. When the person arrested has committed a felony although not in his presence.
3. When a felony has been in fact committed, and he has reasonable cause for believing the person arrested to have committed it.

He must, before making the arrest, inform the person to be arrested of the cause thereof, and require him to submit, except when he is in actual commission of the offense or when he is arrested on pursuit immediately after its commission.

A private person who has arrested another for the commission of a public offense, must, without unnecessary delay, take him before a magistrate or deliver him to a peace officer.

Any person making an arrest must take from the person arrested all offensive weapons which he may have about his person, and must deliver them to the magistrate before whom he is taken.

2. Detention
(Tit. 22, 1343, Okla. Stats. Ann.)

Any merchant, his agent or employee, who has reasonable grounds or probable cause to believe that a person has committed or is committing a wrongful taking of merchandise or money from a mercantile establishment, may detain such person in a reasonable manner for a reasonable length of time for all or any of the following purposes:

(a) Conducting an investigation, including reasonable interrogation of the detained person, as to whether there has been a wrongful taking of such merchandise or money;
(b) Informing the police or other law enforcement officials of the facts relevant to such detention;
(c) Performing a reasonable search of the detained person and his belongings when it appears that the merchandise or money may otherwise be lost; and
(d) Recovering the merchandise or money believed to have been taken wrongfully.
Any such reasonable detention shall not constitute an unlawful arrest or detention,

nor shall it render the merchant, his agent or employee criminally or civilly liable to the person so detained.

3. Shoplifting/Concealment/Larceny
(Tit. 22, 1341, 1344; Tit. 21, 1731, Okla. Stats. Ann.)

"Wrongful taking," includes stealing of merchandise or money and any other wrongful appropriation of merchandise or money.

Any person concealing unpurchased merchandise of any mercantile establishment, either on the premises or outside the premises of such establishment, shall be presumed to have so concealed such merchandise with the intention of committing a wrongful taking of such merchandise within the meaning of Section 1341 of this title, and such concealment or the finding of such unpurchased merchandise concealed upon the person or among the belongings of such person shall be conclusive evidence of reasonable grounds and probable cause for the detention in a reasonable manner and for a reasonable length of time, of such person by a merchant, his agent or employee, and any such reasonable detention shall not be deemed to be unlawful, nor render such merchant, his agent or employee criminally or civilly liable.

Larceny of merchandise held for sale in retail or wholesale establishments shall be punishable as follows:

1. For the first conviction, in the event the value of the goods, edible meat or other corporeal property which has been taken does not exceed Fifty Dollars ($50.00), punishment shall be by imprisonment in the county jail not exceeding thirty (30) days, and by a fine not less than Ten Dollars ($10.00) nor more than One Hundred Dollars ($100.00); provided for the first conviction, in the event more than one item of goods, edible meat or other corporeal property has been taken, punishment shall be by imprisonment in the county jail not to exceed thirty (30) days, and by a fine not less than Fifty Dollars ($50.00) nor more than One Hundred Dollars ($100.00).
2. If it be shown, in the trial of a case in which the value of the goods, edible meat or other corporeal property does not exceed Fifty Dollars ($50.00), that the defendant has been once before convicted of the same offense, he shall, on his second conviction, be punished by confinement in the county jail for not less than thirty (30) days nor more than one (1) year, and by a fine not exceeding One Thousand Dollars ($1,000.00).
3. If it be shown, upon the trial of a case where the value of the goods, edible meat or other corporeal personal property does not exceed Fifty Dollars ($50.00), that the defendant has two or more times before been convicted of the same offense, regardless of the value of the goods, edible meat or other corporeal personal property involved in the first two convictions, upon the third or any subsequent conviction, the punishment shall be by confinement in the State Penitentiary for not less than two (2) nor more than five (5) years.
4. In the event the value of the goods, edible meat or other corporeal property is Fifty Dollars ($50.00) or more, but is less than Five Hundred Dollars ($500.00), the defendant shall be guilty of a felony and shall be punished by incarceration in the county jail for not more than one (1) year or by incarceration in the county jail one or more nights or weekends pursuant to Section 991a-2 of Title 22 of the Oklahoma Statutes, at the option of the court, and shall be subject to a fine of not more than

Five Thousand Dollars ($5,000.00) and ordered to provide restitution to the victim as provided in Section 991a of Title 22 of the Oklahoma Statutes.

5. In the event the value of the goods, edible meat or other corporeal property is Five Hundred Dollars ($500.00) or more, punishment shall be by confinement in the State Penitentiary for not less than one (1) year nor more than five (5) years.

OREGON

1. Arrest by Private Persons
(133.225, 133.255, Oreg. Rev. Stats.)

(1) A private person may arrest another person for any crime committed in the presence of the private person if the private person has probable cause to believe the arrested person committed the crime. A private person making such an arrest shall, without unnecessary delay, take the arrested person before a magistrate or deliver the arrested person to a peace officer.

(2) In order to make the arrest a private person may use physical force as is justifiable . . .

(1) Except as provided in subsection (2) [below] of this section, a private person acting on the person's own account is justified in using physical force upon another person when and to the extent that the person reasonably believes it necessary to make an arrest or to prevent the escape from custody of an arrested person whom the person has arrested . . .

(2) A private person acting under the circumstances prescribed in subsection (1) of this section is justified in using deadly physical force only when the person reasonably believes it necessary for self-defense or to defend a third person from what the person reasonably believes to be the use or imminent use of deadly physical force.

2. Detention
(131.655, Oreg. Rev. Stats.)

(1) Notwithstanding any other provision of law, a peace officer, merchant or merchant's employee who has probable cause for believing that a person has committed theft of property of a store or other mercantile establishment may detain and interrogate the person in regard thereto in a reasonable manner and for a reasonable time.

(2) If a peace officer, merchant or merchant's employee, with probable cause for believing that a person has committed theft of property of a store or other mercantile establishment, detains and interrogates the person in regard thereto, and the person thereafter brings against the peace officer, merchant or merchant's employee any civil or criminal action based upon the detention and interrogation, such probable cause shall be a defense to the action, if the detention and interrogation were done in a reasonable manner and for a reasonable time.

3. Theft
(164.015, 30.870 and 30.875, Oreg. Rev. Stats.)

A person commits theft when, with intent to deprive another of property or to appropriate property to the person or to a third person, the person:

Takes, appropriates, obtains or withholds such property from an owner thereof . . .

An adult or an emancipated minor who takes possession of any merchandise displayed or offered for sale by any mercantile establishment, or who takes from any real property any agricultural produce kept, grown or raised on the property for purposes of sale, without the consent of the owner and with the intention of converting such merchandise or produce to the individual's own use without having paid the purchase price thereof, or who alters the price indicia of such merchandise, shall be civilly liable to the owner for actual damages, for a penalty to the owner in the amount of the retail value of the merchandise or produce not to exceed $500, and for an additional penalty to the owner of not less than $100 nor more than $250.

The parents having custody of an unemancipated minor who takes possession of any merchandise displayed or offered for sale by any mercantile establishment, or who takes from any real property any agricultural produce kept, grown or raised on the property for purposes of sale, without the consent of the owner, and with the intention of converting such merchandise or produce to the minor's own use without having paid the purchase price thereof, or who alters the price indicia of such merchandise or who engages in conduct described in ORS 164.125, 164.132 or 164.373, shall be civilly liable to the owner for actual damages, for a penalty to the owner in the amount of the retail value of the merchandise or produce not to exceed $250, plus an additional penalty to the owner of not less than $100 nor more than $250. Persons operating a foster home certified under [particular provisions of state law] are not liable under this subsection for the acts of children not related to them by blood or marriage and under their care.

(3)   A conviction for theft is not a condition precedent to the maintenance of a civil action under this section.

(4)   A civil liability under this section is not limited by any other law that limits liability of parents of minor children.

PENNSYLVANIA

1. Arrest by Private Persons
(Tit. 18, 508, Pa. Stats. Ann.)

A private person who makes, or assists another private person in making a lawful arrest is justified in the use of any force which he would be justified in using if he were summoned or directed by a peace officer to make such arrest, except that he is justified in the use of deadly force only when he believes that such force is necessary to prevent death or serious bodily injury to himself or another.

2. Detention
(Tit. 18, 3929, Pa. Stats. Ann.)

A peace officer, merchant or merchant's employee or an agent under contract with a merchant, who has probable cause to believe that retail theft has occurred or is occurring on or about a store or other retail mercantile establishment and who has probable cause to believe that a specific person has committed or is committing the retail theft may detain the suspect in a reasonable manner for a reasonable time on or off the premises for all or any of the following purposes: to require the suspect to identify himself, to verify such identification, to determine whether such suspect has in his possession unpurchased merchandise taken from the mercantile establishment and, if so, to recover such merchandise, to inform a peace officer, or to institute criminal proceedings against the suspect. Such detention shall not impose civil or criminal liability upon the peace officer, merchant, employee, or agent so detaining.

3. Retail Theft
(Tit. 18, 3929, Pa. Stats. Ann.)

A person is guilty of a retail theft if he:

(1) takes possession of, carries away, transfers or causes to be carried away or transferred, any merchandise displayed, held, stored or offered for sale by any store or other retail mercantile establishment with the intention of depriving the merchant of the possession, use or benefit of such merchandise without paying the full retail value thereof;

(2) alters, transfers or removes any label, price tag marking, indicia of value or any other markings which aid in determining value affixed to any merchandise displayed, held, stored or offered for sale in a store or other retail mercantile establishment and attempts to purchase such merchandise personally or in consort with another at less than the full retail value with the intention of depriving the merchant of the full retail value of such merchandise;

(3) transfers any merchandise displayed, held, stored or offered for sale by any store or other retail mercantile establishment from the container in or on which the same shall be displayed to any other container with intent to deprive the merchant of all or some part of the full retail value thereof; or

(4) under-rings with the intention of depriving the merchant of the full retail value of the merchandise.

Amounts involved in retail thefts committed pursuant to one scheme or course of conduct, whether from the same store or retail mercantile establishment or several stores or retail mercantile establishments, may be aggregated in determining the grade of the offense.

Any person intentionally concealing unpurchased property of any store or other mercantile establishment, either on the premises or outside the premises of such store, shall be prima facie presumed to have so concealed such property with the intention of depriving the merchant of the possession, use or benefit of such merchandise without paying the full retail value thereof within the meaning of subsection (a), and the finding of such unpurchased property concealed, upon the person or among the belongings of such person, shall be prima facie evidence of intentional concealment, and, if such person conceals, or causes to be concealed, such unpurchased property, upon the person or among the belongings of another, such fact shall also be prima facie evidence of intentional concealment on the part of the person so concealing such property.

To the extent that there is other competent evidence to substantiate the offense, the conviction shall not be avoided because the prosecution cannot produce the stolen merchandise.

RHODE ISLAND

1. Arrest by Private Persons
[No statute]

2. Detention
(11-41-21, R.I. Gen. Laws)

Any merchant who observes any person concealing or attempting to conceal merchandise on his person or amongst his belongings or upon the person or amongst the belongings of another, transporting merchandise beyond the area within the retail mercantile establishment where payment for it is to be made without making payment therefor, removing or altering price tags on merchandise or switching the containers of merchandise may stop such person. Immediately upon stopping such person, the merchant shall identify himself and state his reason for stopping the person. If after his initial confrontation with the person under suspicion, the merchant has reasonable grounds to believe that at the time stopped the person was committing or attempting to commit the crime of shoplifting on his premises, he may detain such person for a reasonable time sufficient to summon a police officer to the premises. In no case shall the detention be for a period exceeding one hour. Said detention must be accomplished in a reasonable manner without unreasonable restraint or excessive force, and may take place only on the premises of the retail mercantile establishment where the alleged shoplifting occurred. Any person so stopped by a merchant pursuant to this section shall promptly identify himself by name and address. Once placed under detention, no other information shall be required of such person and no written and/or signed statement, except as provided in subsection (c), shall be elicited from him until a police officer has taken him into custody. The merchant may, however, examine for the purposes of ascertaining ownership any merchandise which is in plain view which the merchant has reasonable grounds to believe was unlawfully taken or otherwise tampered with . . .

A merchant may request a person detained for shoplifting to sign a statement waiving his right to bring a civil action arising from said detention in return for a signed statement from said merchant waiving his right to bring criminal charges based upon the alleged shoplifting. Any such statement shall state in writing in large print at the top of the form that the person detained has a right to remain silent and a right not to make or sign any statement and a right to call an attorney.

It shall be unlawful to circulate or cause to be circulated any such signed statement or the name of any person signing such statement to a person or persons not employed by the retail mercantile establishment which obtained said statement, other than in defense of a legal action arising from said detention. Any person circulating or causing to be circulated such information shall be civilly liable to the person who signed said statement.

(d) For the purposes of this section, "reasonable grounds" shall include knowledge that a person has concealed unpurchased merchandise of such establishment while on the premises, or has altered or removed identifying labels on such merchandise while on the premises, or is leaving such premises with such unpurchased concealed or altered merchandise in his possession.

(e) In detaining a person whom the merchant has reasonable grounds to believe is committing the crime of shoplifting, the merchant may use a reasonable amount of nondeadly force when and only when such force is necessary to protect himself or to prevent the escape of the person being detained or the loss of his property.

(f)   In any civil action by a person detained under this section against the merchant so detaining him arising out of said detention, evidence that the defendant had reasonable grounds as defined in subsection (d) to believe that the plaintiff was at the time in question committing or attempting to commit the crime of shoplifting [. . .] shall create a rebuttable presumption that the plaintiff was so committing or attempting to commit said crime.

3. Shoplifting
(11-41-20, 11-41-24, R.I. Gen. Laws)

Whoever shall engage in the following shall be guilty of the crime of shoplifting:

(1)   Take possession of, carry away, transfer or cause to be carried away or transferred any merchandise displayed, held, stored, or offered for sale by a retail mercantile establishment with the intention of depriving the merchant of all or any part of the full retail value of such merchandise, or

(2)   Alter, transfer, or remove a label, price tag, marking, indicia of value or any other markings which aid in determining value affixed to any merchandise displayed, held, stored or offered for sale in a retail mercantile establishment and attempt to purchase or purchase such merchandise personally or in consort with another at less than the full retail value with the intention of depriving the merchant of all or any part of the full retail value of such merchandise, or

(3)   Transfer any merchandise displayed, held, stored or offered for sale in a retail mercantile establishment from one container to another in an attempt to purchase or purchase such merchandise personally or in consort with another at less than the full retail value with the intention of depriving the merchant of all or any part of the full retail value of such merchandise, or

(4)   Remove a shopping cart from the premises of a retail mercantile establishment without the consent of the merchant given at the time of such removal with the intention of depriving the merchant of the possession, use or benefit of such cart.

(c)   The fact that a person conceals upon his person, among his belongings, or upon the person or among the belongings of another, merchandise displayed, held, stored or offered for sale in a retail mercantile establishment, for which he has not paid the full retail value, and said merchandise has been taken beyond the area within the retail mercantile establishment where payment for it is to be made shall be prima facie evidence that said person has possessed, carried away or transferred such merchandise with the intention of depriving the merchant of all or part of the full retail value of such merchandise, without paying the full retail value of such merchandise.

(d)   Any person convicted of the crime of shoplifting shall be guilty of a misdemeanor and shall be punished by a fine of not less than fifty dollars ($50.00) or two times the full retail value of the merchandise, whichever is greater, but not more than five hundred dollars ($500) or by imprisonment for not more than one year or both; provided, however, any person convicted of the crime of shoplifting merchandise with a retail value of over one hundred dollars ($100) who has previously been convicted of shoplifting shall be guilty of a felony and shall be punished by a fine of not more than five thousand dollars ($5,000) or by imprisonment of not more than five (5) years or both.

Any person who shall be convicted three (3) times for the crime of shoplifting as defined in Sec. 11-41-20 or larceny as defined in Sec. 11-41-1 or receiving stolen goods as defined in Sec. 11-41-2 or who shall have been convicted three (3) times of any combination of the crimes described herein, shall also be charged as an habitual offender and upon conviction shall be fined not less than two hundred dollars ($200) nor more than five hundred dollars ($500) and shall be imprisoned not less than six (6) months nor more than one (1) year.

SOUTH CAROLINA

1. Arrest by Private Persons
(17-13-10, S.C. Code Ann.)

Upon (a) view of a felony committed, (b) certain information that a felony has been committed or (c) view of a larceny committed, any person may arrest the felon or thief and take him to a judge or magistrate, to be dealt with according to law.

2. Detention
(16-13-140, S.C. Code Ann.)

In any action brought by reason of having been delayed by a merchant or merchant's employee or agent on or near the premises of a mercantile establishment for the purpose of investigation concerning the ownership of any merchandise, it shall be a defense to such action if: (1) The person was delayed in a reasonable manner and for a reasonable time to permit such investigation, and (2) reasonable cause existed to believe that the person delayed had committed the crime of shoplifting.

3. Shoplifting/Civil Liability for Shoplifting
(16-13-110, 16-13-120, and 15-75-40, S.C. Code Ann.)

(A) A person is guilty of shoplifting if he:
   (1) takes possession of, carries away, transfers from one person to another or from one area of a store or other retail mercantile establishment to another area, or causes to be carried away or transferred any merchandise displayed, held, stored, or offered for sale by any store or other retail mercantile establishment with the intention of depriving the merchant of the possession, use, or benefit of the merchandise without paying the full retail value;
   (2) alters, transfers, or removes any label, price tag marking, indicia of value, or any other markings which aid in determining value affixed to any merchandise displayed, held, stored, or offered for sale in a store or other retail mercantile establishment and attempts to purchase the merchandise personally or in consort with another at less than the full retail value with the intention of depriving the merchant of the full retail value of the merchandise;

(3) transfers any merchandise displayed, held, stored, or offered for sale by any store or other retail mercantile establishment from the container in which it is displayed to any other container with intent to deprive the merchant of the full retail value.

(B) A person who violates the provisions of this section is guilty of a:

(1) misdemeanor triable in magistrate's court and, upon conviction, must be fined not more than five hundred dollars or imprisoned not more than thirty days if the value of the shoplifted merchandise is one thousand dollars or less;

(2) felony and, upon conviction, must be fined not more than one thousand dollars or imprisoned not more than five years, or both, if the value of the shoplifted merchandise is more than one thousand dollars but less than five thousand dollars;

(3) felony and, upon conviction, must be imprisoned not more than ten years if the value of the shoplifted merchandise is five thousand dollars or more.

It is permissible to infer that any person wilfully concealing unpurchased goods or merchandise of any store or other mercantile establishment either on the premises or outside the premises of the store has concealed the article with the intention of converting it to his own use without paying the purchase price thereof within the meaning of Sec. 16-13-110. It is also permissible to infer that the finding of the unpurchased goods or merchandise concealed upon the person or among the belongings of the person is evidence of wilful concealment. If the person conceals or causes to be concealed the unpurchased goods or merchandise upon the person or among the belongings of another, it is also permissible to infer that the person so concealing such goods wilfully concealed them with the intention of converting them to his own use without paying the purchase price thereof within the meaning of Sec. 16-13-110.

An adult or emancipated minor who commits shoplifting against the property of a store or other retail mercantile establishment is civilly liable to the operator of the establishment in an amount consisting of:

(1) the retail price of the merchandise if not recovered in merchantable condition up to an amount not to exceed fifteen hundred dollars; plus

(2) a penalty not to exceed the greater of three times the retail price of the merchandise or one hundred fifty dollars. In no event may the penalty exceed five hundred dollars.

(D) Custodial parents or legal guardians of an unemancipated minor who knew or should have known of the minor's propensity to steal are civilly liable for the minor who commits shoplifting against the property of a store or other retail mercantile establishment to the operator of the establishment in an amount consisting of:

(1) the retail price of the merchandise if not recovered in merchantable condition up to an amount not to exceed fifteen hundred dollars; plus

(2) a penalty not to exceed the greater of three times the retail price of the merchandise or one hundred fifty dollars. In no event may the penalty exceed five hundred dollars.

(E) A conviction or a plea of guilty for committing shoplifting is not a prerequisite to the bringing of a civil suit, obtaining a judgment, or collecting that judgment under this section.

(F) The fact that an operator of a store or other retail mercantile establishment may bring an action against an individual as provided in this section does not limit the right of the merchant to demand, orally or in writing, that a person who is liable for damages and penalties under this section remit the damages and penalties before the commencement of a legal action.***

(H)   In an action brought under subsection (D) of this section, the court shall consider in the interest of justice mitigating circumstances that bear directly upon the actions of the custodial parent or legal guardian in supervising the unemancipated minor who committed the shoplifting. These mitigating circumstances may include, but are not limited to, whether or not the unemancipated minor had demonstrated a propensity to steal or tendencies toward kleptomania and whether or not the custodial parent or legal guardian had notice or knowledge of the unemancipated minor's propensity to steal or tendencies toward kleptomania.***

(J)   The provisions of this section may not be construed to prohibit or limit any other cause of action which an operator of a store or other retail mercantile establishment may have against a person who unlawfully takes merchandise from the establishment.***

(L)   A store which utilizes the provisions of this section is prohibited from subsequently filing criminal charges against the individual pursuant to Section 16-13-110.

SOUTH DAKOTA

1. Arrest by Private Persons
(23A-3-3, 23A-3-4, 23-A-3-5, 23A-4-1, S.D. Codified Laws)

Any person may arrest another:

(1)   For a public offense, other than a petty offense, committed or attempted in his presence; or

(2)   For a felony which has been in fact committed although not in his presence, if he has probable cause to believe the person to be arrested committed it.

When arresting a person without a warrant, the person making the arrest must inform the person to be arrested of his authority and the cause of the arrest, and require him to submit, except when the person to be arrested is engaged in the actual commission of an offense or when he is arrested on pursuit immediately after its commission.

An arrest is made by an actual or attempted restraint of the person arrested or by his submission to the custody of the person making the arrest. No person shall subject an arrested person to more physical restraint than is reasonably necessary to effect the arrest. Any person making an arrest may take from the arrested person all dangerous weapons . . . which the arrested person may have about his person.

[A private] person making an arrest shall, without unnecessary delay, take the arrested person before the nearest available committing magistrate or deliver him to the nearest available law enforcement officer.

2. Detention
(22-30A-19.2, S.D. Codified Laws)

Any merchant who has reasonable grounds to believe that a person has committed retail theft may detain such person, on or off the premises of a retail mercantile establishment, in a reasonable manner and for a reasonable length of time:

(1) To request identification;
(2) To verify such identification;
(3) To make reasonable inquiry as to whether such person has in his possession unpurchased merchandise and, to make reasonable investigation of the ownership of such merchandise;
(4) To inform a peace officer of the detention of the person and surrender that person to the custody of a peace officer;
(5) In the case of a minor, to inform a peace officer, the parents, guardian or other private person interested in the welfare of that minor of this detention and to surrender custody of such minor to such person.

A merchant may make a detention as permitted in this section off the premises of a retail mercantile establishment only if such detention is pursuant to an immediate pursuit of such person.

3.   Theft/Civil Liability for Shoplifting
(22-30A-1, S.D. Codified Laws)

Any person who takes, or exercises control over, property of another with intent to deprive him of it, is guilty of theft.

Any adult or emancipated minor [. . .] or the parents or guardian of any unemancipated minor who takes possession of any goods, wares or merchandise displayed or offered for sale by the store or other mercantile establishment without the consent of the owner or seller and with the intention of converting the goods to the person's own use without having paid the purchase price is liable to the owner or seller for the retail value of the merchandise, regardless of whether the merchandise has been recovered in undamaged condition by the merchant. In addition, the merchant is entitled to a penalty of three times the retail value of the merchandise, or fifty dollars, whichever is greater.

Any person who is the victim of retail theft may make a written demand for the amount for which the person who committed the act is liable [under the previous section]. Except for a sole proprietorship, a member of management other than the initial detaining person, shall evaluate the validity of the accusation that the person committed the act and shall approve the accusation in writing before a written demand for payment is issued. The demand for payment shall be mailed by certified mail to the person from whom payment is demanded.

If the person to whom a written demand is made under @ 22-30A-19.3 complies with the written demand within thirty days after its receipt, that person incurs no further civil liability to the merchant. However, if the person to whom a written demand is made fails to respond to a written demand then the penalty allowed in [the demand] may be doubled.

TENNESSEE

1.   Arrest by Private Persons
(40-7-109, 40-7-111, 40-7-113, 39-11-621, Tenn. Code Ann.)

(a) A private person may arrest another:
(1) For a public offense committed in his presence;
(2) When the person arrested has committed a felony, although not in his presence; or

(3) When a felony has been committed, and he has reasonable cause to believe that the person arrested committed it.

(b) A private person who makes an arrest of another pursuant to the provisions of [this statute] shall receive no arrest fee or compensation therefor.

A private person making an arrest shall, at the time of the arrest, inform the person arrested of the cause thereof, except when he is in the actual commission of the offense, or when arrested on pursuit.

(a) A private person who has arrested another for a public offense, shall, without unnecessary delay, take him before a magistrate or deliver him to an officer.

A private citizen, in making an arrest authorized by law, may use force reasonably necessary to accomplish the arrest of an individual who flees or resists the arrest; provided, however, that a private citizen cannot use or threaten to use deadly force except to the extent authorized under self-defense or defense of third person statutes (Secs. 39-11-611 and 39-11-612).

2. Detention
(40-7-116, Tenn. Code Ann.)

(a) A merchant or a merchant's employee or agent or a peace officer who has probable cause to believe that a person has committed or is attempting to commit the offense of theft, as defined in Sec. 39-14-103 [reported below in Section 3], may detain such person on or off the premises of the mercantile establishment if such detention is done for any or all of the following purposes:
(1) To question the person, investigate the surrounding circumstances, obtain a statement, or any combination thereof;
(2) To request or verify identification, or both;
(3) To inform a peace officer of the detention of such person, or surrender that person to the custody of a peace officer, or both;
(4) To inform a peace officer, the parent or parents, guardian or other private person interested in the welfare of a minor of the detention and to surrender the minor to the custody of such person; or
(5) To institute criminal proceedings against the person.
(b) Probable cause to suspect that a person has committed or is attempting to commit the offense of theft may be based on, but not limited to:
(1) Personal observation, including observation via closed circuit television or other visual device;
(2) Report of such personal observation from another merchant;
(3) Activation of an electronic or other type of mechanical device designed to detect theft; or
(4) Personal observation of dressing rooms, including observation via closed circuit television, two-way mirrors, or other visual devices shall be limited to observation by a person of the same sex as the person being observed. No such observation shall be lawful unless notices are posted in such dressing rooms that such monitoring may occur.
(c) A merchant or a merchant's employee or agent or a peace officer who detains, questions or causes the arrest of any person suspected of theft shall not be

criminally or civilly liable for any legal action relating to such detention, questioning or arrest if the merchant or merchant's employee or agent or peace officer:

(1) Has reasonable grounds to suspect that the person has committed or is attempting to commit theft;

(2) Acts in a reasonable manner under the circumstances; and

(3) Detains the suspected person for a reasonable period of time.

(d) The merchant may use a reasonable amount of force necessary to protect himself, to prevent escape of the person detained, or to prevent the loss or destruction of property.

(e) A reasonable period of time, for the purposes of this section, is a period of time long enough to accomplish the purpose set forth in this section, and shall include any time spent awaiting the arrival of a law enforcement officer or the parents or guardian of a juvenile suspect, if the merchant or the merchant's employee or agent has summoned such law enforcement officer, parents or guardian.

3. Theft
(39-14-101, 39-14-144, Tenn. Code Ann.)

Conduct denominated as theft in this part constitutes a single offense embracing the separate offenses heretofore known as: embezzlement, false pretense, fraudulent conversion, larceny, receiving/concealing stolen property, and other similar offenses.

A person commits theft of property if, with intent to deprive the owner of property, the person knowingly obtains or exercises control over the property without the owner's effective consent.

TEXAS

1. Arrest by Private Persons
(Art. 14.01, Tex. Code Ann.)

(a) A peace officer or any other person, may, without a warrant, arrest an offender when the offense is committed in his presence or within his view, if the offense is one classed as a felony or as an offense against the public peace.

(b) A peace officer may arrest an offender without a warrant for any offense committed in his presence or within his view.

2. Detention
[No statute]

3. Theft
(Art. 31.02, 31.03, Tex. Penal Code)

Theft as defined in Section 31.03 of this code constitutes a single offense superseding the separate offenses previously known as theft, theft by false pretext, conversion by a bailee, theft from the person, shoplifting, acquisition of property by threat, swindling,

swindling by worthless check, embezzlement, extortion, receiving or concealing embezzled property, and receiving or concealing stolen property.

(a)   A person commits an offense if he unlawfully appropriates property with intent to deprive the owner of property.

(b)   Appropriation of property is unlawful if:
    (1)   it is without the owner's effective consent;
    (2)   the property is stolen and the actor appropriates the property knowing it was stolen by another; or . . .

(c)   For purposes of Subsection (b) of this section:
    (1)   evidence that the actor has previously participated in recent transactions other than, but similar to, that which the prosecution is based is admissible for the purpose of showing knowledge or intent and the issues of knowledge or intent are raised by the actor's plea of not guilty;
    (2)   the testimony of an accomplice shall be corroborated by proof that tends to connect the actor to the crime, but the actor's knowledge or intent may be established by the uncorroborated testimony of the accomplice; . .
    (8)   an actor who possesses a shopping cart, laundry cart, or container that has a name or mark and is not on the premises of the owner or an adjacent parking area is presumed to have appropriated property without the owner's consent.

UTAH

1.   Arrest by Private Persons
(77-7-3, 77-7-6, 77-7-8, Utah Code Ann.)

A private person may arrest another:

(1)   For a public offense committed or attempted in his presence; or
(2)   When a felony has been committed and he has reasonable cause to believe the person arrested has committed it.

The person making the arrest shall inform the person being arrested of his intention, cause and authority to arrest him. Such notice shall not be required when:

(1)   There is reason to believe the notice will endanger the life or safety of the officer or another person or will likely enable the party being arrested to escape;
(2)   The person being arrested is actually engaged in the commission of, or an attempt to commit, an offense; or
(3)   The person being arrested is pursued immediately after the commission of an offense or an escape.

To make an arrest, a private person, if the offense is a felony, and in all cases, a peace officer, may break the door or window of the building in which the person to be arrested is, or in which there are reasonable grounds for believing him to be. Before making the break, the person shall demand admission and explain the purpose for which admission is desired. Demand and explanation need not be given before breaking under the exceptions in Section 77-7-6 [previous section above] or where there is reason to believe evidence will be secreted or destroyed.

2.   Detention
(76-6-603 and 76-6-604, Utah Code Ann.)

Any merchant who has probable cause to believe that a person has committed retail theft may detain such person, on or off the premises of a retail mercantile establishment, in a reasonable manner and for a reasonable length of time for all or any of the following purposes:

(1)   To make reasonable inquiry as to whether such person has in his possession unpurchased merchandise and to make reasonable investigation of the ownership of such merchandise;

(2)   To request identification;

(3)   To verify such identification;

(4)   To make a reasonable request of such person to place or keep in full view any merchandise such individual may have removed, or which the merchant has reason to believe he may have removed, from its place of display or elsewhere, whether for examination, purchase or for any other reasonable purpose;

(5)   To inform a peace officer of the detention of the person and surrender that person to the custody of a peace officer;

(6)   In the case of a minor, to inform a peace officer, the parents, guardian or other private person interested in the welfare of that minor immediately, if possible, of this detention and to surrender custody of such minor to such person.

A merchant may make a detention as permitted herein off the premises of a retail mercantile establishment only if such detention is pursuant to an immediate pursuit of such person.

In any action for false arrest, false imprisonment, unlawful detention, defamation of character, assault, trespass, or invasion of civil rights brought by any person detained by the merchant, it shall be a defense to such action that the merchant detaining such person had probable cause to believe that the person had committed retail theft and that the merchant acted reasonably under all circumstances.

3.   Retail Theft
(76-6-602, 78-11-15, and 78-11-16, Utah Code Ann.)

A person commits the offense of retail theft when he knowingly:

(1)   Takes possession of, conceals, carries away, transfers or causes to be carried away or transferred, any merchandise displayed, held, stored or offered for sale in a retail mercantile establishment with the intention of retaining such merchandise or with the intention of depriving the merchant permanently of the possession, use or benefit of such merchandise without paying the retail value of such merchandise; or

(2)   Alters, transfers, or removes any label, price tag, marking, indicia of value or any other markings which aid in determining value of any merchandise displayed, held, stored or offered for sale, in a retail mercantile establishment and attempts to purchase such merchandise personally or in consort with another at less than the retail value with the intention of depriving the merchant of the retail value of such merchandise; or

(3) Transfers any merchandise displayed, held, stored or offered for sale in a retail mercantile establishment from the container in or on which such merchandise is displayed to any other container with the intention of depriving the merchant of the retail value of such merchandise; or

(4) Under-rings with the intention of depriving the merchant of the retail value of the merchandise; or

(5) Removes a shopping cart from the premises of a retail mercantile establishment with the intent of depriving the merchant of the possession, use or benefit of such cart.

VERMONT

1. Arrest by Private Persons
[No statute].

2. Detention
(Tit. 13, 2576, Vt. Stats. Ann.)

(a) Any merchant who has reasonable cause to believe that a person has committed or attempted to commit retail theft may detain the person on or in the immediate vicinity of the premises of a retail mercantile establishment, affording the person the opportunity to be detained in a place out of public view if available, in a reasonable manner which may include the use of reasonable force and for a reasonable length of time for any of the following purposes:

(1) To request and verify identification;

(2) To make reasonable inquiry as to whether the person has in his possession unpurchased merchandise and, if unpurchased, to recover the merchandise;

(3) To inform a law enforcement officer of the detention of the person and surrender that person to the custody of a law enforcement officer; and

(4) In the case of a minor, to inform a law enforcement officer, and, if known or determined, the parent or parents, guardian or other person having supervision of the minor of his detention and to surrender custody of the minor to the law enforcement officer, parent, guardian or other person.

(b) Any person detained under (a) (3) or (a) (4) of this section shall, if a telephone is available, have the right to make one local telephone call of reasonable duration. The merchant shall advise the person detained of this right.

3. Retail Theft
(Tit. 13, 2575, 2577, 2578, and 2574, Vt. Stats. Ann.)

A person commits the offense of retail theft when he, with intent of depriving the merchant wrongfully of the lawful possession of his merchandise,

(1) takes and carries away or causes to be taken and carried away or aids and abets the carrying away of, any merchandise from a retail mercantile establishment without paying the retail value of the merchandise; or

(2) alters, transfers or removes or causes to be altered, transferred or removed or aids and abets the alteration, transfer or removal of any label, price tag, indicia of value or any other markings affixed to any merchandise in a retail mercantile establishment and purchases the merchandise for less than its retail value; or

(3) transfers or causes to be transferred or aids and abets in the transfer of any merchandise in a retail mercantile establishment from one container or location to another container or location and purchases the merchandise for less than its retail value.

(a) A person convicted of the offense of retail theft of merchandise having a retail value not in excess of $100.00 shall be punished by a fine of not more than $300.00 or imprisonment for not more than six months, or both.

(b) Upon the second or subsequent conviction of the offense of retail theft of merchandise having a retail value not in excess of $100.00, a person shall be punished by a fine of not more than $500.00 or imprisonment for not more than two years, or both.

(c) A person convicted of the offense of retail theft of merchandise having a retail value in excess of $100.00 shall be punished by a fine of not more than $500.00 or imprisonment for not more than ten years, or both.

A sentencing court may order reasonable restitution where merchandise stolen is not recovered or is recovered in damaged condition. Damages shall be calculated based on retail value.

A merchant has the right to request in a reasonable manner any person at his retail mercantile establishment to place and keep in full view any merchandise which the person has removed from its place of display, for any purpose. Notice of this request shall be conspicuously posted by the merchant in said retail mercantile establishment.

VIRGINIA

1. Arrest by Private Persons
[No statute]

2. Detention
(18.2-105, 18.2-105.1, Va. Code)

A merchant, agent or employee of the merchant, who causes the arrest or detention of any person [. . .] shall not be held civilly liable for unlawful detention, if such detention does not exceed one hour, slander, malicious prosecution, false imprisonment, false arrest, or assault and battery of the person so arrested or detained, whether such arrest or detention takes place on the premises of the merchant, or after close pursuit from such premises by such merchant, his agent or employee, provided that, in causing the arrest or detention of such person, the merchant, agent or employee of the merchant, had at the time of such arrest or detention probable cause to believe that the person had shoplifted or committed willful concealment of goods or merchandise. The activation of an electronic article surveillance device as a result of a person exiting the premises or an area within the premises of a merchant where an electronic article surveillance device is located shall constitute probable cause for the detention of such person by such merchant, his agent or employee, provided such person is detained only in a reasonable manner and only for such time as is necessary for an inquiry into the circumstances surrounding the activation of the device, and provided that clear and visible notice is posted at each exit and location within the premises where such a device is located indicating the presence of an antishoplifting or inventory control device. For purposes of this section, "electronic article surveillance device" means an electronic device designed and operated for the purpose of detecting the removal from the premises, or a protected area within such premises, of specially marked or tagged merchandise.

A merchant, agent or employee of the merchant, who has probable cause to believe that a person has shoplifted [. . .] on the premises of the merchant, may detain such person for a period not to exceed one hour pending arrival of a law-enforcement officer.

3.   Shoplifting/Concealment/Cart Removal
(18.2-103, 18.2-102.1, Va. Code Ann.)

Whoever, without authority, with the intention of converting goods or merchandise to his own or another's use without having paid the full purchase price thereof, or of defrauding the owner of the value of the goods or merchandise, (i) willfully conceals or takes possession of the goods or merchandise of any store or other mercantile establishment, or (ii) alters the price tag or other price marking on such goods or merchandise, or transfers the goods from one container to another, or (iii) counsels, assists, aids or abets another in the performance of any of the above acts, when the value of the goods or merchandise involved in the offense is less than $200, shall be guilty of petit larceny and, when the value of the goods or merchandise involved in the offense is $200 or more, shall be guilty of grand larceny. The willful concealment of goods or merchandise of any store or other mercantile establishment, while still on the premises thereof, shall be prima facie evidence of an intent to convert and defraud the owner thereof out of the value of the goods or merchandise.

It shall be unlawful for any person to remove a shopping cart from the premises, of the owner of such shopping cart without the consent, of the owner or of his agent, servant, or employee given at the time of such removal. For the purpose of this section, the premises shall include all the parking area set aside by the owner, or on behalf of the owner, for the parking of cars for the convenience of the patrons of the owner.

WASHINGTON

1.   Arrest by Private Persons
[No statute]

2.   Detention
(Sec. 4.24.220, Wash. Rev. Code)

In any civil action brought by reason of any person having been detained on or in the immediate vicinity of the premises of a mercantile establishment for the purpose of investigation or questioning as to the ownership of any merchandise, it shall be a defense of such action that the person was detained in a reasonable manner and for not more than a reasonable time to permit such investigation or questioning by a peace officer or by the owner of the mercantile establishment, his authorized employee or agent, and that such peace officer, owner, employee or agent had reasonable grounds to believe that the person so detained was committing or attempting to commit larceny or shoplifting on such premises of such merchandise. As used in this section, "reasonable grounds" shall include, but not be limited to, knowledge that a person has concealed possession of unpurchased merchandise of a mercantile establishment, and a "reasonable time" shall mean the time necessary to permit the person detained to make a statement or to refuse to make a statement, and the time necessary to examine employees and records of the mercantile establishment relative to the ownership of the merchandise.

3. Theft/Shoplifting
(9A-56.020 and 4.24.230, Wash. Rev. Code)

"Theft" means:

(a)   To wrongfully obtain or exert unauthorized control over the property or services of another or the value thereof, with intent to deprive him of such property or services; or

An adult or emancipated minor who takes possession of any goods, wares, or merchandise displayed or offered for sale by any wholesale or retail store or other mercantile establishment without the consent of the owner or seller, and with the intention of converting such goods, wares, or merchandise to his own use without having paid the purchase price thereof shall be liable in addition to actual damages, for a penalty to the owner or seller in the amount of the retail value thereof not to exceed one thousand dollars, plus an additional penalty of not less than one hundred dollars nor more than two hundred dollars, plus all reasonable attorney's fees and court costs expended by the owner or seller. A customer who orders a meal in a restaurant or other eating establishment, receives at least a portion thereof, and then leaves without paying, is subject to liability under this section. A person who shall receive any food, money, credit, lodging, or accommodation at any hotel, motel, boardinghouse, or lodging house, and then leaves without paying the proprietor, manager, or authorized employee thereof, is subject to liability under this section.

(2)   The parent or legal guardian having the custody of an unemancipated minor who takes possession of any goods, wares, or merchandise displayed or offered for sale by any wholesale or retail store or other mercantile establishment without the consent of the owner or seller and with the intention of converting such goods, wares, or merchandise to his own use without having paid the purchase price thereof, shall be liable as a penalty to the owner or seller for the retail value of such goods, wares, or merchandise not to exceed five hundred dollars plus an additional penalty of not less than one hundred dollars nor more than two hundred dollars, plus all reasonable attorney's fees and court costs expended by the owner or seller. The parent or legal guardian having the custody of an unemancipated minor, who orders a meal in a restaurant or other eating establishment, receives at least a portion thereof, and then leaves without paying, is subject to liability under this section. The parent or legal guardian having the custody of an unemancipated minor, who receives any food, money, credit, lodging, or accommodation at any hotel, motel, boarding house, or lodging house, and then leaves without paying the proprietor, manager, or authorized employee thereof, is subject to liability under this section. For the purposes of this subsection, liability shall not be imposed upon any governmental entity, private agency, or foster parent assigned responsibility for the minor child pursuant to court order or action of the department of social and health services.

(4)   A conviction for [theft] shall not be a condition precedent to maintenance of a civil action authorized by this section.

(5) An owner or seller demanding payment of a penalty under subsection (1) or (2) of this section shall give written notice to the person or persons from whom the penalty is sought. The notice shall state:

"IMPORTANT NOTICE: The payment of any penalty demanded of you does not prevent criminal prosecution under a related criminal provision."

This notice shall be boldly and conspicuously displayed, in at least the same size type as is used in the demand, and shall be sent with the demand for payment of a penalty described [above].

WEST VIRGINIA

1. Arrest by Private Persons
[No statute]

2. Detention
(61-3A-4, W. Va. Code)

An act of shoplifting as defined herein, is hereby declared to constitute a breach of peace and any owner of merchandise, his agent or employee, or any law-enforcement officer who has reasonable ground to believe that a person has committed shoplifting, may detain such person in a reasonable manner and for a reasonable length of time not to exceed thirty minutes, for the purpose of investigating whether or not such person has committed or attempted to commit shoplifting. Such reasonable detention shall not constitute an arrest nor shall it render the owner of merchandise, his agent or employee, liable to the person detained.

3. Shoplifting/Civil Liability for Shoplifting
(61-3A-1, 61-3A-5, W. Va. Code)

(a) A person commits the offense of shoplifting if, with intent to appropriate merchandise without paying the merchant's stated price for the merchandise, such person, alone or in concert with another person, knowingly:
   (1) Conceals the merchandise upon his or her person or in another manner; or
   (2) Removes or causes the removal of merchandise from the mercantile establishment or beyond the last station for payment; or
   (3) Alters, transfers or removes any price marking affixed to the merchandise; or
   (4) Transfers the merchandise from one container to another; or
   (5) Causes the cash register or other sales recording device to reflect less than the merchant's stated price for the merchandise; or
   (6) Removes a shopping cart from the premises of the mercantile establishment.
(b) A person also commits the offense of shoplifting if such person, alone or in concert with another person, knowingly and with intent obtains an exchange or refund or attempts to obtain an exchange or refund for merchandise which has not been purchased from the mercantile establishment.
(a) General rule.—Any person who commits any of the acts described in section one [61-3A-1] of this article shall be civilly liable:

(1)   To restore the merchandise to the mercantile establishment; and

(2)   If such merchandise is not recoverable or is damaged, for actual damages, including the value of the merchandise involved in the shoplifting; and

(3)   For other actual damages arising from the incident, not including the loss of time or loss of wages incurred by the mercantile establishment or any merchant in connection with the apprehension and processing of the suspect; and

(4)   In all cases, for a penalty to be paid to the mercantile establishment in the amount of fifty dollars or double the value of the merchandise, whichever is higher.

(b)   Costs and attorneys' fees.—A merchant who is a prevailing party under this section is entitled to costs.

(c)   Effect of conviction.—A conviction for the offense of theft by shoplifting is not a prerequisite to the maintenance of a civil action authorized by this section. However, a merchant who has recovered the penalty prescribed by section three of this article is not entitled to recover the penalty imposed by this section.

(d)   Right to demand payment.—The fact that a mercantile establishment may bring an action against an individual as provided in this section does not limit the right of such establishment to demand, orally or in writing, that a person who is liable for damages or a penalty under this section remit said damages or penalty prior to the commencement of any legal action.

WISCONSIN

1.   Arrest by Private Persons
[No statute]

2.   Detention
(943.50, Wis. Stat. Ann.)

A merchant, a merchant's adult employee or a merchant's security agent who has reasonable cause for believing that a person has violated this section in his or her presence may detain the person in a reasonable manner for a reasonable length of time to deliver the person to a peace officer, or to his or her parent or guardian in the case of a minor. The detained person must be promptly informed of the purpose for the detention and be permitted to make phone calls, but he or she shall not be interrogated or searched against his or her will before the arrival of a peace officer who may conduct a lawful interrogation of the accused person. The merchant, merchant's adult employee or merchant's security agent may release the detained person before the arrival of a peace officer or parent or guardian. Any merchant, merchant's adult employee or merchant's security agent who acts in good faith in any act authorized under this section is immune from civil or criminal liability for those acts.

3.   Retail Theft/Cart Removal/Civil Liability for Retail Theft
(943.50, 943.51, and 943.55, Wis. Stat. Ann.)

Whoever intentionally alters indicia of price or value of merchandise or who takes and carries away, transfers, conceals or retains possession of merchandise held for resale by a merchant or property of the merchant without his or her consent and with intent to deprive the merchant permanently of possession, or the full purchase price, of the merchandise may be penalized as provided [below].

The intentional concealment of unpurchased merchandise which continues from one floor to another or beyond the last station for receiving payments in a merchant's store is evidence of intent to deprive the merchant permanently of possession of such merchandise without paying the purchase price thereof. The discovery of unpurchased merchandise concealed upon the person or among the belongings of such person or concealed by a person upon the person or among the belongings of another is evidence of intentional concealment on the part of the person so concealing such goods.

In any action or proceeding for violation of this section, duly identified and authenticated photographs of merchandise which was the subject of the violation may be used as evidence in lieu of producing the merchandise.

Whoever violates this section is guilty of: A Class A misdemeanor, if the value of the merchandise does not exceed $1,000.

A Class E felony, if the value of the merchandise exceeds $1,000 but not $2,500.

A Class C felony, if the value of the merchandise exceeds $2,500.

In addition to the other penalties provided for violation of this section, a judge may order a violator to pay restitution . . .

(1) Any person who incurs injury to his or her business or property as a result [of Retail Theft] may bring a civil action against any individual 14 years of age or older who caused the loss for all of the following:
   (a) The retail value of the merchandise unless it is returned undamaged and unused. A person may recover under this paragraph only if he or she exercises due diligence in demanding the return of the merchandise immediately after he or she discovers the loss and the identity of the person who has the merchandise.
   (b) Any actual damages not covered under par. (a).

(2) In addition to sub. (1), if the person who incurs the loss prevails, the judgment in the action may grant any of the following:
   (a) 1. Except as provided in subd. 1m, exemplary damages of not more than 3 times the amount under sub. (1).
       1m If the action is brought against a minor or against the parent who has custody of their minor child for the loss caused by the minor, the exemplary damages may not exceed 2 times the amount under sub. (1).
       2. No additional proof is required for an award of exemplary damages under this paragraph.
   (b) Notwithstanding the limitations of s. 799.25 or 814.04, all actual costs of the action, including reasonable attorney fees.

(3) Notwithstanding sub. (2) and except as provided in sub. (3m), the total amount awarded for exemplary damages and reasonable attorney fees may not exceed $500.
   (3m) Notwithstanding sub. (2), the total amount awarded for exemplary damages and reasonable attorney fees may not exceed $300 if the action is brought against a minor or against the parent who has custody of their minor child for the loss caused by the minor.
   (3r) Any recovery under this section shall be reduced by the amount recovered as restitution for the same act . . .

(4)   The plaintiff has the burden of proving by a preponderance of the evidence that [Retail theft] occurred . . . A conviction [for Retail theft] is not a condition precedent to bringing an action, obtaining a judgment or collecting that judgment under this section.

Whoever intentionally removes a shopping cart or stroller from either the shopping area or a parking area adjacent to the shopping area to another place without authorization of the owner or person in charge and with the intent to deprive the owner permanently of possession of such property shall forfeit an amount not to exceed $50.

WYOMING

1. Arrest by Private Persons
(7-8-101, Wyo. Stats)

A person who is not a peace officer may arrest another for:

(i)   A felony committed in his presence;
(ii)   A felony which has been committed, even though not in his presence, if he has probable cause to believe the person to be arrested committed it; or
(iii) [Certain specified misdemeanors including larceny or property destruction] committed in his presence:

2. Detention
(6-3-405, Wyo. Stats.)

(a)   A peace officer, merchant or merchant's employee who has reasonable cause to believe a person is violating W.S. 6-3-404 may detain and interrogate the person in regard to the suspected violation in a reasonable manner and for a reasonable time.
(b)   In a civil or criminal action for slander, false arrest, false imprisonment, assault, battery or wrongful detention based upon a detention and interrogation pursuant to this section, it is a defense that the peace officer, merchant or merchant's employee had reasonable cause to believe the person was violating W.S. 6-3-404 and the detention and interrogation were conducted in a reasonable manner and for a reasonable time.

3. Shoplifting/Civil Liability for Shoplifting
(6-3-404, 1-1-127, Wyo. Stats.)

(a)   A person who willfully conceals or takes possession of property offered for sale by a wholesale or retail store without the knowledge or consent of the owner and with intent to convert the property to his own use without paying the purchase price is guilty of:
(i)   A felony punishable by imprisonment for not more than ten (10) years, a fine of not more than ten thousand dollars ($10,000.00), or both, if the value of the property is five hundred dollars ($500.00) or more; or

... (iii)   A misdemeanor punishable by imprisonment for not more than six (6) months, a fine of not more than seven hundred fifty dollars ($750.00), or both, if the value of the property is less than five hundred dollars ($500.00).

(b)   A person who alters, defaces, changes or removes a price tag or marker on or about property offered for sale by a wholesale or retail store with intent to obtain the property at less than the marked or listed price is guilty of:

    (i)   A felony punishable by imprisonment for not more than ten (10) years, a fine of not more than ten thousand dollars ($10,000.00), or both, if the difference between the marked or listed price and the amount actually paid is five hundred dollars ($500.00) or more; or

    ... (iii)   A misdemeanor punishable by imprisonment for not more than six (6) months, a fine of not more than seven hundred fifty dollars ($750.00), or both, if the difference between the marked or listed price and the amount actually paid is less than five hundred dollars ($500.00).

(a)   A person over ten (10) years of age who violates [prohibitions on shoplifting] is civilly liable to the merchant of the property in an amount consisting of:

    (i)   Return of the property in original condition or actual damages equal to the full marked or listed price of the property; plus

    (ii)   A civil liability of twice the amount of the full marked or listed price of the property but not less than fifty dollars ($50.00) nor more than one thousand dollars ($1,000.00); plus

    (iii)   Reasonable attorney's fees and court costs.

(b)   If an unemancipated minor violates [prohibitions on shoplifting], the parents or guardian of the child shall be civilly liable as provided by subsection (a) of this section, provided liability under this subsection shall not apply to foster parents, to parents whose parental custody and control of the child have been terminated by court order prior to the violation or to any governmental or private agency that has been appointed guardian for the minor child pursuant to court order or action of the department of family services. Civil liability under this subsection is not subject to the limitation on liability provided by [particular provisions of state law] or any other law that limits the liability of parents for damages caused by an unemancipated minor.

(c)   A conviction or a plea of guilty to a violation of [prohibitions on shoplifting] is not a prerequisite to the bringing of a civil suit under this section.

... (e)   In order to recover damages and any civil liability under this act, the merchant of the property shall also notify law enforcement officials.

Index

Abandoned property, seizure, 38–39
Aggravated assault, 206
Americans With Disabilities Act, drug and alcohol screening, 89
Apartment buildings, security, liability, 198
Appellate court, 223–225, 227–229
Arraignment, 214
Arrest, citizen, 21–29
  authorization for, 21–22
  citizen assistance in police arrests, 26
  force permissible, 26–27
  of juveniles, 28–29
  legislative enactments, 22–23
  liability for, 25, 147–156
  Miranda warning, 72–75
  "offense" defined, 23–24
  postarrest procedures, 28, 211–215
  reasonable grounds, 22, 24–25
  search of arrestees, 44–45
Arrestee
  Miranda warning, 71–75
  obligations, 16
  rights during arrest, 15–16
  search by private citizens, 44–45
Arrest, illegal. *See also* Liability
  confessions, 69, 78–79
  contractual release, 160–163
  false imprisonment, 173–176
  lawful custody, 71
  legal consequences, 145–160, 173–176
  security officer, 25, 147–156, 173–176
Arrest, police, 1–21
  citizen assistance, 26
  by federal officers, 11, 17, 146
  force permissible, 11–14
  hearsay evidence and informants' tips, 4–5, 7
  jurisdiction, 10–11
  legal alternatives to, 17–18
  liability for, 145–147
  Miranda warning, 71, 74, 75
  obligations of persons about to be arrested, 16
  police obligations, 7–9, 15

  postarrest procedures, 28, 211–215
  quashing an arrest warrant, 9–10
  reasonable grounds, 3–4, 5–6
  resisting arrest, 16
  rights of arrested persons, 15–16
  search and seizure, 31–44
  by special police, 18–21
  "stop" short of an arrest, 5
  timing, 14
  with a warrant, 6–10, 11
  without a warrant, 2–6, 10–11, 145
Arrest, by security officers. *See* Arrest, citizen
Arrest warrant, 6
  federal, 11
  obtaining, 6, 8
  police obligations, 7–9
  quashing, 9–10
  reasonable grounds for, 6–7
  validity of, 8, 9, 11
Assault and battery, 170–173, 194, 206
Assimilative Crimes Act, 225
Attempt (to commit a crime), 206
Automobile searches, 43–44

Bail, 211–212
Battery, 206
Blackmail, 208
Breaking and entering, 206
Bribery, 206, 207
Burglary, 206, 207
Business owners, civil liability, 187–203

Campus police, 19–21, 74
Case preparation. *See* Criminal case preparation
Circuit court, 223
Citizen's arrest. *See* Arrest, citizen
Civil Rights Act of 1871, illegal search and seizure, 164
Civil Rights Act of 1964, psychological testing, 135–136
Civil Rights Act of 1991, 140, 142
Civil Rights Act, criminal history used by employer, 125–126

Civil rights statutes, 146, 149–155
Closing arguments, 217–218
Coercive tactics, interrogation, 69–70, 72
Color of law, 149–155, 164
Commercial bribery, 207
Common law, 2, 117–118, 205
Complaint, 6, 49–51
Compounding a crime, 207
Computers, electronic eavesdropping, 102
Concealed surveillance. *See* Surveillance
Confession
    electronic recording of, 78–79
    lawful custody, 71
    Miranda warning, 71
    oral, 79
    trickery and deceit to obtain, 70
    voluntariness, 69–70, 72
    written, 78
Confidence game, 207
Conspiracy, 207
Contraband, 31, 37–38
Counterfeit currency transactions, 207
Courts, 221–229
    federal appellate, 227–229
    federal trial, 225–227
    juvenile, 223, 226–227
    state appellate, 223–225
    state trial, 222–223
Credit card misuse, 207–208
Crimes, types, 205–209
Crime scene, protection by security officer, 232–234
Criminal case preparation, 231–241
    crime scene, protection of, 232–234
    evidence, proper preservation of, 234–235
    proof of corporate existence, 236
    proof of value of merchandise, 236
    prosecuting attorney, security officer cooperates with, 237–238
    security officer as witness, 238–241
    witnesses' statements, 235–236
Criminal history, 117–129
    access to FBI records, 119–121
    access to federal and state records, 121–124
    access to public records, 117–119
    of applicants and employees, 124–128
    arrest versus conviction, 121–122, 124–125, 142–143
    and civil rights, 125–126
    of customers, 126, 128–129
    expungement, 123, 125
    Freedom of Information Act, 119
    interbusiness trading of, 126–129
    juveniles, 123
    used by employer, 124–128
Criminal law principles
    entrapment, 210–222
    intent, 209–210
    presumption, 210
Criminal law procedures
    appeal process, 223–224, 227–229

arraignment and plea, 214
between arrest and trial, 211–215
case preparation, 231–241
closing arguments, 217–218
courts, 221–229
crime scene, protection of, 232–234
evidence, defendant's, 217
evidence, proper preservation of, 234–235
evidence, prosecution's, 217
grand jury, 212, 213–214
habeas corpus writ, 213
jury selection, 217
motion for a new trial, 218
motion to quash indictment, 214
motion to suppress evidence, 215
opening statements, 217
postarrest requirements, 28, 211–215
preliminary hearing, 15, 211, 212
pretrial motions, 214–215
right to an attorney, 212
right to bail, 211–212
sentencing, 218–219
trial, 215–219
verdict, 218
witnesses' statements, 235–236

Deadly force
    fleeing felon, 12–13, 176–177
    security officer, 13, 27, 176–178
Defamation
    criminal history information, 126, 127
    interrogations, 77
    liability, security guard, 182–186
Detention and inquiry
    by off-duty (moonlighting) police officer, 156–157
    customers and other nonemployees, 57–66, 153–155
    employees, 66–68
    false imprisonment, 173–176
    force permissible in, 60
    liability for, 62–63, 66–67, 154
    location of, 60–61
    reasonable grounds for, 58–60
    time permissible for, 60
Discriminatory employment practices
    Civil Rights Act of 1964, 135–136
    disparate impact, 137, 138–140
    disparate treatment, 137
    drug screening, 89
    guidelines, 140–142
    psychological testing, 135–140
    surveillance photography, 101
    use of criminal history, 125–126
Disorderly conduct, 208
Disparate impact, 137, 138–140
Disparate treatment, 137
District court, 223, 225–227
Dram shop liability, 193–194
Drug Free Workplace Act of 1988 (DFWA), 81–82

Drug testing, 81–89
  case law, 83–87
  federal laws mandating, 81–83
  implementation, 88–89
  state statutory restrictions, 87–88

Electronic eavesdropping, 102–105
Electronic monitoring. *See* Surveillance
Electronic theft detection, 105, 175
Embezzlement, 208
Emergency search, 42–43
Employee Polygraph Protection Act (1988),
  93–95
Employees
  detention and inquiry, 66–68
  drug testing, 81–89
  employer liability in selection and retention,
    193, 201–202
  psychological testing, 131–143
  right to view employee records, 123–124
  search of desks and lockers, 41, 47, 68
  search and seizure, 41–42, 45–47, 54–55
Employer. *See also* Liability, employer
  concealed surveillance, 97–106
  criminal history of applicants and employ-
    ees, 117–129
  drug screening, 81–89
  eavesdropping, 102–105
  plain view seizure, 46
  polygraph testing, 93–95
  search and seizure, 41–42, 45–47, 54–55
  vicarious liability, 156–160, 170–186
Entrapment, 210–222
Equal Employment Opportunity Commission
  (EEOC), 125, 136, 142
Escape, definition, 25
Evidence
  during trial, 217
  illegally seized by security officer, 166–167
  proper preservation, 234–235
  suppression of, 164–166, 215
Excessive force, 11–12
Exclusionary rule, 31, 54, 164–165, 166
Expungement, 123, 125
Extortion, 208
Extradition, 11

False arrest. *See* Arrest, illegal
False imprisonment, 173–176
Federal Bureau of Investigation (FBI), 119–121
Federal courts, 225–229
Federal Juvenile Delinquency Act, 227
Federal officers, arrests by, 11, 17, 146
Federal Rehabilitation Act, drug and alcohol
  screening, 89
Federal Tort Claim Act, 146
Felony
  definition, 2, 205
  judicial procedure, 212, 213–214, 219, 223
Field search, 32

Fingerprints, 120, 123
Firearms related claims, liability, 176–178
Fleeing felon, 12–13, 176–177
Following, surveillance, 100–101
Force
  deadly force, 12–13, 27, 176–177
  excessive force, 11–12
Force, permissible
  to arrest, 11–14, 26–27
  interrogations, coercive tactics, 69–70, 72
  owner regaining personal property, 55–56
  to protect property, 13
  to search, 35–36
Forgery, 207, 208
Fourth Amendment
  concealed surveillance, 102
  deadly force, 177
  drug screening, 83–84, 86–87
  eavesdropping, 102
  force needed, 12
  search and seizure, 3, 39, 41, 48, 54–55
Freedom of Information Act (1966), 119
Fresh pursuit, 10, 11
Frisking, 36–37

Garbage, search and seizure, 38–39
Grand jury, 212, 213–214
Grand larceny, 208

Habeas corpus writ, 213
Hearsay evidence, 4–5, 7, 50
Hobbs Act, 208
Hospitals, security, liability, 194–196
Hotel, security, liability, 199–200
Hot pursuit, 10, 11, 42

Immunity statutes, 62–64
Indictment, 213, 214
Informants, 4–5, 7, 50
Innkeepers, security, liability, 199, 200, 202
Intent (to commit a crime), 209–210
Interrogation, police
  coercive tactics, 69–70
  lawful custody, 71
  Miranda warning, 71
Interrogation, by security officer
  campus police, 74
  coercive tactics, 72
  electronic recording of confession, 78–79
  emotional distress, 77–78
  juveniles, 79
  Miranda requirements, exemption, 72–75
  by off-duty (moonlighting) police officer, 74
  privacy, 75–76
  slander/defamation, 77
  written confession, 78
Intimidation, 208
Investigation techniques
  drug testing, 81–89
  dyes or powder, used for identification,
    105–106

Investigation techniques (Continued)
fingerprints, 120
polygraph test, 90–95
sensitized merchandise tags, 106, 175

Judicial procedures. *See* Criminal law procedures
Judiciary Act of 1789, 225
Jurisdiction, 10–11
Jury, 216, 217
Justice of the peace, 223
Juveniles
arrest, 28–29
court jurisdictions, 223, 226–227
criminal history, 123
interrogation, 79

Labor management issues, 109–112
Landlord, liability, 197–203
Larceny, 208
Lawful custody, confession, 71
Liability, arrest
false arrest/false imprisonment, 173–176
immunity, 62–64
police, 7, 16, 145–147
security officer, 25, 147–156, 173–176
Liability, employer
armed robbery on premises, 187, 189
criminal history information, 126, 127
drive-by shooting of patrons, 190
for employee selection and retention, 193, 201–202
in a hospital, 194–196
hotels, 197–203
for inadequate security duties, 187–203
landlords, 197–203
negligence where liquor is served, 193–194
preventive measures, 196
rape of patron, 191–193
for wrongful actions of security officers, 156–160, 170–186
Liability, police
illegal arrest, 145–147
warrant, executing, 7
Liability, security officer
arrest, 25, 147–156, 173–176
assault and battery, 170–173
defamation/slander, 182–186
detention and inquiry, 62–63, 66–67
ejecting a patron from a store, 108, 153
false arrest/false imprisonment, 173–176
firearms claims, 176–178
inadequate security duties, 187–203
invasion of privacy, 186
malicious prosecution, 178–182
Lie detector test. *See* Polygraph test

Major trial court, 223
Malicious mischief, 208
Malicious prosecution, liability, 178–182

Merchandise
detention statutes, 56–68
proof of value, 236
search and seizure, 44, 46, 54–56
sensitized merchandise tags, 105, 175
Minor offense, 226
Minor trial courts, 222–223
Miranda warning
for campus security officers, 21, 74
interrogations, 71, 72–75
for police, 71, 74, 75
for police officers under investigation, 75
for security officers, 72–75
Misdemeanor
definition, 2, 205
judicial procedure, 211, 213, 223
Misprison of felony, 207
Motel, security, liability, 199–200
Motion for a new trial, 218
Motion to quash indictment, 214
Motion to suppress evidence, 215

National Labor Relations Board (NLRD), on picketing, 112
Nolo contendere plea, 214
Notice to appear, 2, 17–18

Off-duty police officers, 74, 156–157
Offense, 23–24, 25

Peeking, 97–100
Periodic imprisonment, 219
Perjury, 209
Personal property, right of owner to regain, 55–56, 57
Petty larceny, 208
Photography
crime scene, 234
surveillance, 101–102
Picketing, 109–112
Pickpocketing, 209
Plain view seizure, 37–38, 46
Polygraph test, 90–95
admissibility, of test results, 95
examiners, 91
legal status, 93–95
technique, 90–93
Preliminary hearing, 15, 211, 212
Presumption (of guilt), 210
Pretrial motions, 214–215
Privacy
concealed surveillance, 97–99, 101
criminal history, 124
drug screening, 83–85, 86
during search and seizure, 38, 47
employee desks and lockers, 41, 47, 68
of garbage, 38–39
interrogations, 75–76
invasion of privacy, liability, 186
shadowing, 100–101
Probable cause. *See* Reasonable grounds

Proof of corporate existence, 236
Proof of value of merchandise, 236
Protest activities, 109–115
Psychological Equal Employment Opportunity
    Commission, guidelines, 140–142
Psychological testing, 131–143
    Civil Rights Act of 1964, 135–136
    Civil Rights Act of 1991, 140, 142
    discriminatory employment practices,
        135–140
    reliability, 133–135
Public housing authority, security, liability,
    200–201
Public records, 117–119
Purse snatching, 209

Qualified privilege, 77
Quasi-crimes, 205

Reasonable force. See Force, permissible
Reasonable grounds (probable cause)
    for arrest warrant, 6–7
    for citizen's arrest, 22, 25–26
    detention statutes, 58–59
    for police arrest, 3–4
    search warrant, 48, 49
Reid Report, 131–133
Resisting arrest, 16
Retail theft, 209
Robbery, 209

Scientific investigations. See also Investigative
    techniques; Psychological testing
    drug testing, 81–89
    polygraph test, 90–95
Search and seizure, citizen, 44–48
    of arrestees, 44–45
    of company-owned merchandise, 44, 46,
        54–56
    employee consent, 46
    of employee desks and lockers, 47, 68
    of employees on premises, 45–46, 48
    false imprisonment, 173–176
    liability, 166
    of nonemployees on premises, 45
    stop-and-frisk privilege, 48
Search and seizure, employer, 41–42, 45–47,
    54–55
    concealed surveillance, 97–106
    drug screening, 83–87
    employee consent, 46
Search and seizure, police, 31–44
    abandoned property, 38–39
    automobile searches, 43–44
    consent for, 39–43
    contraband in plain view, 37–38
    emergency search, 42–43
    force permissible, 35–36
    hot pursuit, 42
    illegal, 164–166
    liability, 164

    reasonable expectation of privacy, 38
    search incident to arrest, 31–34
    stop-and-frisk privilege, 36–37
Search warrant, 31, 34, 48–55
    complaint for, 49–51
    execution, 52–54
    quashing, 51
    search by private individuals, 54
    things subject to seizure, 52
    validity, 51, 53
Security companies, 157–160
Security officer. See also Liability, security
        officer
    arrest by, 21–29, 147–156
    assault and battery, liability, 170–173
    color of law, 149–155, 164
    crime scene, protection of, 232–234
    criminal case preparation, 231–241
    deadly force, 13, 27, 176–178
    defamation/slander, liability, 182–186
    detention and inquiry, 62–63, 66–67
    drug screening of, 85, 86
    ejecting store patrons, 107–109, 153
    evidence, proper preservation of, 234–235
    false arrest, 25, 145–160, 173–176
    firearms, liability, 176–178
    hospitals, 194–196
    inadequate security duties, 187–203
    interrogations, 72–79
    invasion of privacy, liability, 186
    juvenile arrests, 28–29
    juvenile interrogation, 79
    malicious prosecution, liability, 178–182
    Miranda warning, 72–75
    notes, 236
    proof of corporate existence, 236
    proof of value of merchandise, 236
    prosecuting attorney, cooperates with,
        237–238
    search of employees, 45–48
    search of nonemployees absent an arrest,
        45
    search and seizure, 54–55, 166–170
    stop-and-frisk privilege, 48
    surveillance, 100–101
    vicarious liability of employer, 156–160,
        170–186
    as witness, 238–241
    witnesses' statements, 235–236
Sensitized merchandise tags, 105
Sentencing, 218–219
Shadowing, 100–101
Shoplifting, 209
    arrest, 24–25, 173–175
    concealed surveillance, 99–100
    criminal history of customers, 128
    detention statutes, 58–68, 153–155, 168
    intent to steal, 209–210
    malicious prosecution, 179–182
    Miranda warning, 73–74
    search and seizure, 44–45, 55–56

Sit-in protest, 113–114
Slander
    criminal history information, 126, 127
    interrogations, 77
    liability, security officer, 182–186
Special police, arrests by, 18–21
State courts, 222–225
Stolen property, possessing/receiving, 209
Stop-and-frisk, 36–37, 48
Summons, 2, 17–18
Superior courts, 223
Suppression of evidence, 164–166, 215
Supreme Court (U.S.), 228–229
Surveillance, 97
    concealed, 97–106, 175–176
    electronic eavesdropping, 102–105
    electronic theft detection, 105
    in fitting rooms, 99–100
    fluorescent powder, 105–106
    following, 100–101
    peeking, 97–100
    photography, 101–102
    in washroom, 97–99

Tailing, 100–101

Temporary detention. See Detention and inquiry
Testing. See Psychological testing; Scientific investigations
Theft, 209
Theft detection, electronic. See Electronic theft detection
Trespass, 209
Trial, 215–219
True bill, 213

Ultraviolet light search, for theft, 105–106
Union activities
    picketing, 109–112
    presence at interrogation, 75–76, 77
Unnecessary delay, 15

Verdict, 218
Vicarious liability, 156–160, 170–186

Warrant. See Arrest warrant; Search warrant
Witnesses, 235–236, 238–241
Work release, 219
Writ of certiorari, 229
Writ of habeas corpus, 213